魔法先生

ネギま!

MAGISTER NEGI MAGI

5

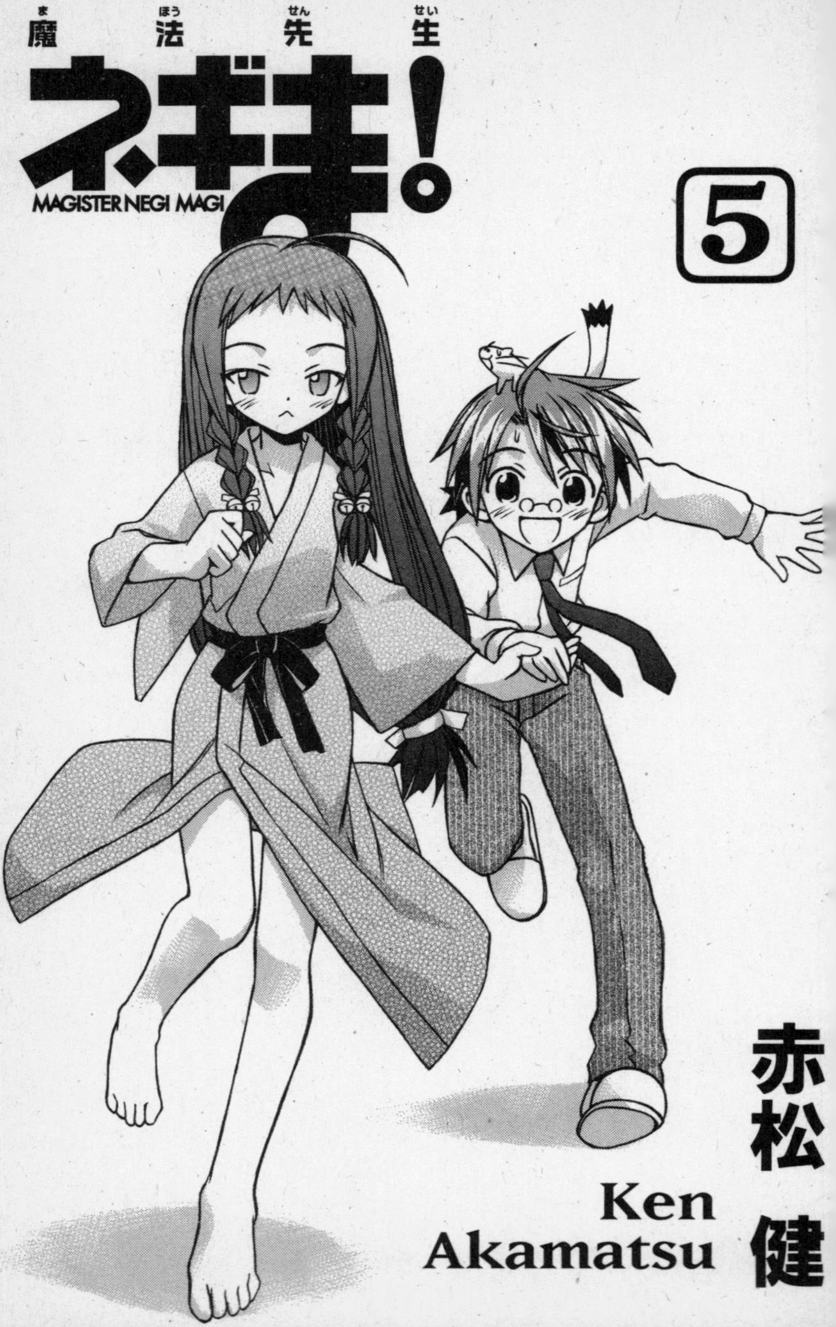

赤松健

Ken Akamatsu

CONTENTS

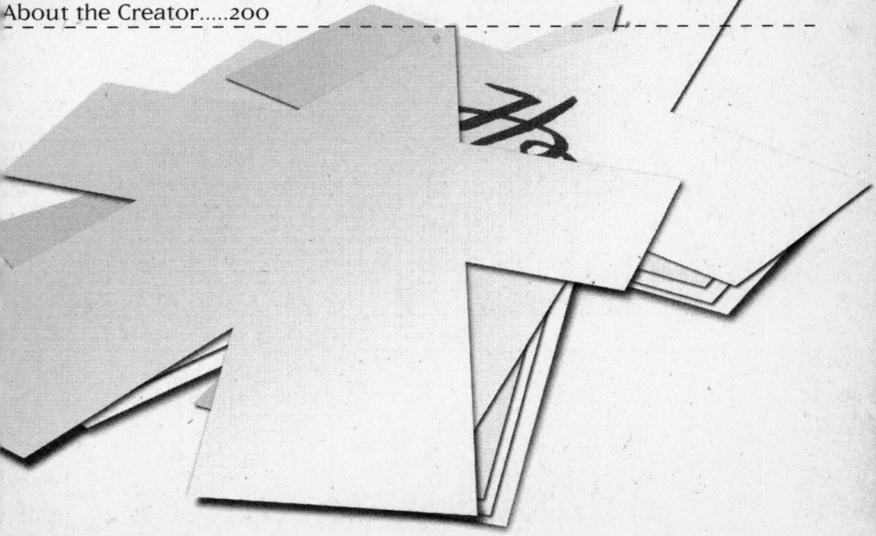

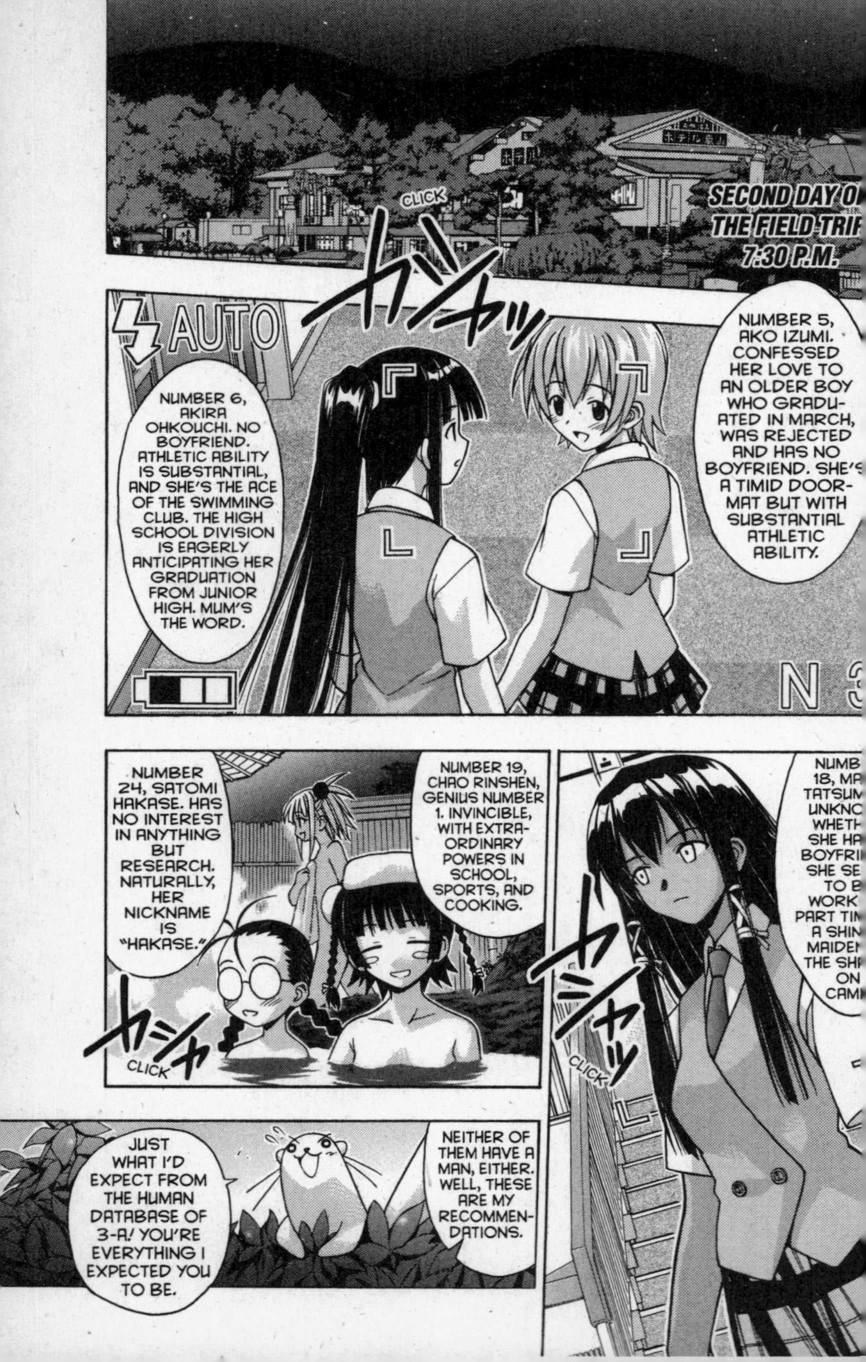
SECOND DAY O
THE FIELD TRI
7:30 P.M.
CLICK
NUMBER 5, AKO IZUMI. CONFESSED HER LOVE TO AN OLDER BOY WHO GRADU-ATED IN MARCH, WAS REJECTED AND HAS NO BOYFRIEND. SHE'S A TIMID DOOR-MAT BUT WITH SUBSTANTIAL ATHLETIC ABILITY.
NUMBER 6, AKIRA OHKOUCHI. NO BOYFRIEND. ATHLETIC ABILITY IS SUBSTANTIAL, AND SHE'S THE ACE OF THE SWIMMING CLUB. THE HIGH SCHOOL DIVISION IS EAGERLY ANTICIPATING HER GRADUATION FROM JUNIOR HIGH. MUM'S THE WORD.
AUTO
N 3
NUMB 18, MA TATSUM UNKNO WHETH SHE HA BOYFRI SHE SE TO B WORK PART TIM A SHIN MAIDEN THE SHR ON CAMI
CLICK
NUMBER 19, CHAO RINSHEN, GENIUS NUMBER 1. INVINCIBLE, WITH EXTRA-ORDINARY POWERS IN SCHOOL, SPORTS, AND COOKING.
NUMBER 24, SATOMI HAKASE. HAS NO INTEREST IN ANYTHING BUT RESEARCH. NATURALLY, HER NICKNAME IS "HAKASE."
CLICK
NEITHER OF THEM HAVE A MAN, EITHER. WELL, THESE ARE MY RECOMMEN-DATIONS.
JUST WHAT I'D EXPECT FROM THE HUMAN DATABASE OF 3-A! YOU'RE EVERYTHING I EXPECTED YOU TO BE.

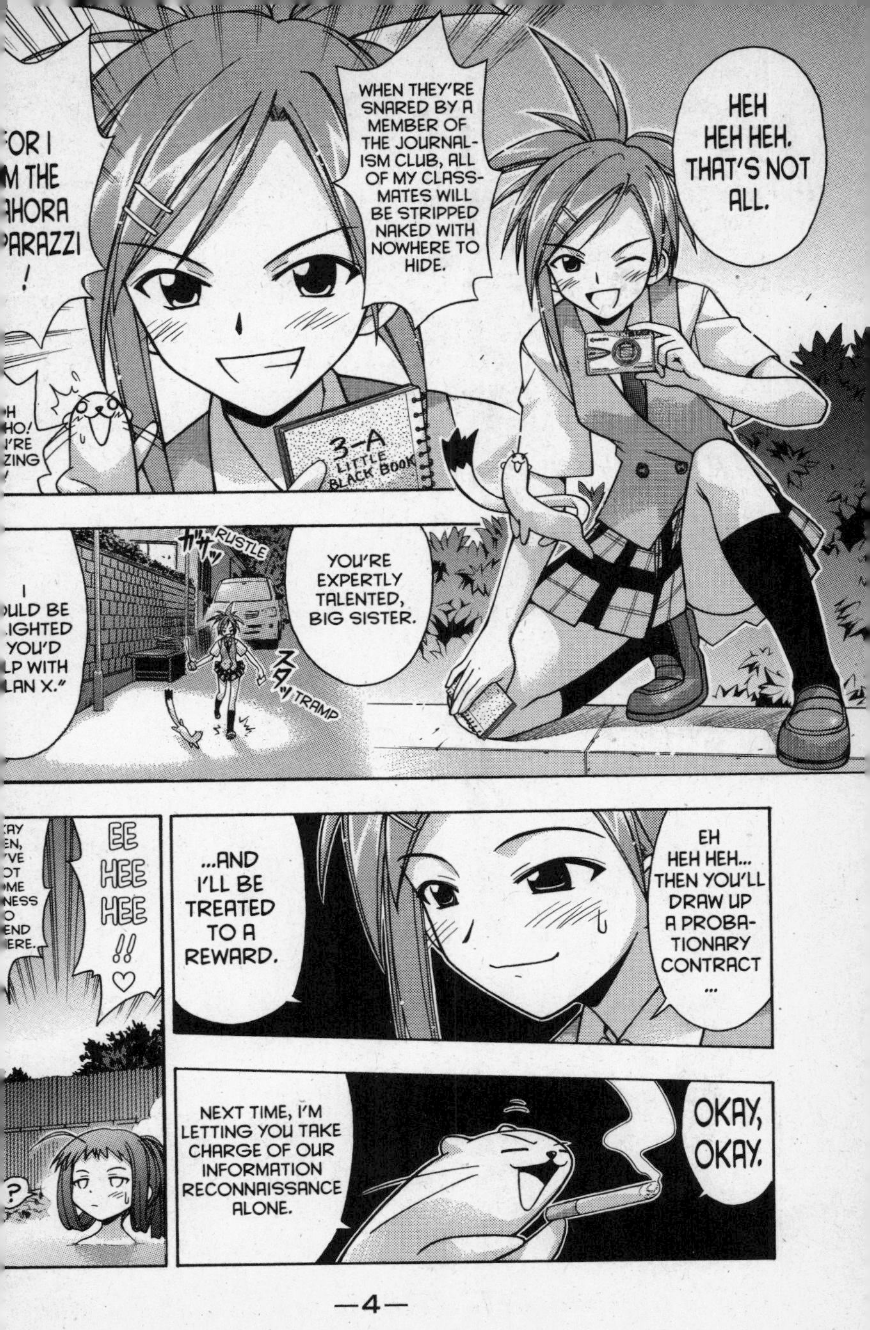
HEH HEH HEH. THAT'S NOT ALL.
WHEN THEY'RE SNARED BY A MEMBER OF THE JOURNALISM CLUB, ALL OF MY CLASSMATES WILL BE STRIPPED NAKED WITH NOWHERE TO HIDE.
3-A LITTLE BLACK BOOK
FOR I M THE AHORA PARAZZI !
H HO! U'RE ZING
ガサッ RUSTLE
YOU'RE EXPERTLY TALENTED, BIG SISTER.
スタッ TRAMP
I OULD BE LIGHTED YOU'D LP WITH LAN X."
EH HEH HEH... THEN YOU'LL DRAW UP A PROBATIONARY CONTRACT ...
...AND I'LL BE TREATED TO A REWARD.
OKAY, OKAY.
NEXT TIME, I'M LETTING YOU TAKE CHARGE OF OUR INFORMATION RECONNAISSANCE ALONE.
EE HEE HEE !! ♡
KAY EN, 'VE OT ME NESS O END ERE.
?

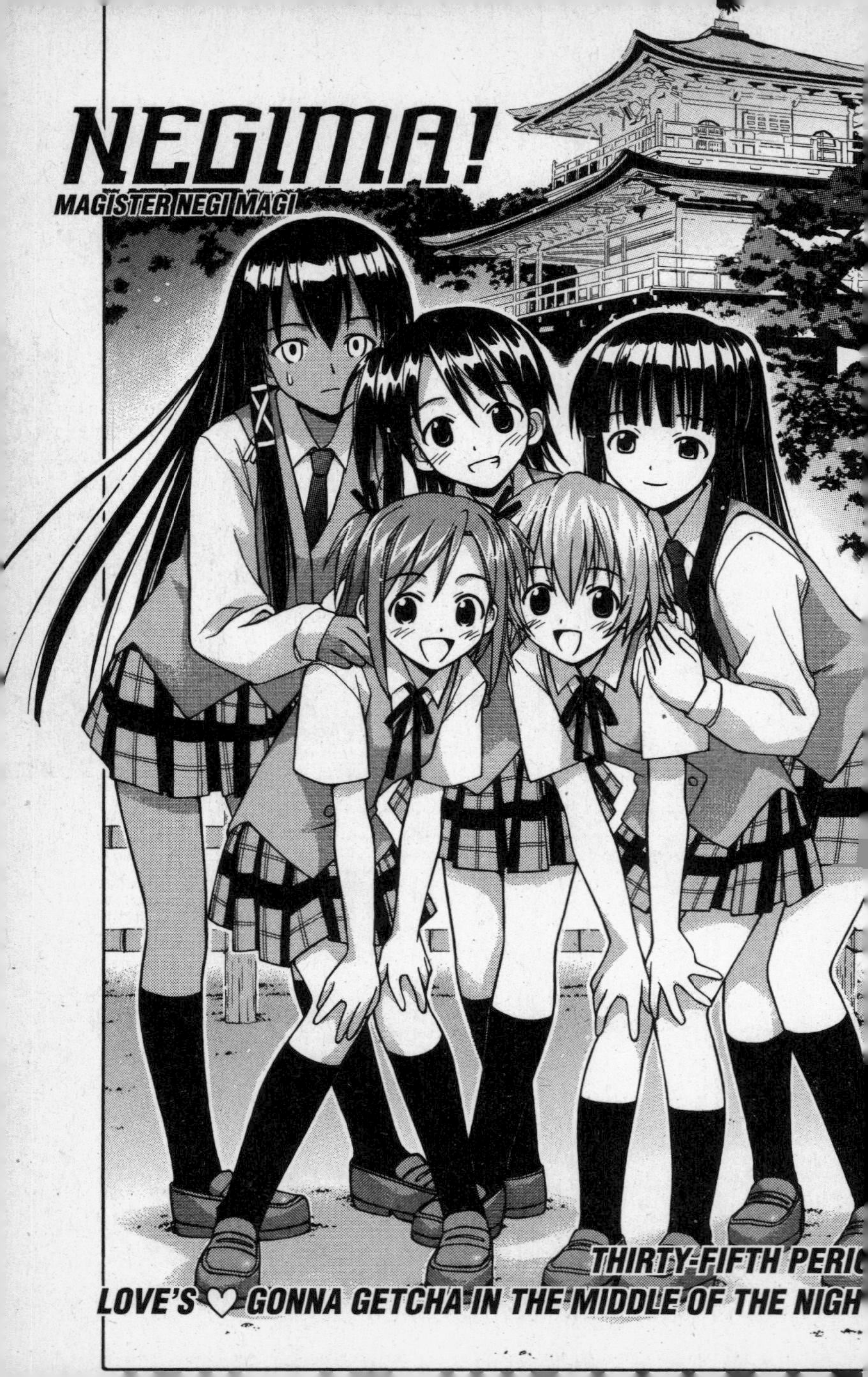
NEGIMA!
MAGISTER NEGI MAGI
THIRTY-FIFTH PERIO
LOVE'S ♡ GONNA GETCHA IN THE MIDDLE OF THE NIGH

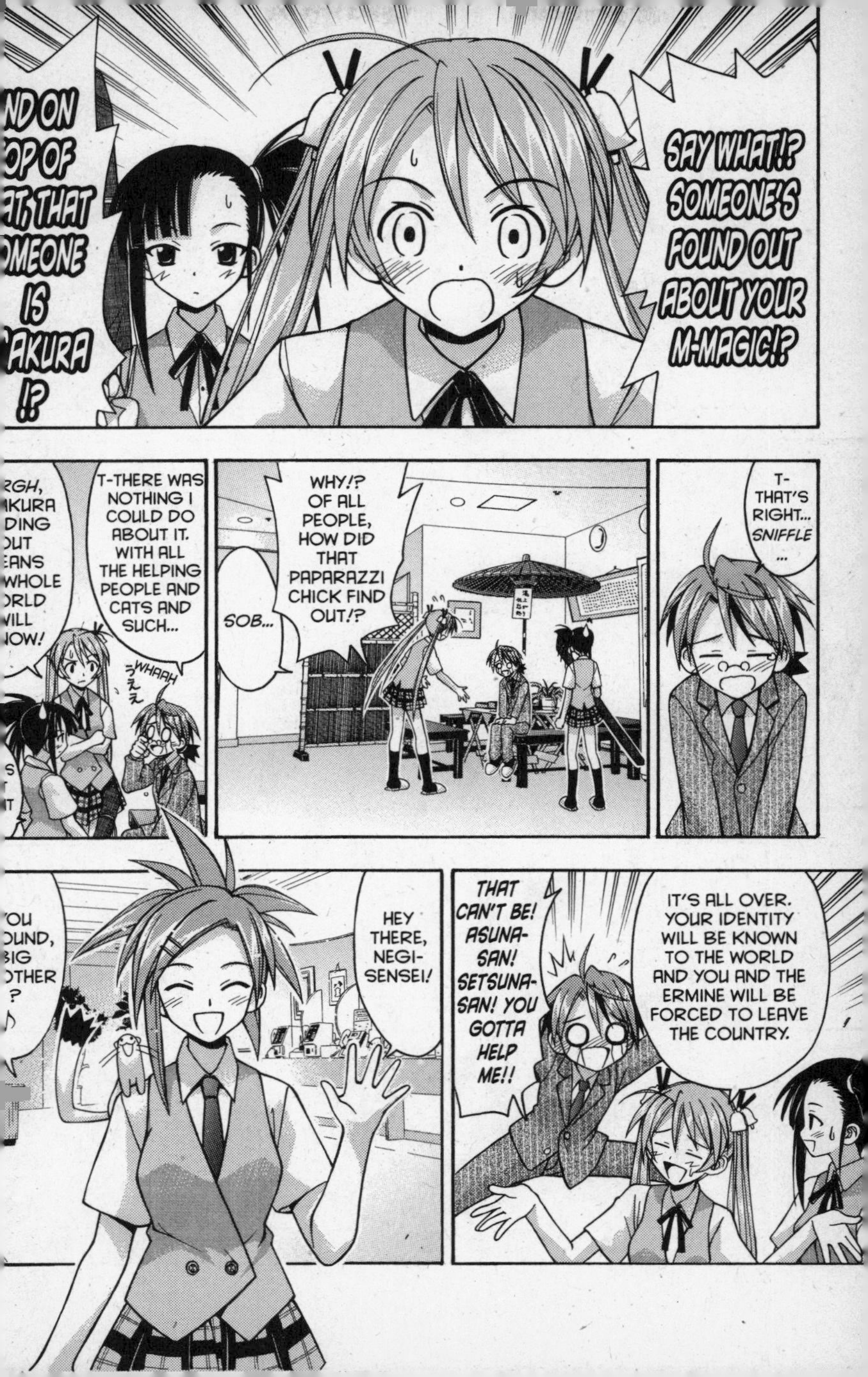
SAY WHAT!? SOMEONE'S FOUND OUT ABOUT YOUR M-MAGIC!?
ND ON OP OF AT, THAT OMEONE IS AKURA !?
T-THAT'S RIGHT... SNIFFLE ...
WHY!? OF ALL PEOPLE, HOW DID THAT PAPARAZZI CHICK FIND OUT!?
SOB...
T-THERE WAS NOTHING I COULD DO ABOUT IT. WITH ALL THE HELPING PEOPLE AND CATS AND SUCH...
WHAAAH
RGH, AKURA DING OUT EANS WHOLE ORLD WILL NOW!
IT'S ALL OVER. YOUR IDENTITY WILL BE KNOWN TO THE WORLD AND YOU AND THE ERMINE WILL BE FORCED TO LEAVE THE COUNTRY.
THAT CAN'T BE! ASUNA-SAN! SETSUNA-SAN! YOU GOTTA HELP ME!!
HEY THERE, NEGI-SENSEI!
OU OUND, BIG OTHER ? ♪

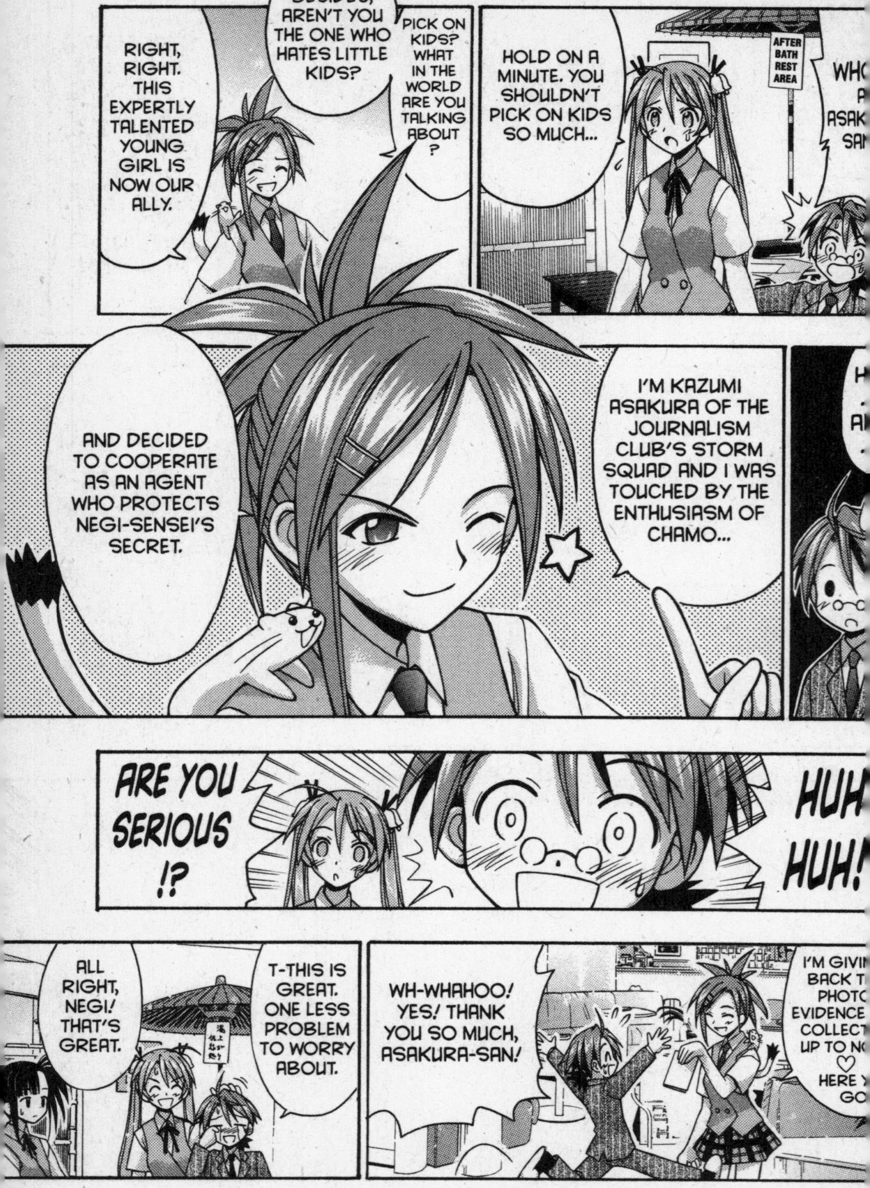
AFTER BATH REST AREA
HOLD ON A MINUTE. YOU SHOULDN'T PICK ON KIDS SO MUCH...
PICK ON KIDS? WHAT IN THE WORLD ARE YOU TALKING ABOUT?
BESIDES, AREN'T YOU THE ONE WHO HATES LITTLE KIDS?
RIGHT, RIGHT. THIS EXPERTLY TALENTED YOUNG GIRL IS NOW OUR ALLY.
I'M KAZUMI ASAKURA OF THE JOURNALISM CLUB'S STORM SQUAD AND I WAS TOUCHED BY THE ENTHUSIASM OF CHAMO...
AND DECIDED TO COOPERATE AS AN AGENT WHO PROTECTS NEGI-SENSEI'S SECRET.
HUH HUH!
ARE YOU SERIOUS !?
WH-WHAHOO! YES! THANK YOU SO MUCH, ASAKURA-SAN!
T-THIS IS GREAT. ONE LESS PROBLEM TO WORRY ABOUT.
ALL RIGHT, NEGI! THAT'S GREAT.

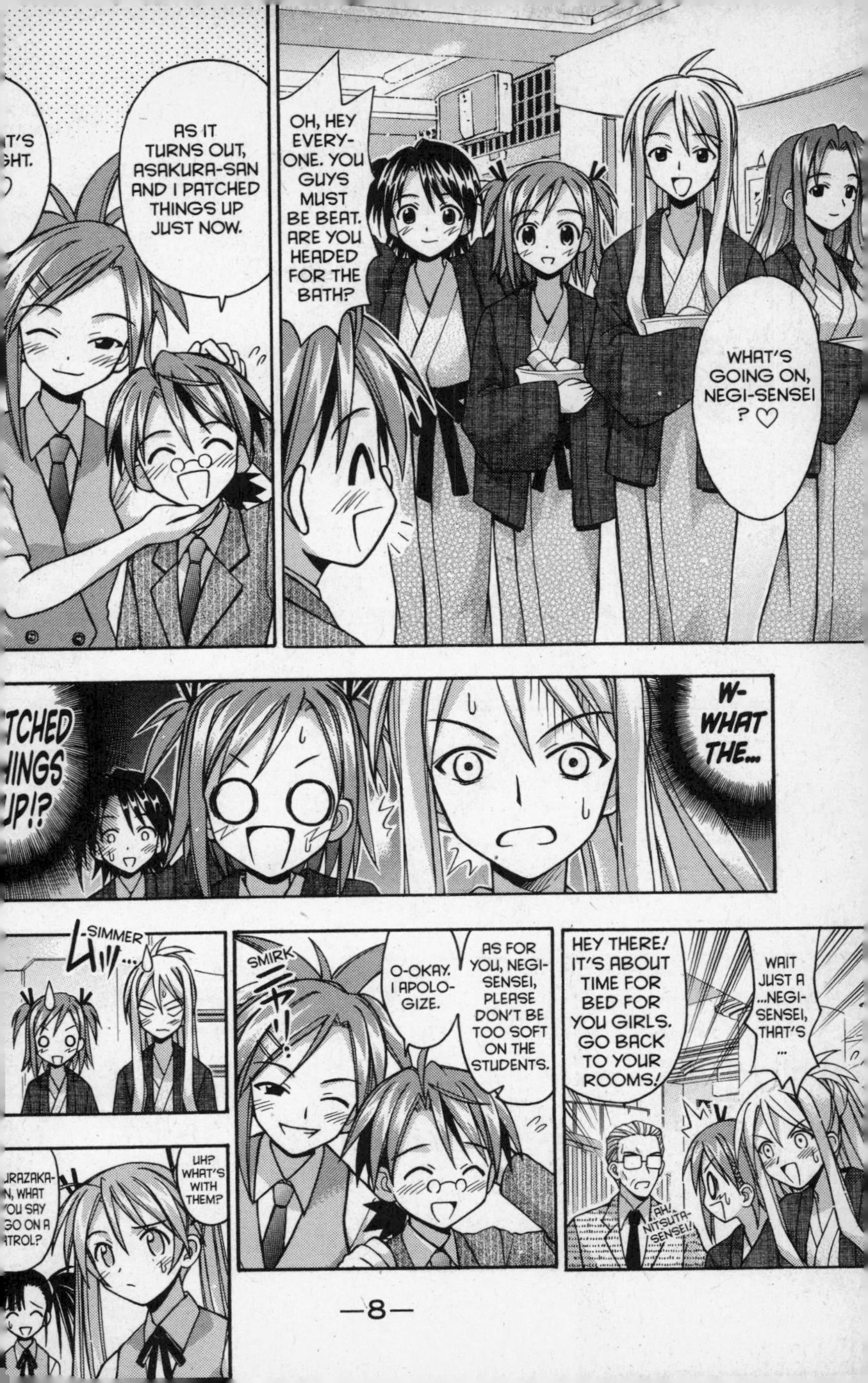
OH, HEY EVERY-ONE. YOU GUYS MUST BE BEAT. ARE YOU HEADED FOR THE BATH?
WHAT'S GOING ON, NEGI-SENSEI? ♡
AS IT TURNS OUT, ASAKURA-SAN AND I PATCHED THINGS UP JUST NOW.
T'S GHT. ♡
W-WHAT THE...
TCHED HINGS UP!?
WAIT JUST A ...NEGI-SENSEI, THAT'S ...
HEY THERE! IT'S ABOUT TIME FOR BED FOR YOU GIRLS. GO BACK TO YOUR ROOMS!
AH! NITSUTA-SENSEI!
AS FOR YOU, NEGI-SENSEI, PLEASE DON'T BE TOO SOFT ON THE STUDENTS.
O-OKAY. I APOLOGIZE.
SMIRK
SIMMER
UH? WHAT'S WITH THEM?
URAZAKA-N, WHAT YOU SAY GO ON A ATROL?

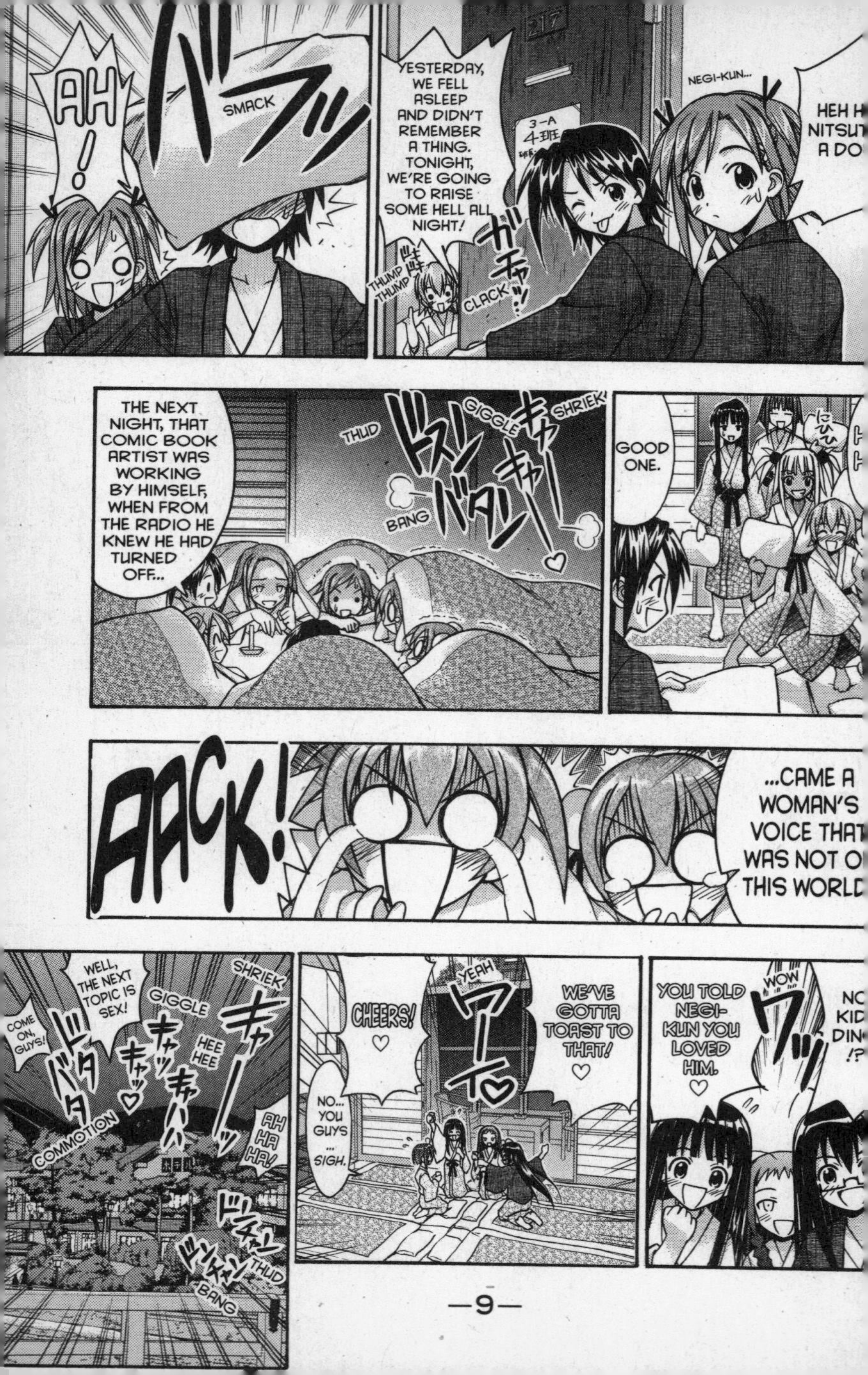
HEH H
NITSUT
A DO
NEGI-KUN...
YESTERDAY, WE FELL ASLEEP AND DIDN'T REMEMBER A THING. TONIGHT, WE'RE GOING TO RAISE SOME HELL ALL NIGHT!
3-A
THUMP THUMP
CLACK
SMACK
AH!
GOOD ONE.
SHRIEK
GIGGLE
THUD
BANG
THE NEXT NIGHT, THAT COMIC BOOK ARTIST WAS WORKING BY HIMSELF, WHEN FROM THE RADIO HE KNEW HE HAD TURNED OFF...
...CAME A WOMAN'S VOICE THAT WAS NOT O THIS WORLD
AACK!
NO KID DIN !?
WOW
YOU TOLD NEGI-KUN YOU LOVED HIM.
YEAH
WE'VE GOTTA TOAST TO THAT!
CHEERS!
NO... YOU GUYS ... SIGH.
SHRIEK
WELL, THE NEXT TOPIC IS SEX!
GIGGLE
COME ON, GUYS!
HEE HEE
AH HA HA!
COMMOTION
THUD
BANG

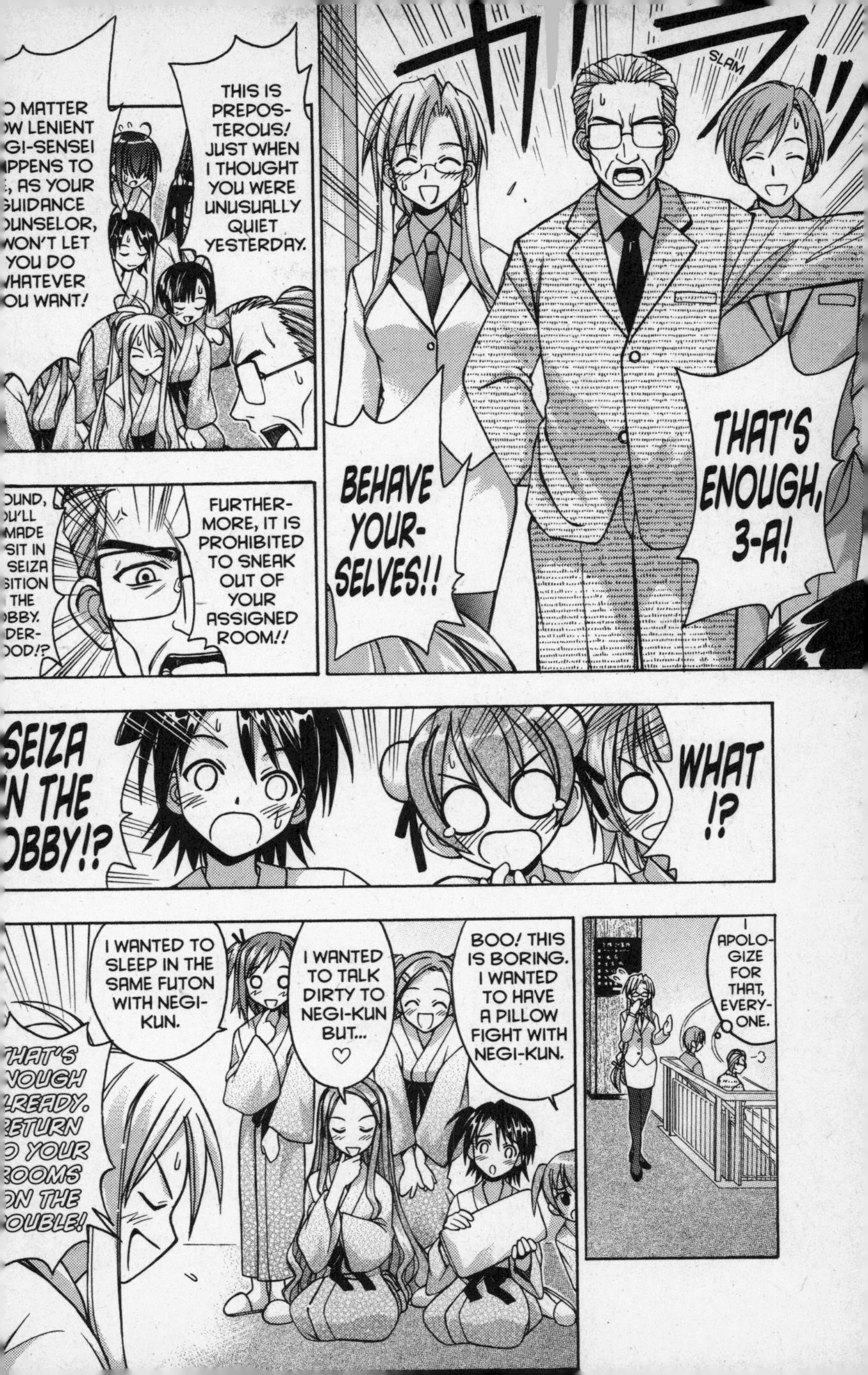
SLAM
THAT'S ENOUGH, 3-A!
BEHAVE YOURSELVES!!
THIS IS PREPOSTEROUS! JUST WHEN I THOUGHT YOU WERE UNUSUALLY QUIET YESTERDAY.
O MATTER W LENIENT GI-SENSEI PPENS TO , AS YOUR GUIDANCE OUNSELOR, WON'T LET YOU DO HATEVER OU WANT!
FURTHERMORE, IT IS PROHIBITED TO SNEAK OUT OF YOUR ASSIGNED ROOM!!
OUND, U'LL MADE SIT IN SEIZA SITION THE OBBY. DER- OOD!?
WHAT!?
SEIZA N THE OBBY!?
I APOLOGIZE FOR THAT, EVERYONE.
BOO! THIS IS BORING. I WANTED TO HAVE A PILLOW FIGHT WITH NEGI-KUN.
I WANTED TO TALK DIRTY TO NEGI-KUN BUT... ♡
I WANTED TO SLEEP IN THE SAME FUTON WITH NEGI-KUN.
THAT'S NOUGH LREADY. RETURN O YOUR ROOMS ON THE OUBLE!

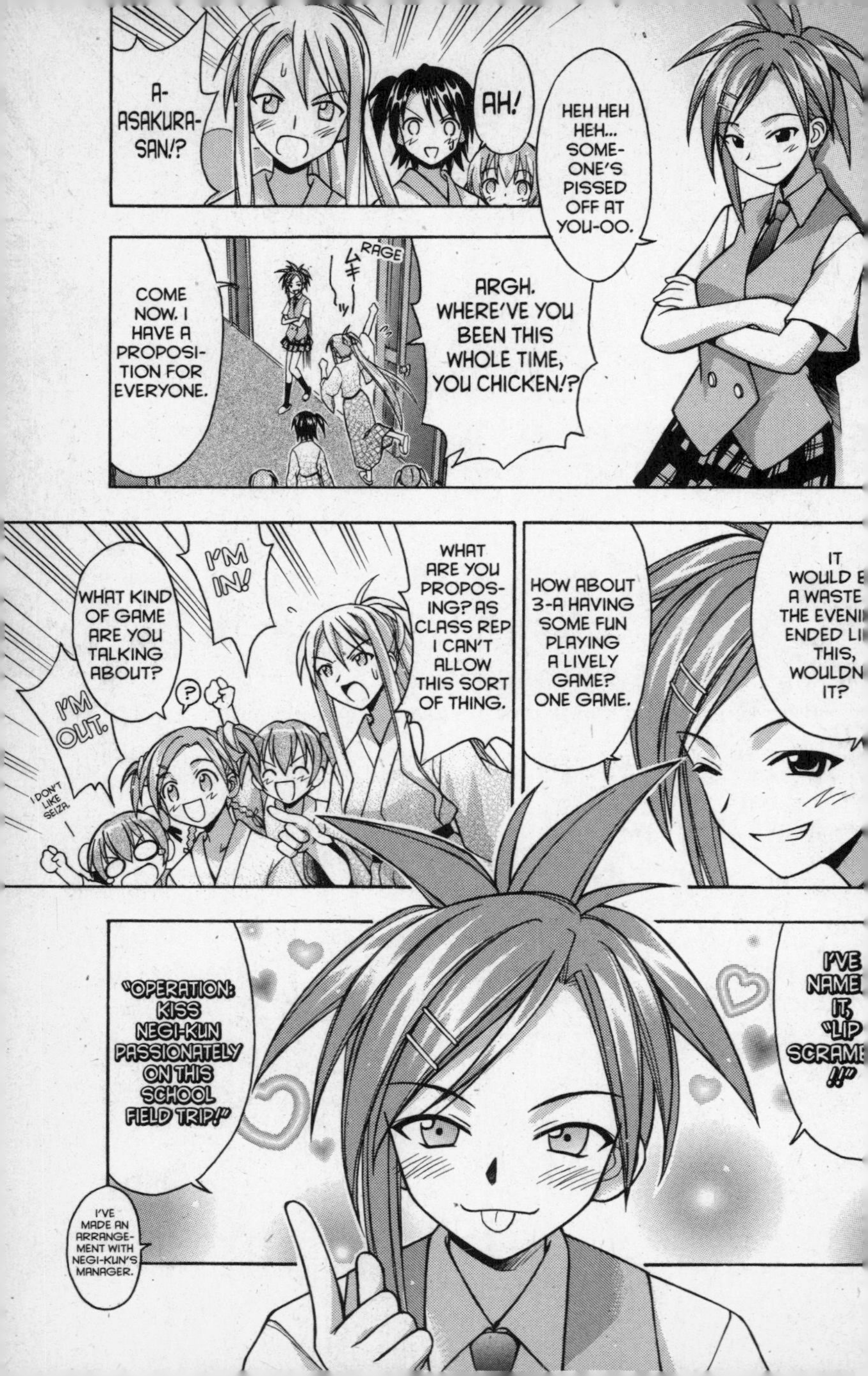
HEH HEH HEH... SOME-ONE'S PISSED OFF AT YOU-OO.
AH!
A-ASAKURA-SAN!?
RAGE
ARGH. WHERE'VE YOU BEEN THIS WHOLE TIME, YOU CHICKEN!?
COME NOW. I HAVE A PROPOSITION FOR EVERYONE.
IT WOULD B A WASTE THE EVENI ENDED LI THIS, WOULDN IT?
HOW ABOUT 3-A HAVING SOME FUN PLAYING A LIVELY GAME? ONE GAME.
WHAT ARE YOU PROPOSING? AS CLASS REP I CAN'T ALLOW THIS SORT OF THING.
I'M IN!
WHAT KIND OF GAME ARE YOU TALKING ABOUT?
?
I'M OUT.
I DON'T LIKE SEIZA.
I'VE NAME IT, "LIP SCRAMB!!"
"OPERATION: KISS NEGI-KUN PASSIONATELY ON THIS SCHOOL FIELD TRIP!"
I'VE MADE AN ARRANGEMENT WITH NEGI-KUN'S MANAGER.

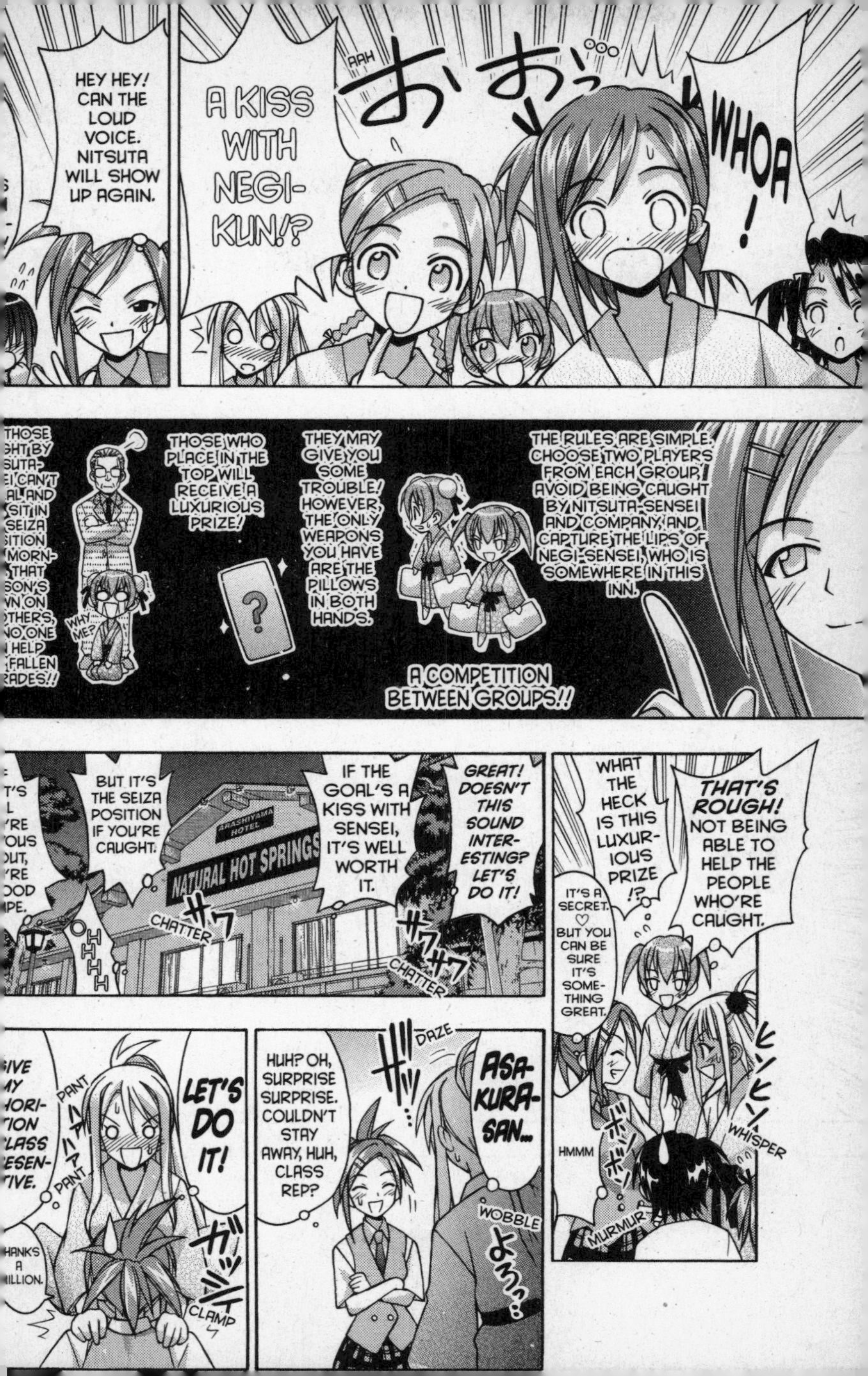
WHOA!
AAH
おおっ
A KISS WITH NEGI-KUN!?
HEY HEY! CAN THE LOUD VOICE. NITSUTA WILL SHOW UP AGAIN.
THE RULES ARE SIMPLE. CHOOSE TWO PLAYERS FROM EACH GROUP, AVOID BEING CAUGHT BY NITSUTA-SENSEI AND COMPANY, AND CAPTURE THE LIPS OF NEGI-SENSEI, WHO IS SOMEWHERE IN THIS INN.
A COMPETITION BETWEEN GROUPS!!
THEY MAY GIVE YOU SOME TROUBLE! HOWEVER, THE ONLY WEAPONS YOU HAVE ARE THE PILLOWS IN BOTH HANDS.
THOSE WHO PLACE IN THE TOP WILL RECEIVE A LUXURIOUS PRIZE!
WHY ME?
THAT'S ROUGH! NOT BEING ABLE TO HELP THE PEOPLE WHO'RE CAUGHT.
WHAT THE HECK IS THIS LUXURIOUS PRIZE!?
IT'S A SECRET. ♡ BUT YOU CAN BE SURE IT'S SOMETHING GREAT.
WHISPER
HMMM
MURMUR
GREAT! DOESN'T THIS SOUND INTERESTING? LET'S DO IT!
IF THE GOAL'S A KISS WITH SENSEI, IT'S WELL WORTH IT.
ARASHIYAMA HOTEL
NATURAL HOT SPRINGS
CHATTER
CHATTER
BUT IT'S THE SEIZA POSITION IF YOU'RE CAUGHT.
OHHHH
ASA-KURA-SAN...
DAZE
HUH? OH, SURPRISE SURPRISE. COULDN'T STAY AWAY, HUH, CLASS REP?
WOBBLE
LET'S DO IT!
PANT
PANT
CLAMP

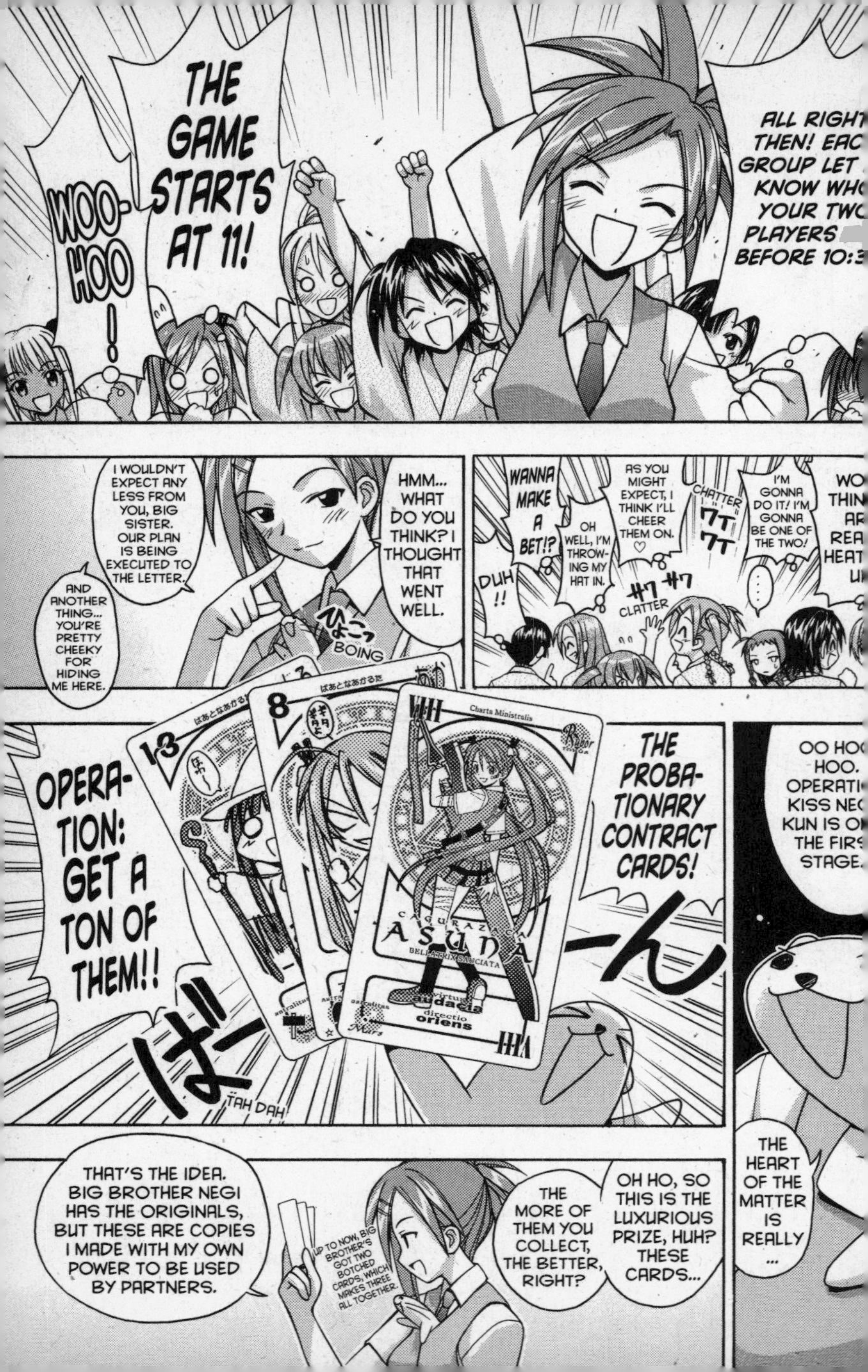
ALL RIGHT THEN! EAC GROUP LET KNOW WH YOUR TWO PLAYERS BEFORE 10:3
THE GAME STARTS AT 11!
WOO-HOO!
WO THIN AR REA HEAT U
I'M GONNA DO IT! I'M GONNA BE ONE OF THE TWO!
...
CHATTER
AS YOU MIGHT EXPECT, I THINK I'LL CHEER THEM ON. ♡
OH WELL, I'M THROWING MY HAT IN.
WANNA MAKE A BET!?
DUH !!
CLATTER
HMM... WHAT DO YOU THINK? I THOUGHT THAT WENT WELL.
I WOULDN'T EXPECT ANY LESS FROM YOU, BIG SISTER. OUR PLAN IS BEING EXECUTED TO THE LETTER.
AND ANOTHER THING... YOU'RE PRETTY CHEEKY FOR HIDING ME HERE.
BOING
OO HO HOO. OPERATI KISS NE KUN IS O THE FIRS STAGE.
THE HEART OF THE MATTER IS REALLY ...
THE PROBATIONARY CONTRACT CARDS!
Charta Ministralis
CAGURAZACA ASUNA
BELLATRIX SAUCIATA
audacia
directio oriens
Mars
OPERATION: GET A TON OF THEM!!
TAH DAH
OH HO, SO THIS IS THE LUXURIOUS PRIZE, HUH? THESE CARDS...
THE MORE OF THEM YOU COLLECT, THE BETTER, RIGHT?
THAT'S THE IDEA. BIG BROTHER NEGI HAS THE ORIGINALS, BUT THESE ARE COPIES I MADE WITH MY OWN POWER TO BE USED BY PARTNERS.
UP TO NOW, BIG BROTHER'S GOT TWO BOTCHED CARDS, WHICH MAKES THREE ALL TOGETHER.

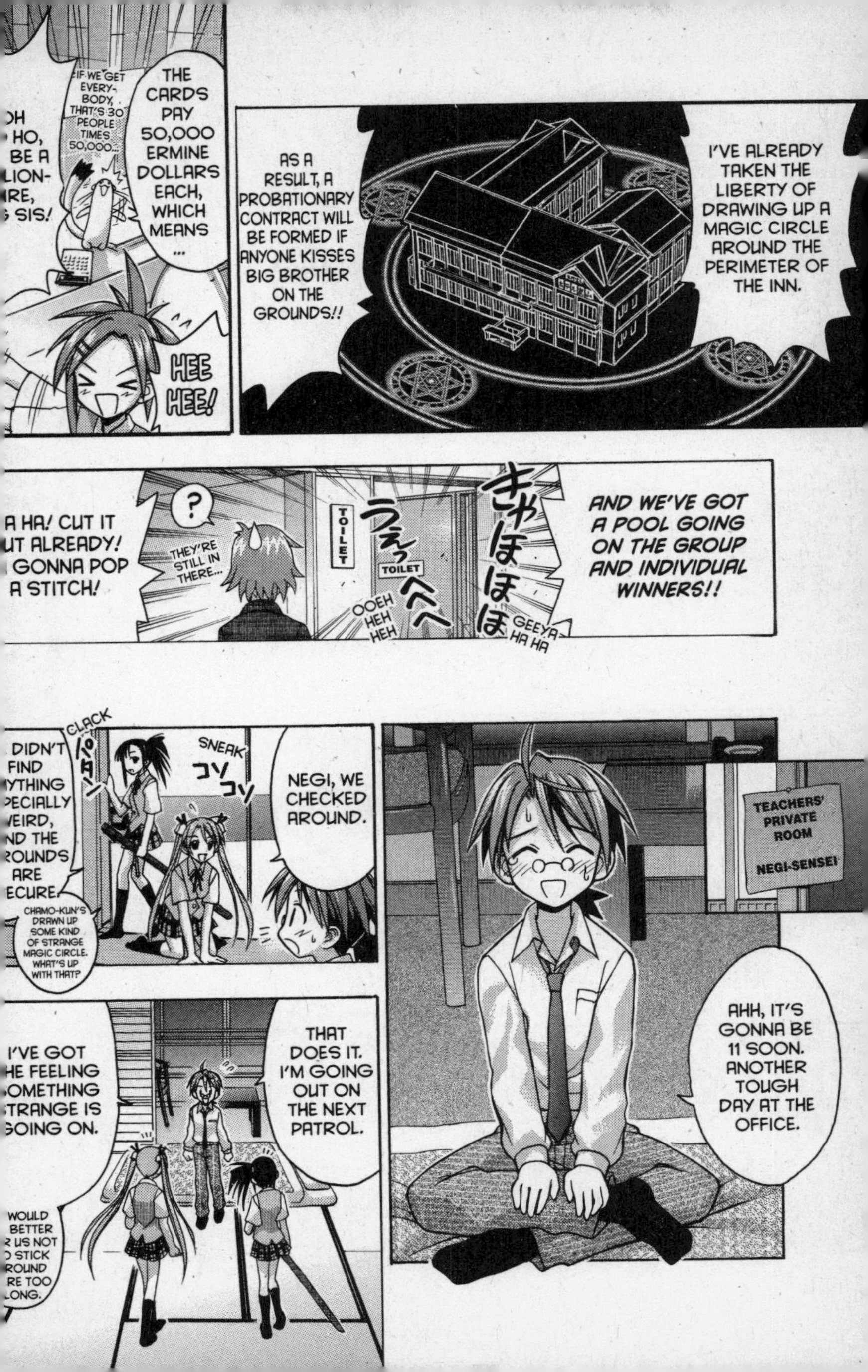
I'VE ALREADY TAKEN THE LIBERTY OF DRAWING UP A MAGIC CIRCLE AROUND THE PERIMETER OF THE INN.
AS A RESULT, A PROBATIONARY CONTRACT WILL BE FORMED IF ANYONE KISSES BIG BROTHER ON THE GROUNDS!!
THE CARDS PAY 50,000 ERMINE DOLLARS EACH, WHICH MEANS ...
IF WE GET EVERY-BODY, THAT'S 30 PEOPLE TIMES 50,000...
OH HO, BE A LION-AIRE, SIS!
HEE HEE!
AND WE'VE GOT A POOL GOING ON THE GROUP AND INDIVIDUAL WINNERS!!
きゃほほほ
GEEYA-HA HA
うえっへへへ
OOEH HEH HEH
TOILET
TOILET
?
THEY'RE STILL IN THERE...
A HA! CUT IT UT ALREADY! GONNA POP A STITCH!
TEACHERS' PRIVATE ROOM
NEGI-SENSEI
AHH, IT'S GONNA BE 11 SOON. ANOTHER TOUGH DAY AT THE OFFICE.
NEGI, WE CHECKED AROUND.
SNEAK
コソコソ
CLACK
パタン
DIDN'T FIND YTHING PECIALLY EIRD, ND THE ROUNDS ARE ECURE.
CHAMO-KUN'S DRAWN UP SOME KIND OF STRANGE MAGIC CIRCLE. WHAT'S UP WITH THAT?
THAT DOES IT. I'M GOING OUT ON THE NEXT PATROL.
I'VE GOT HE FEELING OMETHING TRANGE IS OING ON.
WOULD BETTER R US NOT O STICK ROUND RE TOO LONG.

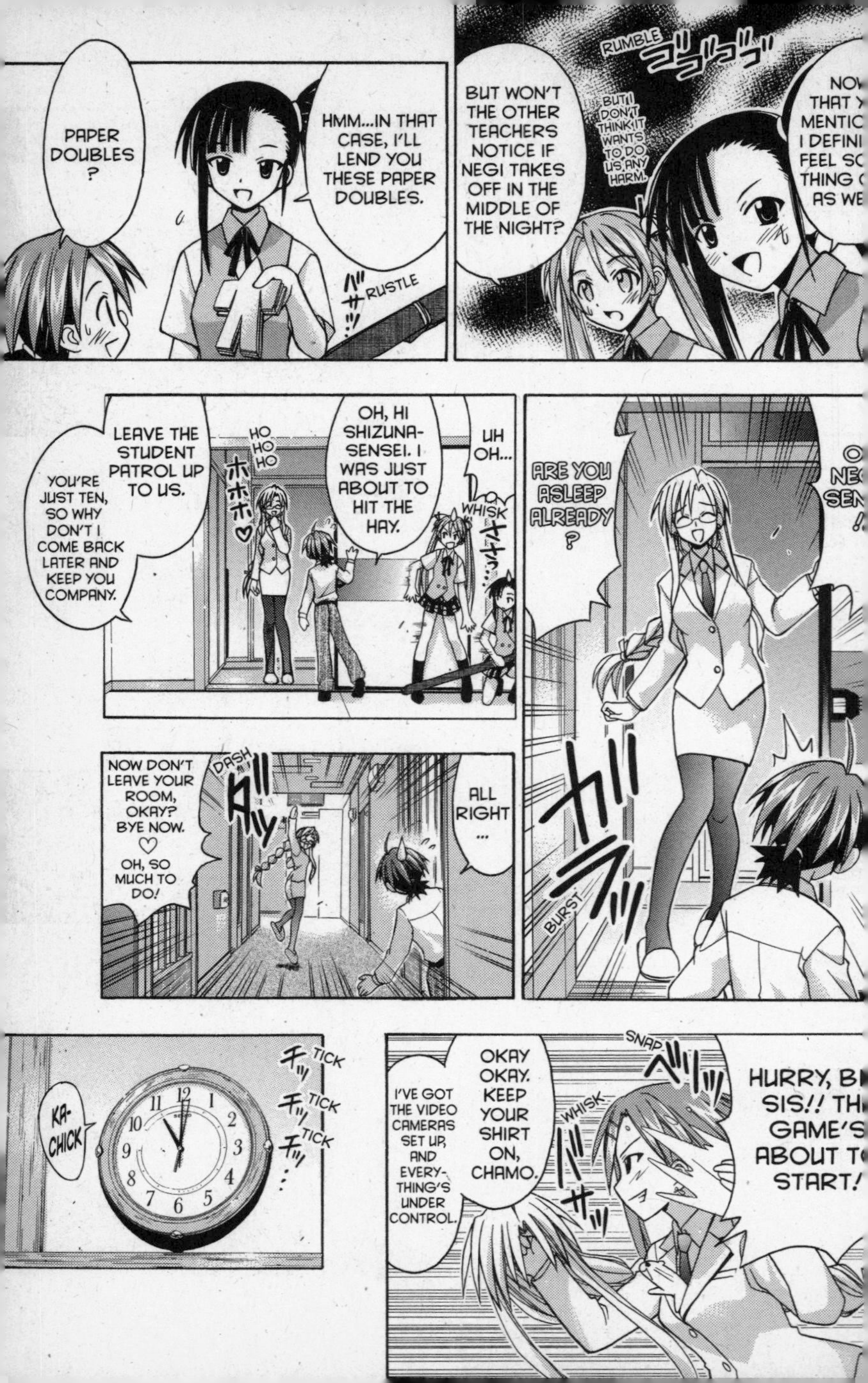
RUMBLE
ゴゴゴゴ
NOW THAT Y
MENTIC
I DEFINI
FEEL SC
THING C
AS WE
BUT I DON'T THINK IT WANTS TO DO US ANY HARM.
BUT WON'T THE OTHER TEACHERS NOTICE IF NEGI TAKES OFF IN THE MIDDLE OF THE NIGHT?
HMM...IN THAT CASE, I'LL LEND YOU THESE PAPER DOUBLES.
バサッ RUSTLE
PAPER DOUBLES?
O
NEG
SEN
!
ARE YOU ASLEEP ALREADY?
ガラッ
BURST
UH OH...
さささっ WHISK
OH, HI SHIZUNA-SENSEI. I WAS JUST ABOUT TO HIT THE HAY.
HO HO HO
ホホホ♡
LEAVE THE STUDENT PATROL UP TO US.
YOU'RE JUST TEN, SO WHY DON'T I COME BACK LATER AND KEEP YOU COMPANY.
ALL RIGHT...
DASH
NOW DON'T LEAVE YOUR ROOM, OKAY? BYE NOW. ♡
OH, SO MUCH TO DO!
HURRY, B
SIS!! TH
GAME'S
ABOUT T
START!
SNAP
ベッ
OKAY OKAY. KEEP YOUR SHIRT ON, CHAMO.
WHISK
バサッ
I'VE GOT THE VIDEO CAMERAS SET UP, AND EVERYTHING'S UNDER CONTROL.
チッ TICK
チッ TICK
チッ TICK
KA-CHICK

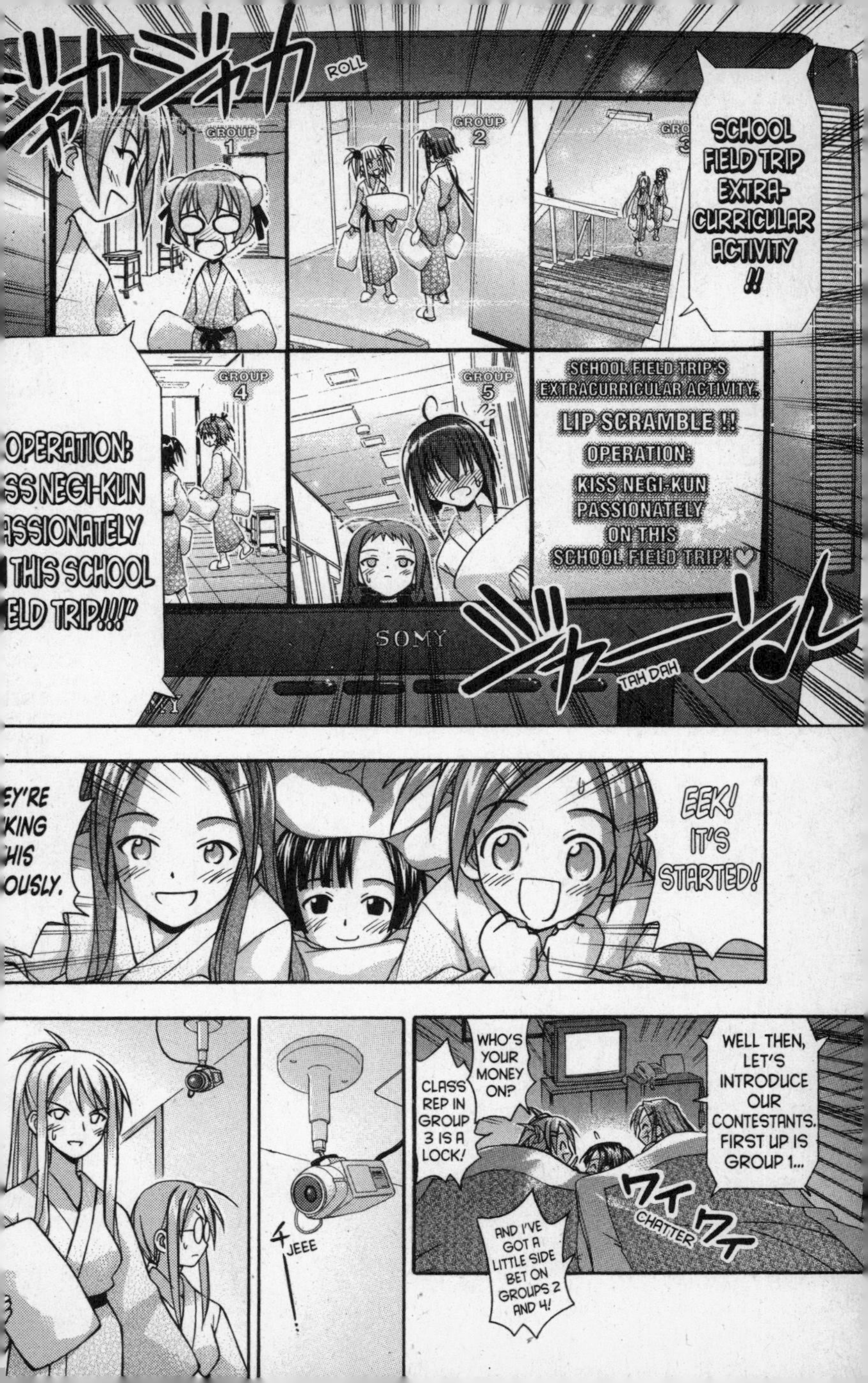

SCHOOL FIELD TRIP EXTRA-CURRICULAR ACTIVITY !!
ジャカジャカ
ROLL
GROUP 3
GROUP 2
GROUP 1
SCHOOL FIELD TRIP'S EXTRACURRICULAR ACTIVITY.
LIP SCRAMBLE !!
OPERATION: KISS NEGI-KUN PASSIONATELY ON THIS SCHOOL FIELD TRIP! ♡
GROUP 5
GROUP 4
OPERATION:
SS NEGI-KUN
ASSIONATELY
THIS SCHOOL
ELD TRIP!!!"
SOMY
ジャーン
TAH DAH
EEK! IT'S STARTED!
EY'RE
KING
HIS
OUSLY.
WELL THEN, LET'S INTRODUCE OUR CONTESTANTS. FIRST UP IS GROUP 1...
WHO'S YOUR MONEY ON?
CLASS REP IN GROUP 3 IS A LOCK!
ワイワイ
CHATTER
AND I'VE GOT A LITTLE SIDE BET ON GROUPS 2 AND 4!
JEEE

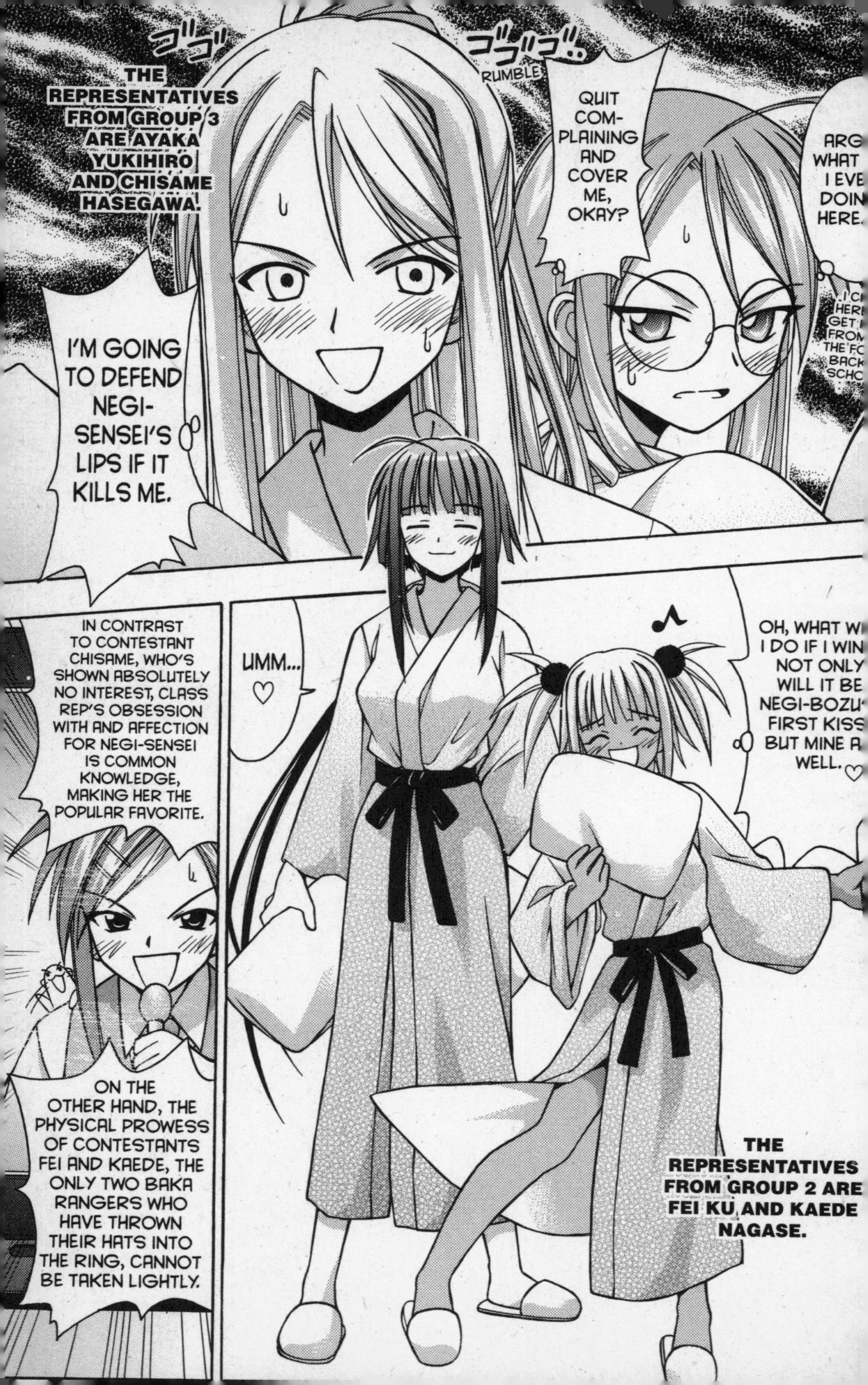
ARG WHAT I EVE DOIN HERE.
QUIT COMPLAINING AND COVER ME, OKAY?
RUMBLE
THE REPRESENTATIVES FROM GROUP 3 ARE AYAKA YUKIHIRO AND CHISAME HASEGAWA.
I'M GOING TO DEFEND NEGI-SENSEI'S LIPS IF IT KILLS ME.
OH, WHAT WI I DO IF I WIN NOT ONLY WILL IT BE NEGI-BOZU FIRST KISS BUT MINE A WELL. ♡
UMM... ♡
THE REPRESENTATIVES FROM GROUP 2 ARE FEI KU AND KAEDE NAGASE.
IN CONTRAST TO CONTESTANT CHISAME, WHO'S SHOWN ABSOLUTELY NO INTEREST, CLASS REP'S OBSESSION WITH AND AFFECTION FOR NEGI-SENSEI IS COMMON KNOWLEDGE, MAKING HER THE POPULAR FAVORITE.
ON THE OTHER HAND, THE PHYSICAL PROWESS OF CONTESTANTS FEI AND KAEDE, THE ONLY TWO BAKA RANGERS WHO HAVE THROWN THEIR HATS INTO THE RING, CANNOT BE TAKEN LIGHTLY.

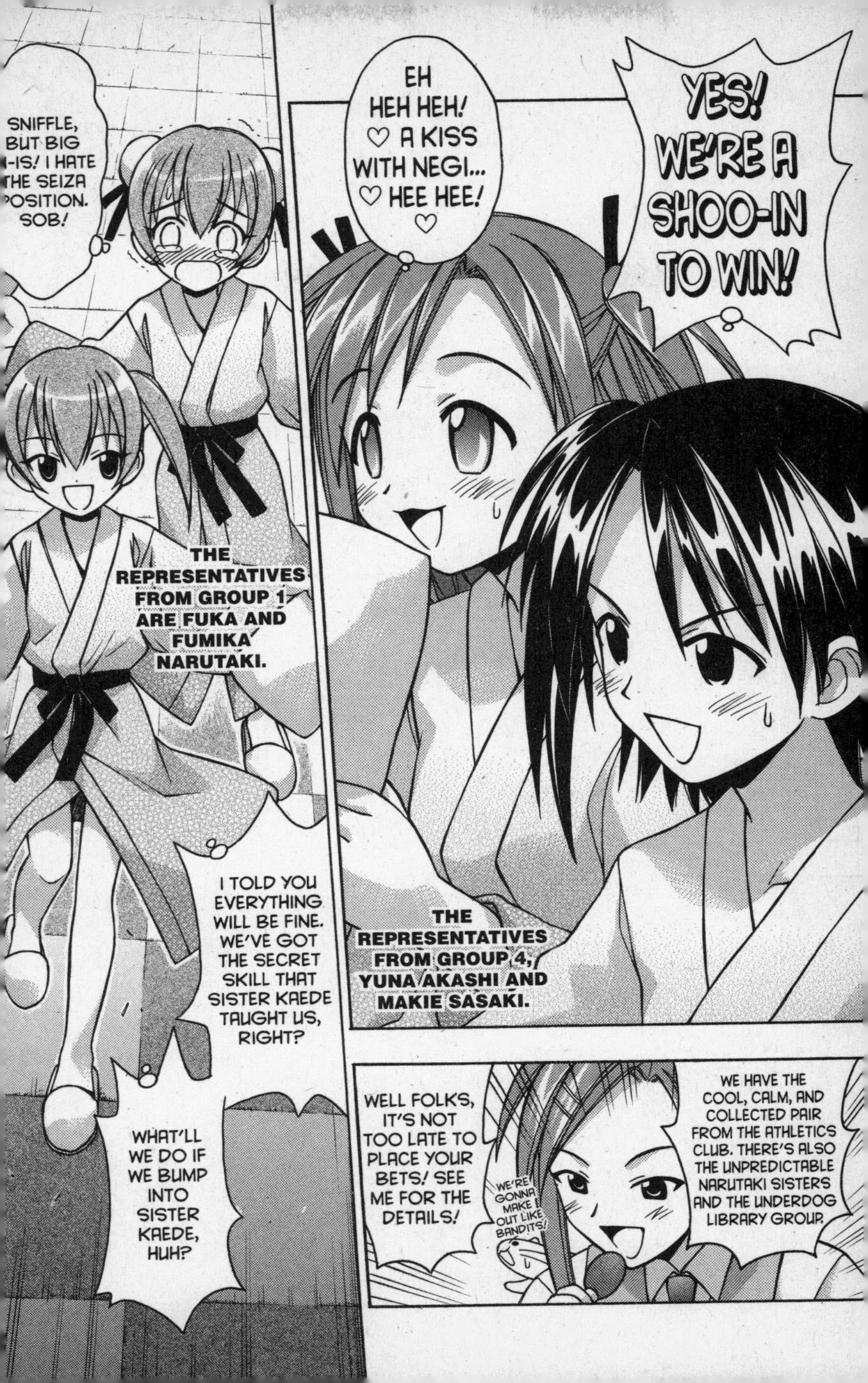
YES! WE'RE A SHOO-IN TO WIN!
EH HEH HEH! ♡ A KISS WITH NEGI... ♡ HEE HEE! ♡
THE REPRESENTATIVES FROM GROUP 4, YUNA AKASHI AND MAKIE SASAKI.
WE HAVE THE COOL, CALM, AND COLLECTED PAIR FROM THE ATHLETICS CLUB. THERE'S ALSO THE UNPREDICTABLE NARUTAKI SISTERS AND THE UNDERDOG LIBRARY GROUP.
WE'RE GONNA MAKE OUT LIKE BANDITS!
WELL FOLKS, IT'S NOT TOO LATE TO PLACE YOUR BETS! SEE ME FOR THE DETAILS!
SNIFFLE, BUT BIG -IS! I HATE THE SEIZA OSITION. SOB!
THE REPRESENTATIVES FROM GROUP 1 ARE FUKA AND FUMIKA NARUTAKI.
I TOLD YOU EVERYTHING WILL BE FINE. WE'VE GOT THE SECRET SKILL THAT SISTER KAEDE TAUGHT US, RIGHT?
WHAT'LL WE DO IF WE BUMP INTO SISTER KAEDE, HUH?

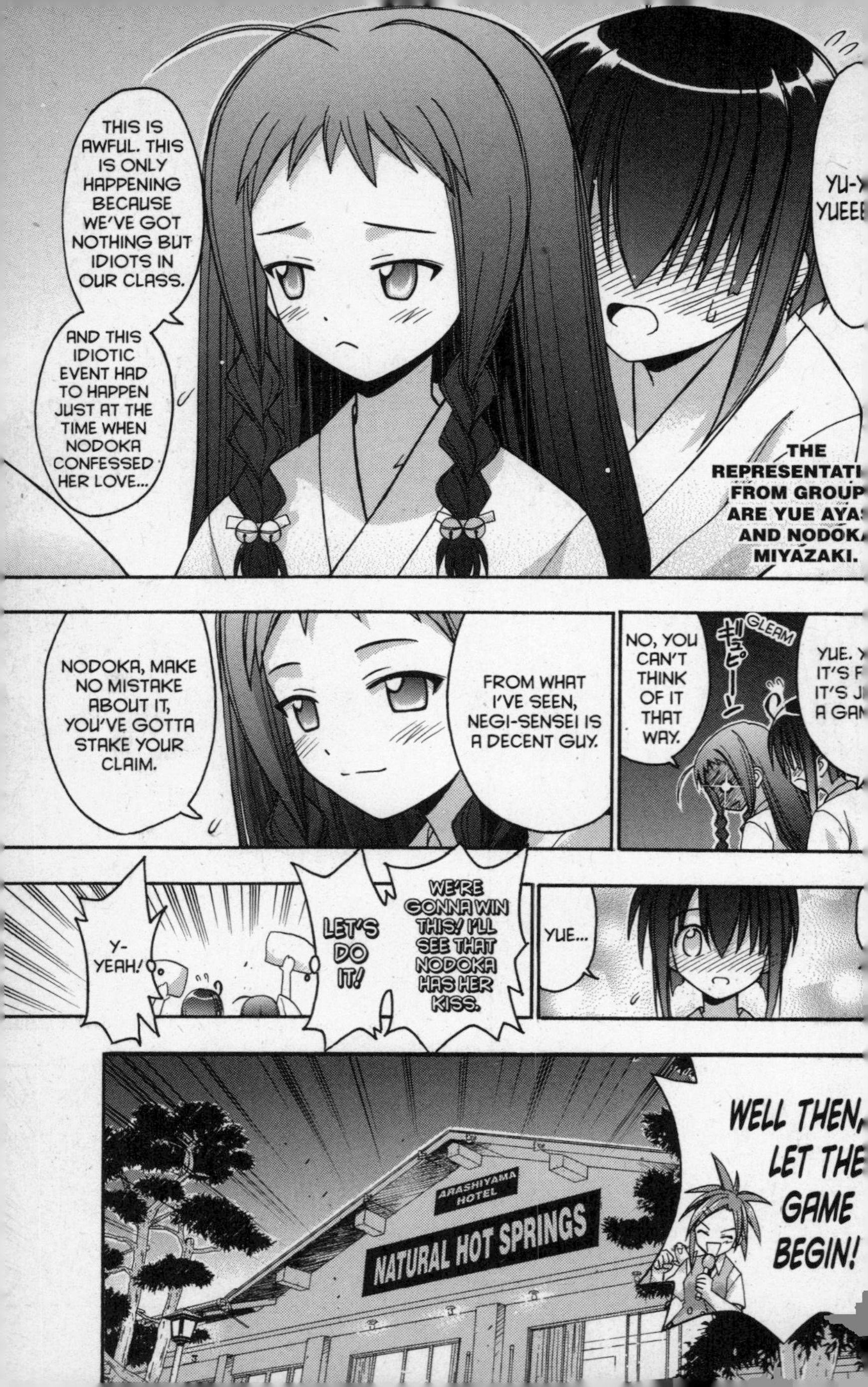
YU-Y
YUEEE
THE REPRESENTATI FROM GROUP ARE YUE AYA AND NODOKA MIYAZAKI.
THIS IS AWFUL. THIS IS ONLY HAPPENING BECAUSE WE'VE GOT NOTHING BUT IDIOTS IN OUR CLASS.
AND THIS IDIOTIC EVENT HAD TO HAPPEN JUST AT THE TIME WHEN NODOKA CONFESSED HER LOVE...
YUE. Y
IT'S F
IT'S J
A GA
GLEAM
NO, YOU CAN'T THINK OF IT THAT WAY.
FROM WHAT I'VE SEEN, NEGI-SENSEI IS A DECENT GUY.
NODOKA, MAKE NO MISTAKE ABOUT IT, YOU'VE GOTTA STAKE YOUR CLAIM.
YUE...
WE'RE GONNA WIN THIS! I'LL SEE THAT NODOKA HAS HER KISS.
LET'S DO IT!
Y- YEAH!
WELL THEN, LET THE GAME BEGIN!
ARASHIYAMA HOTEL
NATURAL HOT SPRINGS

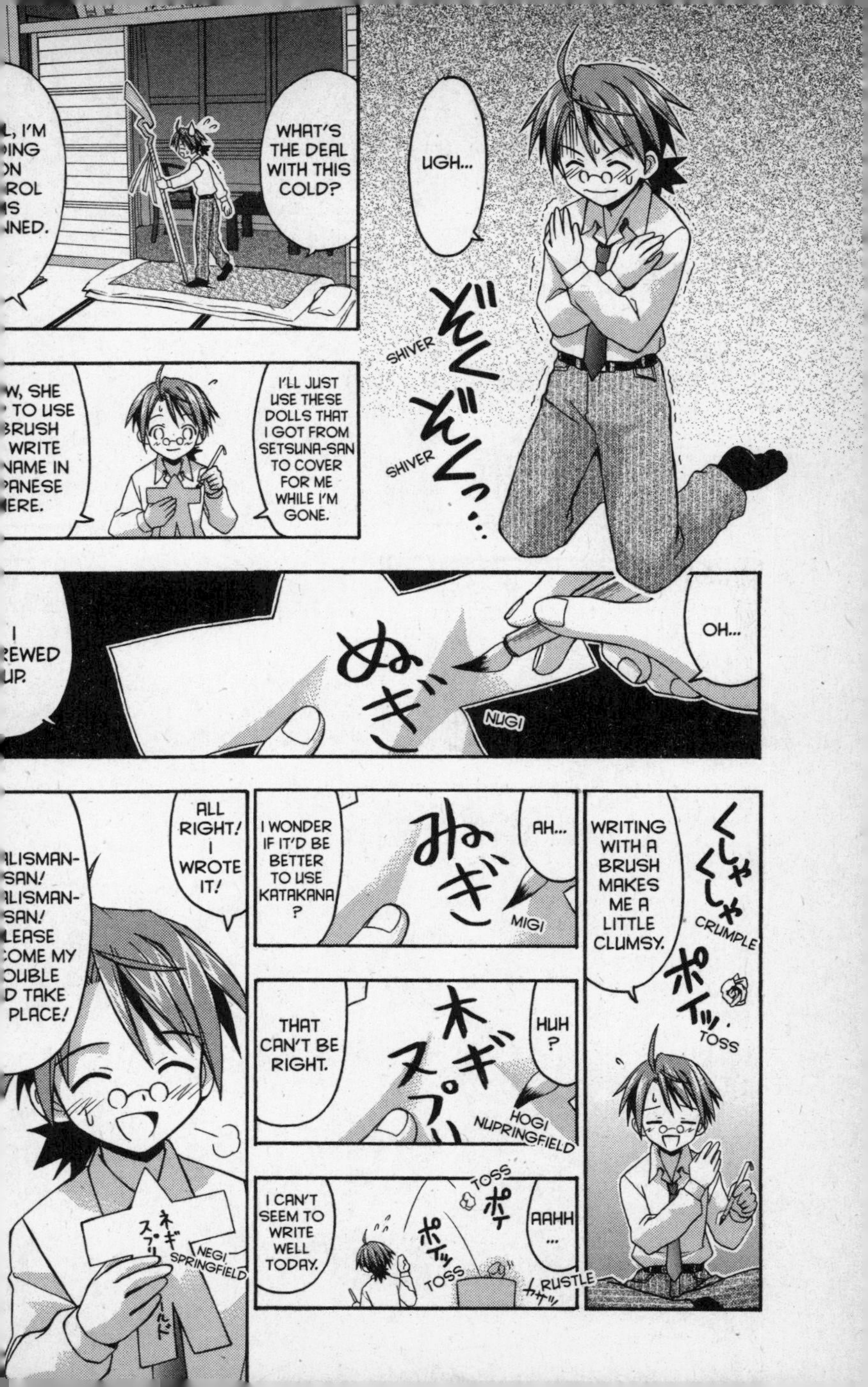

UGH...
ぞくぞくっ...
SHIVER
SHIVER
WHAT'S THE DEAL WITH THIS COLD?
L, I'M DING ON ROL S NNED.
I'LL JUST USE THESE DOLLS THAT I GOT FROM SETSUNA-SAN TO COVER FOR ME WHILE I'M GONE.
W, SHE TO USE BRUSH WRITE NAME IN PANESE ERE.
OH...
ぬぎ
NUGI
I REWED UP.
WRITING WITH A BRUSH MAKES ME A LITTLE CLUMSY.
くしゃくしゃ
CRUMPLE
ポイッ
TOSS
AH...
みぎ
MIGI
I WONDER IF IT'D BE BETTER TO USE KATAKANA?
HUH?
ホギヌプリ
HOGI NUPRINGFIELD
THAT CAN'T BE RIGHT.
AAHH...
ポイ
TOSS
ポイッ
TOSS
カサッ
RUSTLE
I CAN'T SEEM TO WRITE WELL TODAY.
ALL RIGHT! I WROTE IT!
ALISMAN-SAN! ALISMAN-SAN! LEASE COME MY OUBLE D TAKE PLACE!
ネギスプリ
NEGI SPRINGFIELD

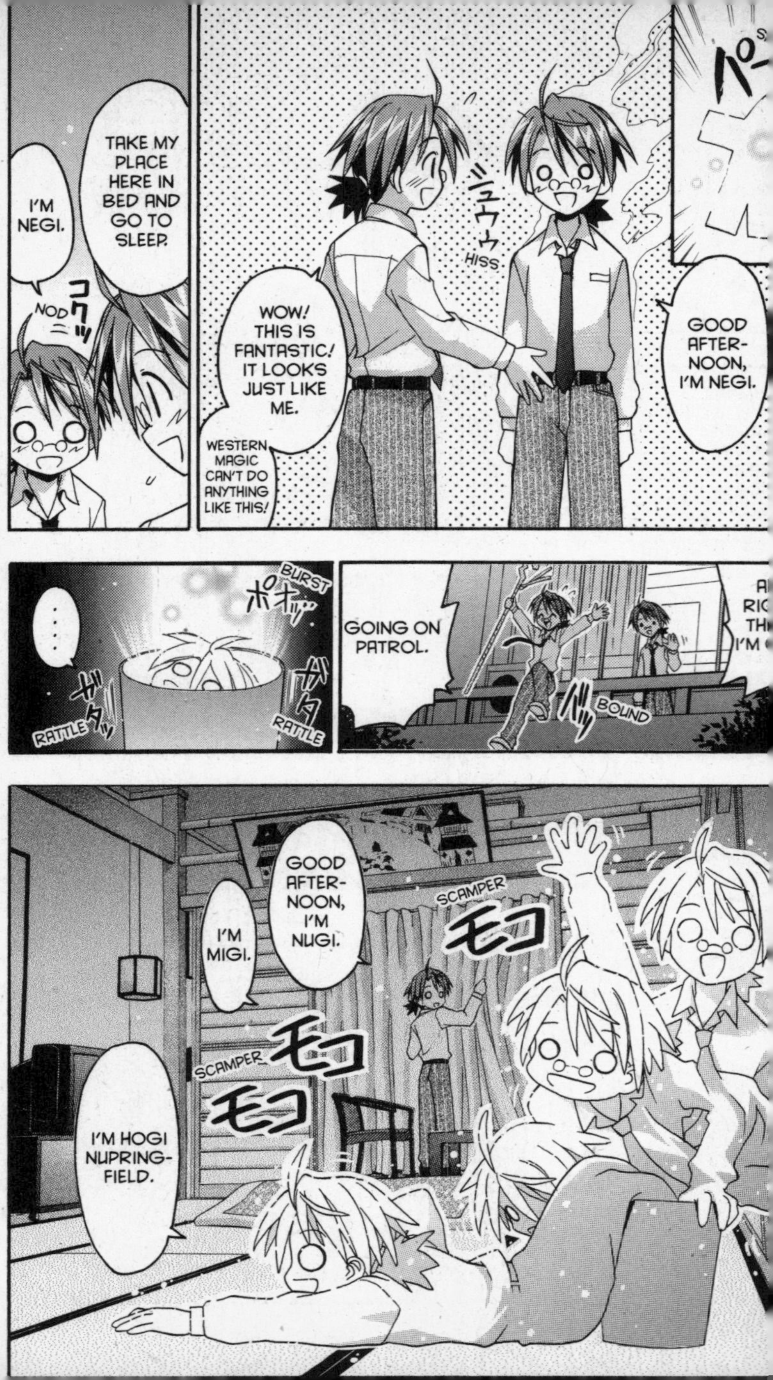
GOOD AFTERNOON, I'M NEGI.
HISS
WOW! THIS IS FANTASTIC! IT LOOKS JUST LIKE ME.
WESTERN MAGIC CAN'T DO ANYTHING LIKE THIS!
TAKE MY PLACE HERE IN BED AND GO TO SLEEP.
I'M NEGI.
NOD
GOING ON PATROL.
BOUND
BURST
RATTLE
RATTLE
. . . .
SCAMPER
GOOD AFTERNOON, I'M NUGI.
I'M MIGI.
SCAMPER
I'M HOGI NUPRINGFIELD.

"OPERATION KISS NEGI-KUN PASSIONATELY ON THIS SCHOOL FIELD TRIP" PLAYER INTRODUCTIONS.

GROUP 1: FUMIKA AND FUKA
WE'VE GOT A SECRET PLAN!! IF YOU WANNA ROCK THE BOAT, WE'RE YOUR TEAM!

GROUP 2: KAEDE AND FEI KU
THEIR COMBAT POWERS MAKE THEM THE BIG FAVORITES! BUT DO THEY LACK THE WILL TO WIN?

GROUP 3: CLASS REP AND CHISAME
THERE ARE DOUBTS ABOUT THEIR TEAMWORK, BUT IF THEY CAN WORK TOGETHER THERE'S NO STOPPING THEM.

GROUP 4: YUNA AND MAKIE
WE'VE GOT SUPREME BALANCE!! WE'LL NEVER GIVE AN INCH!!

GROUP 5: NODOKA AND YUE
THEY WANT IT BAD ENOUGH!! THEY'LL TAKE ON THE CHALLENGE USING THEIR INTELLECT AND HEART!!

THIRTY-SIXTH PERIOD: THE LABYRINTH OF LIP

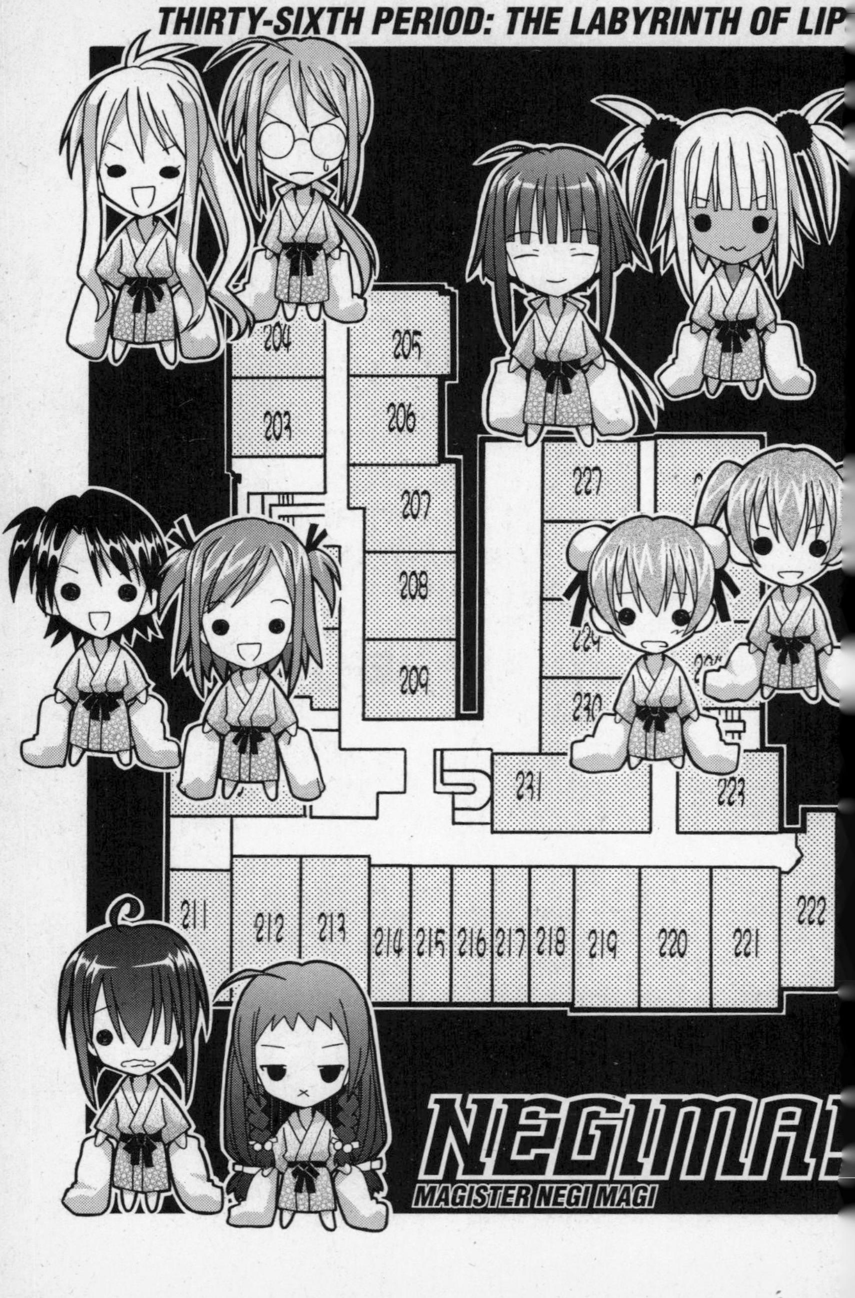
204
205
203
206
227
207
208
224
209
230
231
223
211
212
213
214
215
216
217
218
219
220
221
222
NEGIMA
MAGISTER NEGI MAGI

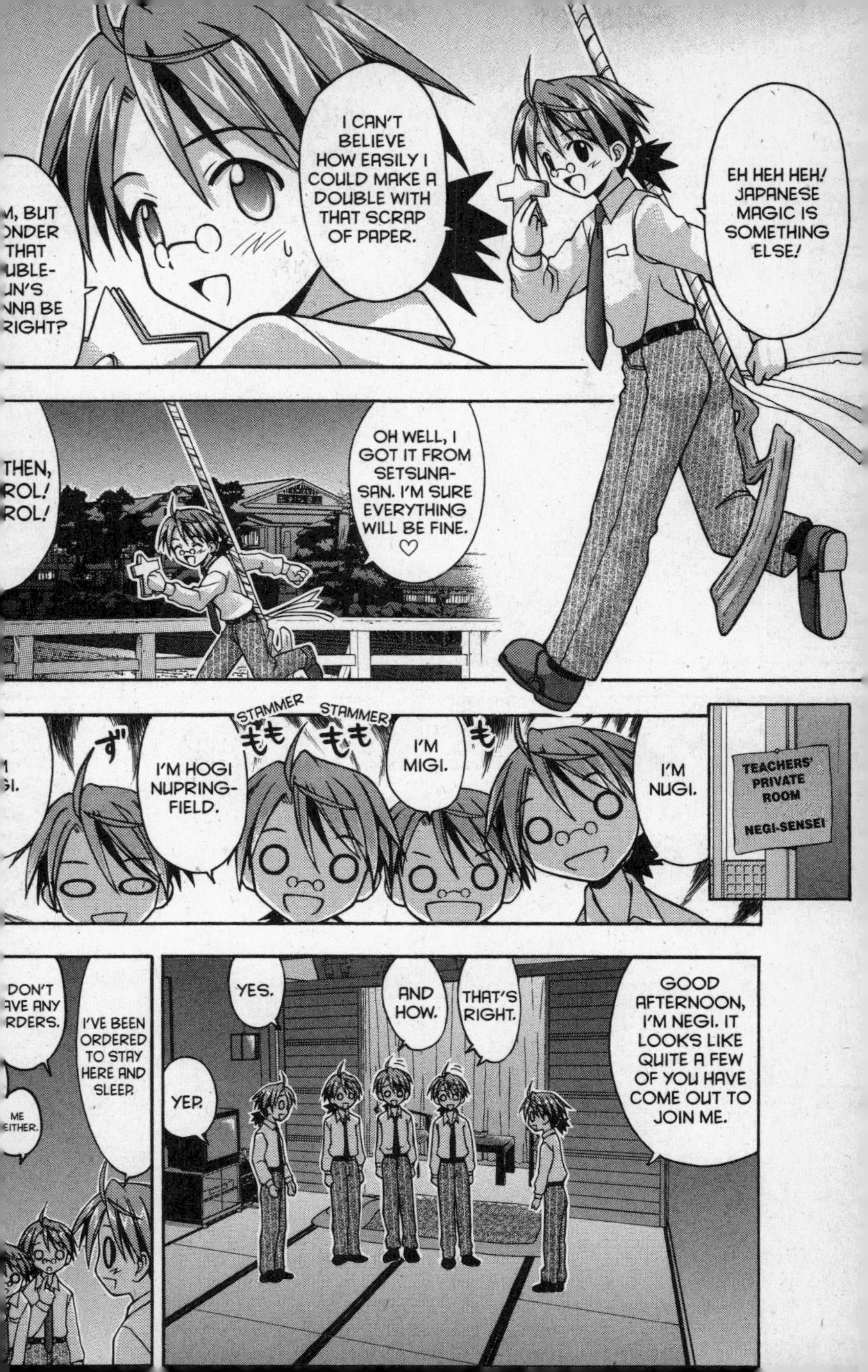
EH HEH HEH! JAPANESE MAGIC IS SOMETHING ELSE!
I CAN'T BELIEVE HOW EASILY I COULD MAKE A DOUBLE WITH THAT SCRAP OF PAPER.
M, BUT ONDER THAT UBLE- UN'S NNA BE RIGHT?
OH WELL, I GOT IT FROM SETSUNA-SAN. I'M SURE EVERYTHING WILL BE FINE. ♡
THEN, ROL! ROL!
TEACHERS' PRIVATE ROOM NEGI-SENSEI
I'M NUGI.
も
I'M MIGI.
STAMMER もも
STAMMER もも
I'M HOGI NUPRING-FIELD.
ず
GOOD AFTERNOON, I'M NEGI. IT LOOKS LIKE QUITE A FEW OF YOU HAVE COME OUT TO JOIN ME.
THAT'S RIGHT.
AND HOW.
YES.
YEP.
I'VE BEEN ORDERED TO STAY HERE AND SLEEP.
DON'T AVE ANY RDERS.
ME EITHER.

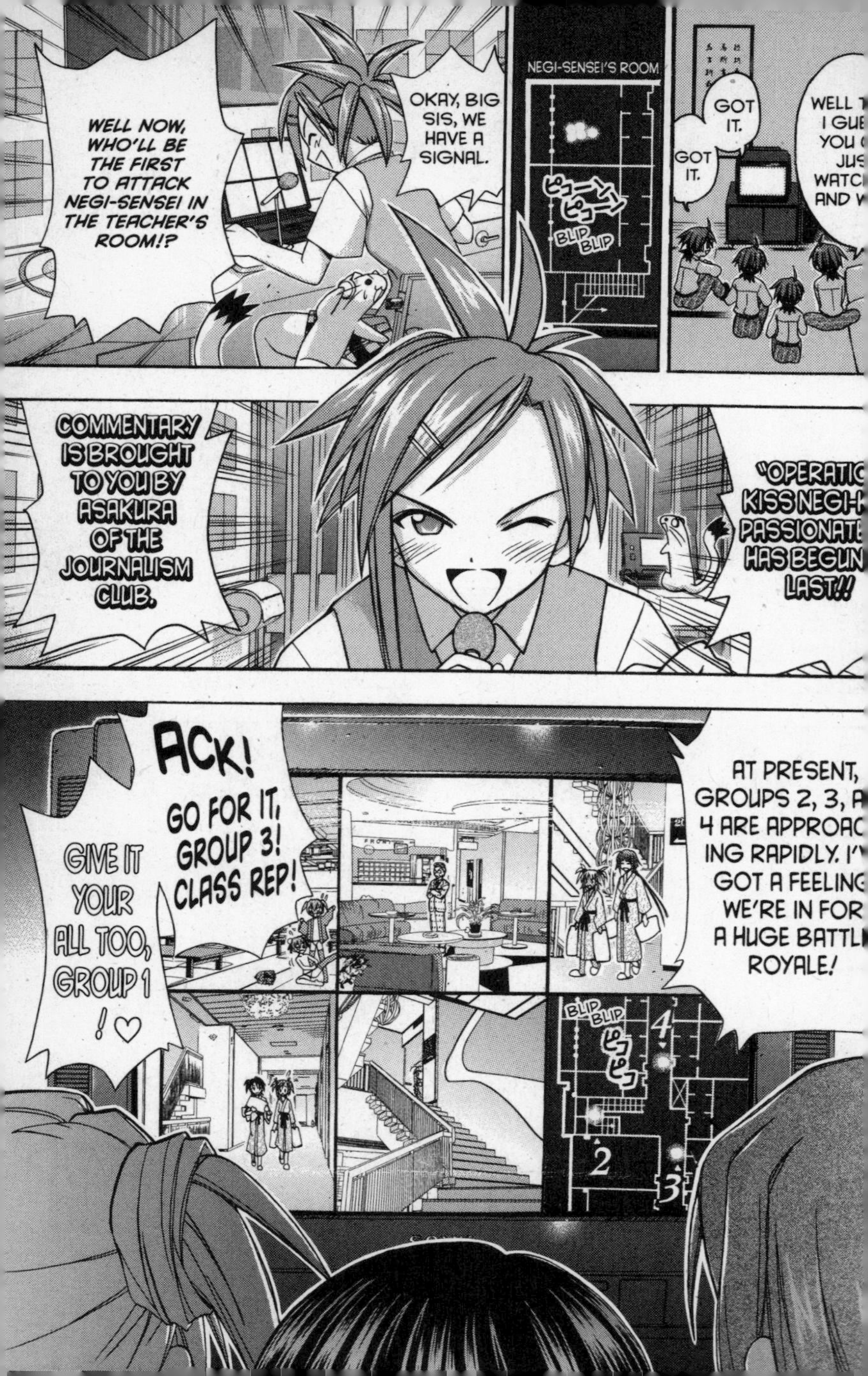
WELL T I GUE YOU C JUS WATCH AND W
GOT IT.
GOT IT.
NEGI-SENSEI'S ROOM
BLIP BLIP
OKAY, BIG SIS, WE HAVE A SIGNAL.
WELL NOW, WHO'LL BE THE FIRST TO ATTACK NEGI-SENSEI IN THE TEACHER'S ROOM!?
"OPERATIO KISS NEGI-K PASSIONATE HAS BEGUN LAST!!
COMMENTARY IS BROUGHT TO YOU BY ASAKURA OF THE JOURNALISM CLUB.
AT PRESENT, GROUPS 2, 3, A 4 ARE APPROAC ING RAPIDLY. I'V GOT A FEELING WE'RE IN FOR A HUGE BATTL ROYALE!
BLIP BLIP
4
2
3
ACK!
GO FOR IT, GROUP 3! CLASS REP!
GIVE IT YOUR ALL TOO, GROUP 1! ♡

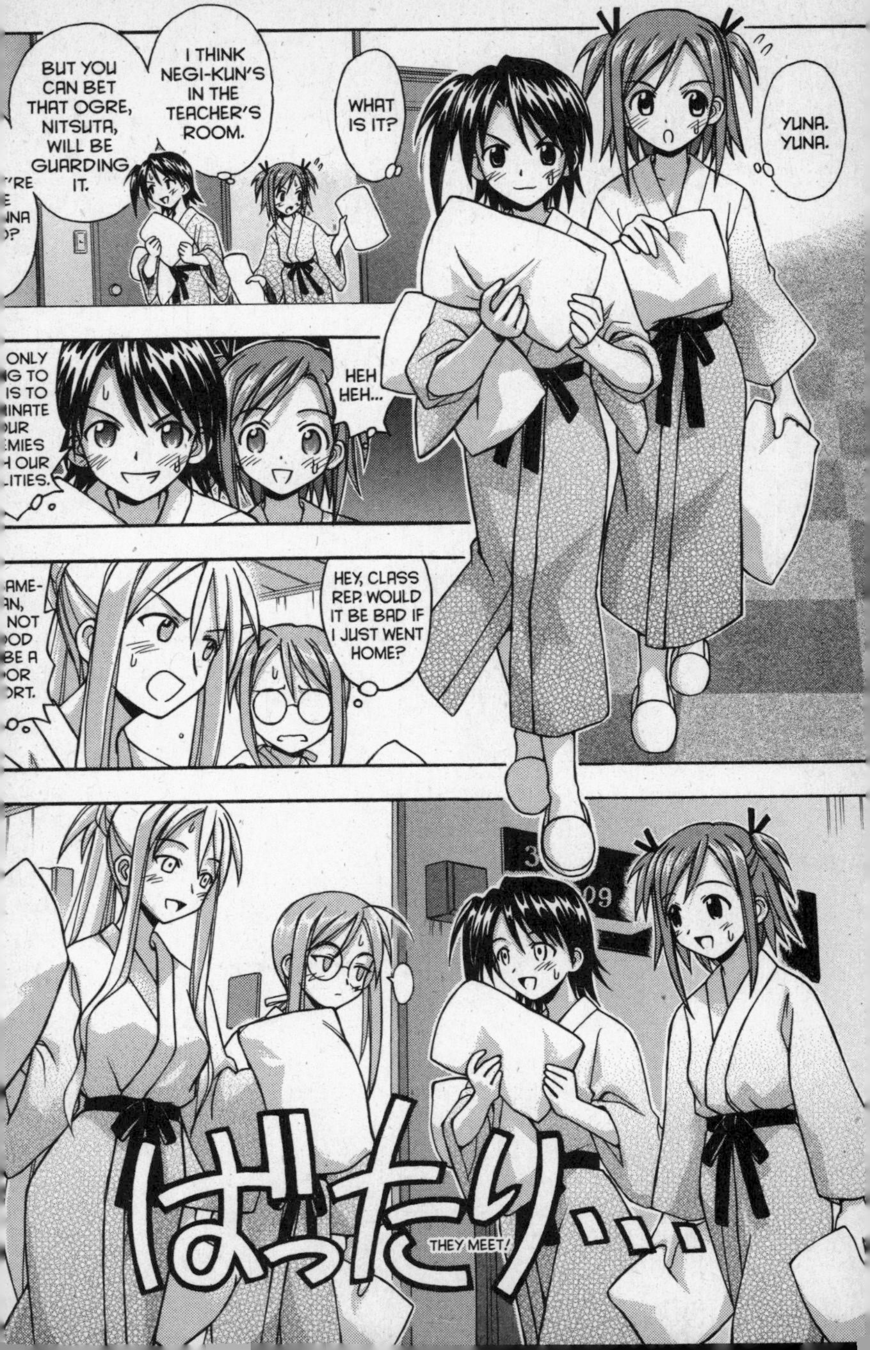
YUNA. YUNA.
WHAT IS IT?
I THINK NEGI-KUN'S IN THE TEACHER'S ROOM.
BUT YOU CAN BET THAT OGRE, NITSUTA, WILL BE GUARDING IT.
HEH HEH...
HEY, CLASS REP. WOULD IT BE BAD IF I JUST WENT HOME?
はったり…
THEY MEET!

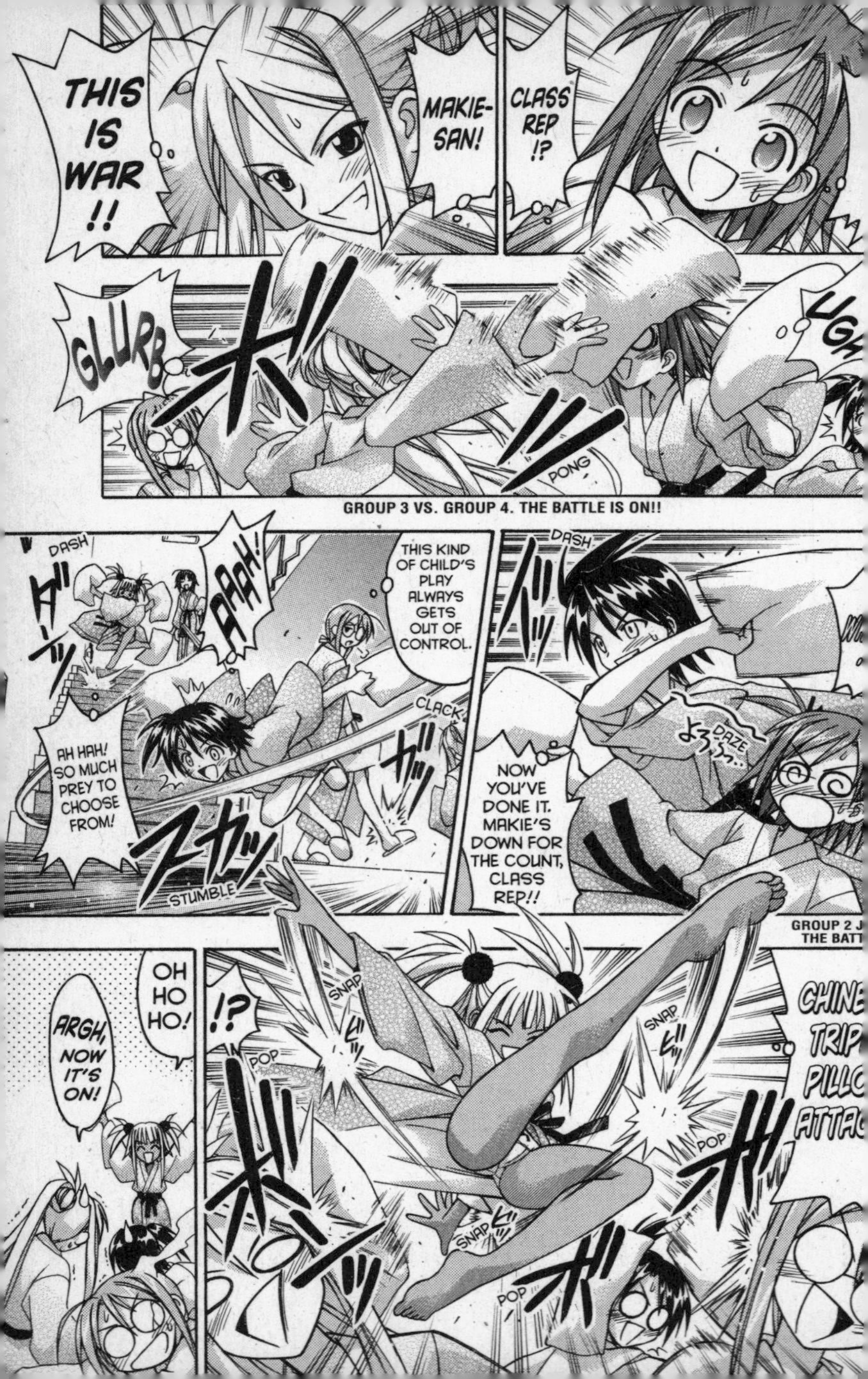
CLASS REP !?
MAKIE-SAN!
THIS IS WAR !!
UGH
GLURB
PONG
GROUP 3 VS. GROUP 4. THE BATTLE IS ON!!
DASH
DAZE
NOW YOU'VE DONE IT. MAKIE'S DOWN FOR THE COUNT, CLASS REP!!
THIS KIND OF CHILD'S PLAY ALWAYS GETS OUT OF CONTROL.
AAAH!
DASH
CLACK
AH HAH! SO MUCH PREY TO CHOOSE FROM!
STUMBLE
SNAP
SNAP
POP
POP
SNAP
POP
!?
OH HO HO!
ARGH, NOW IT'S ON!

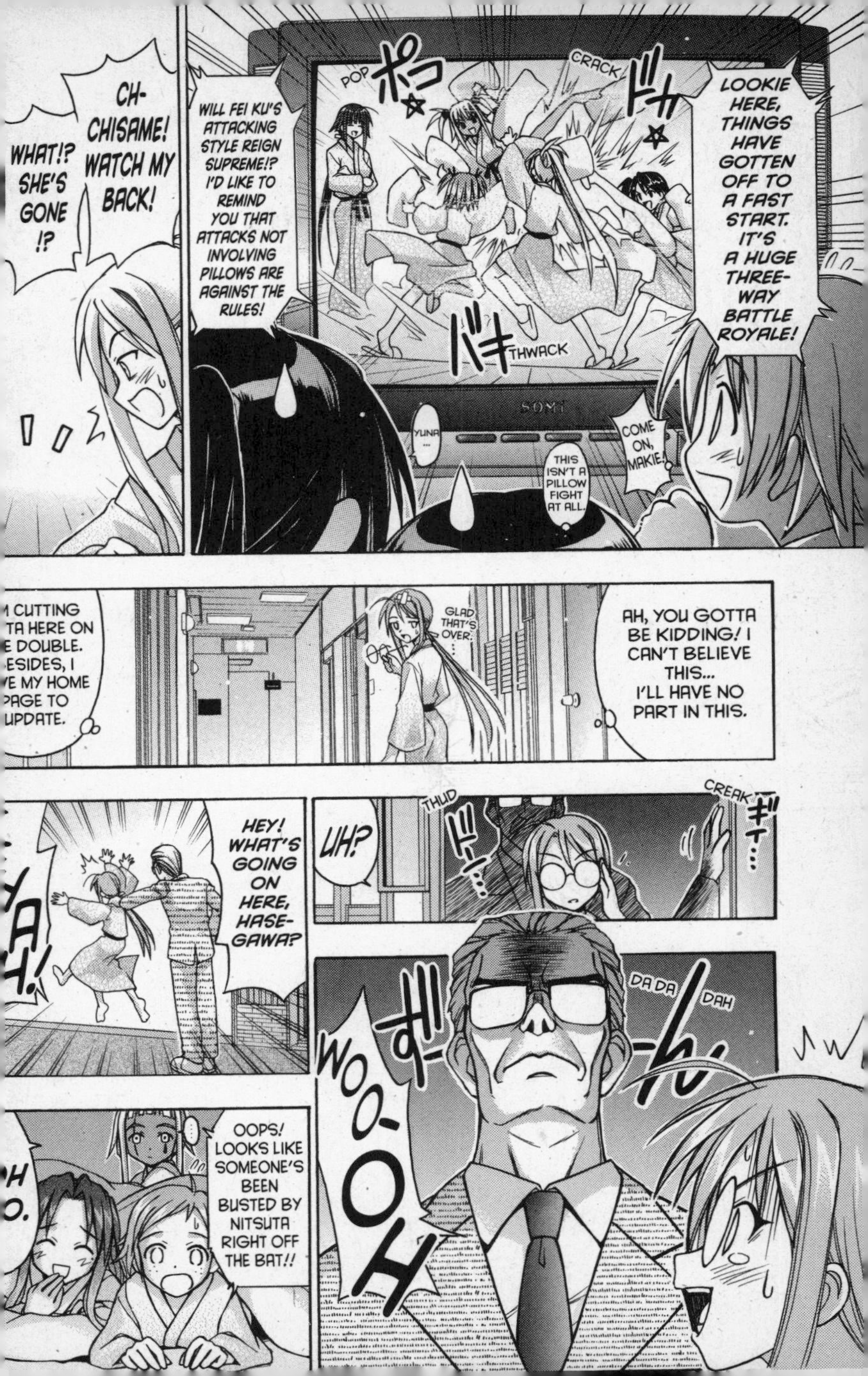
LOOKIE HERE, THINGS HAVE GOTTEN OFF TO A FAST START. IT'S A HUGE THREE-WAY BATTLE ROYALE!
CRACK
POP
WILL FEI KU'S ATTACKING STYLE REIGN SUPREME!? I'D LIKE TO REMIND YOU THAT ATTACKS NOT INVOLVING PILLOWS ARE AGAINST THE RULES!
THWACK
COME ON, MAKIE!
THIS ISN'T A PILLOW FIGHT AT ALL.
YUNA...
CH-CHISAME! WATCH MY BACK!
WHAT!? SHE'S GONE !?
AH, YOU GOTTA BE KIDDING! I CAN'T BELIEVE THIS... I'LL HAVE NO PART IN THIS.
GLAD THAT'S OVER...
M CUTTING TA HERE ON E DOUBLE. ESIDES, I VE MY HOME PAGE TO UPDATE.
CREAK
THUD
UH?
DA DA DAH
WOOO-OH
HEY! WHAT'S GOING ON HERE, HASE-GAWA?
OOPS! LOOKS LIKE SOMEONE'S BEEN BUSTED BY NITSUTA RIGHT OFF THE BAT!!

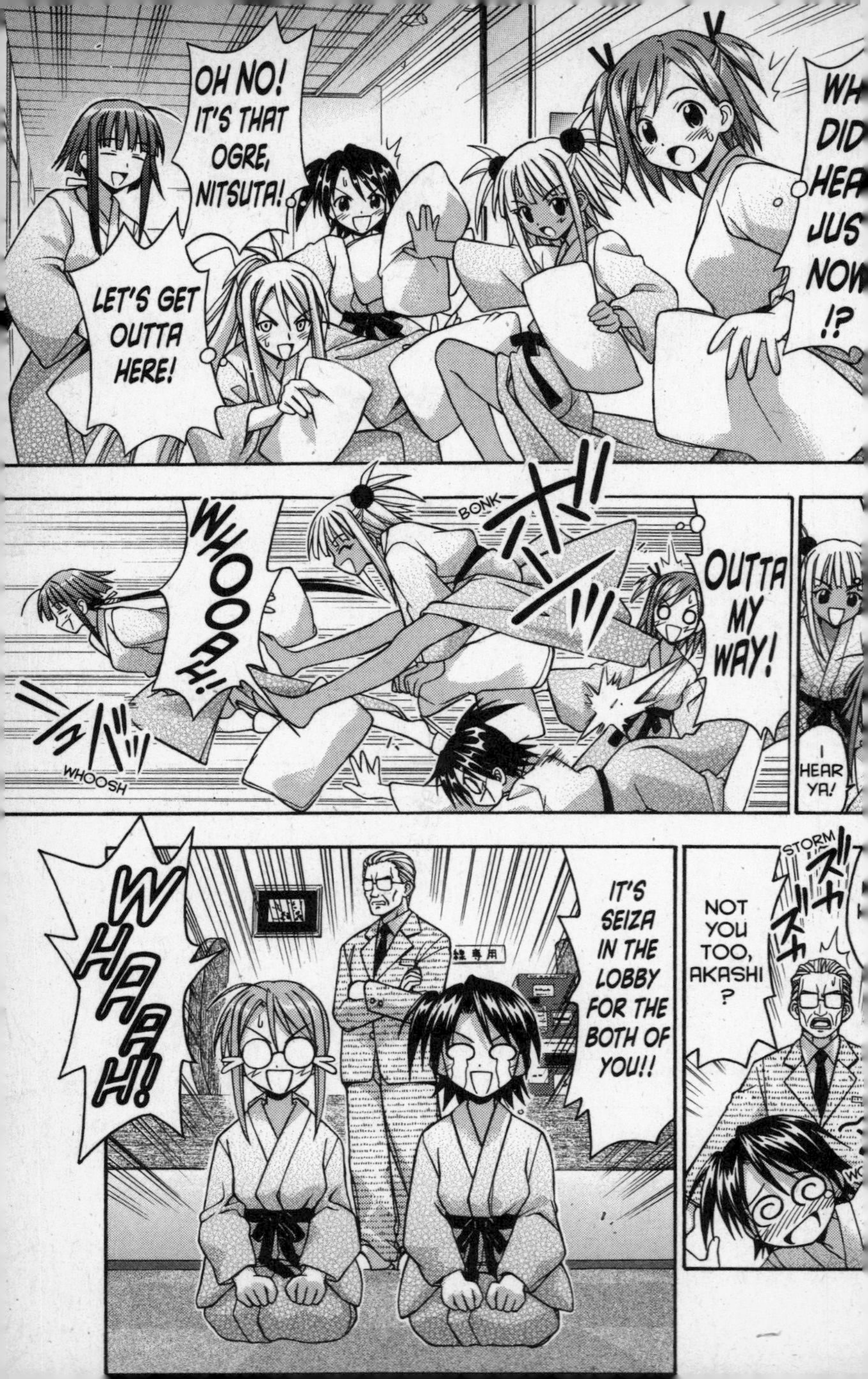
WH DID HEA JUS NOW !?
OH NO! IT'S THAT OGRE, NITSUTA!
LET'S GET OUTTA HERE!
I HEAR YA!
OUTTA MY WAY!
BONK
WHOOOAH!!
WHOOSH
STORM
NOT YOU TOO, AKASHI?
IT'S SEIZA IN THE LOBBY FOR THE BOTH OF YOU!!
WHAAAH!

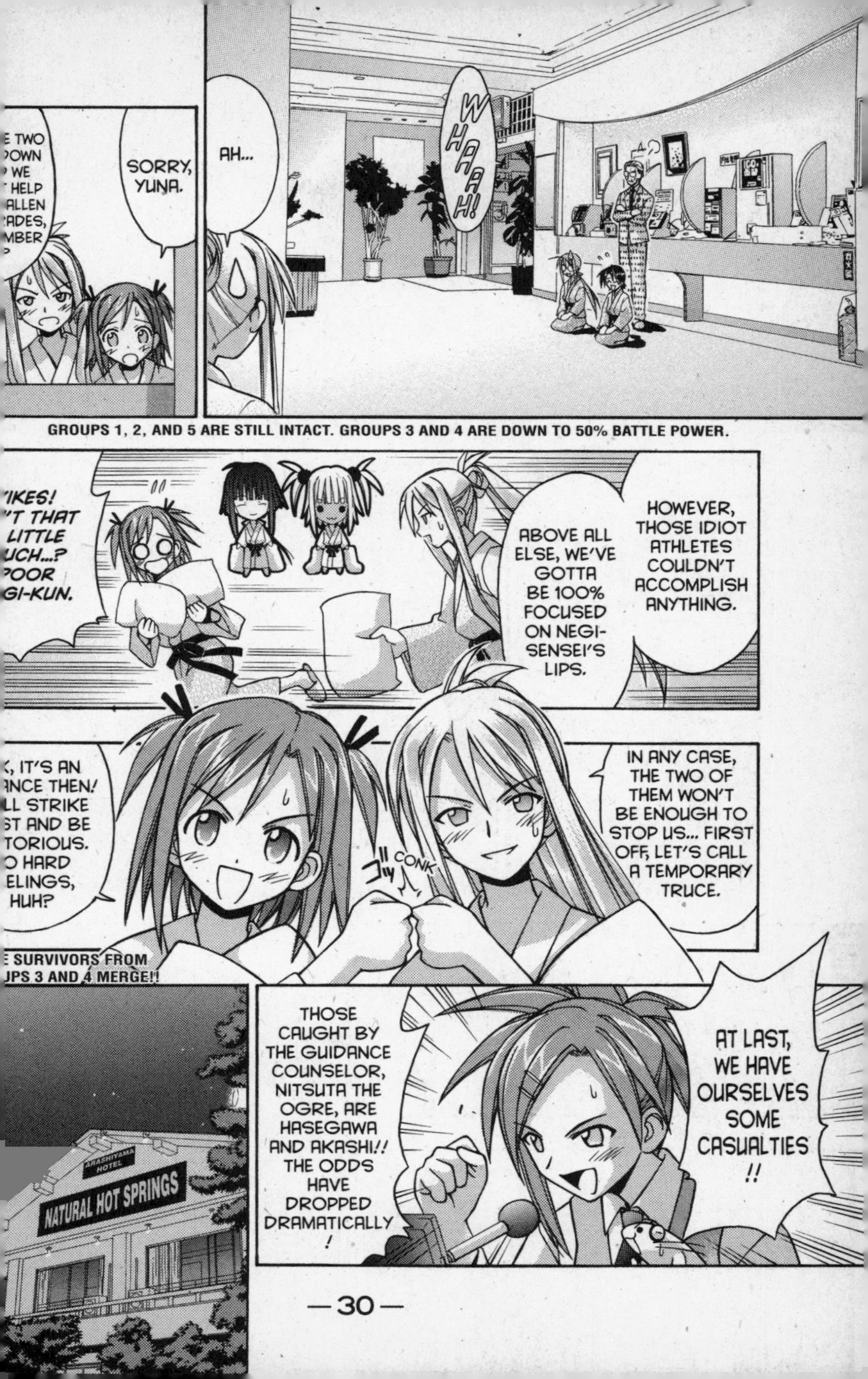
WHAAAH!
AH...
SORRY, YUNA.
E TWO
DOWN
WE
HELP
ALLEN
RADES,
MBER
GROUPS 1, 2, AND 5 ARE STILL INTACT. GROUPS 3 AND 4 ARE DOWN TO 50% BATTLE POWER.
HOWEVER, THOSE IDIOT ATHLETES COULDN'T ACCOMPLISH ANYTHING.
ABOVE ALL ELSE, WE'VE GOTTA BE 100% FOCUSED ON NEGI-SENSEI'S LIPS.
IKES! 'T THAT LITTLE UCH...? POOR GI-KUN.
IN ANY CASE, THE TWO OF THEM WON'T BE ENOUGH TO STOP US... FIRST OFF, LET'S CALL A TEMPORARY TRUCE.
CONK
, IT'S AN ANCE THEN! LL STRIKE ST AND BE TORIOUS. O HARD ELINGS, HUH?
E SURVIVORS FROM UPS 3 AND 4 MERGE!!
AT LAST, WE HAVE OURSELVES SOME CASUALTIES !!
THOSE CAUGHT BY THE GUIDANCE COUNSELOR, NITSUTA THE OGRE, ARE HASEGAWA AND AKASHI!! THE ODDS HAVE DROPPED DRAMATICALLY !
ARASHIYAMA HOTEL
NATURAL HOT SPRINGS

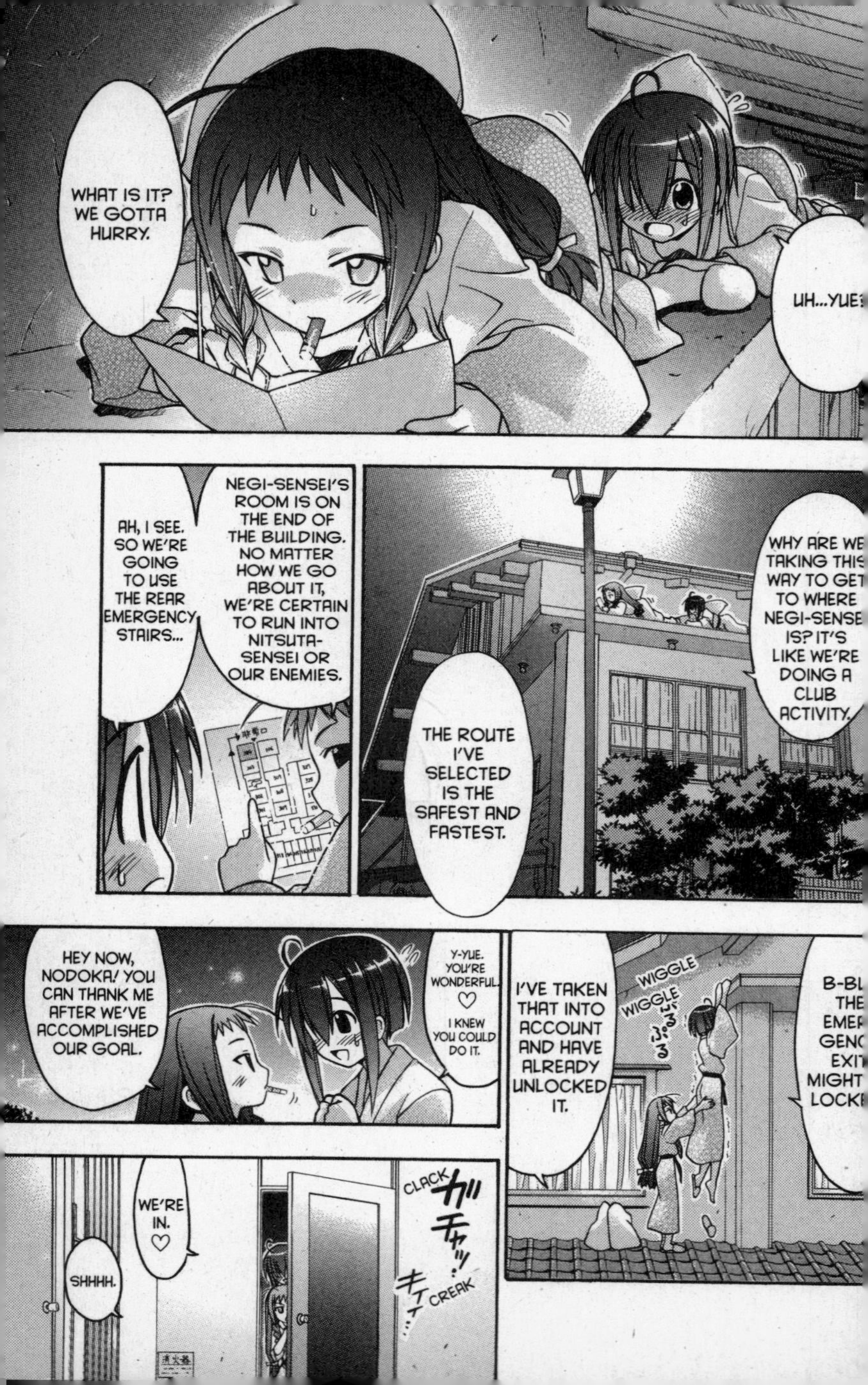
UH...YUE
WHAT IS IT? WE GOTTA HURRY.
WHY ARE WE TAKING THIS WAY TO GET TO WHERE NEGI-SENSE IS? IT'S LIKE WE'RE DOING A CLUB ACTIVITY.
THE ROUTE I'VE SELECTED IS THE SAFEST AND FASTEST.
NEGI-SENSEI'S ROOM IS ON THE END OF THE BUILDING. NO MATTER HOW WE GO ABOUT IT, WE'RE CERTAIN TO RUN INTO NITSUTA-SENSEI OR OUR ENEMIES.
AH, I SEE. SO WE'RE GOING TO USE THE REAR EMERGENCY STAIRS...
B-BL THE EMER GENC EXIT MIGHT LOCK
WIGGLE WIGGLE
ぷるぷる
I'VE TAKEN THAT INTO ACCOUNT AND HAVE ALREADY UNLOCKED IT.
Y-YUE. YOU'RE WONDERFUL ♡
I KNEW YOU COULD DO IT.
HEY NOW, NODOKA! YOU CAN THANK ME AFTER WE'VE ACCOMPLISHED OUR GOAL.
CLACK ガチャッ
CREAK キィィ…
WE'RE IN. ♡
SHHHH.

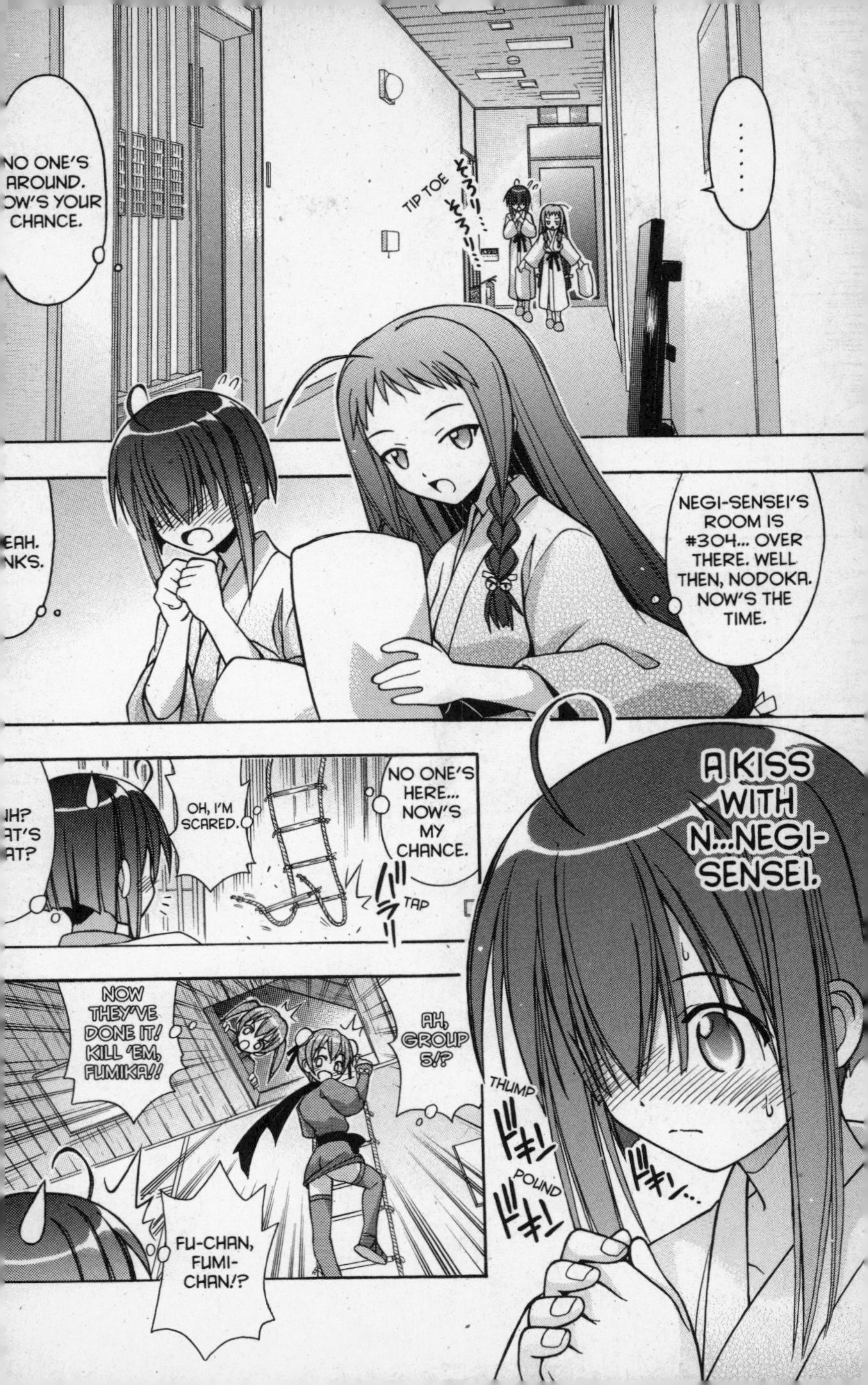
......
TIP TOE
そろり…そろり…
NO ONE'S AROUND. OW'S YOUR CHANCE.
NEGI-SENSEI'S ROOM IS #304... OVER THERE. WELL THEN, NODOKA. NOW'S THE TIME.
EAH. NKS.
A KISS WITH N...NEGI-SENSEI.
THUMP
ドキン
POUND
ドキン
ドキン…
NO ONE'S HERE... NOW'S MY CHANCE.
TAP
OH, I'M SCARED.
NH? AT'S AT?
AH, GROUP 5!?
NOW THEY'VE DONE IT! KILL 'EM, FUMIKA!!
FU-CHAN, FUMI-CHAN!?

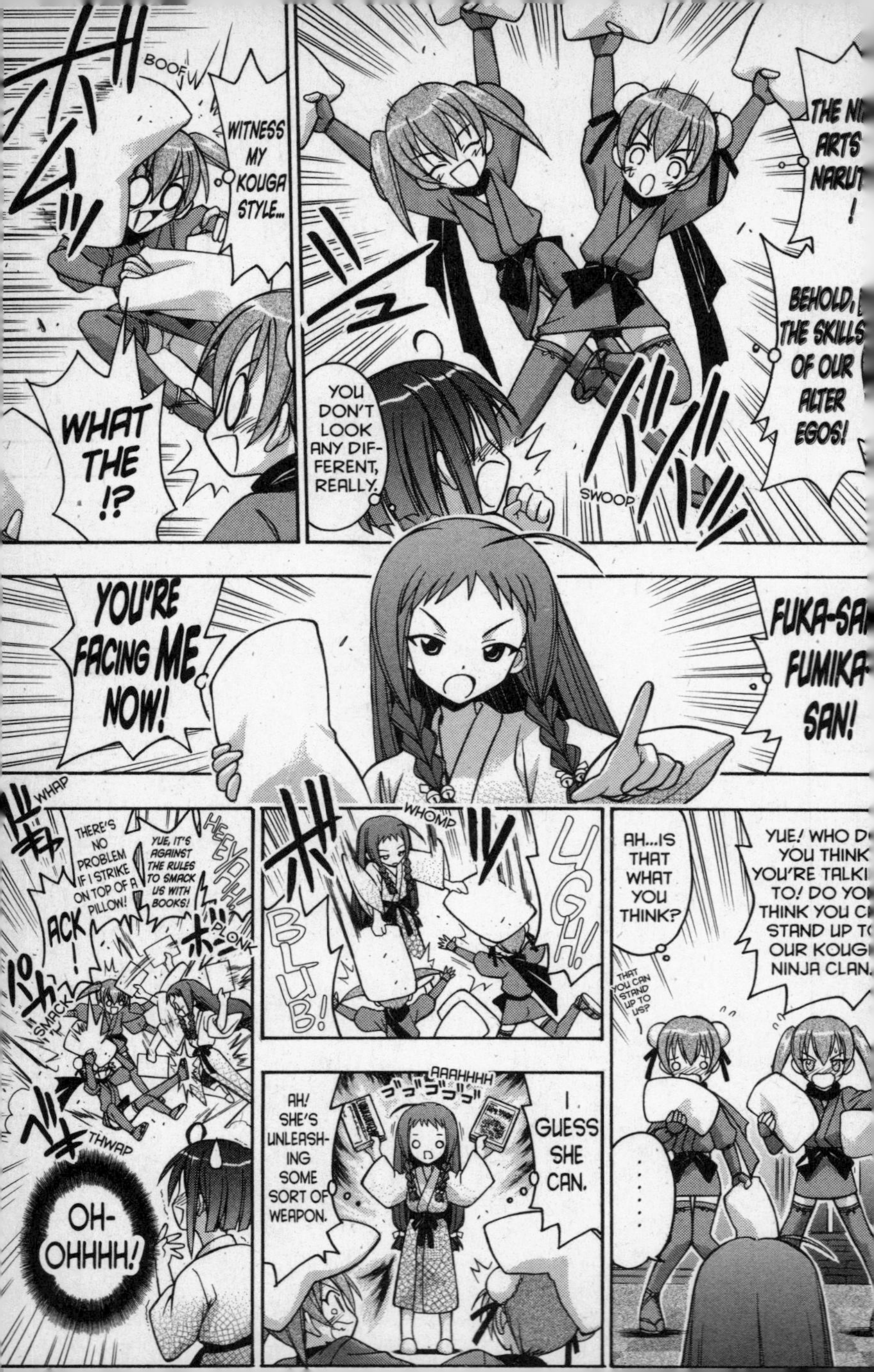
THE NI ARTS NARUT !
BEHOLD, THE SKILLS OF OUR ALTER EGOS!
SWOOP
YOU DON'T LOOK ANY DIF- FERENT, REALLY.
BOOF
WITNESS MY KOUGA STYLE...
WHAT THE !?
FUKA-SA FUMIKA- SAN!
YOU'RE FACING ME NOW!
YUE! WHO D YOU THINK YOU'RE TALKI TO! DO YO THINK YOU C STAND UP TO OUR KOUG NINJA CLAN.
AH...IS THAT WHAT YOU THINK?
THAT YOU CAN STAND UP TO US?
......
WHOMP
UGH!
BLUB!
AAAHHHH
I GUESS SHE CAN.
AH! SHE'S UNLEASH- ING SOME SORT OF WEAPON.
WHAP
YUE, IT'S AGAINST THE RULES TO SMACK US WITH BOOKS!
HEEYAH!
THERE'S NO PROBLEM IF I STRIKE ON TOP OF A PILLOW!
PLONK
ACK !
SMACK
THWAP
OH- OHHHH!

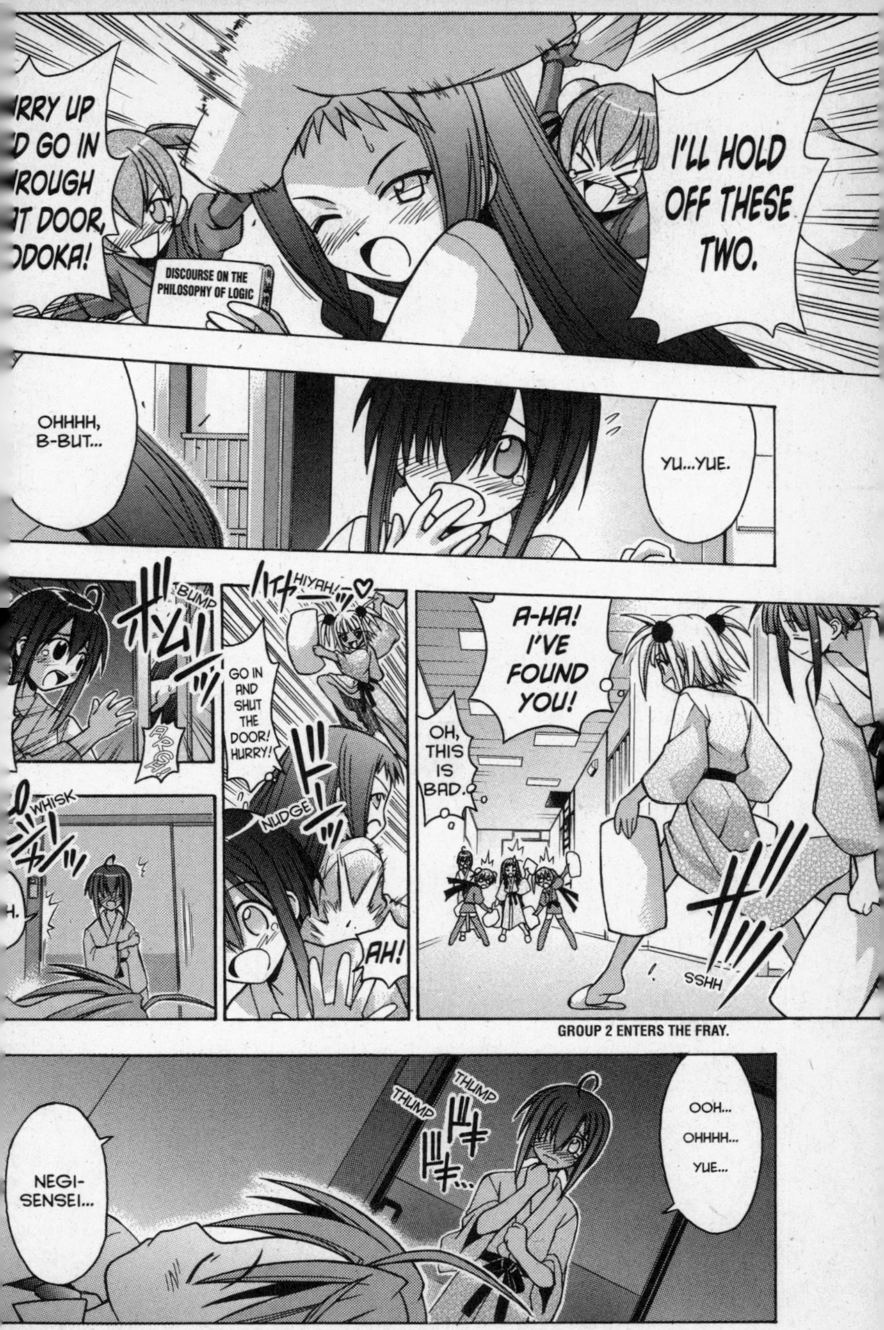
I'LL HOLD OFF THESE TWO.
RRY UP D GO IN ROUGH T DOOR, DOKA!
DISCOURSE ON THE PHILOSOPHY OF LOGIC
YU...YUE.
OHHHH, B-BUT...
A-HA! I'VE FOUND YOU!
OH, THIS IS BAD.
SSHH
HIYAH!
GO IN AND SHUT THE DOOR! HURRY!
NUDGE
AH!
BUMP
ARGH!
WHISK
H.
GROUP 2 ENTERS THE FRAY.
OOH... OHHHH... YUE...
THUMP
THUMP
NEGI-SENSEI...

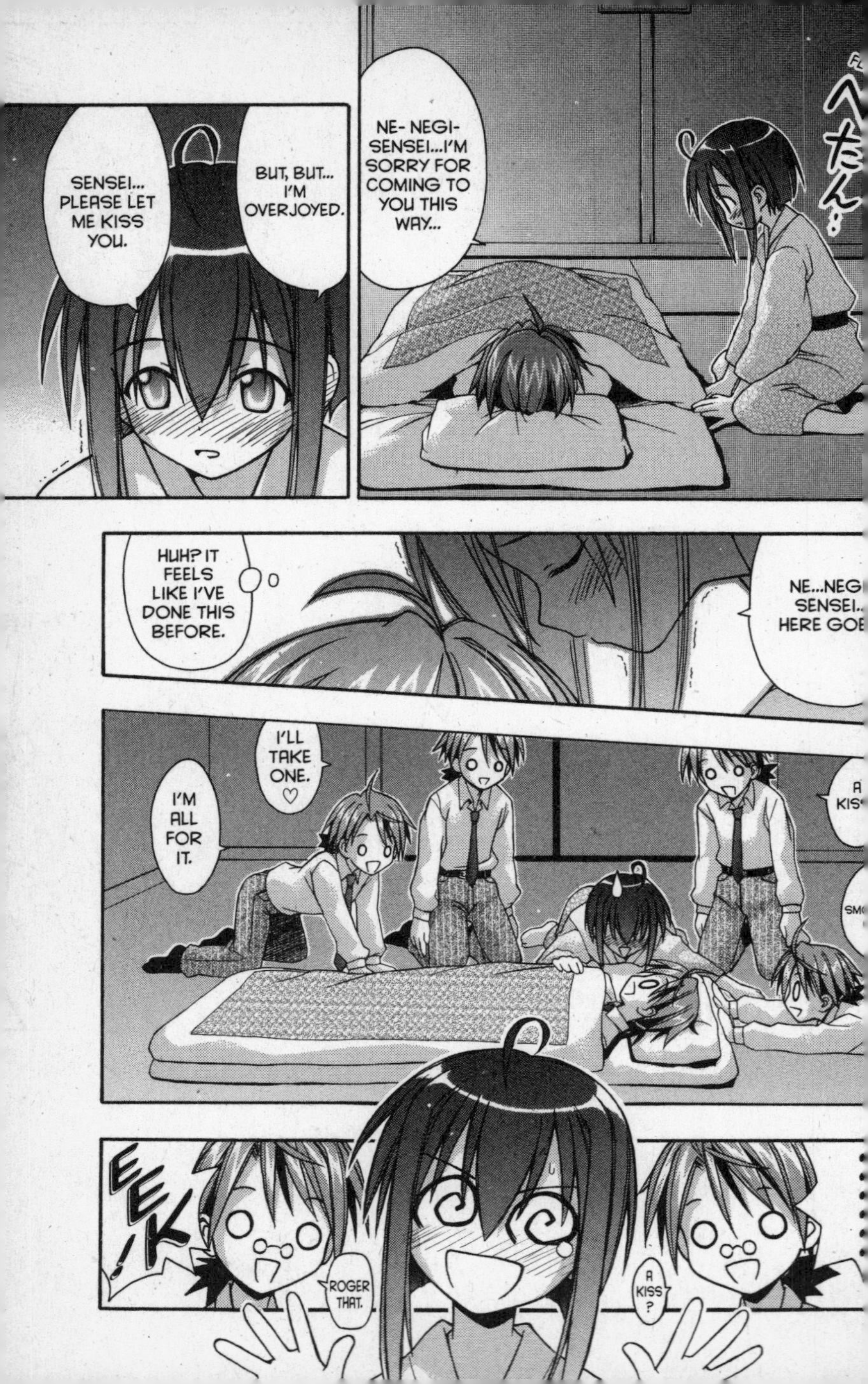
FL
へたん…
NE- NEGI-SENSEI...I'M SORRY FOR COMING TO YOU THIS WAY...
BUT, BUT... I'M OVERJOYED.
SENSEI... PLEASE LET ME KISS YOU.
NE...NEGI SENSEI.. HERE GOE
HUH? IT FEELS LIKE I'VE DONE THIS BEFORE.
A KIS
SM
I'LL TAKE ONE. ♡
I'M ALL FOR IT.
A KISS?
ROGER THAT.
EEEK!

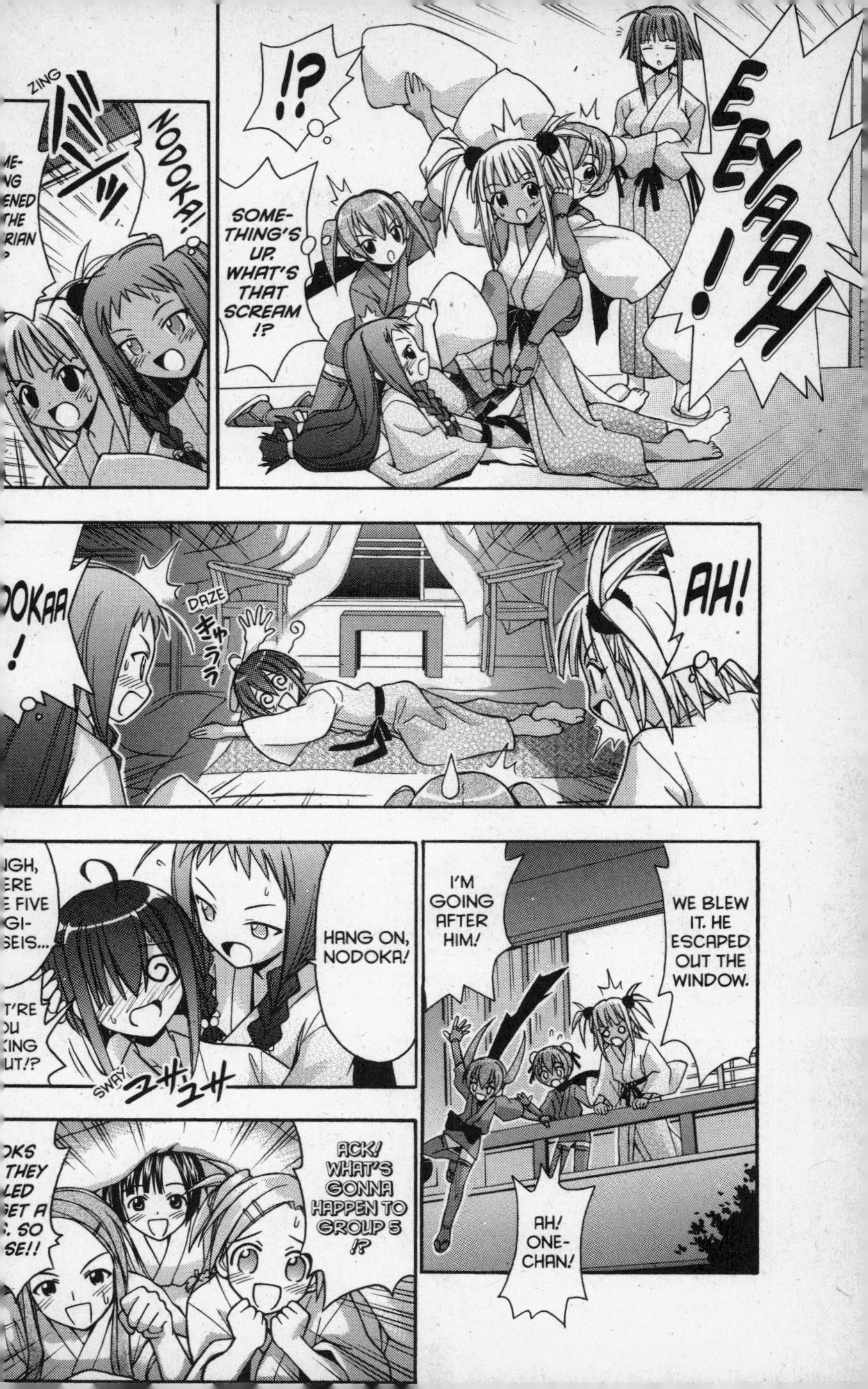
EEYAAAH!
!?
SOME-THING'S UP. WHAT'S THAT SCREAM!?
ZING
NODOKA!
ME- NG ENED THE RIAN
AH!
DAZE
OOKAA!
WE BLEW IT. HE ESCAPED OUT THE WINDOW.
I'M GOING AFTER HIM!
AH! ONE-CHAN!
HANG ON, NODOKA!
IGH, ERE E FIVE GI-SEIS...
T'RE OU KING UT!?
SWAY
ACK! WHAT'S GONNA HAPPEN TO GROUP 5!?
OKS THEY LED GET A . SO SE!!

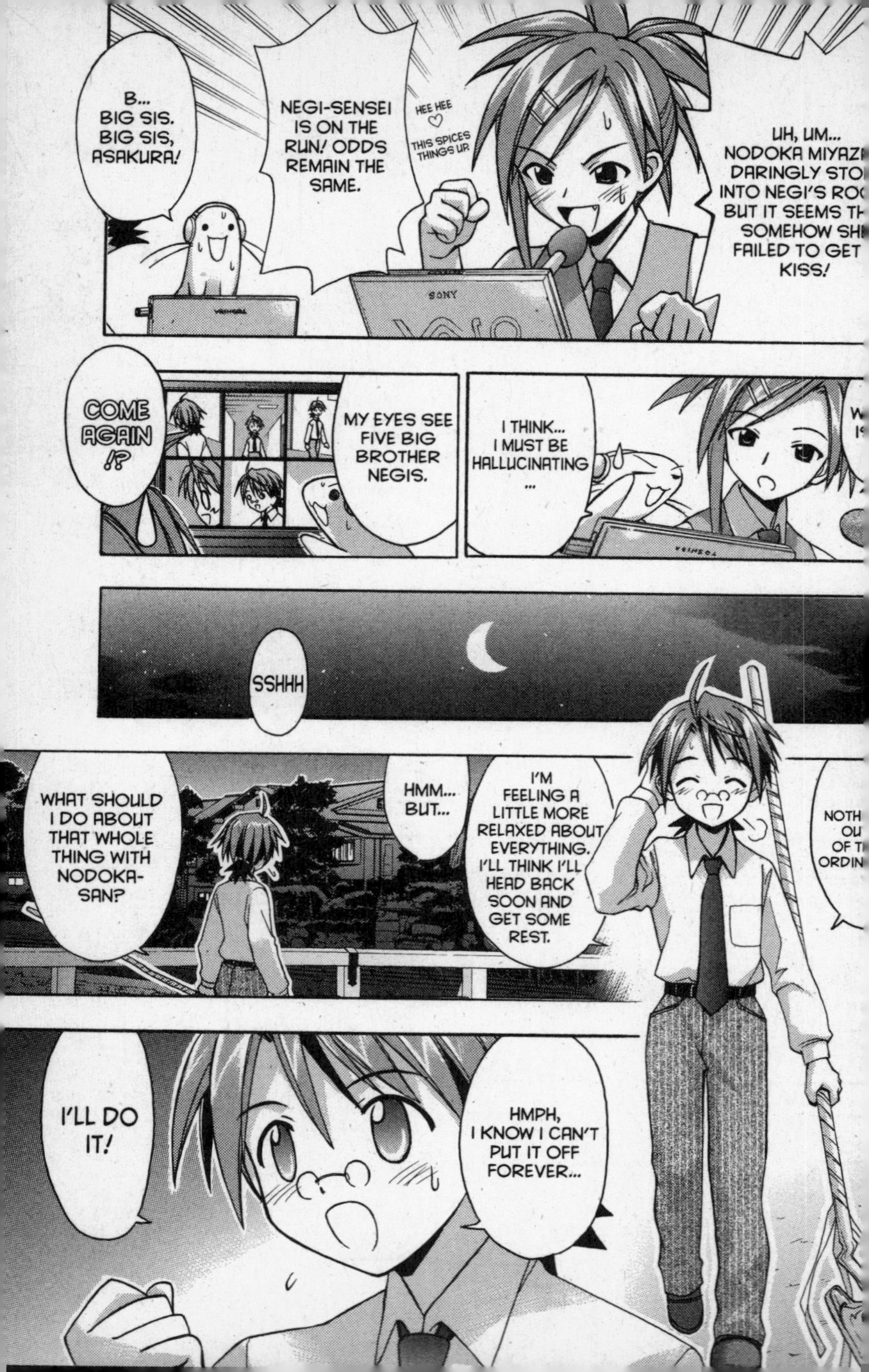
UH, UM... NODOKA MIYAZ DARINGLY STO INTO NEGI'S RO BUT IT SEEMS T SOMEHOW SH FAILED TO GET KISS!
HEE HEE ♡ THIS SPICES THINGS UP.
NEGI-SENSEI IS ON THE RUN! ODDS REMAIN THE SAME.
SONY
B... BIG SIS. BIG SIS, ASAKURA!
I THINK... I MUST BE HALLUCINATING ...
MY EYES SEE FIVE BIG BROTHER NEGIS.
COME AGAIN !?
SSHHH
I'M FEELING A LITTLE MORE RELAXED ABOUT EVERYTHING. I'LL THINK I'LL HEAD BACK SOON AND GET SOME REST.
HMM... BUT...
WHAT SHOULD I DO ABOUT THAT WHOLE THING WITH NODOKA-SAN?
HMPH, I KNOW I CAN'T PUT IT OFF FOREVER...
I'LL DO IT!

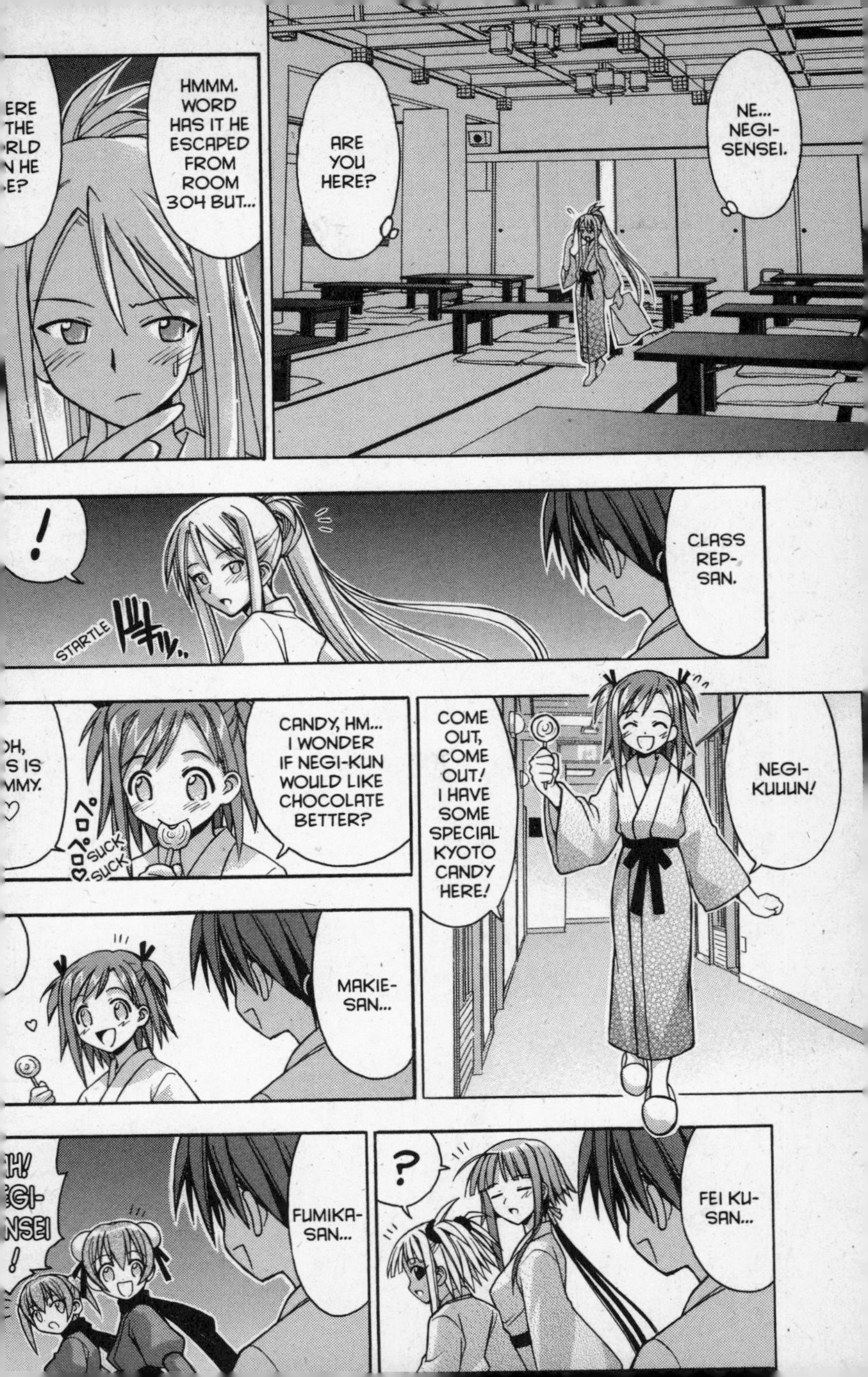
NE... NEGI-SENSEI.
ARE YOU HERE?
HMMM. WORD HAS IT HE ESCAPED FROM ROOM 304 BUT...
CLASS REP-SAN.
!
STARTLE
NEGI-KUUUN!
COME OUT, COME OUT! I HAVE SOME SPECIAL KYOTO CANDY HERE!
CANDY, HM... I WONDER IF NEGI-KUN WOULD LIKE CHOCOLATE BETTER?
SUCK SUCK
MAKIE-SAN...
FEI KU-SAN...
?
FUMIKA-SAN...

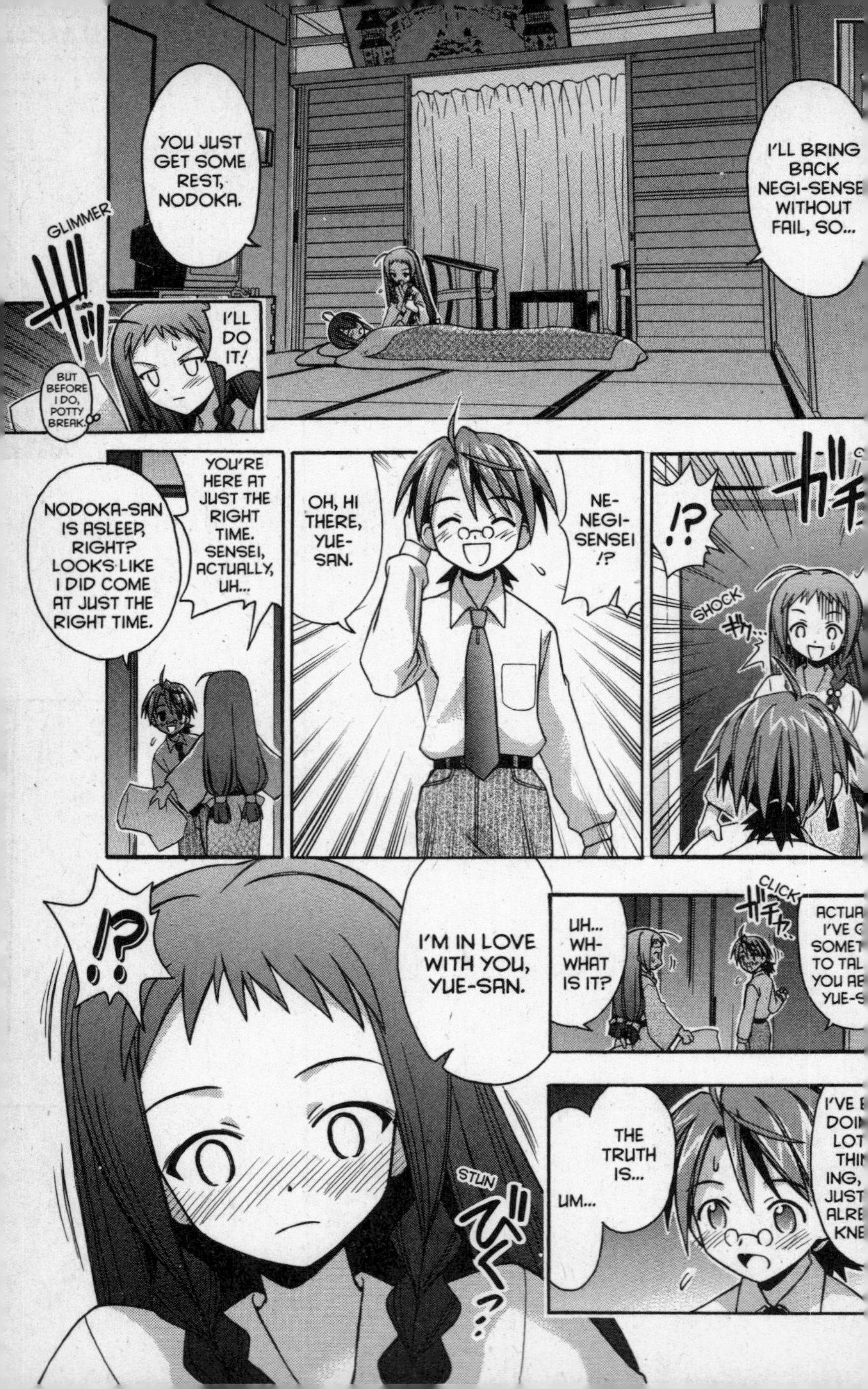
I'LL BRING BACK NEGI-SENSE WITHOUT FAIL, SO...
YOU JUST GET SOME REST, NODOKA.
GLIMMER
I'LL DO IT!
BUT BEFORE I DO, POTTY BREAK.
!?
SHOCK
NE-NEGI-SENSEI!?
OH, HI THERE, YUE-SAN.
YOU'RE HERE AT JUST THE RIGHT TIME. SENSEI, ACTUALLY, UH...
NODOKA-SAN IS ASLEEP, RIGHT? LOOKS LIKE I DID COME AT JUST THE RIGHT TIME.
CLICK
ACTUA I'VE G SOMET TO TAL YOU AB YUE-S
UH... WH-WHAT IS IT?
I'VE DOI LOT THI ING, JUST ALRE KNE
THE TRUTH IS...
UM...
I'M IN LOVE WITH YOU, YUE-SAN.
!?
STUN

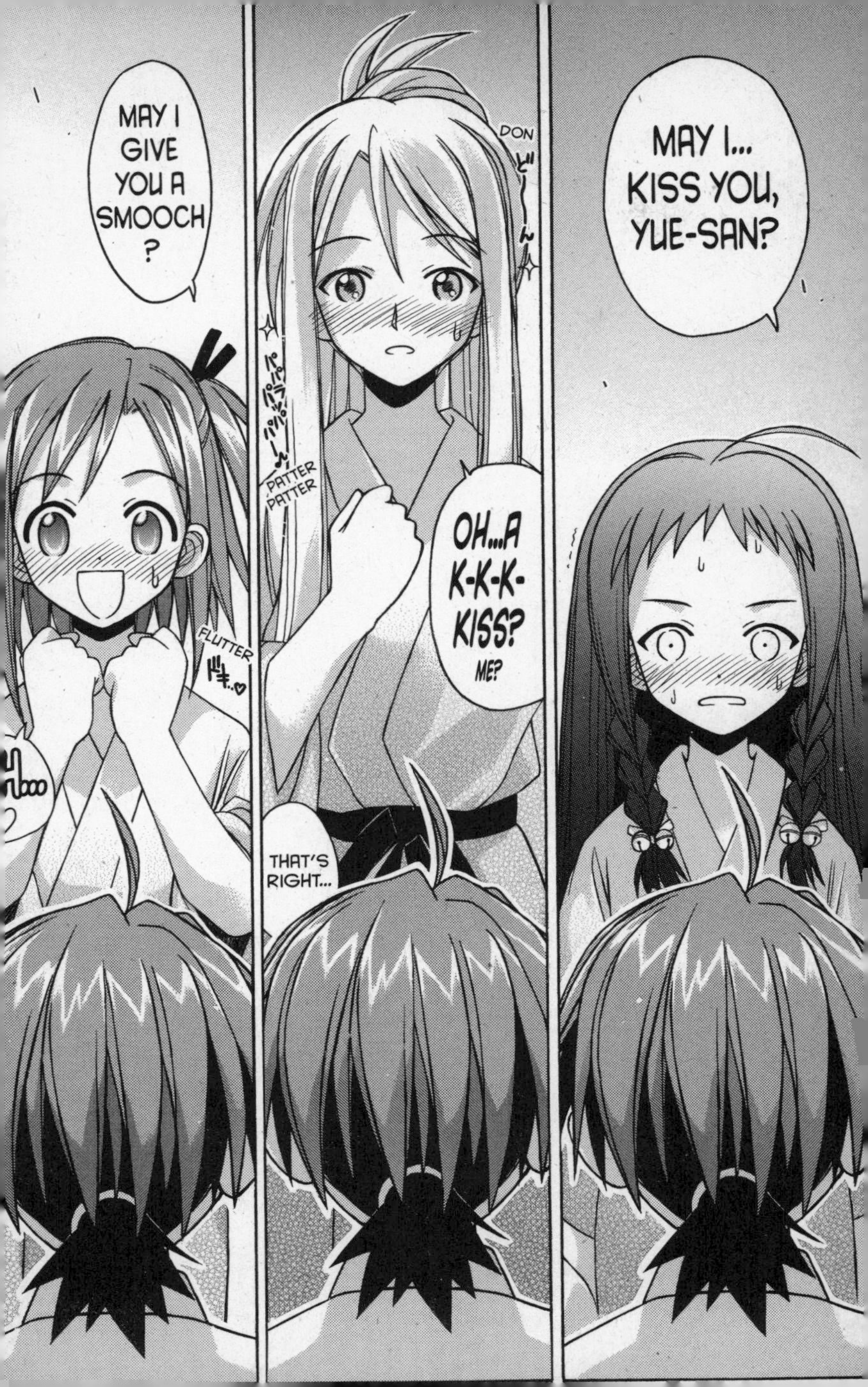
MAY I... KISS YOU, YUE-SAN?
DON
PATTER PATTER
OH...A K-K-K-KISS?
ME?
THAT'S RIGHT...
MAY I GIVE YOU A SMOOCH?
FLUTTER

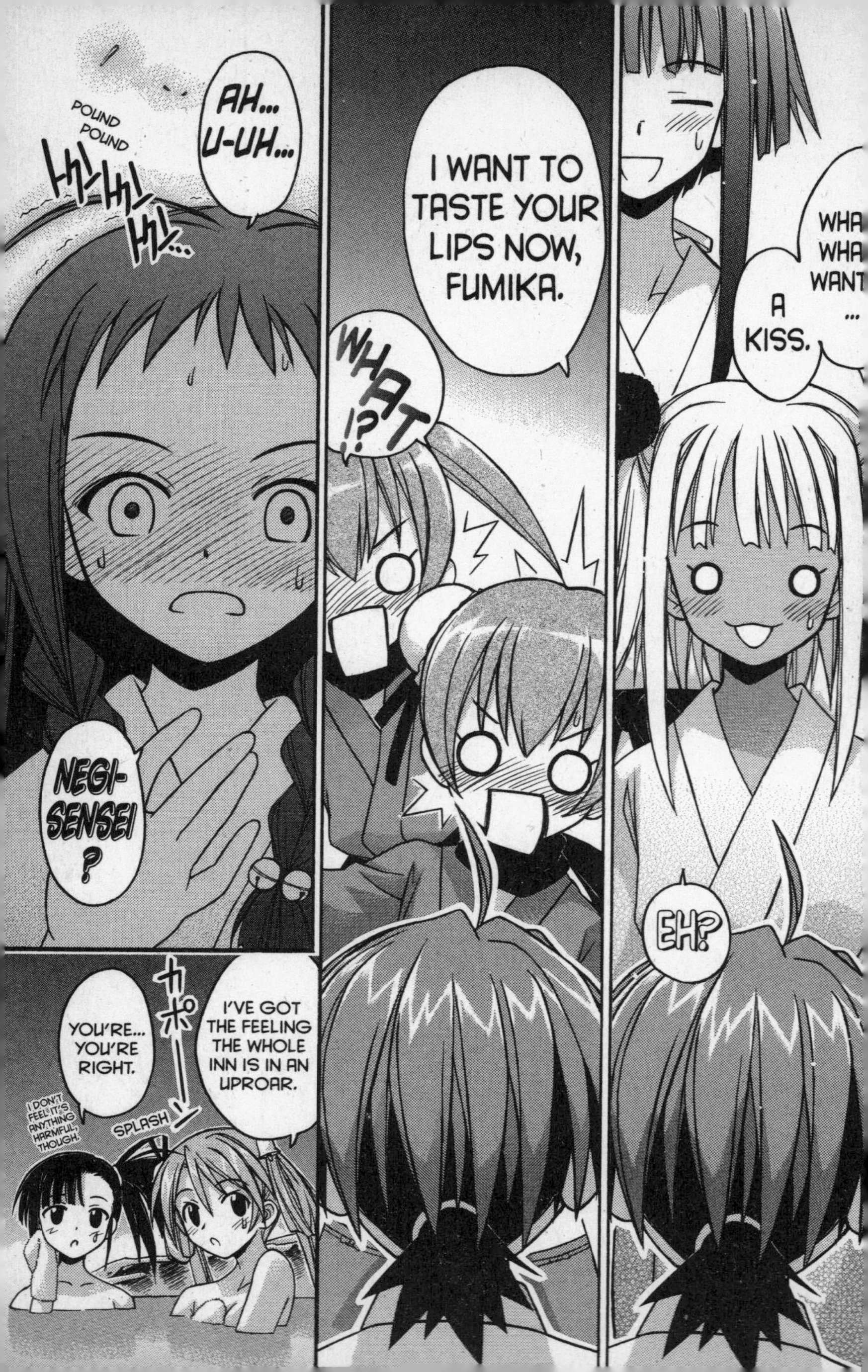
WHA
WHA
WANT
...
A KISS.
EH?
I WANT TO TASTE YOUR LIPS NOW, FUMIKA.
WHAT !?
AH... U-UH...
POUND POUND
NEGI-SENSEI ?
I'VE GOT THE FEELING THE WHOLE INN IS IN AN UPROAR.
SPLASH
YOU'RE... YOU'RE RIGHT.
I DON'T FEEL IT'S ANYTHING HARMFUL, THOUGH.

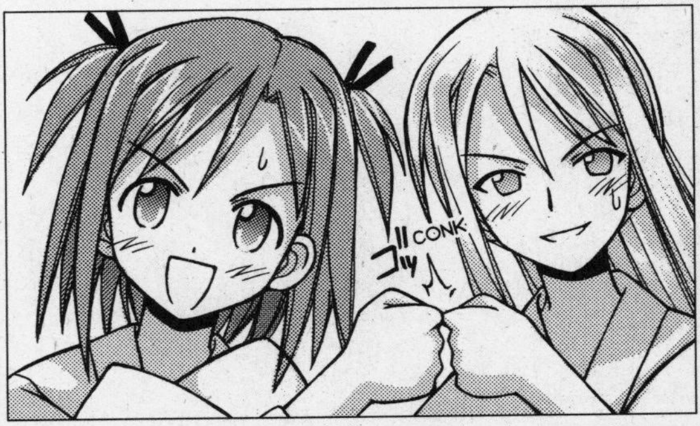
ゴッ
CONK

NEGIMA!

MAGISTER NEGI MAGI

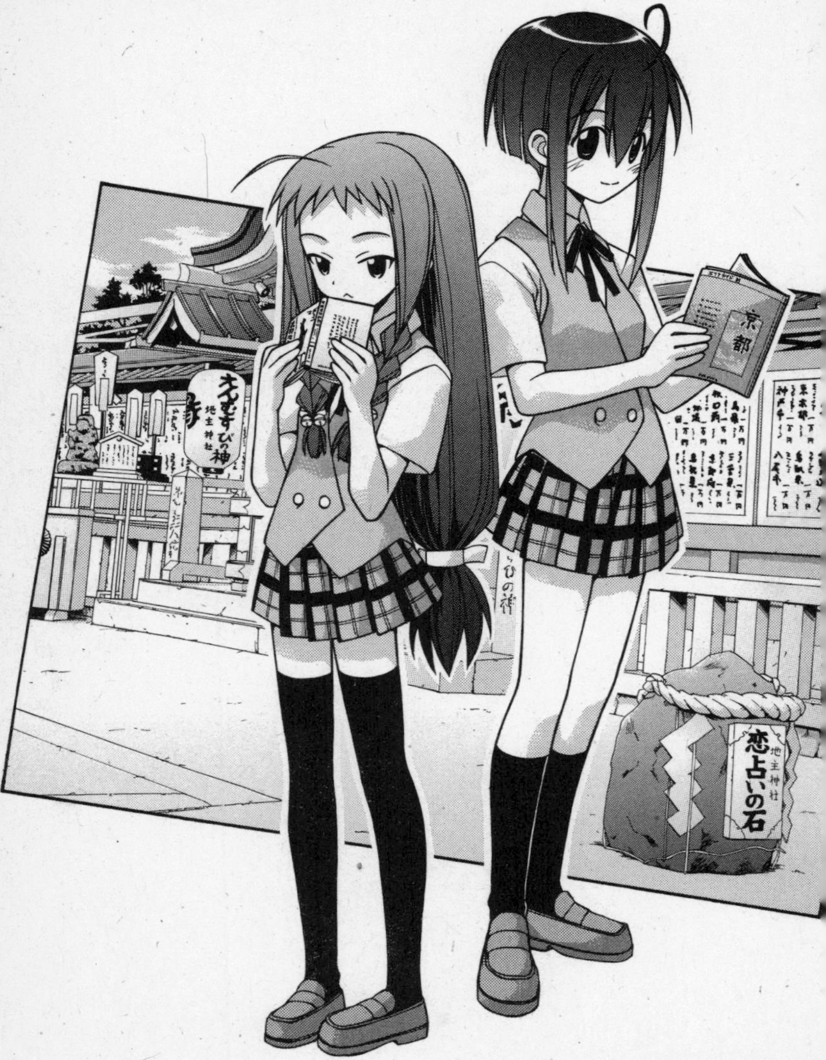
京
都
地主神社
恋占いの石

THIRTY-SEVENTH PERIOD:
WHO DOES NEGI'S KISS BELONG TO!?

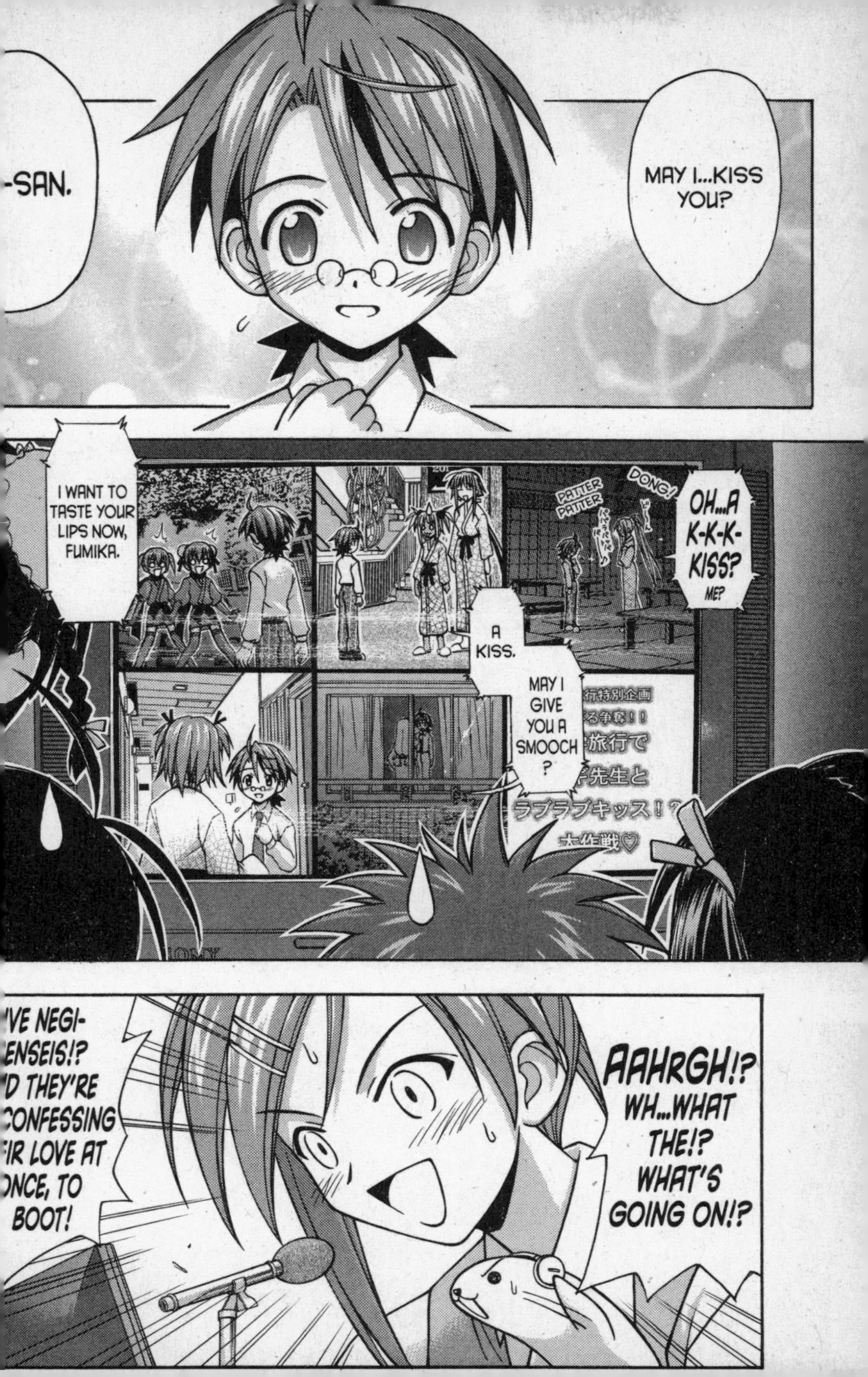
MAY I...KISS YOU?
-SAN.
OH...A K-K-K-KISS? ME?
DONG!
PATTER PATTER
A KISS.
MAY I GIVE YOU A SMOOCH?
I WANT TO TASTE YOUR LIPS NOW, FUMIKA.
ラブラブキッス！？
AAHRGH!? WH...WHAT THE!? WHAT'S GOING ON!?
VE NEGI-ENSEIS!? D THEY'RE CONFESSING EIR LOVE AT NCE, TO BOOT!

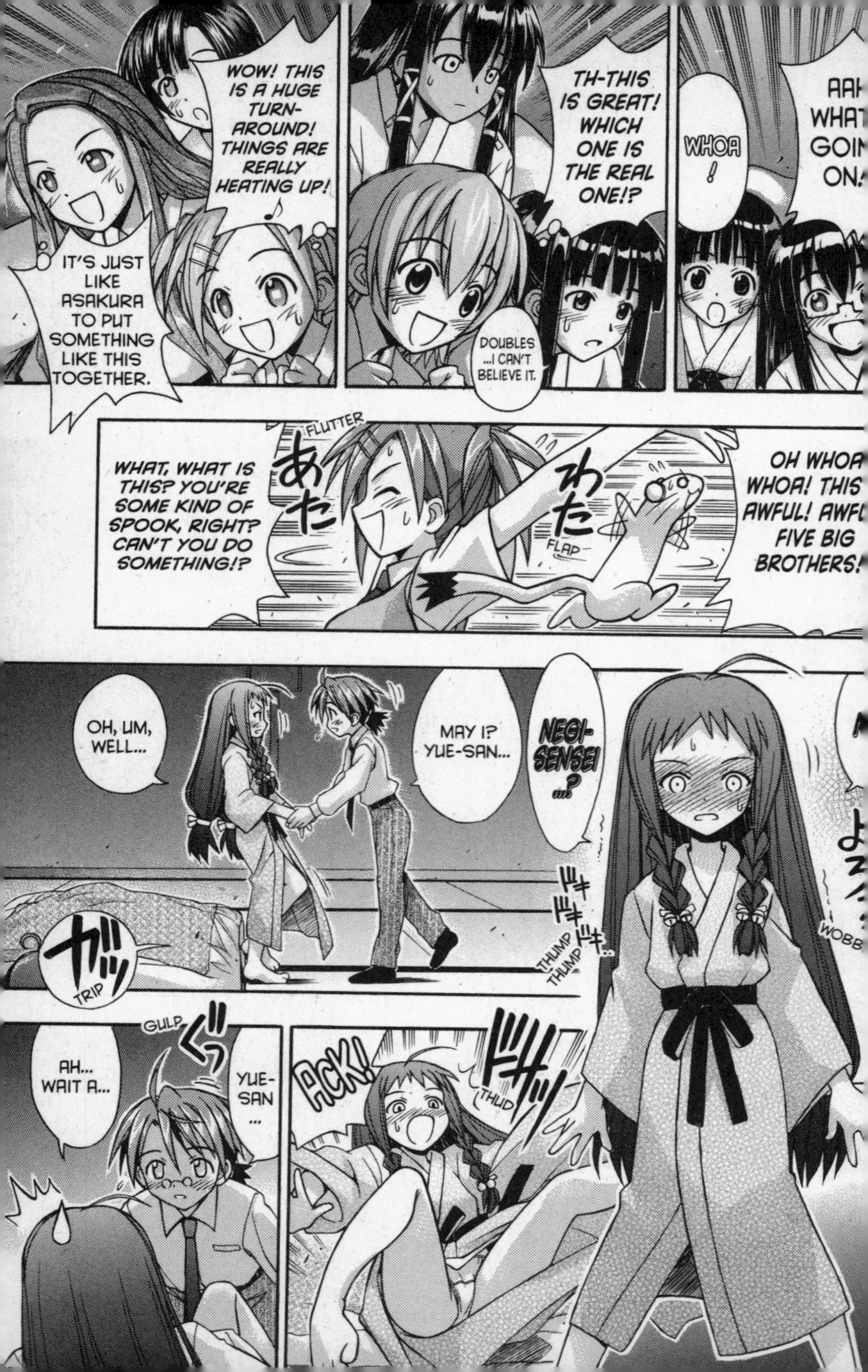
AAH WHAT GOIN ON.
WHOA!
TH-THIS IS GREAT! WHICH ONE IS THE REAL ONE!?
DOUBLES ...I CAN'T BELIEVE IT.
WOW! THIS IS A HUGE TURN-AROUND! THINGS ARE REALLY HEATING UP! ♪
IT'S JUST LIKE ASAKURA TO PUT SOMETHING LIKE THIS TOGETHER.
OH WHOA WHOA! THIS AWFUL! AWF FIVE BIG BROTHERS!
わた
FLAP
あた
FLUTTER
WHAT, WHAT IS THIS? YOU'RE SOME KIND OF SPOOK, RIGHT? CAN'T YOU DO SOMETHING!?
WOBB
NEGI-SENSEI...?
ドキドキドキ...
THUMP THUMP
MAY I? YUE-SAN...
OH, UM, WELL...
ガッ
TRIP
ドサッ
THUD
ACK!
ぐっ
GULP
YUE-SAN...
AH... WAIT A...

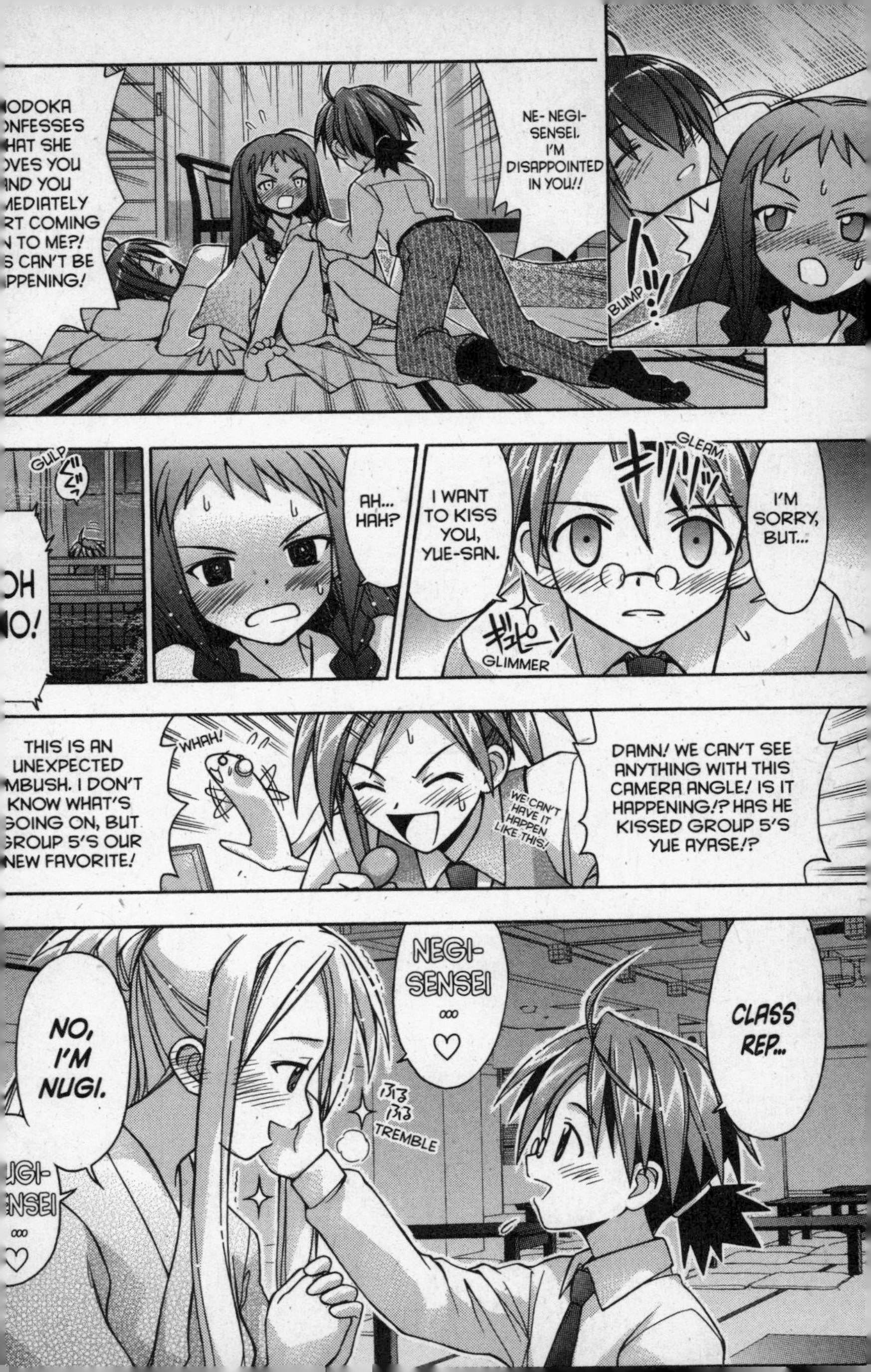
BUMP
NE- NEGI-SENSEI. I'M DISAPPOINTED IN YOU!!
ODOKA ONFESSES HAT SHE OVES YOU ND YOU MEDIATELY RT COMING N TO ME?! S CAN'T BE PPENING!
GLEAM
I'M SORRY, BUT...
I WANT TO KISS YOU, YUE-SAN.
GLIMMER
AH... HAH?
GULP
OH O!
DAMN! WE CAN'T SEE ANYTHING WITH THIS CAMERA ANGLE! IS IT HAPPENING!? HAS HE KISSED GROUP 5'S YUE AYASE!?
WE CAN'T HAVE IT HAPPEN LIKE THIS!
WHAH!
THIS IS AN UNEXPECTED MBUSH. I DON'T KNOW WHAT'S GOING ON, BUT GROUP 5'S OUR NEW FAVORITE!
CLASS REP...
NEGI-SENSEI ... ♡
TREMBLE
NO, I'M NUGI.
UGI-ENSEI ... ♡

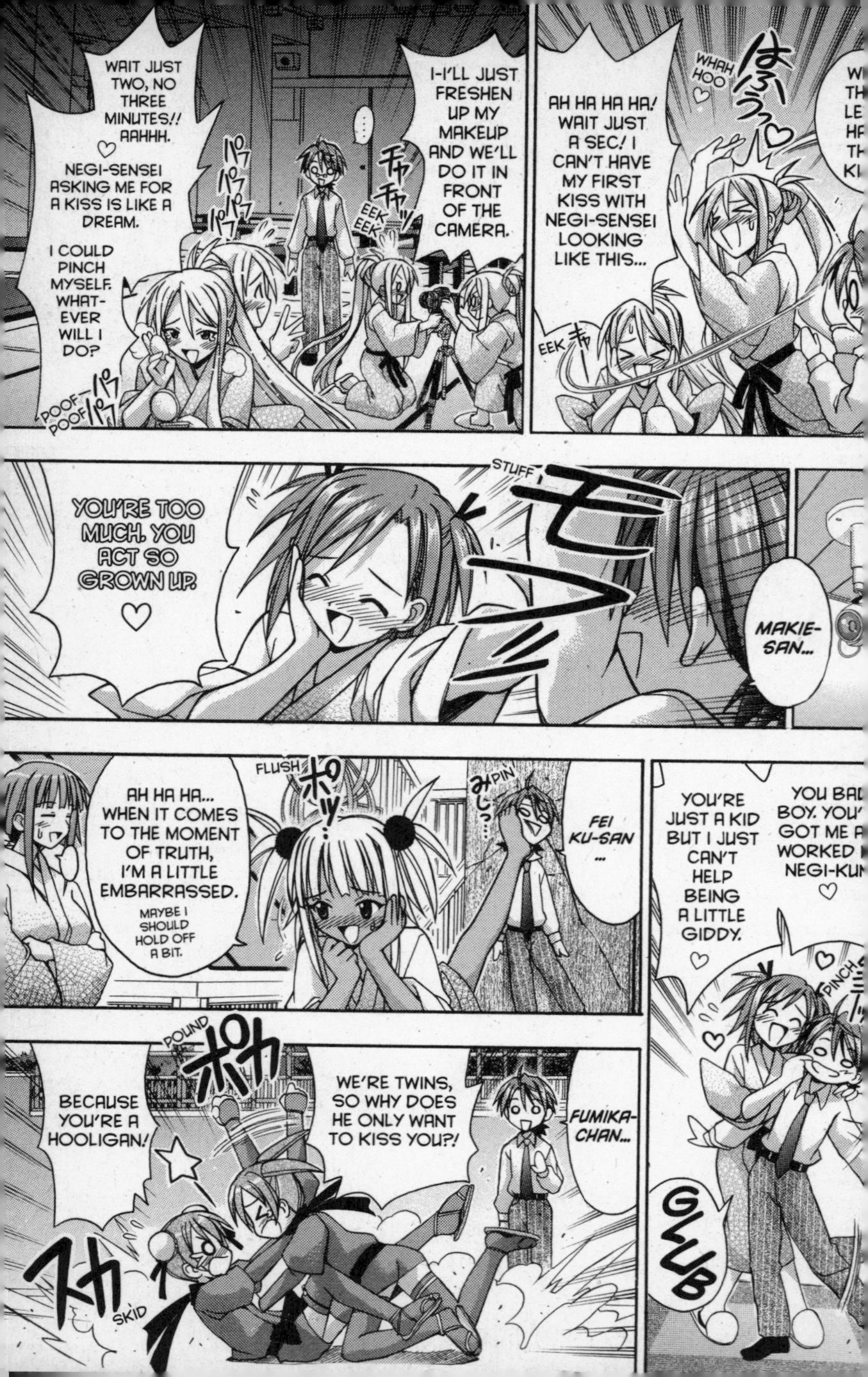
WHAH HOO
AH HA HA HA! WAIT JUST A SEC! I CAN'T HAVE MY FIRST KISS WITH NEGI-SENSEI LOOKING LIKE THIS...
EEK
I-I'LL JUST FRESHEN UP MY MAKEUP AND WE'LL DO IT IN FRONT OF THE CAMERA.
EEK EEK
...
WAIT JUST TWO, NO THREE MINUTES!! AAHHH.
NEGI-SENSEI ASKING ME FOR A KISS IS LIKE A DREAM.
I COULD PINCH MYSELF. WHATEVER WILL I DO?
POOF POOF
STUFF
MAKIE-SAN...
YOU'RE TOO MUCH. YOU ACT SO GROWN UP.
YOU'RE JUST A KID BUT I JUST CAN'T HELP BEING A LITTLE GIDDY.
PINCH
GLUB
FEI KU-SAN ...
PIN
FLUSH
AH HA HA... WHEN IT COMES TO THE MOMENT OF TRUTH, I'M A LITTLE EMBARRASSED.
MAYBE I SHOULD HOLD OFF A BIT.
FUMIKA-CHAN...
WE'RE TWINS, SO WHY DOES HE ONLY WANT TO KISS YOU?!
POUND
BECAUSE YOU'RE A HOOLIGAN!
SKID

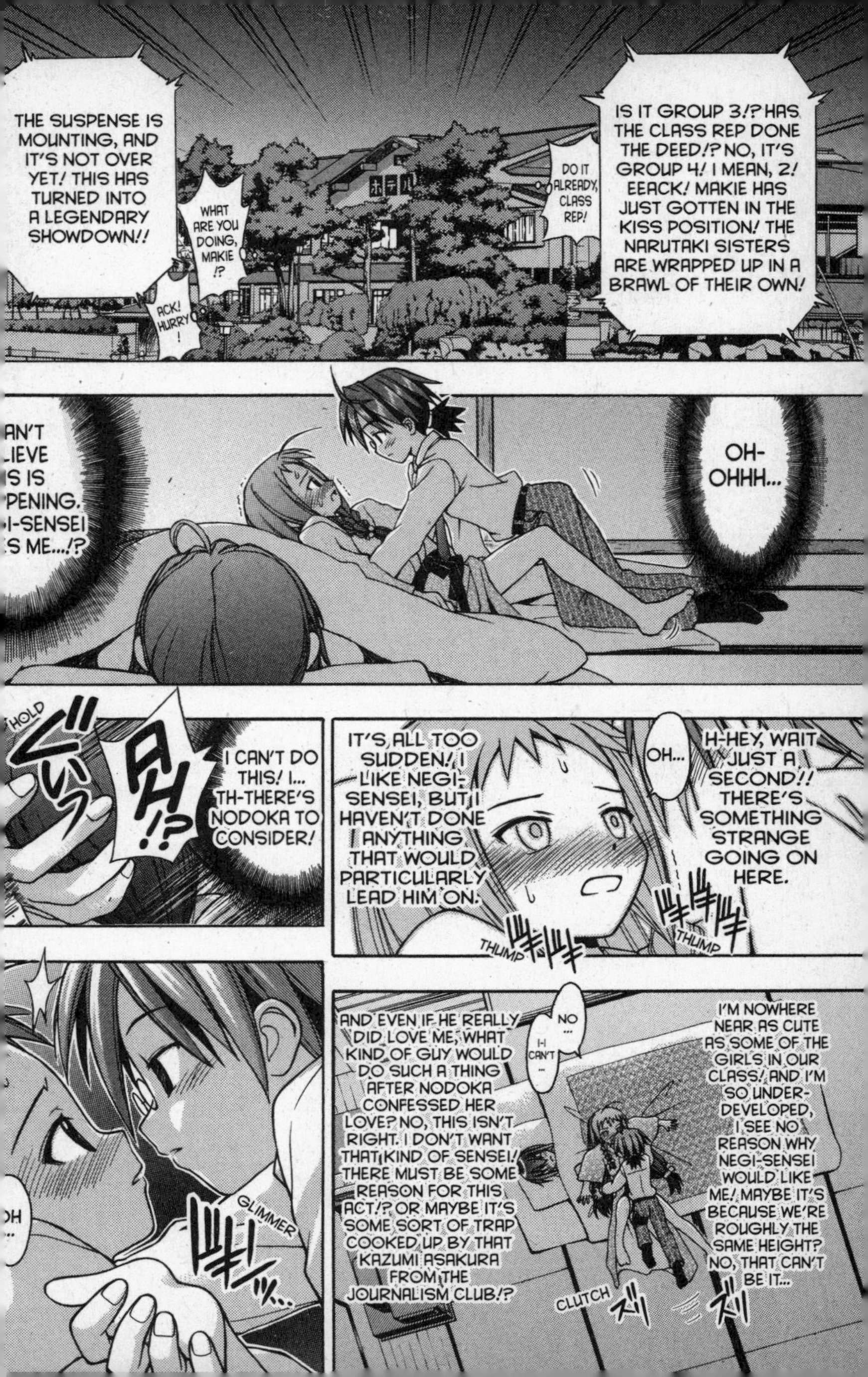
IS IT GROUP 3!? HAS THE CLASS REP DONE THE DEED!? NO, IT'S GROUP 4! I MEAN, 2! EEACK! MAKIE HAS JUST GOTTEN IN THE KISS POSITION! THE NARUTAKI SISTERS ARE WRAPPED UP IN A BRAWL OF THEIR OWN!
DO IT ALREADY, CLASS REP!
THE SUSPENSE IS MOUNTING, AND IT'S NOT OVER YET! THIS HAS TURNED INTO A LEGENDARY SHOWDOWN!!
WHAT ARE YOU DOING, MAKIE!?
ACK! HURRY!
OH-OHHH...
AN'T LIEVE IS IS PENING. I-SENSEI S ME...!?
H-HEY, WAIT JUST A SECOND!! THERE'S SOMETHING STRANGE GOING ON HERE.
OH...
IT'S ALL TOO SUDDEN! I LIKE NEGI-SENSEI, BUT I HAVEN'T DONE ANYTHING THAT WOULD PARTICULARLY LEAD HIM ON.
THUMP
THUMP
I CAN'T DO THIS! I... TH-THERE'S NODOKA TO CONSIDER!
AH!?
HOLD
I'M NOWHERE NEAR AS CUTE AS SOME OF THE GIRLS IN OUR CLASS! AND I'M SO UNDER-DEVELOPED, I SEE NO REASON WHY NEGI-SENSEI WOULD LIKE ME! MAYBE IT'S BECAUSE WE'RE ROUGHLY THE SAME HEIGHT? NO, THAT CAN'T BE IT...
NO...
I-I CAN'T...
AND EVEN IF HE REALLY DID LOVE ME, WHAT KIND OF GUY WOULD DO SUCH A THING AFTER NODOKA CONFESSED HER LOVE? NO, THIS ISN'T RIGHT. I DON'T WANT THAT KIND OF SENSEI! THERE MUST BE SOME REASON FOR THIS ACT!? OR MAYBE IT'S SOME SORT OF TRAP COOKED UP BY THAT KAZUMI ASAKURA FROM THE JOURNALISM CLUB!?
CLUTCH
GLIMMER
OH...

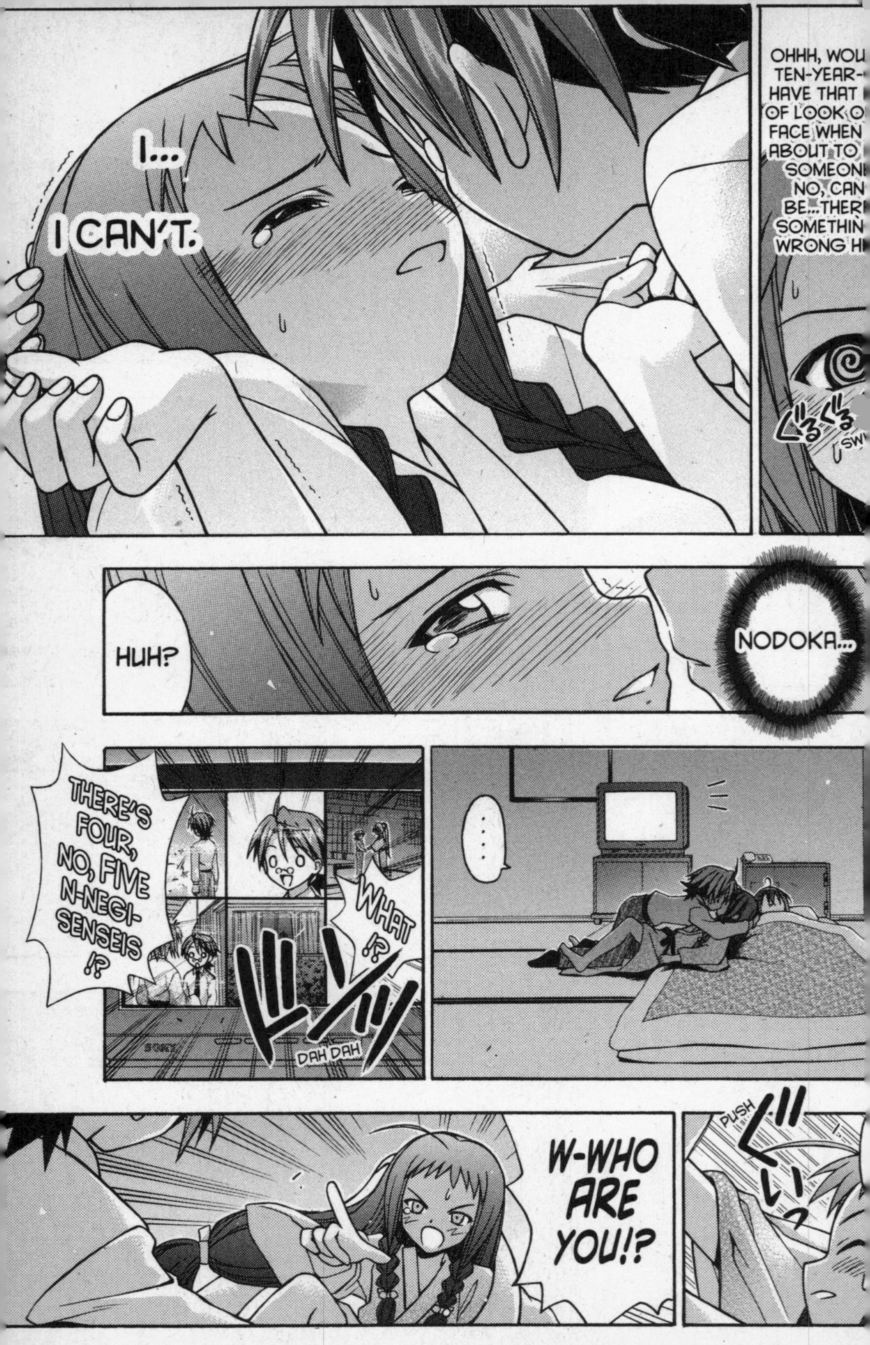

OHHH, WOU
TEN-YEAR-
HAVE THAT
OF LOOK O
FACE WHEN
ABOUT TO
SOMEON
NO, CAN
BE...THER
SOMETHIN
WRONG H
ぐるぐる
I...
I CAN'T.
NODOKA...
HUH?
. . . .
WHAT!?
THERE'S FOUR, NO, FIVE N-NEGI-SENSEIS!?
ドドッ
DAH DAH
ぐいっ
PUSH
W-WHO ARE YOU!?

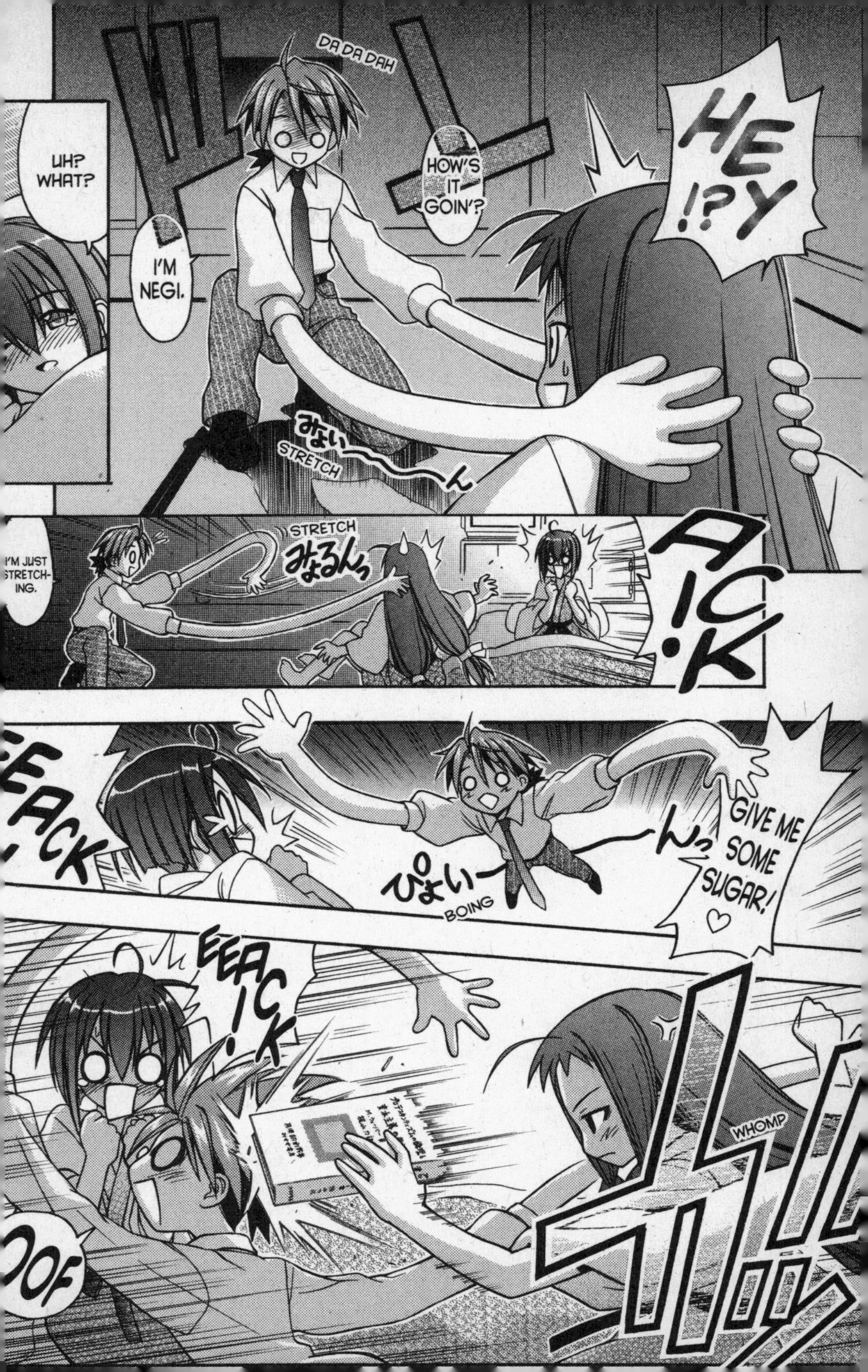
HEY!?
DA DA DAH
HOW'S IT GOIN'?
I'M NEGI.
みょい〜〜ん
STRETCH
UH? WHAT?
ACK!
STRETCH
みょるんっ
I'M JUST STRETCHING.
GIVE ME SOME SUGAR! ♡
んっ
ぴょい
BOING
EEACK!
WHOMP
EEACK!
OOF

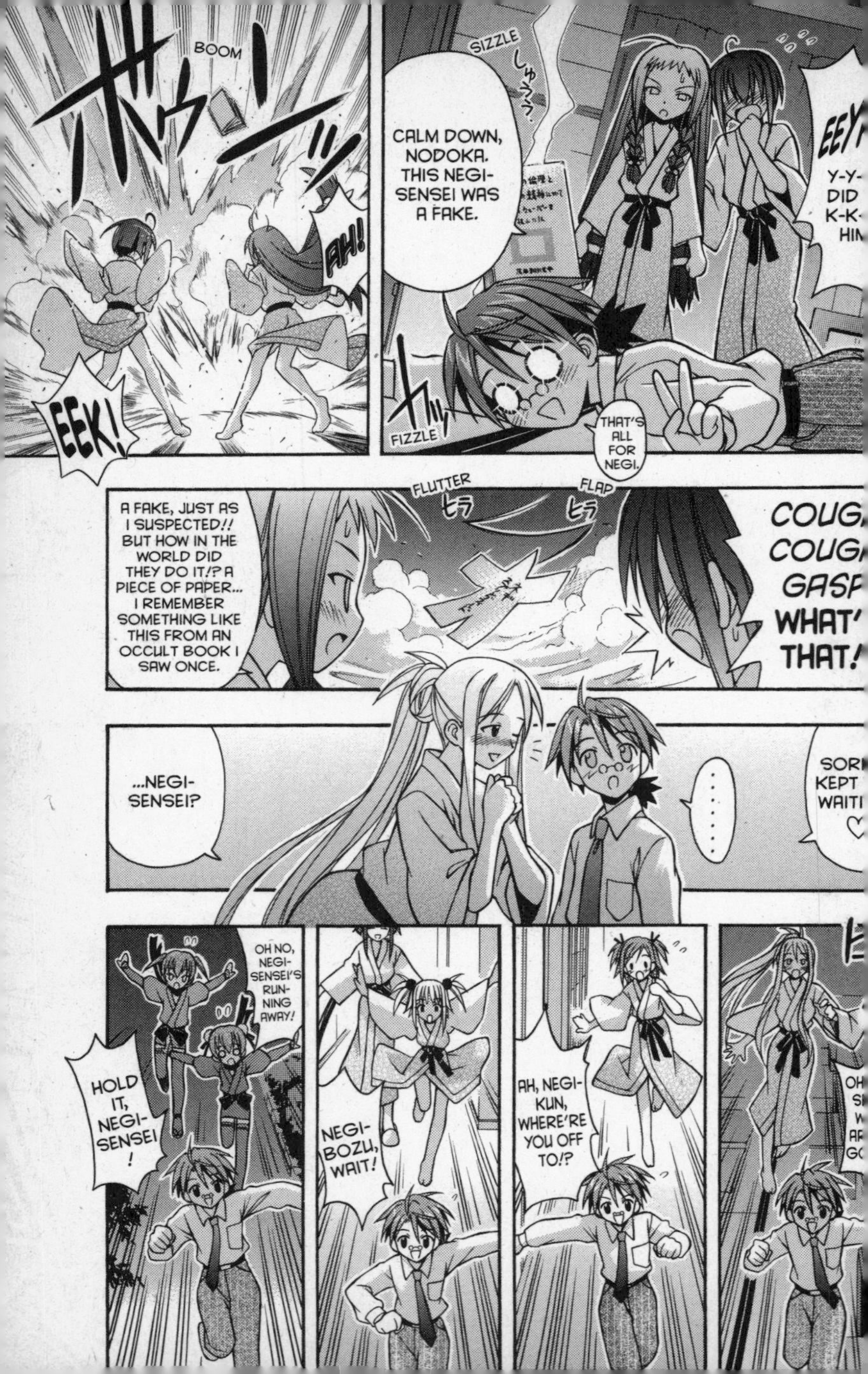
SIZZLE
しゅううう
CALM DOWN, NODOKA. THIS NEGI-SENSEI WAS A FAKE.
EEY
Y-Y- DID K-K- HIM
FIZZLE
THAT'S ALL FOR NEGI.
BOOM
AH!
EEK!
COUG COUG GASP WHAT' THAT!
FLUTTER
FLAP
A FAKE, JUST AS I SUSPECTED!! BUT HOW IN THE WORLD DID THEY DO IT!? A PIECE OF PAPER... I REMEMBER SOMETHING LIKE THIS FROM AN OCCULT BOOK I SAW ONCE.
SORR KEPT WAITI ♡
......
...NEGI-SENSEI?
AH, NEGI-KUN, WHERE'RE YOU OFF TO!?
NEGI-BOZU, WAIT!
OH NO, NEGI-SENSEI'S RUNNING AWAY!
HOLD IT, NEGI-SENSEI!

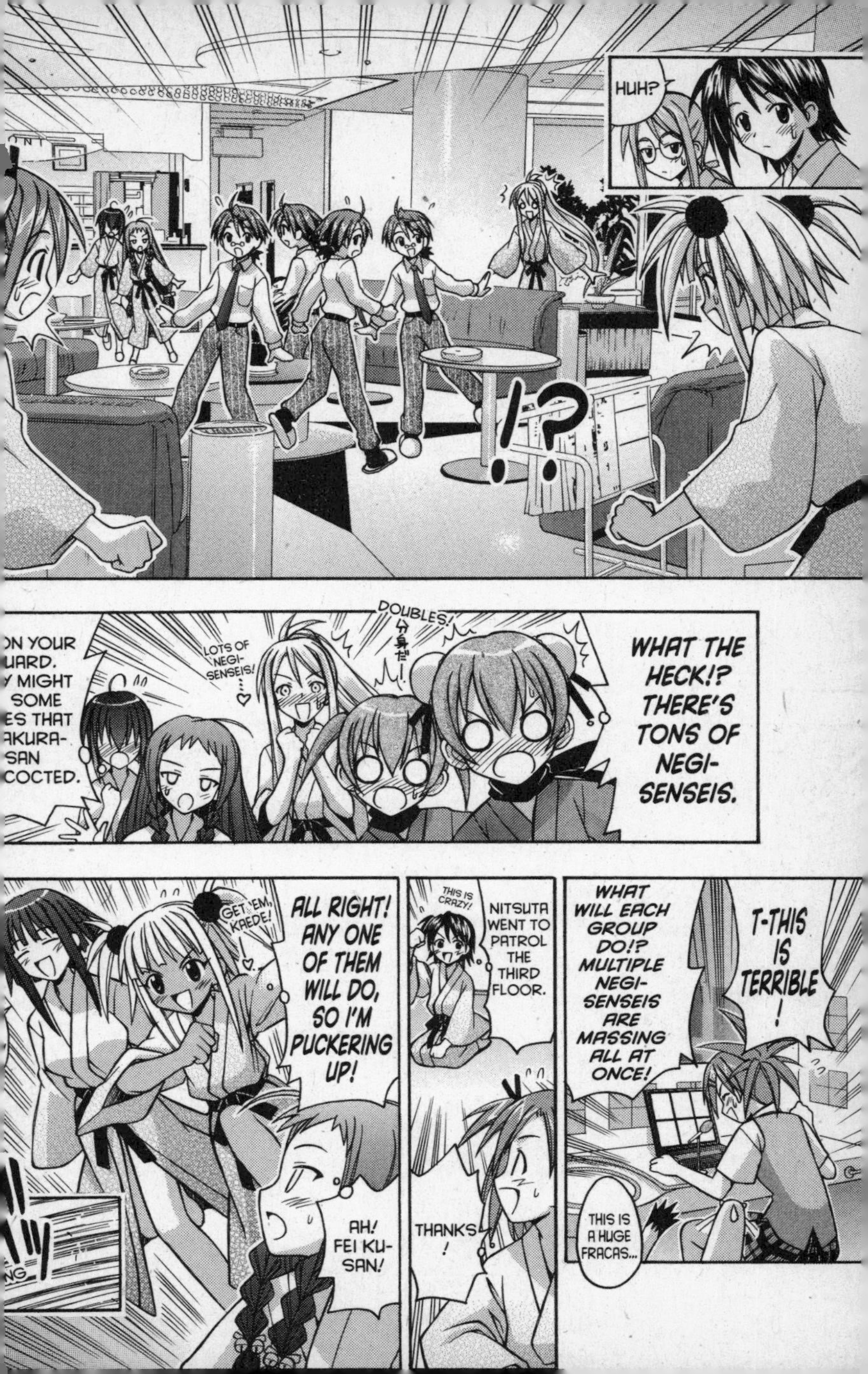
HUH?
!?
WHAT THE HECK!? THERE'S TONS OF NEGI-SENSEIS.
DOUBLES!
分身だ!
LOTS OF NEGI-SENSEIS!...♡
T-THIS IS TERRIBLE!
WHAT WILL EACH GROUP DO!? MULTIPLE NEGI-SENSEIS ARE MASSING ALL AT ONCE!
THIS IS A HUGE FRACAS...
NITSUTA WENT TO PATROL THE THIRD FLOOR.
THIS IS CRAZY!
THANKS!
ALL RIGHT! ANY ONE OF THEM WILL DO, SO I'M PUCKERING UP!
GET 'EM, KAEDE! ♡
AH! FEI KU-SAN!

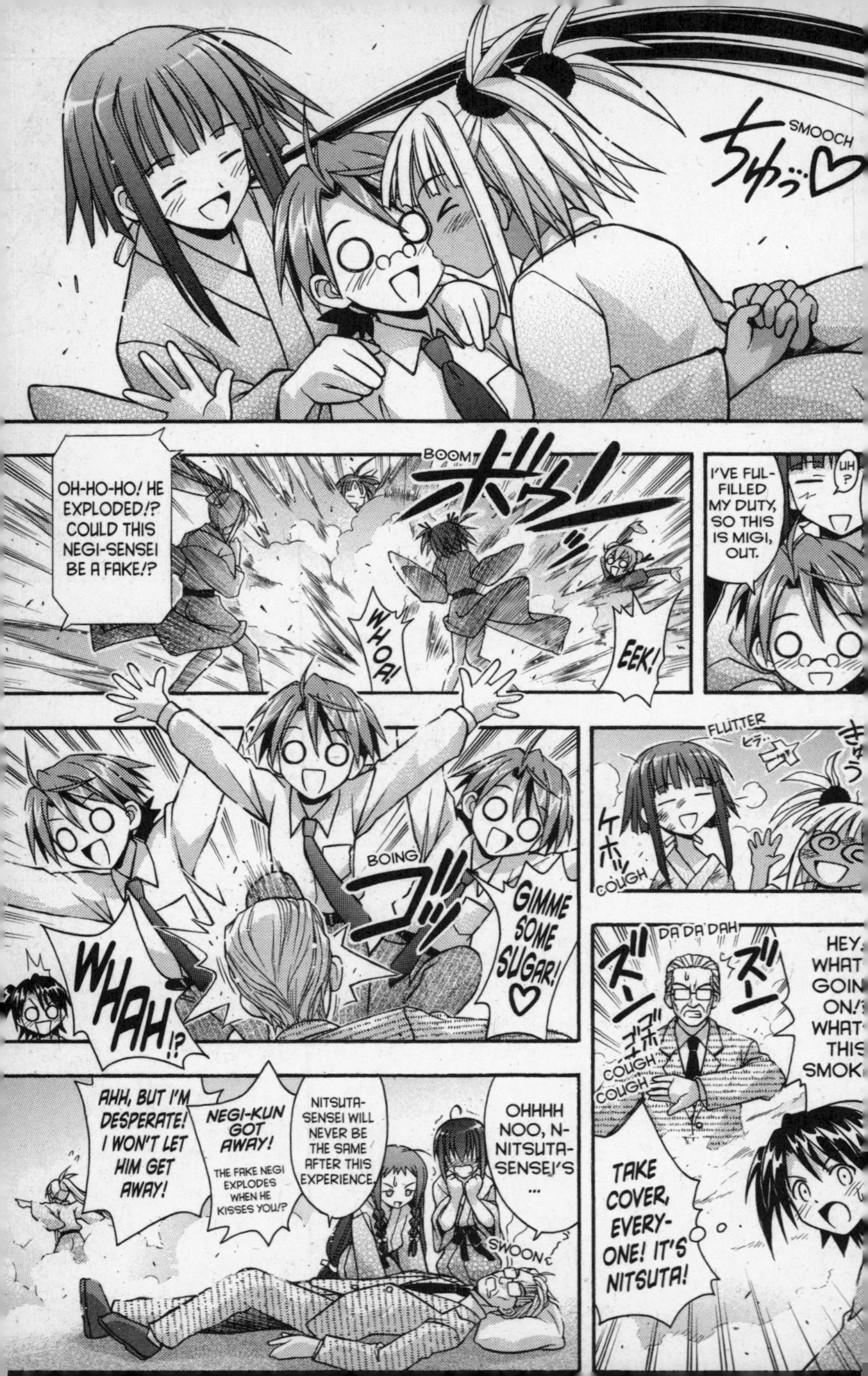
SMOOCH
UH?
I'VE FULFILLED MY DUTY, SO THIS IS MIGI, OUT.
BOOM
OH-HO-HO! HE EXPLODED!? COULD THIS NEGI-SENSEI BE A FAKE!?
WHOA!
EEK!
FLUTTER
COUGH
GIMME SOME SUGAR! ♡
BOING
WHAH!?
DA DA DAH
HEY. WHAT GOIN ON!? WHAT THIS SMOK
COUGH COUGH
TAKE COVER, EVERYONE! IT'S NITSUTA!
OHHHH NOO, N-NITSUTA-SENSEI'S ...
NITSUTA-SENSEI WILL NEVER BE THE SAME AFTER THIS EXPERIENCE.
NEGI-KUN GOT AWAY!
THE FAKE NEGI EXPLODES WHEN HE KISSES YOU!?
AHH, BUT I'M DESPERATE! I WON'T LET HIM GET AWAY!
SWOON

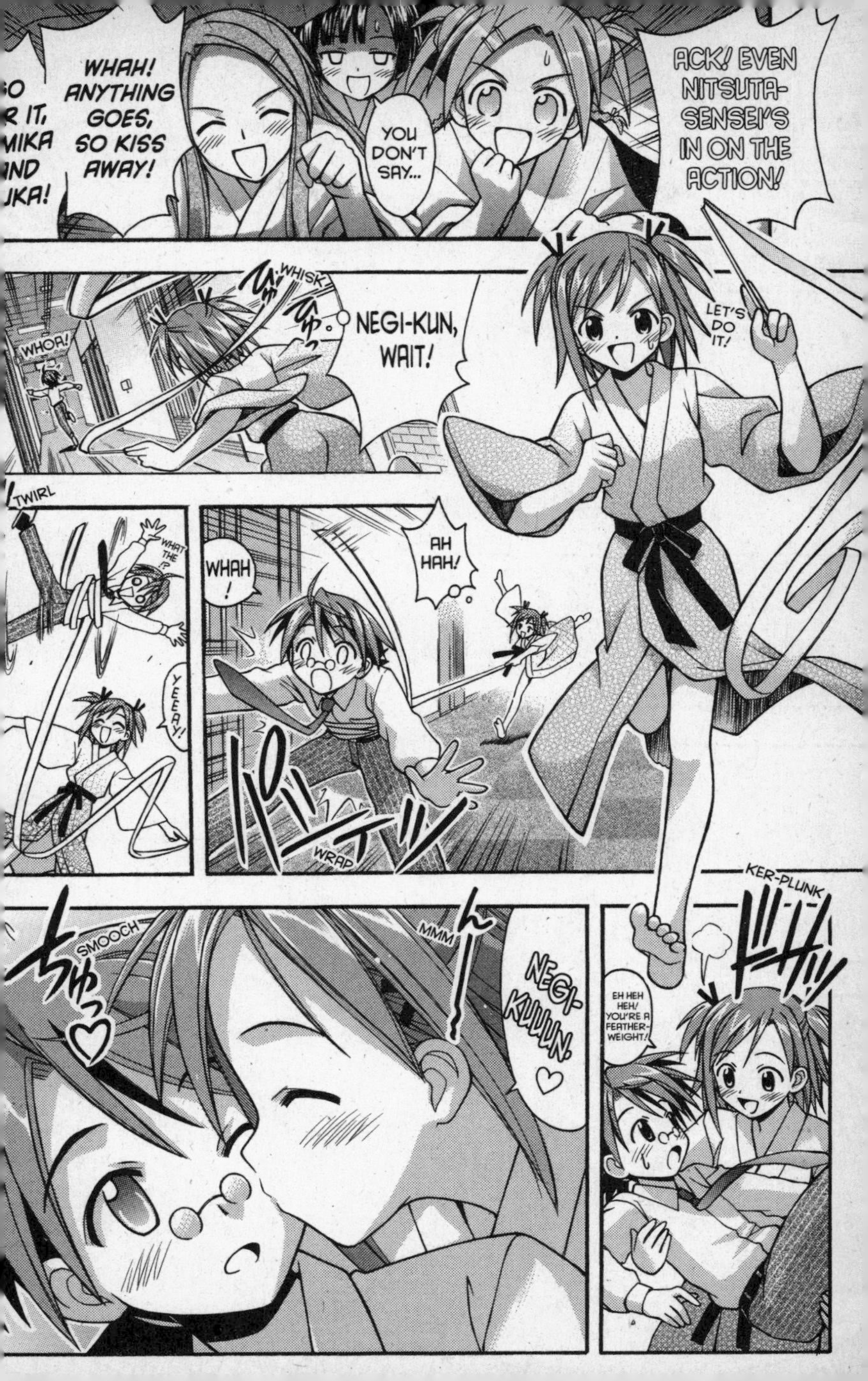
ACK! EVEN NITSUTA-SENSEI'S IN ON THE ACTION!
YOU DON'T SAY...
WHAH! ANYTHING GOES, SO KISS AWAY!
LET'S DO IT!
NEGI-KUN, WAIT!
WHISK
WHOA!
AH HAH!
WHAH!
WRAP
TWIRL
WHAT THE !?
YEEEAY!
KER-PLUNK
EH HEH HEH! YOU'RE A FEATHER-WEIGHT!
NEGI-KUUUN.
MMM
SMOOCH

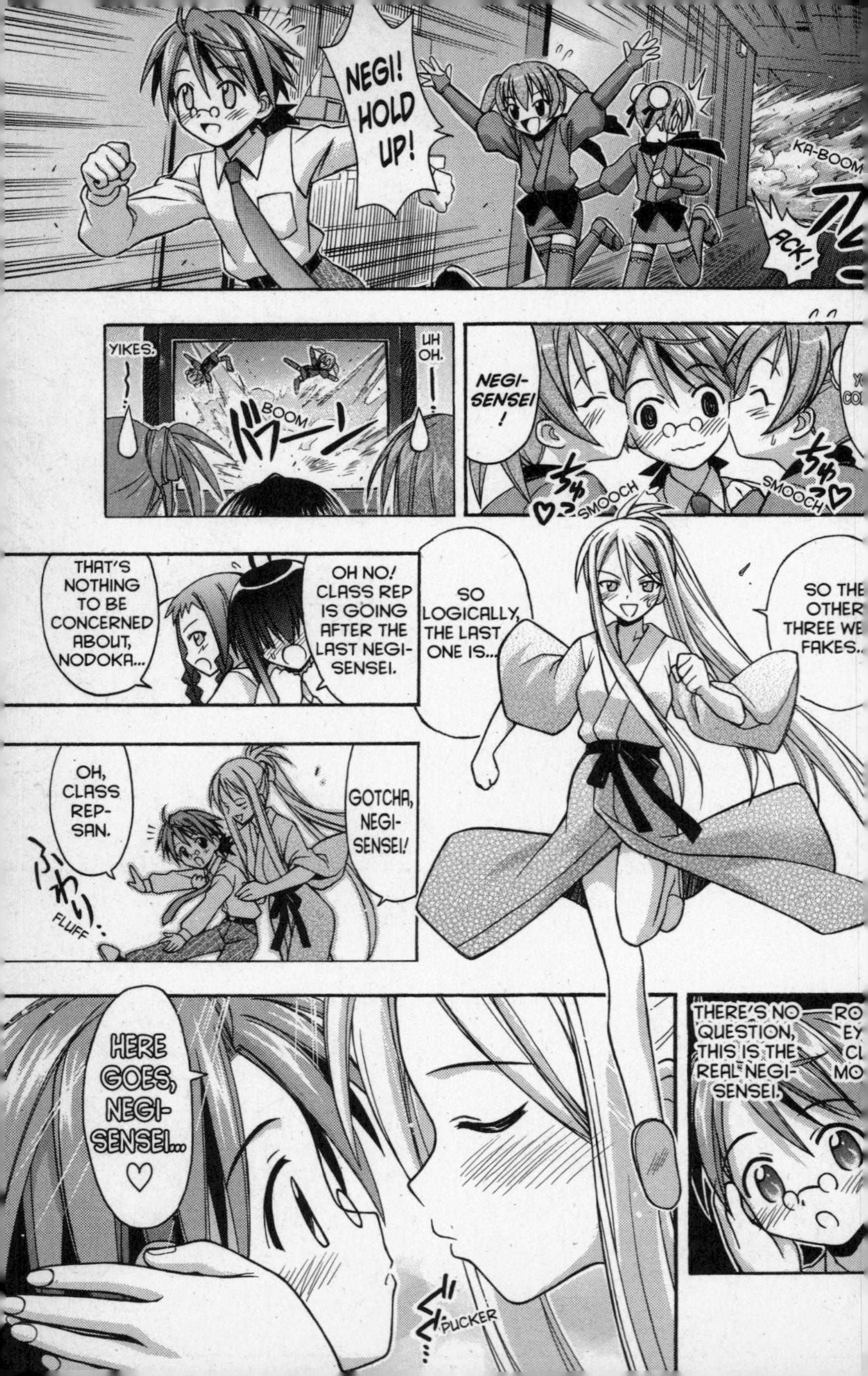
NEGI! HOLD UP!
KA-BOOM
ACK!
NEGI-SENSEI!
SMOOCH
SMOOCH
UH OH.
BOOM
YIKES.
SO THE OTHER THREE WE FAKES..
SO LOGICALLY, THE LAST ONE IS...
OH NO! CLASS REP IS GOING AFTER THE LAST NEGI-SENSEI.
THAT'S NOTHING TO BE CONCERNED ABOUT, NODOKA...
GOTCHA, NEGI-SENSEI!
OH, CLASS REP-SAN.
FLUFF
THERE'S NO QUESTION, THIS IS THE REAL NEGI-SENSEI.
HERE GOES, NEGI-SENSEI... ♡
PUCKER

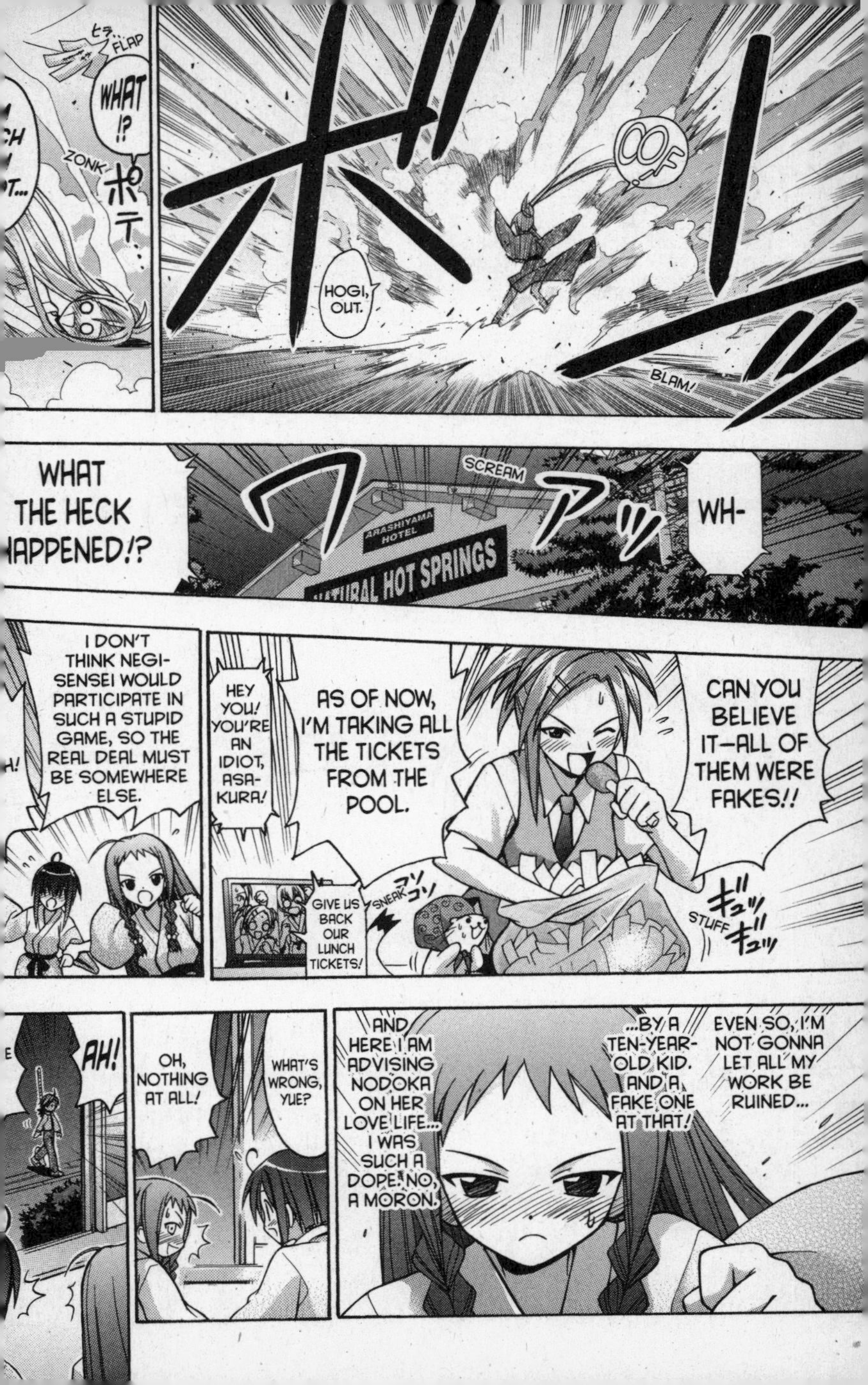
ズドーン
OOF
HOGI, OUT.
BLAM!
ヒラ.. FLAP
WHAT !?
ZONK
ポテ...
WH-
ワアッ
SCREAM
ARASHIYAMA HOTEL
NATURAL HOT SPRINGS
WHAT THE HECK HAPPENED!?
CAN YOU BELIEVE IT—ALL OF THEM WERE FAKES!!
AS OF NOW, I'M TAKING ALL THE TICKETS FROM THE POOL.
HEY YOU! YOU'RE AN IDIOT, ASA-KURA!
ギュッ ギュッ
STUFF
コソ コソ
SNEAK
GIVE US BACK OUR LUNCH TICKETS!
I DON'T THINK NEGI-SENSEI WOULD PARTICIPATE IN SUCH A STUPID GAME, SO THE REAL DEAL MUST BE SOMEWHERE ELSE.
EVEN SO, I'M NOT GONNA LET ALL MY WORK BE RUINED...
...BY A TEN-YEAR-OLD KID. AND A FAKE ONE AT THAT!
AND HERE I AM ADVISING NODOKA ON HER LOVE LIFE... I WAS SUCH A DOPE. NO, A MORON.
WHAT'S WRONG, YUE?
OH, NOTHING AT ALL!
AH!

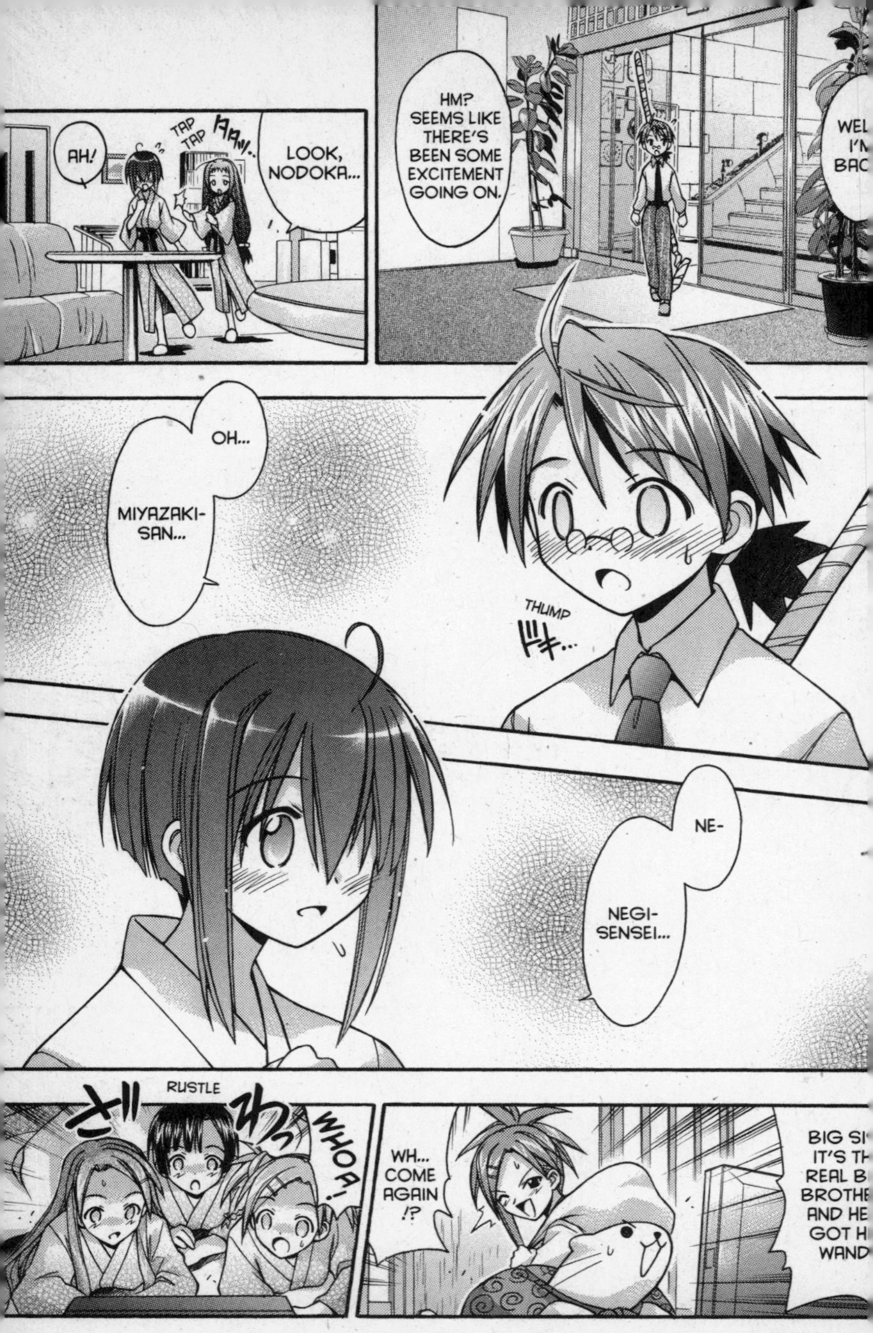
WEL
I'M
BAC
HM? SEEMS LIKE THERE'S BEEN SOME EXCITEMENT GOING ON.
LOOK, NODOKA...
TAP TAP
AH!
THUMP
OH... MIYAZAKI-SAN...
NE- NEGI-SENSEI...
BIG SI IT'S TH REAL B BROTHE AND HE GOT H WAND
WH... COME AGAIN !?
RUSTLE
WHOA!

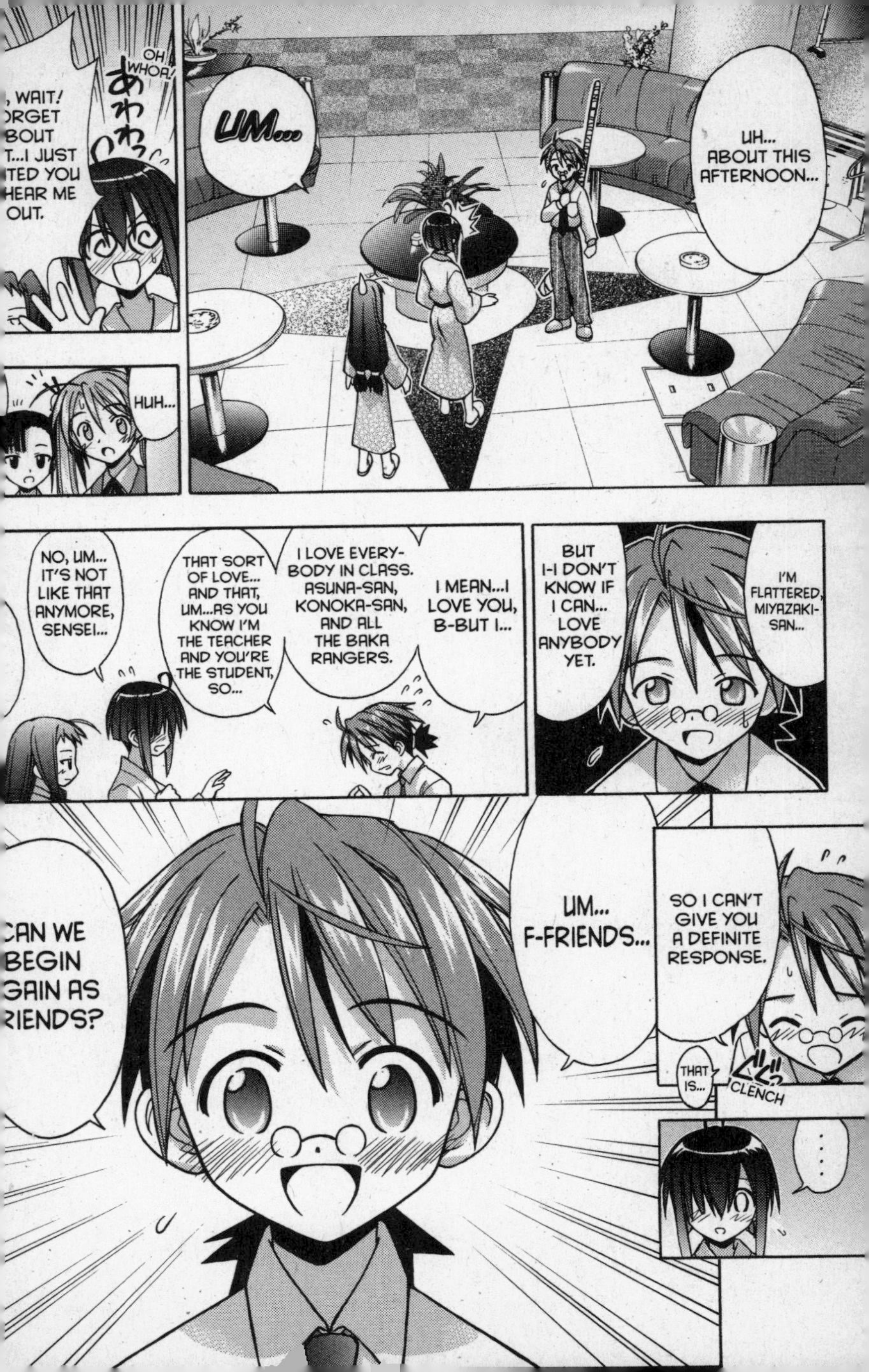
UH... ABOUT THIS AFTERNOON...
UM...
OH WHOA!
あわわっ
, WAIT! ORGET BOUT T...I JUST TED YOU HEAR ME OUT.
HUH...
I'M FLATTERED, MIYAZAKI-SAN...
BUT I-I DON'T KNOW IF I CAN... LOVE ANYBODY YET.
I MEAN...I LOVE YOU, B-BUT I...
I LOVE EVERY-BODY IN CLASS. ASUNA-SAN, KONOKA-SAN, AND ALL THE BAKA RANGERS.
THAT SORT OF LOVE... AND THAT, UM...AS YOU KNOW I'M THE TEACHER AND YOU'RE THE STUDENT, SO...
NO, UM... IT'S NOT LIKE THAT ANYMORE, SENSEI...
SO I CAN'T GIVE YOU A DEFINITE RESPONSE.
THAT IS...
ぐぐっ
CLENCH
...
UM... F-FRIENDS...
CAN WE BEGIN GAIN AS RIENDS?

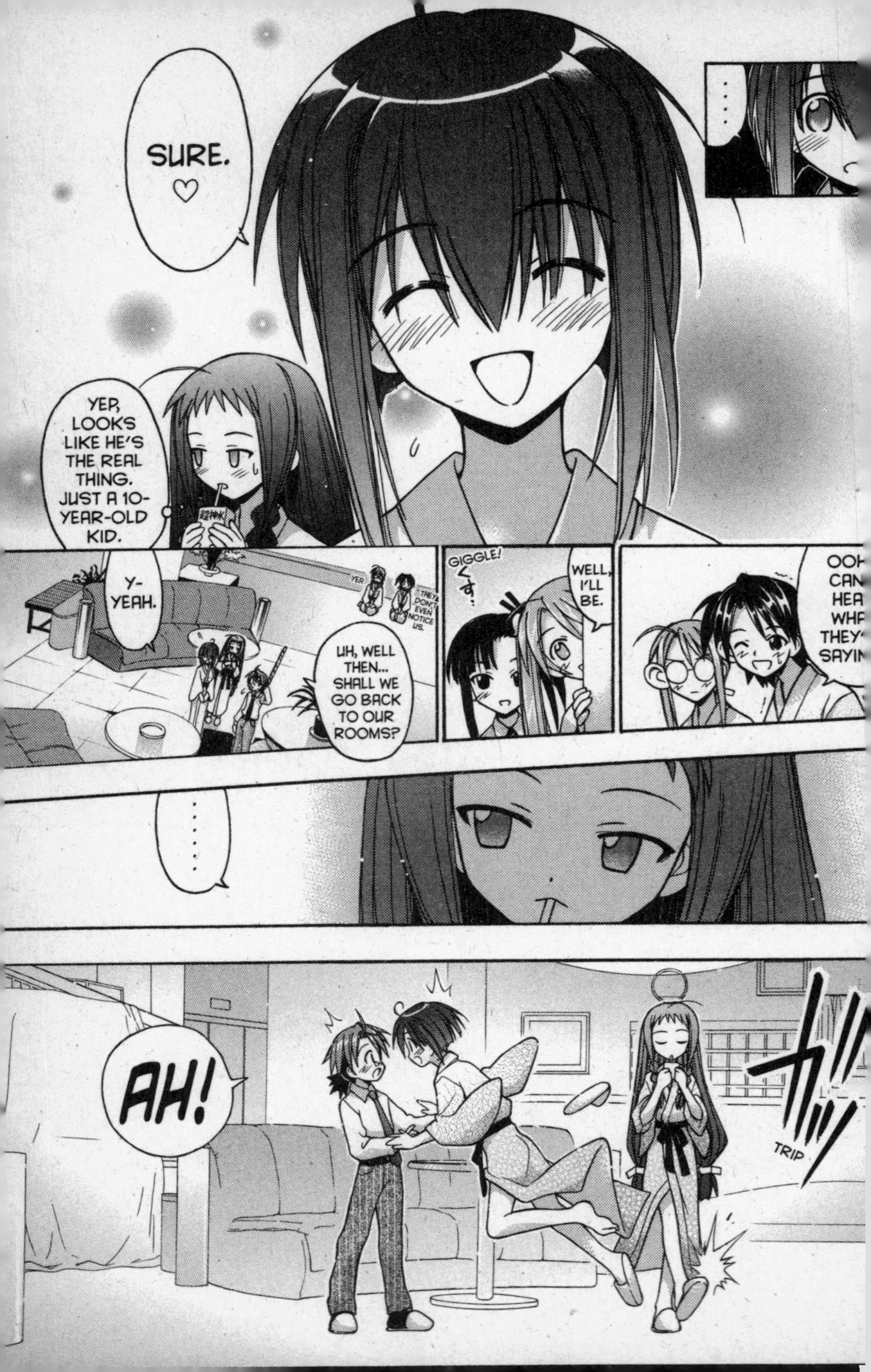
. . . .
SURE. ♡
YEP, LOOKS LIKE HE'S THE REAL THING. JUST A 10-YEAR-OLD KID.
OOH CAN HEA WHA THEY' SAYIN
GIGGLE! くすっ
WELL, I'LL BE.
YEP
THEY DON'T EVEN NOTICE US.
Y-YEAH.
UH, WELL THEN... SHALL WE GO BACK TO OUR ROOMS?
. . . . . .
AH!
TRIP

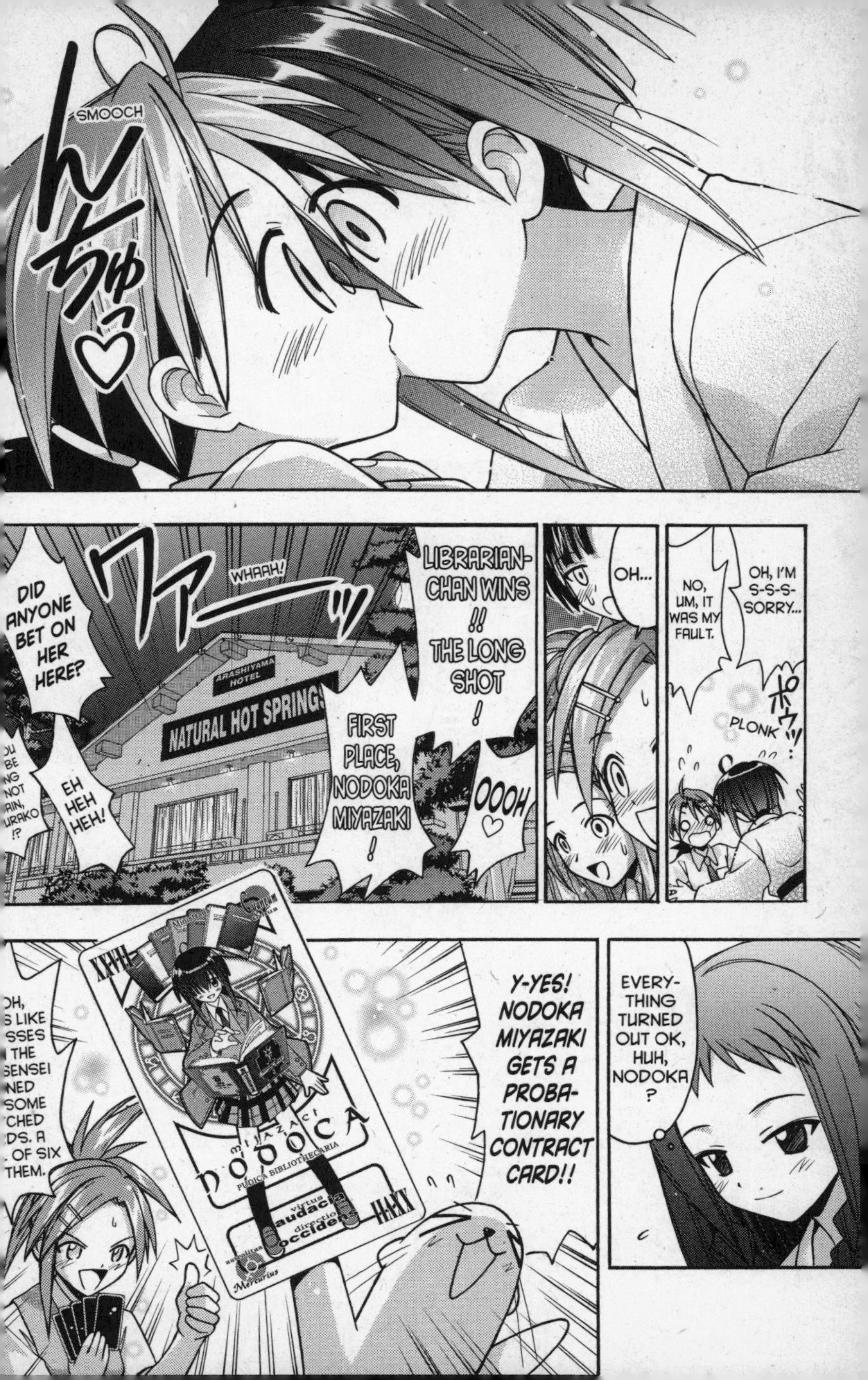
んちゅっ♡
SMOOCH
OH, I'M S-S-S-SORRY...
NO, UM, IT WAS MY FAULT.
ポウッ
PLONK
OH...
LIBRARIAN-CHAN WINS!! THE LONG SHOT!
FIRST PLACE, NODOKA MIYAZAKI!
OOOH♡
ワァーッ
WHAAH!
ARASHIYAMA HOTEL
NATURAL HOT SPRINGS
DID ANYONE BET ON HER HERE?
EH HEH HEH!
EVERY-THING TURNED OUT OK, HUH, NODOKA?
Y-YES! NODOKA MIYAZAKI GETS A PROBA-TIONARY CONTRACT CARD!!
MIYAZAKI NODOCA
PUDICA BIBLIOTHECARIA
virtus audacia
directio occidens
Mercurius

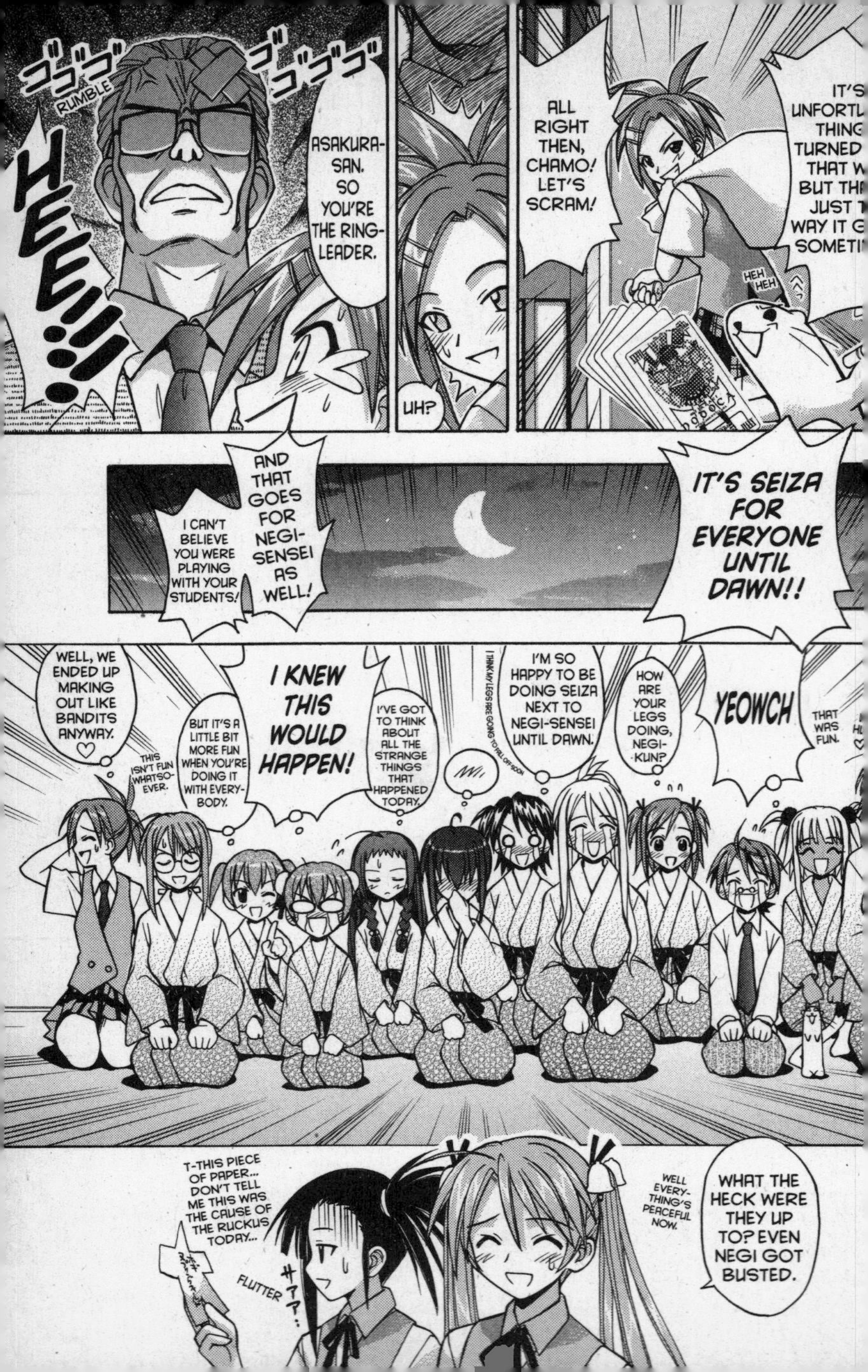
IT'S UNFORTL THING TURNED THAT W BUT THA JUST T WAY IT G SOMETI
ALL RIGHT THEN, CHAMO! LET'S SCRAM!
HEH HEH
UH?
ASAKURA-SAN. SO YOU'RE THE RING-LEADER.
ゴゴゴゴ
ゴゴゴ
RUMBLE
HEEY!!!
IT'S SEIZA FOR EVERYONE UNTIL DAWN!!
AND THAT GOES FOR NEGI-SENSEI AS WELL!
I CAN'T BELIEVE YOU WERE PLAYING WITH YOUR STUDENTS!
THAT WAS FUN.
YEOWCH
HOW ARE YOUR LEGS DOING, NEGI-KUN?
I'M SO HAPPY TO BE DOING SEIZA NEXT TO NEGI-SENSEI UNTIL DAWN.
I THINK MY LEGS ARE GOING TO FALL OFF SOON
I'VE GOT TO THINK ABOUT ALL THE STRANGE THINGS THAT HAPPENED TODAY.
I KNEW THIS WOULD HAPPEN!
BUT IT'S A LITTLE BIT MORE FUN WHEN YOU'RE DOING IT WITH EVERY-BODY.
THIS ISN'T FUN WHATSO-EVER.
WELL, WE ENDED UP MAKING OUT LIKE BANDITS ANYWAY. ♡
WHAT THE HECK WERE THEY UP TO? EVEN NEGI GOT BUSTED.
WELL EVERY-THING'S PEACEFUL NOW.
T-THIS PIECE OF PAPER... DON'T TELL ME THIS WAS THE CAUSE OF THE RUCKUS TODAY...
サァァ
FLUTTER

A SCHOOL FIELD TRIP'S GROUPS 4 AND 5

GROUP 4
(GROUP LEADER)
YUNA AKASHI

AKO IZUMI
AKIRA OHKOUCHI
MAKIE SASAKI
MANA TATSUMIYA

GROUP 5
(GROUP LEADER)
ASUNA KAGURAZAKA

YUE AYASE
KONOKA KONOE
HARUNA SAOTOME
SETSUNA SAKURAZAKI
NODOKA MIYAZAKI

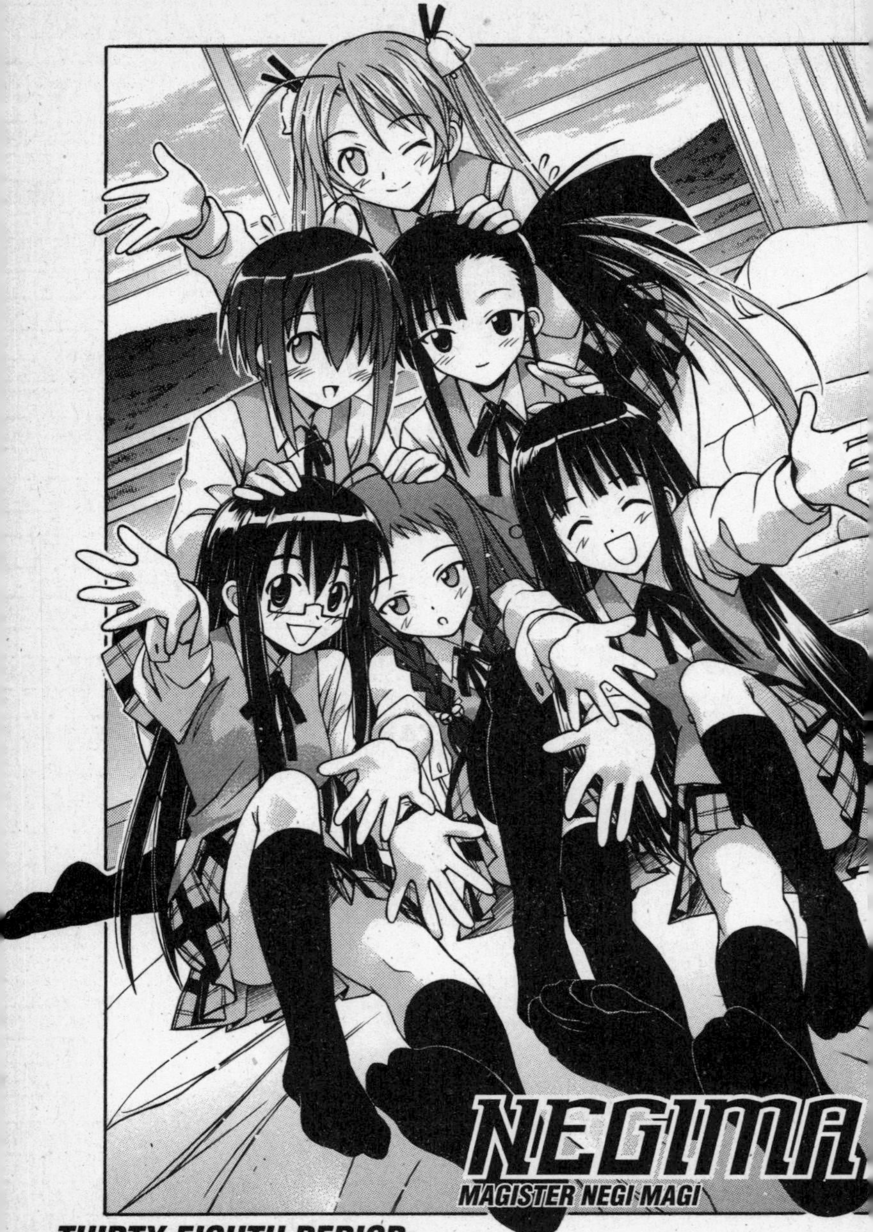
NEGIMA
MAGISTER NEGI MAGI

THIRTY-EIGHTH PERIOD:
NODOKA AND THE SECRET PICTURE DIARY

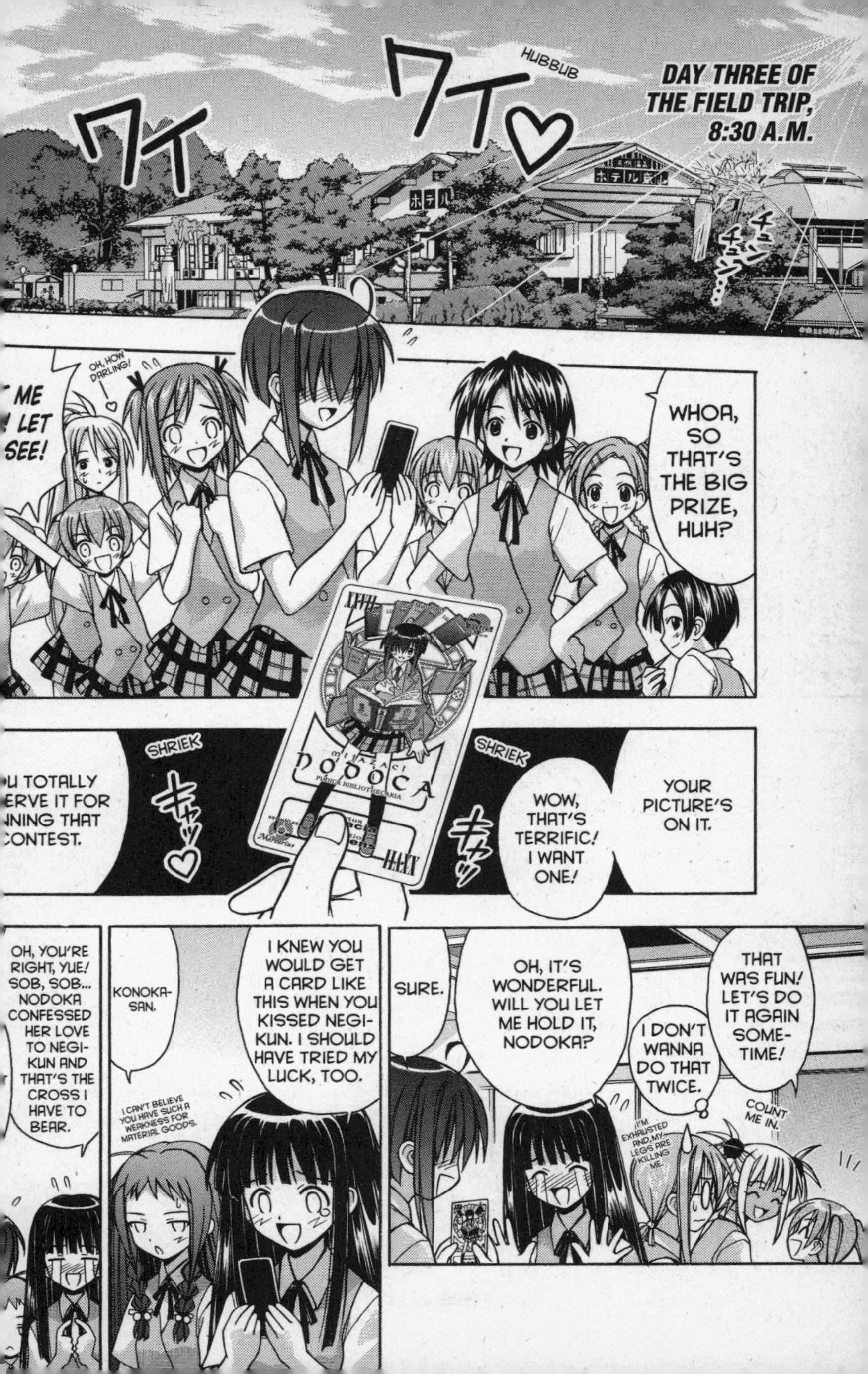
DAY THREE OF THE FIELD TRIP, 8:30 A.M.
HUBBUB
ワイ ワイ♡
WHOA, SO THAT'S THE BIG PRIZE, HUH?
OH, HOW DARLING!
T ME
LET
SEE!
YOUR PICTURE'S ON IT.
WOW, THAT'S TERRIFIC! I WANT ONE!
SHRIEK
NODOCA
PUDICA BIBLIOTHECARIA
SHRIEK
U TOTALLY ERVE IT FOR NNING THAT CONTEST.
THAT WAS FUN! LET'S DO IT AGAIN SOME-TIME!
I DON'T WANNA DO THAT TWICE.
COUNT ME IN.
I'M EXHAUSTED AND MY LEGS ARE KILLING ME.
OH, IT'S WONDERFUL. WILL YOU LET ME HOLD IT, NODOKA?
SURE.
I KNEW YOU WOULD GET A CARD LIKE THIS WHEN YOU KISSED NEGI-KUN. I SHOULD HAVE TRIED MY LUCK, TOO.
KONOKA-SAN.
I CAN'T BELIEVE YOU HAVE SUCH A WEAKNESS FOR MATERIAL GOODS.
OH, YOU'RE RIGHT, YUE! SOB, SOB... NODOKA CONFESSED HER LOVE TO NEGI-KUN AND THAT'S THE CROSS I HAVE TO BEAR.

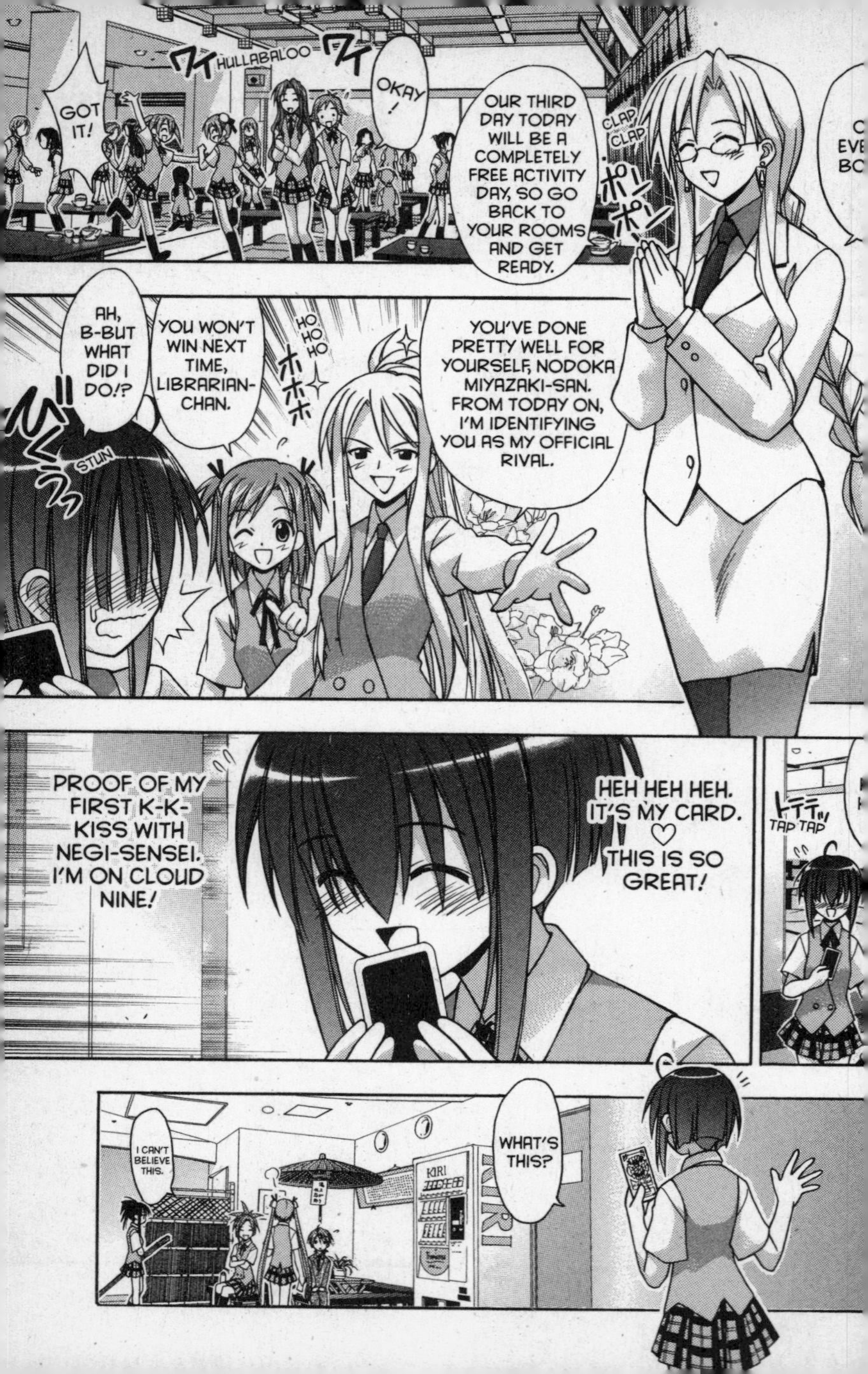
CLAP CLAP
ポン ポン
OUR THIRD DAY TODAY WILL BE A COMPLETELY FREE ACTIVITY DAY, SO GO BACK TO YOUR ROOMS AND GET READY.
OKAY!
ワイ HULLABALOO=ワイ
GOT IT!
YOU'VE DONE PRETTY WELL FOR YOURSELF, NODOKA MIYAZAKI-SAN. FROM TODAY ON, I'M IDENTIFYING YOU AS MY OFFICIAL RIVAL.
HO HO HO
ホホホ
YOU WON'T WIN NEXT TIME, LIBRARIAN-CHAN.
AH, B-BUT WHAT DID I DO!?
STUN
TAP TAP
HEH HEH HEH. IT'S MY CARD. ♡ THIS IS SO GREAT!
PROOF OF MY FIRST K-K-KISS WITH NEGI-SENSEI. I'M ON CLOUD NINE!
WHAT'S THIS?
KIRI
I CAN'T BELIEVE THIS.

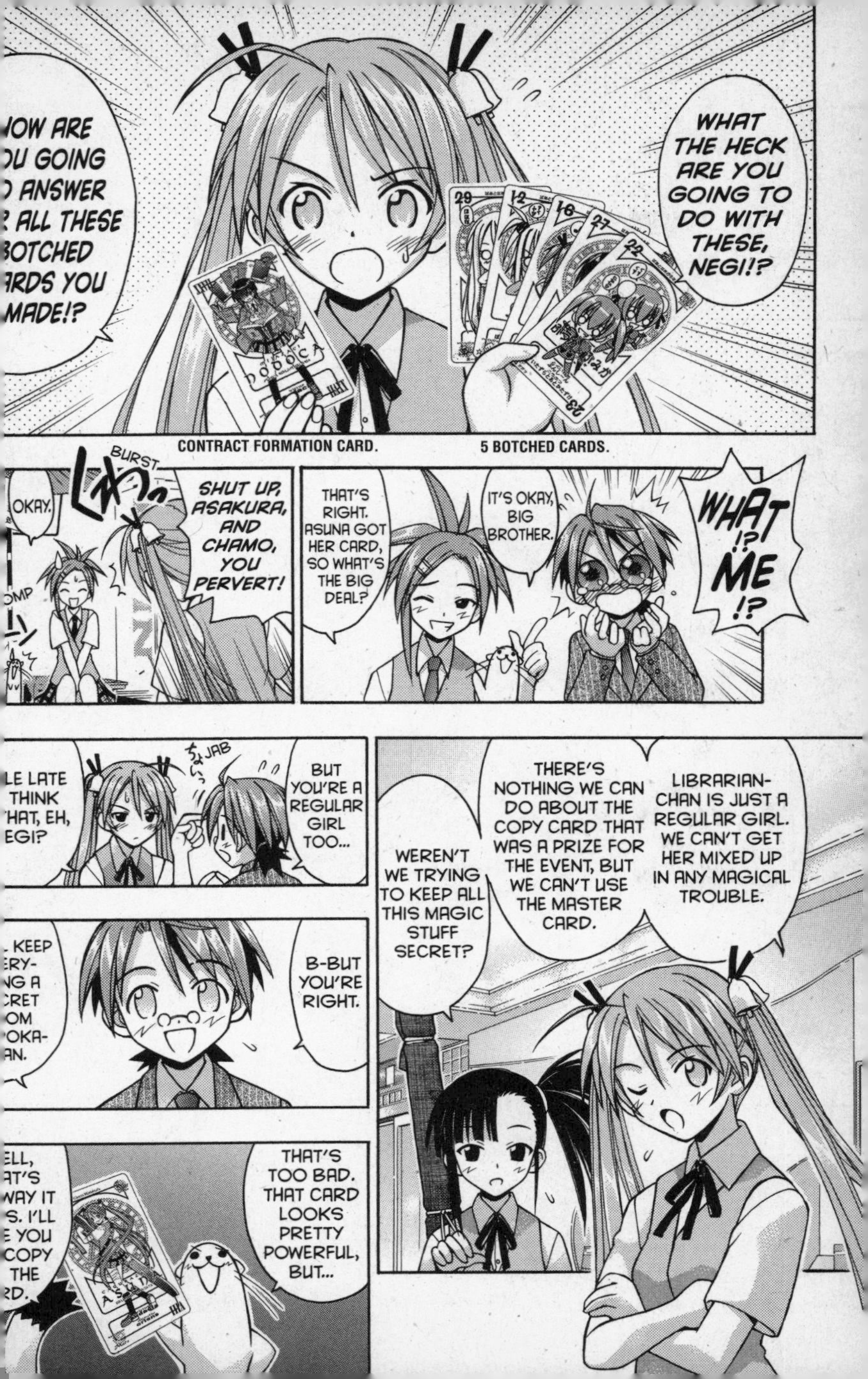
WHAT THE HECK ARE YOU GOING TO DO WITH THESE, NEGI!?
IOW ARE OU GOING O ANSWER R ALL THESE BOTCHED ARDS YOU MADE!?
CONTRACT FORMATION CARD.
5 BOTCHED CARDS.
WHAT !? ME !?
IT'S OKAY, BIG BROTHER.
THAT'S RIGHT. ASUNA GOT HER CARD, SO WHAT'S THE BIG DEAL?
SHUT UP, ASAKURA, AND CHAMO, YOU PERVERT!
BURST
OKAY.
LIBRARIAN-CHAN IS JUST A REGULAR GIRL. WE CAN'T GET HER MIXED UP IN ANY MAGICAL TROUBLE.
THERE'S NOTHING WE CAN DO ABOUT THE COPY CARD THAT WAS A PRIZE FOR THE EVENT, BUT WE CAN'T USE THE MASTER CARD.
WEREN'T WE TRYING TO KEEP ALL THIS MAGIC STUFF SECRET?
BUT YOU'RE A REGULAR GIRL TOO...
JAB
LE LATE THINK THAT, EH, EGI?
B-BUT YOU'RE RIGHT.
L KEEP ERY- NG A CRET OM OKA- AN.
THAT'S TOO BAD. THAT CARD LOOKS PRETTY POWERFUL, BUT...
ELL, AT'S WAY IT S. I'LL E YOU COPY THE RD.

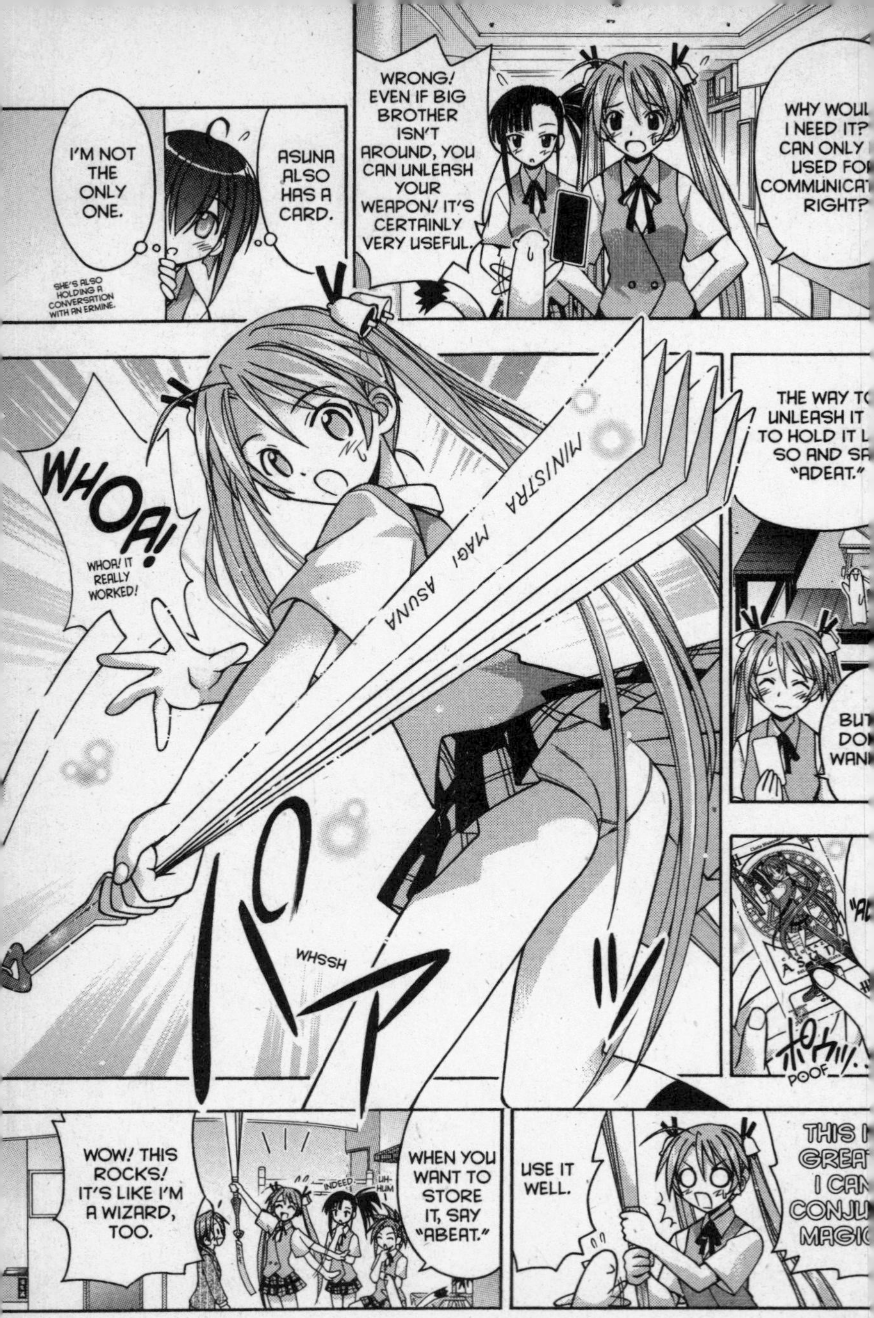
WHY WOUL
I NEED IT?
CAN ONLY
USED FOR
COMMUNICAT
RIGHT?
WRONG! EVEN IF BIG BROTHER ISN'T AROUND, YOU CAN UNLEASH YOUR WEAPON! IT'S CERTAINLY VERY USEFUL.
ASUNA ALSO HAS A CARD.
I'M NOT THE ONLY ONE.
SHE'S ALSO HOLDING A CONVERSATION WITH AN ERMINE.
THE WAY TO
UNLEASH IT
TO HOLD IT L
SO AND SA
"ADEAT."
BUT
DO
WAN
"AD
POOF
WHOA!
WHOA! IT REALLY WORKED!
MINISTRA MAGI ASUNA
WHSSH
THIS I
GREAT
I CAN
CONJU
MAGIC
USE IT WELL.
WHEN YOU WANT TO STORE IT, SAY "ABEAT."
UH-HUM
INDEED
WOW! THIS ROCKS! IT'S LIKE I'M A WIZARD, TOO.

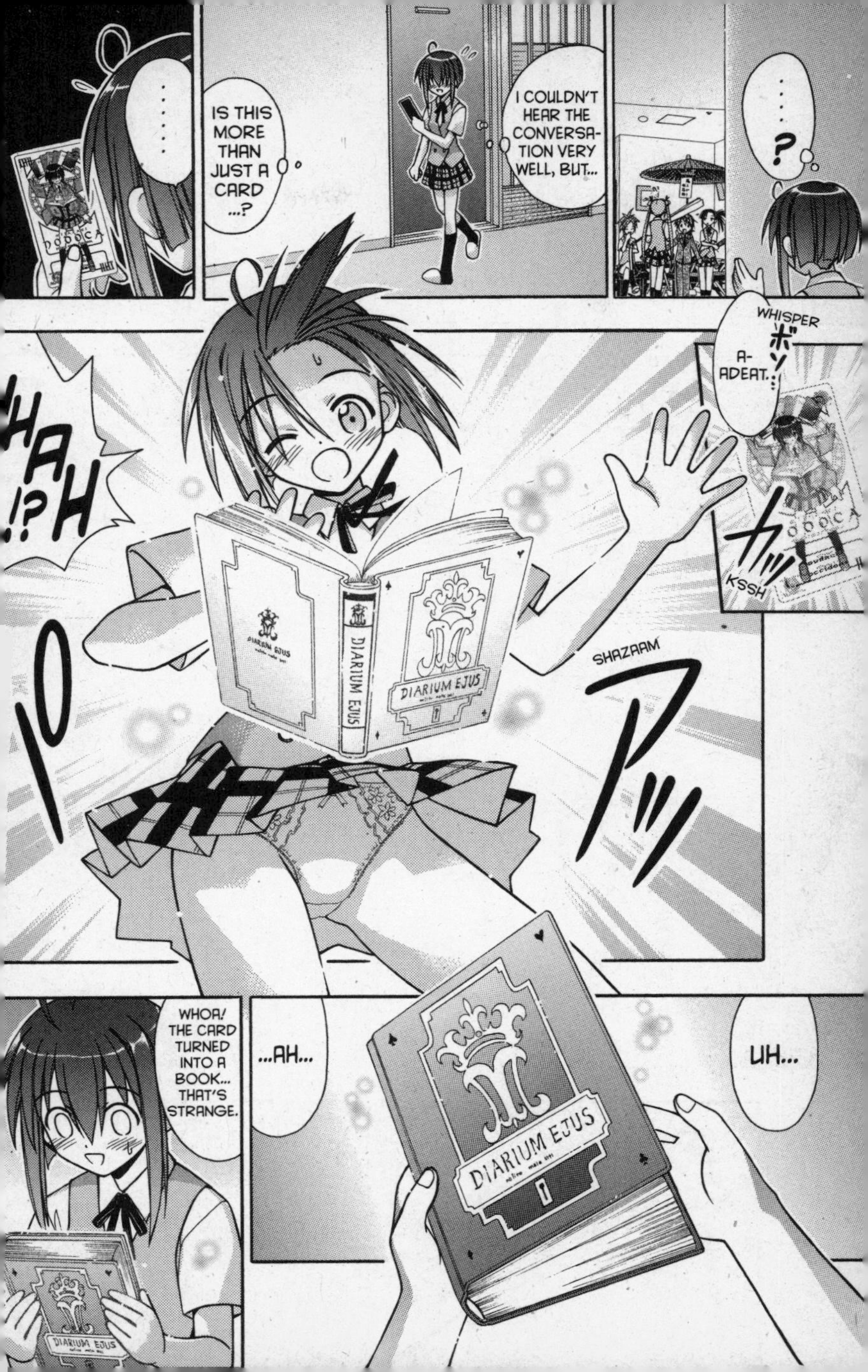
...?
I COULDN'T HEAR THE CONVERSATION VERY WELL, BUT...
IS THIS MORE THAN JUST A CARD ...?
......
A-ADEAT...
WHISPER ボソ
KSSH カッ
SHAZAAM アッ
HAH!?
DIARIUM EJUS
UH...
...AH...
WHOA! THE CARD TURNED INTO A BOOK... THAT'S STRANGE.
DIARIUM EJUS

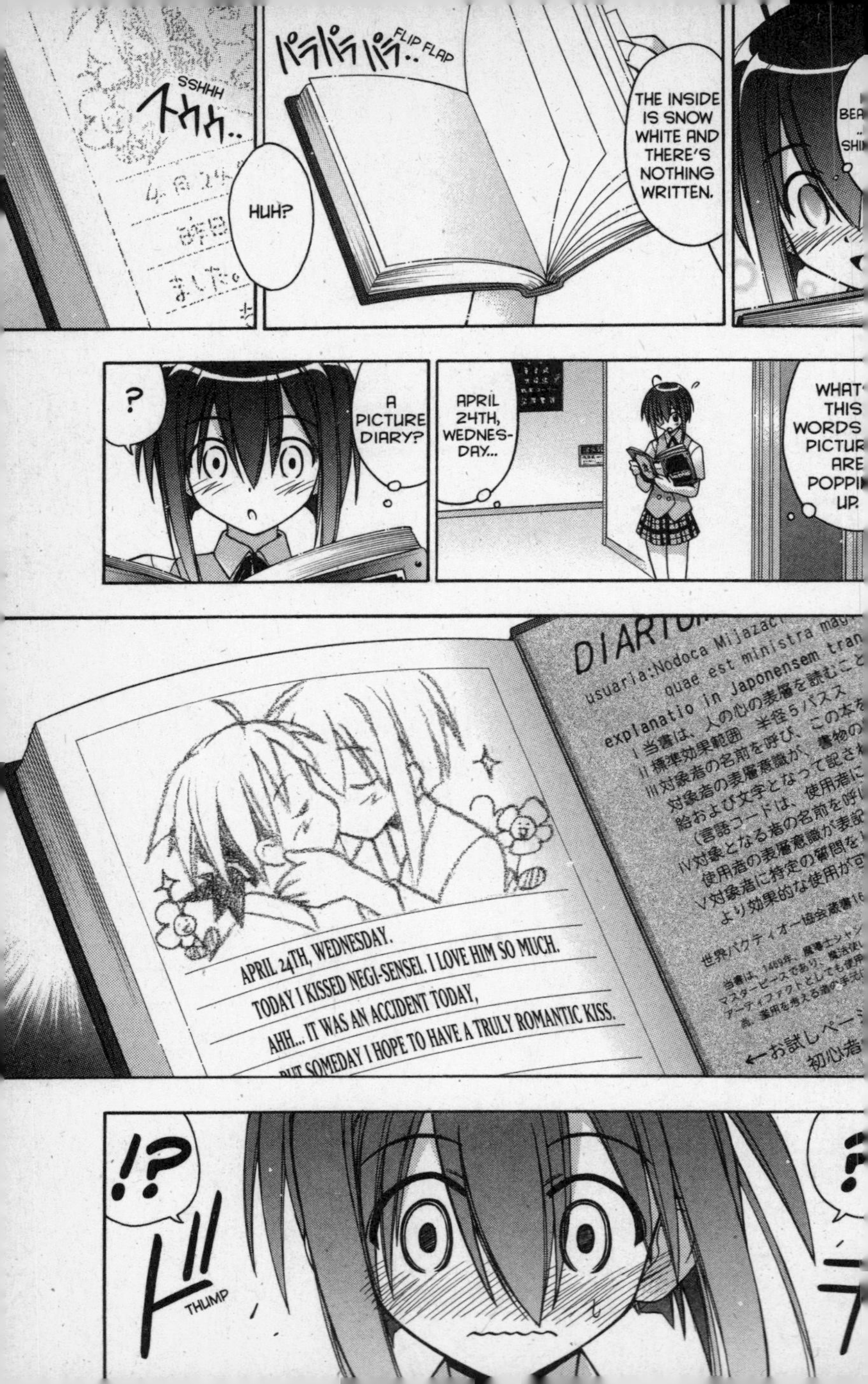

THE INSIDE IS SNOW WHITE AND THERE'S NOTHING WRITTEN.
パラパラパラ‥ FLIP FLAP
HUH?
スゥゥ‥ SSHHH
WHAT THIS WORDS PICTUR ARE POPPIN UP.
APRIL 24TH, WEDNES-DAY...
A PICTURE DIARY?
?
usuaria:Nodoca Mijazac
quae est ministra mag
explanatio in Japonensem tran
APRIL 24TH, WEDNESDAY.
TODAY I KISSED NEGI-SENSEI. I LOVE HIM SO MUCH.
AHH... IT WAS AN ACCIDENT TODAY,
BUT SOMEDAY I HOPE TO HAVE A TRULY ROMANTIC KISS.
THUMP
!?

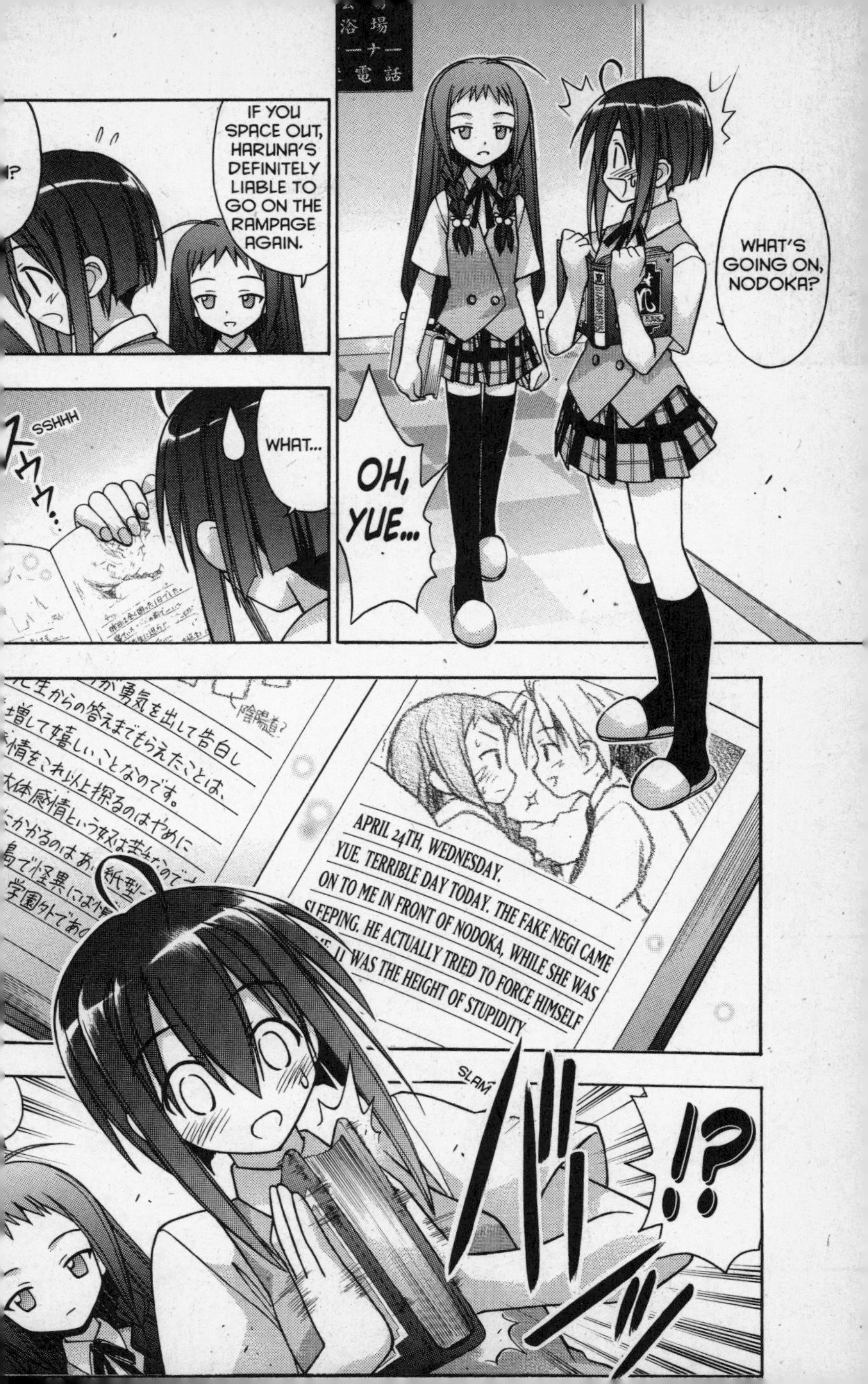
WHAT'S GOING ON, NODOKA?
OH, YUE...
IF YOU SPACE OUT, HARUNA'S DEFINITELY LIABLE TO GO ON THE RAMPAGE AGAIN.
!?
SSHHH
WHAT...
APRIL 24TH, WEDNESDAY.
YUE. TERRIBLE DAY TODAY. THE FAKE NEGI CAME ON TO ME IN FRONT OF NODOKA, WHILE SHE WAS SLEEPING. HE ACTUALLY TRIED TO FORCE HIMSELF
IT WAS THE HEIGHT OF STUPIDITY
SLAM
!?

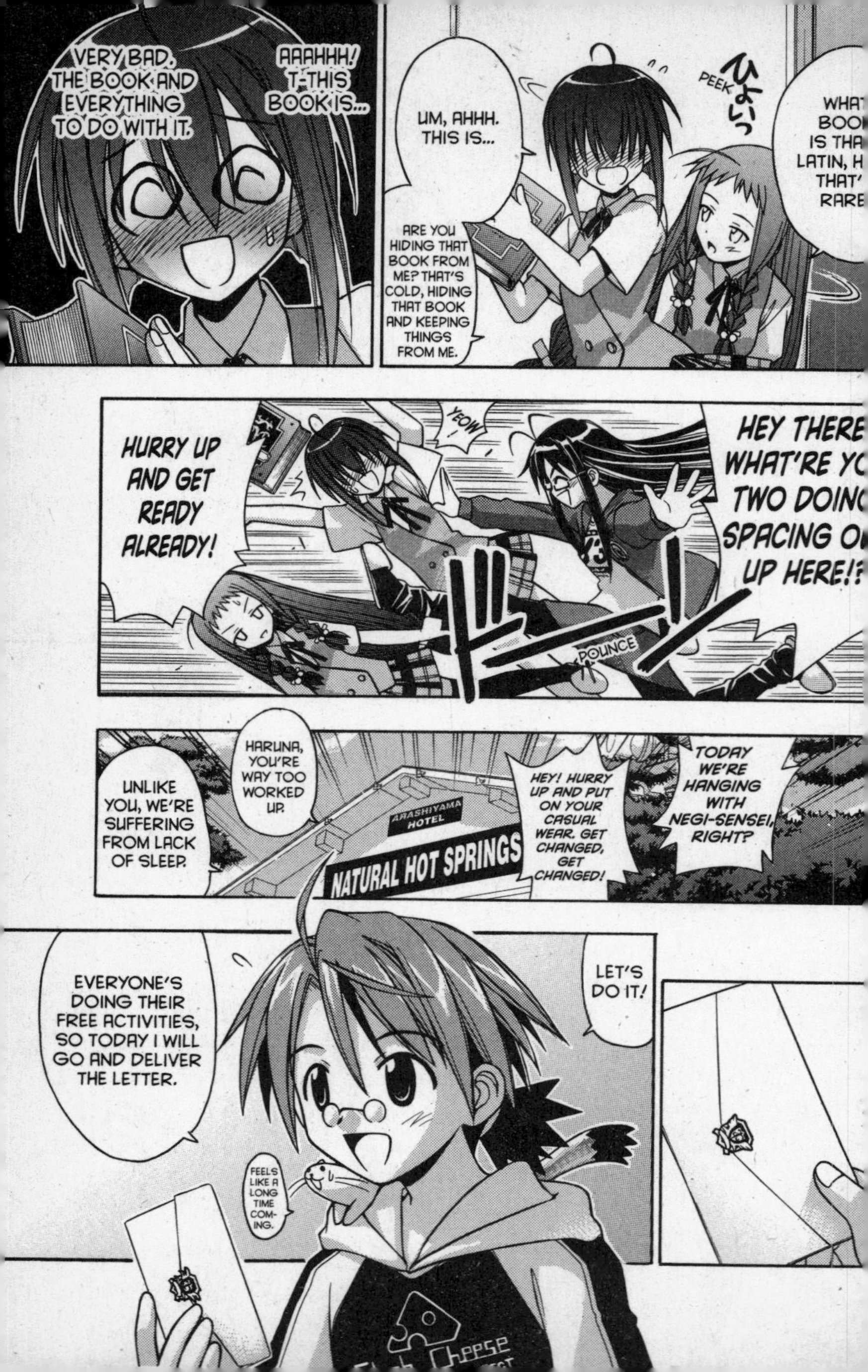
WHAT BOOK IS THA LATIN, H THAT' RARE
PEEK
UM, AHHH. THIS IS...
ARE YOU HIDING THAT BOOK FROM ME? THAT'S COLD, HIDING THAT BOOK AND KEEPING THINGS FROM ME.
AAAHHH! T-THIS BOOK IS...
VERY BAD. THE BOOK AND EVERYTHING TO DO WITH IT.
HEY THERE WHAT'RE YO TWO DOINC SPACING O UP HERE!?
YEOW
POUNCE
HURRY UP AND GET READY ALREADY!
TODAY WE'RE HANGING WITH NEGI-SENSEI, RIGHT?
HEY! HURRY UP AND PUT ON YOUR CASUAL WEAR. GET CHANGED, GET CHANGED!
HARUNA, YOU'RE WAY TOO WORKED UP.
UNLIKE YOU, WE'RE SUFFERING FROM LACK OF SLEEP.
ARASHIYAMA HOTEL
NATURAL HOT SPRINGS
LET'S DO IT!
EVERYONE'S DOING THEIR FREE ACTIVITIES, SO TODAY I WILL GO AND DELIVER THE LETTER.
FEELS LIKE A LONG TIME COMING.

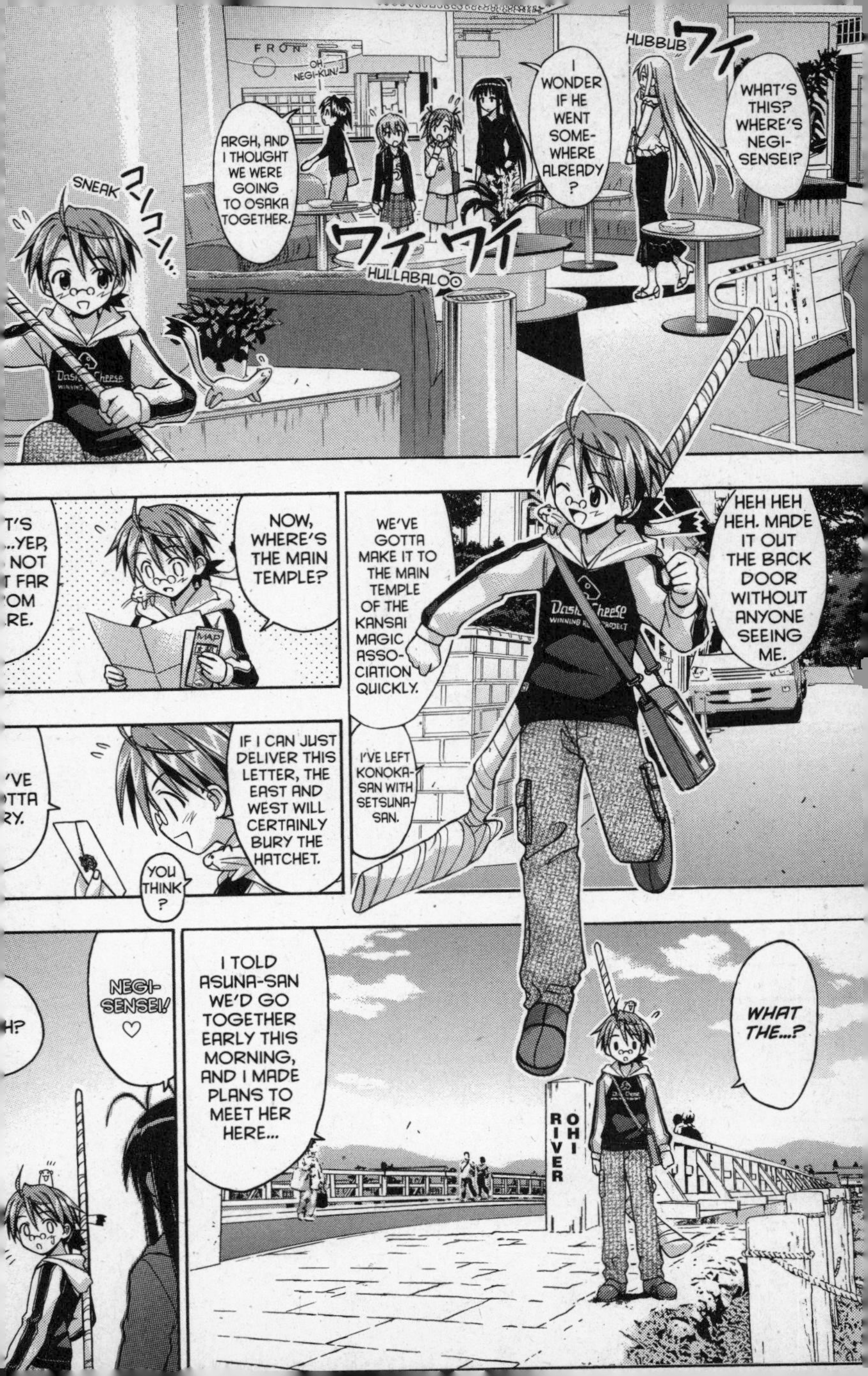
HUBBUB ワイ
WHAT'S THIS? WHERE'S NEGI-SENSEI?
I WONDER IF HE WENT SOMEWHERE ALREADY?
FRON
OH, NEGI-KUN!
ARGH, AND I THOUGHT WE WERE GOING TO OSAKA TOGETHER.
ワイ ワイ
HULLABALOO
SNEAK
HEH HEH HEH. MADE IT OUT THE BACK DOOR WITHOUT ANYONE SEEING ME.
WE'VE GOTTA MAKE IT TO THE MAIN TEMPLE OF THE KANSAI MAGIC ASSOCIATION QUICKLY.
I'VE LEFT KONOKA-SAN WITH SETSUNA-SAN.
NOW, WHERE'S THE MAIN TEMPLE?
MAP
T'S ...YEP, NOT T FAR ROM RE.
IF I CAN JUST DELIVER THIS LETTER, THE EAST AND WEST WILL CERTAINLY BURY THE HATCHET.
YOU THINK?
'VE OTTA RY.
WHAT THE...?
OHI RIVER
I TOLD ASUNA-SAN WE'D GO TOGETHER EARLY THIS MORNING, AND I MADE PLANS TO MEET HER HERE...
NEGI-SENSEI! ♡
H?

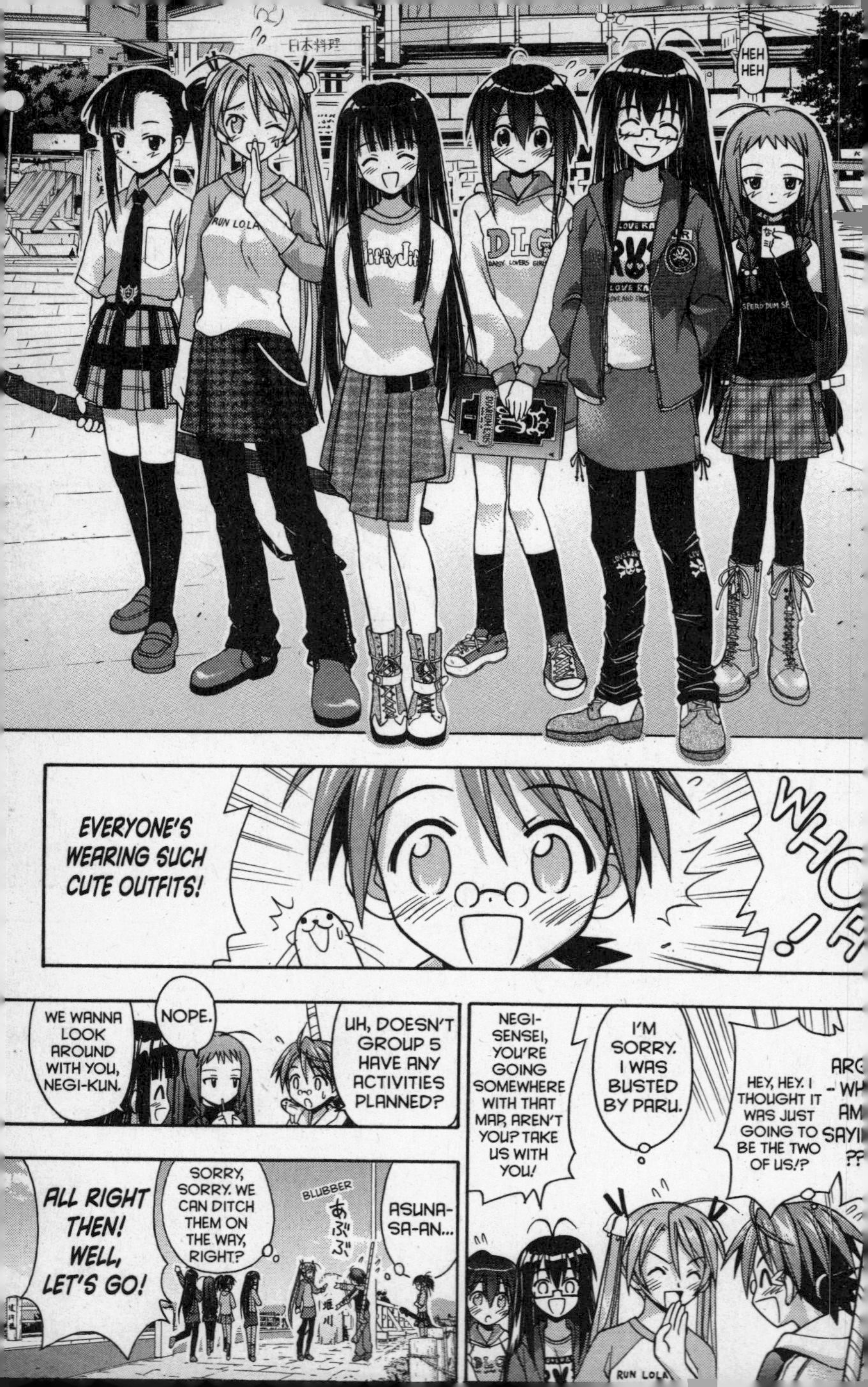
HEH HEH
日本料理
WHOA!
EVERYONE'S WEARING SUCH CUTE OUTFITS!
ARG - WH AM SAYI ??
HEY, HEY. I THOUGHT IT WAS JUST GOING TO BE THE TWO OF US!?
I'M SORRY. I WAS BUSTED BY PARU.
NEGI-SENSEI, YOU'RE GOING SOMEWHERE WITH THAT MAP, AREN'T YOU? TAKE US WITH YOU!
UH, DOESN'T GROUP 5 HAVE ANY ACTIVITIES PLANNED?
NOPE.
WE WANNA LOOK AROUND WITH YOU, NEGI-KUN.
ASUNA-SA-AN...
BLUBBER あぶぶ
SORRY, SORRY. WE CAN DITCH THEM ON THE WAY, RIGHT?
ALL RIGHT THEN! WELL, LET'S GO!

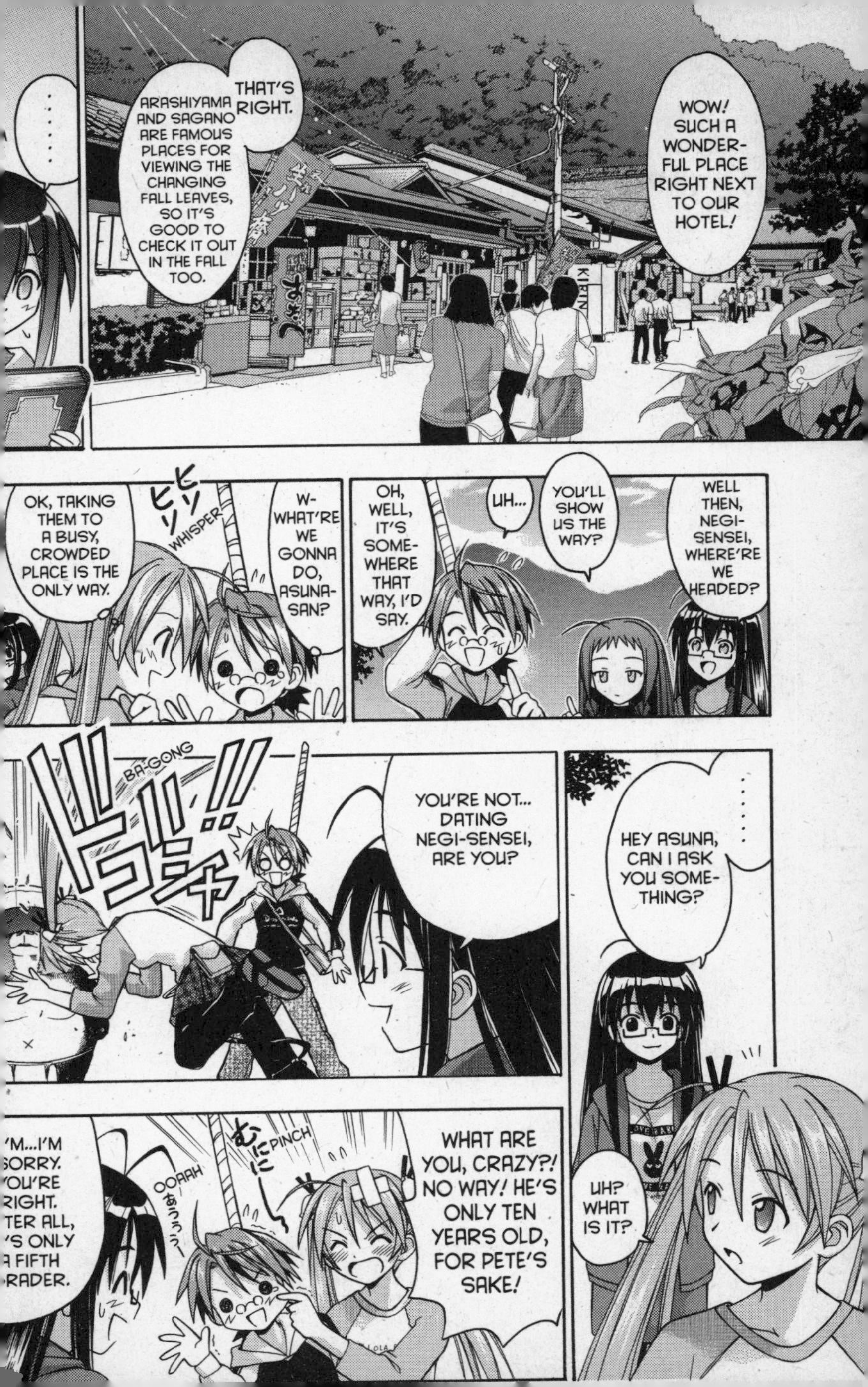
WOW! SUCH A WONDERFUL PLACE RIGHT NEXT TO OUR HOTEL!
THAT'S RIGHT.
ARASHIYAMA AND SAGANO ARE FAMOUS PLACES FOR VIEWING THE CHANGING FALL LEAVES, SO IT'S GOOD TO CHECK IT OUT IN THE FALL TOO.
KIRIN
......
WELL THEN, NEGI-SENSEI, WHERE'RE WE HEADED?
YOU'LL SHOW US THE WAY?
UH...
OH, WELL, IT'S SOMEWHERE THAT WAY, I'D SAY.
W-WHAT'RE WE GONNA DO, ASUNA-SAN?
ヒソ ヒソ
WHISPER
OK, TAKING THEM TO A BUSY, CROWDED PLACE IS THE ONLY WAY.
......
HEY ASUNA, CAN I ASK YOU SOMETHING?
UH? WHAT IS IT?
YOU'RE NOT... DATING NEGI-SENSEI, ARE YOU?
ドゴシャ!!
BA-GONG
WHAT ARE YOU, CRAZY?! NO WAY! HE'S ONLY TEN YEARS OLD, FOR PETE'S SAKE!
むにー
PINCH
あうぅぅー
OOAAH
'M...I'M SORRY. YOU'RE RIGHT. TER ALL, 'S ONLY A FIFTH RADER.

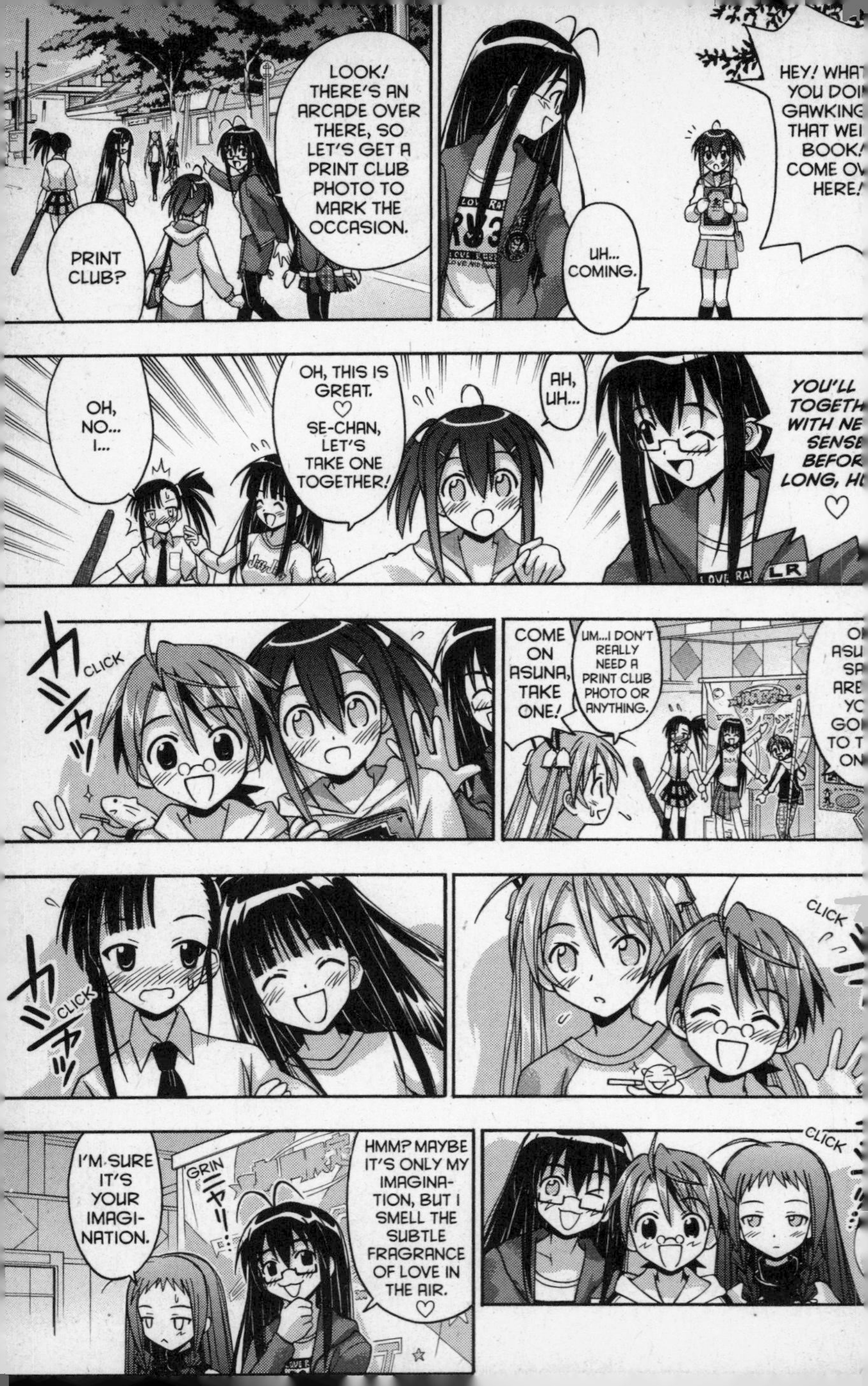
HEY! WHAT YOU DOI GAWKING THAT WEI BOOK! COME OV HERE!
UH... COMING.
LOOK! THERE'S AN ARCADE OVER THERE, SO LET'S GET A PRINT CLUB PHOTO TO MARK THE OCCASION.
PRINT CLUB?
YOU'LL TOGETH WITH NE SENSE BEFOR LONG, HU ♡
AH, UH...
OH, THIS IS GREAT. ♡ SE-CHAN, LET'S TAKE ONE TOGETHER!
OH, NO... I...
OH ASU SA ARE YO GO TO T ON
UM...I DON'T REALLY NEED A PRINT CLUB PHOTO OR ANYTHING.
COME ON ASUNA, TAKE ONE!
CLICK
CLICK
CLICK
CLICK
HMM? MAYBE IT'S ONLY MY IMAGINA-TION, BUT I SMELL THE SUBTLE FRAGRANCE OF LOVE IN THE AIR. ♡
GRIN
I'M SURE IT'S YOUR IMAGI-NATION.

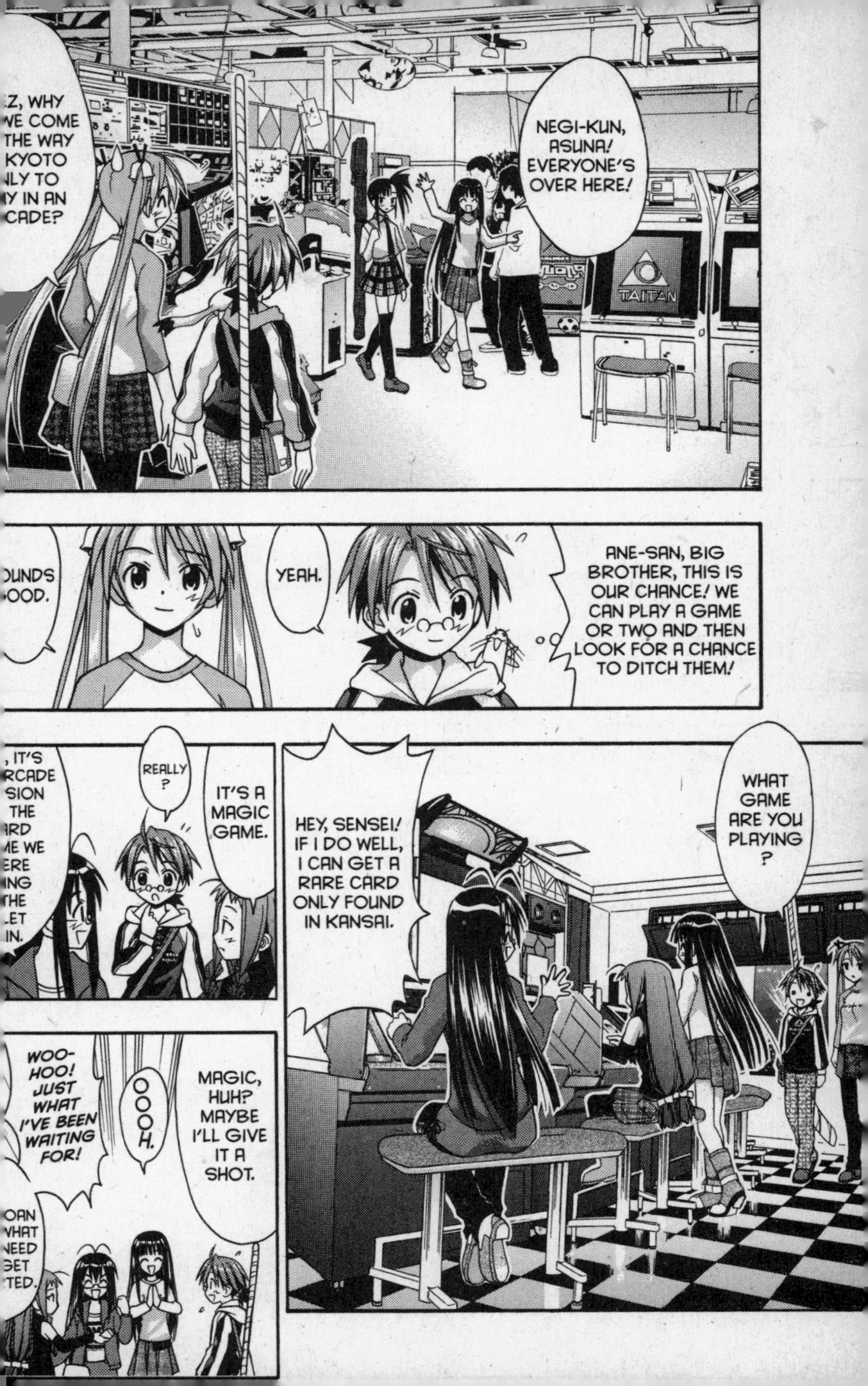
NEGI-KUN, ASUNA! EVERYONE'S OVER HERE!
EZ, WHY WE COME THE WAY KYOTO NLY TO Y IN AN CADE?
ANE-SAN, BIG BROTHER, THIS IS OUR CHANCE! WE CAN PLAY A GAME OR TWO AND THEN LOOK FOR A CHANCE TO DITCH THEM!
YEAH.
OUNDS OOD.
WHAT GAME ARE YOU PLAYING?
HEY, SENSEI! IF I DO WELL, I CAN GET A RARE CARD ONLY FOUND IN KANSAI.
IT'S A MAGIC GAME.
REALLY?
, IT'S RCADE SION THE RD ME WE ERE NG THE LET IN.
MAGIC, HUH? MAYBE I'LL GIVE IT A SHOT.
OOOH.
WOO-HOO! JUST WHAT I'VE BEEN WAITING FOR!
OAN WHAT NEED GET TED.

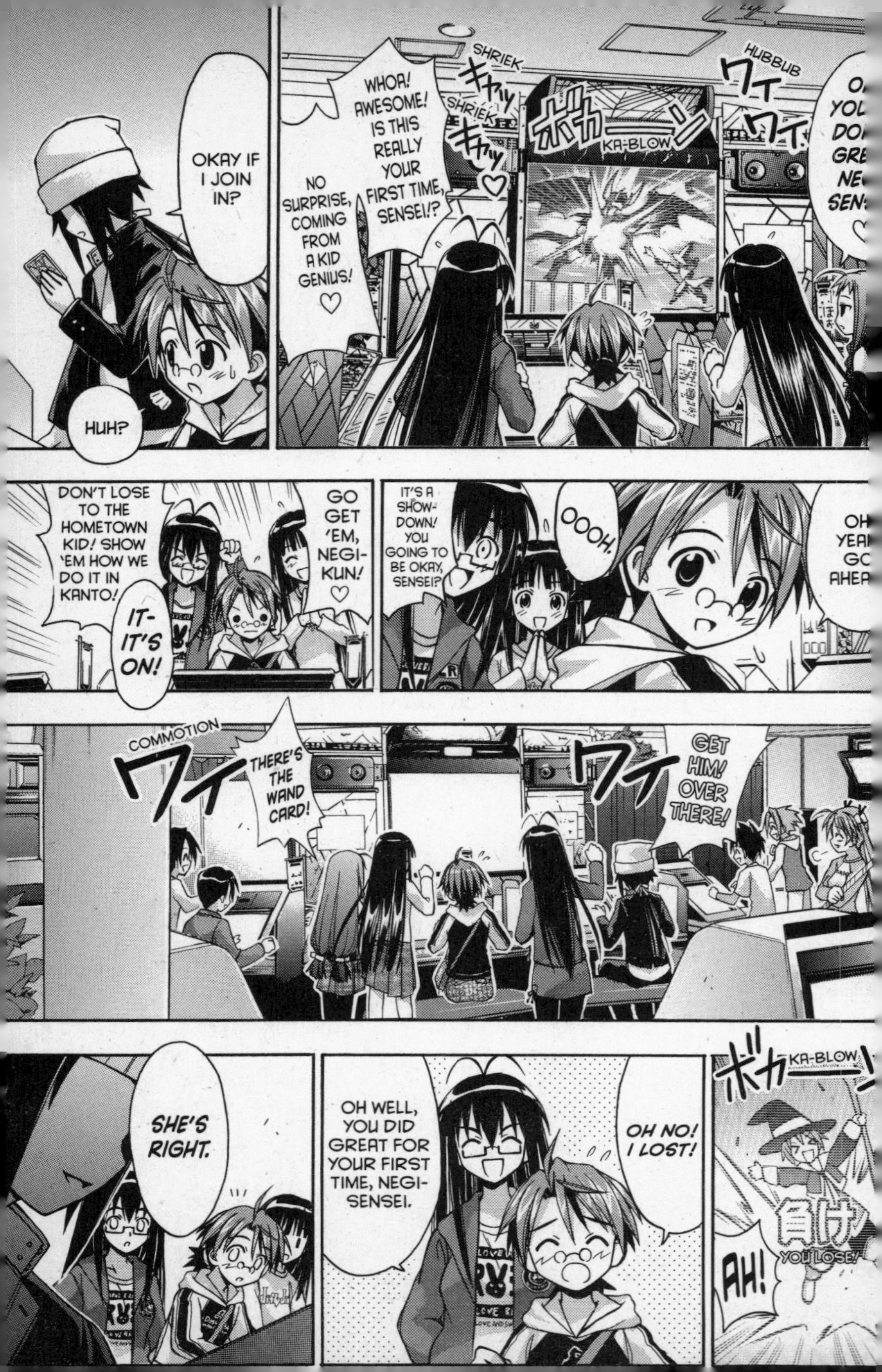
HUBBUB
ワイワイ
KA-BLOW
ボカーン
SHRIEK
キャッ
SHRIEK
キャッ ♡
WHOA! AWESOME! IS THIS REALLY YOUR FIRST TIME, SENSEI!?
NO SURPRISE, COMING FROM A KID GENIUS! ♡
OKAY IF I JOIN IN?
HUH?
OOOH.
IT'S A SHOW-DOWN! YOU GOING TO BE OKAY, SENSEI?
GO GET 'EM, NEGI-KUN! ♡
DON'T LOSE TO THE HOMETOWN KID! SHOW 'EM HOW WE DO IT IN KANTO!
IT-IT'S ON!
GET HIM! OVER THERE!
ワイ
THERE'S THE WAND CARD!
COMMOTION
ワイ
KA-BLOW
ボカーン
負け
YOU LOSE!
AH!
OH NO! I LOST!
OH WELL, YOU DID GREAT FOR YOUR FIRST TIME, NEGI-SENSEI.
SHE'S RIGHT.

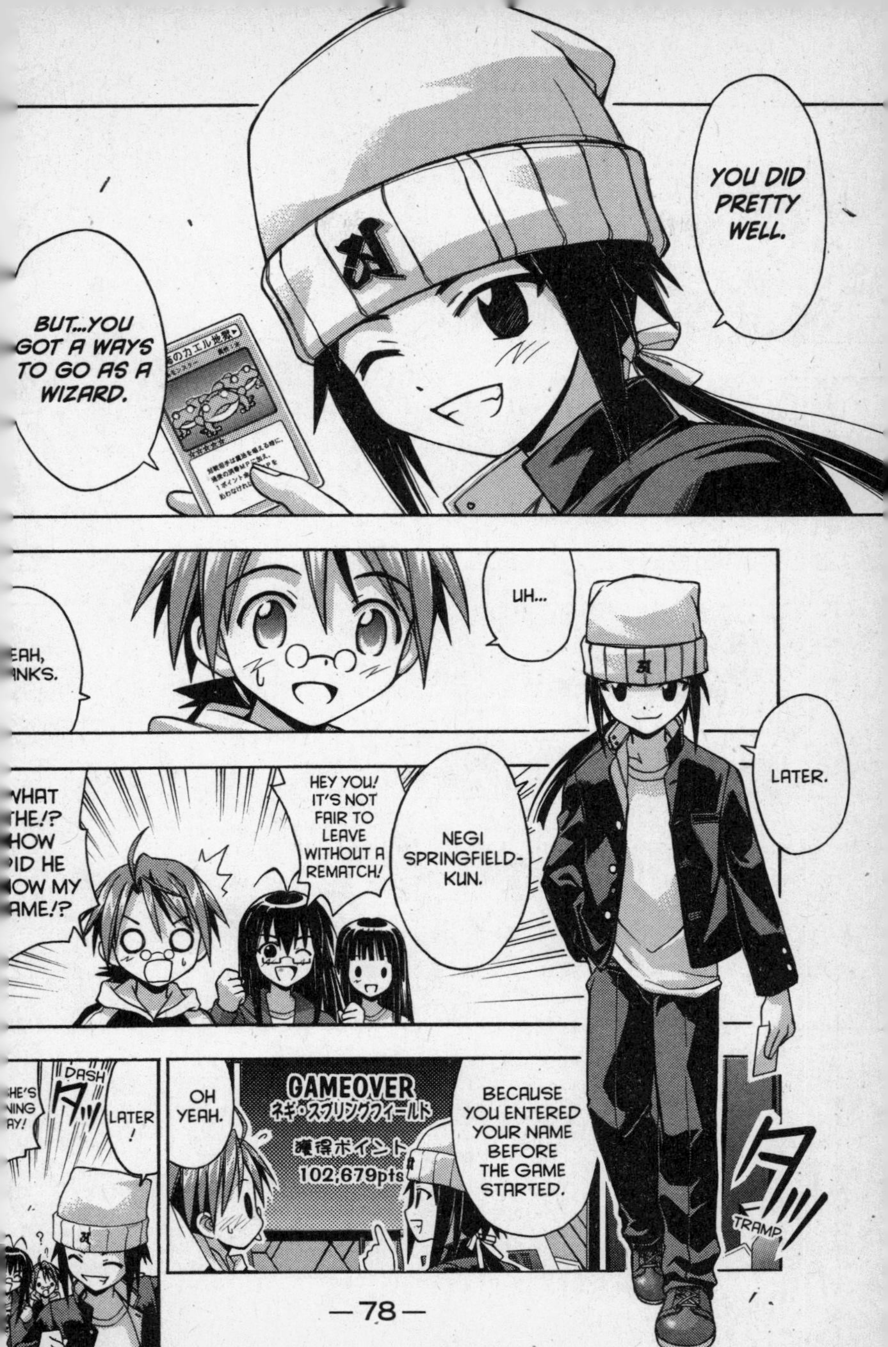
YOU DID PRETTY WELL.
BUT...YOU GOT A WAYS TO GO AS A WIZARD.
LATER.
TRAMP
UH...
EAH, ANKS.
NEGI SPRINGFIELD-KUN.
HEY YOU! IT'S NOT FAIR TO LEAVE WITHOUT A REMATCH!
WHAT THE!? HOW DID HE NOW MY AME!?
BECAUSE YOU ENTERED YOUR NAME BEFORE THE GAME STARTED.
GAMEOVER
ネギ・スプリングフィールド
獲得ポイント
102,679pts
OH YEAH.
LATER!
DASH
HE'S NING AY!

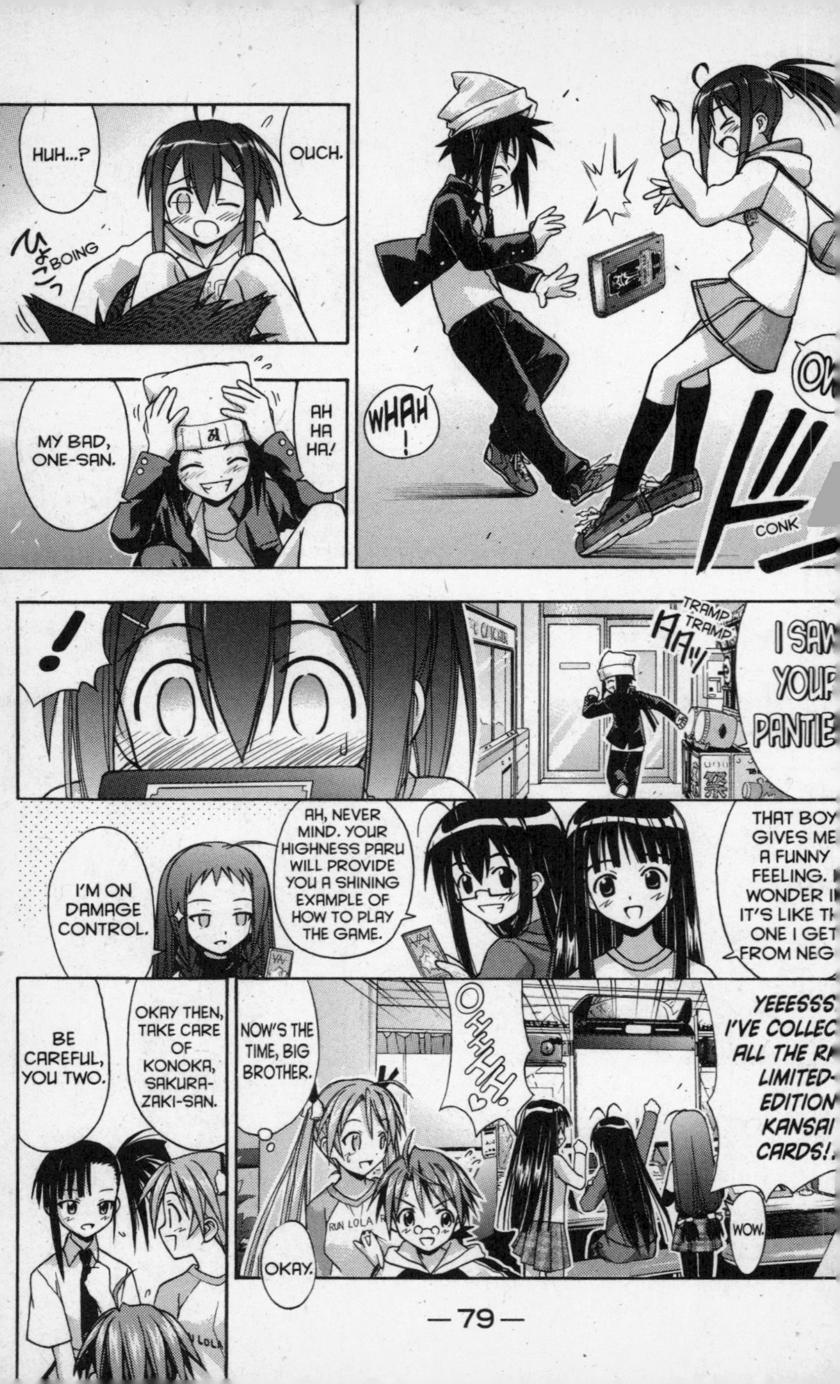
OW
WHAH!
CONK
OUCH.
HUH...?
BOING
AH HA HA!
MY BAD, ONE-SAN.
TRAMP TRAMP
I SAW YOUR PANTIE
!
THAT BOY GIVES ME A FUNNY FEELING. I WONDER I IT'S LIKE TH ONE I GET FROM NEG
AH, NEVER MIND. YOUR HIGHNESS PARU WILL PROVIDE YOU A SHINING EXAMPLE OF HOW TO PLAY THE GAME.
I'M ON DAMAGE CONTROL.
YEEESSS I'VE COLLEC ALL THE R LIMITED- EDITION KANSAI CARDS!
OHHHH!
WOW.
NOW'S THE TIME, BIG BROTHER.
OKAY.
OKAY THEN, TAKE CARE OF KONOKA, SAKURA-ZAKI-SAN.
BE CAREFUL, YOU TWO.

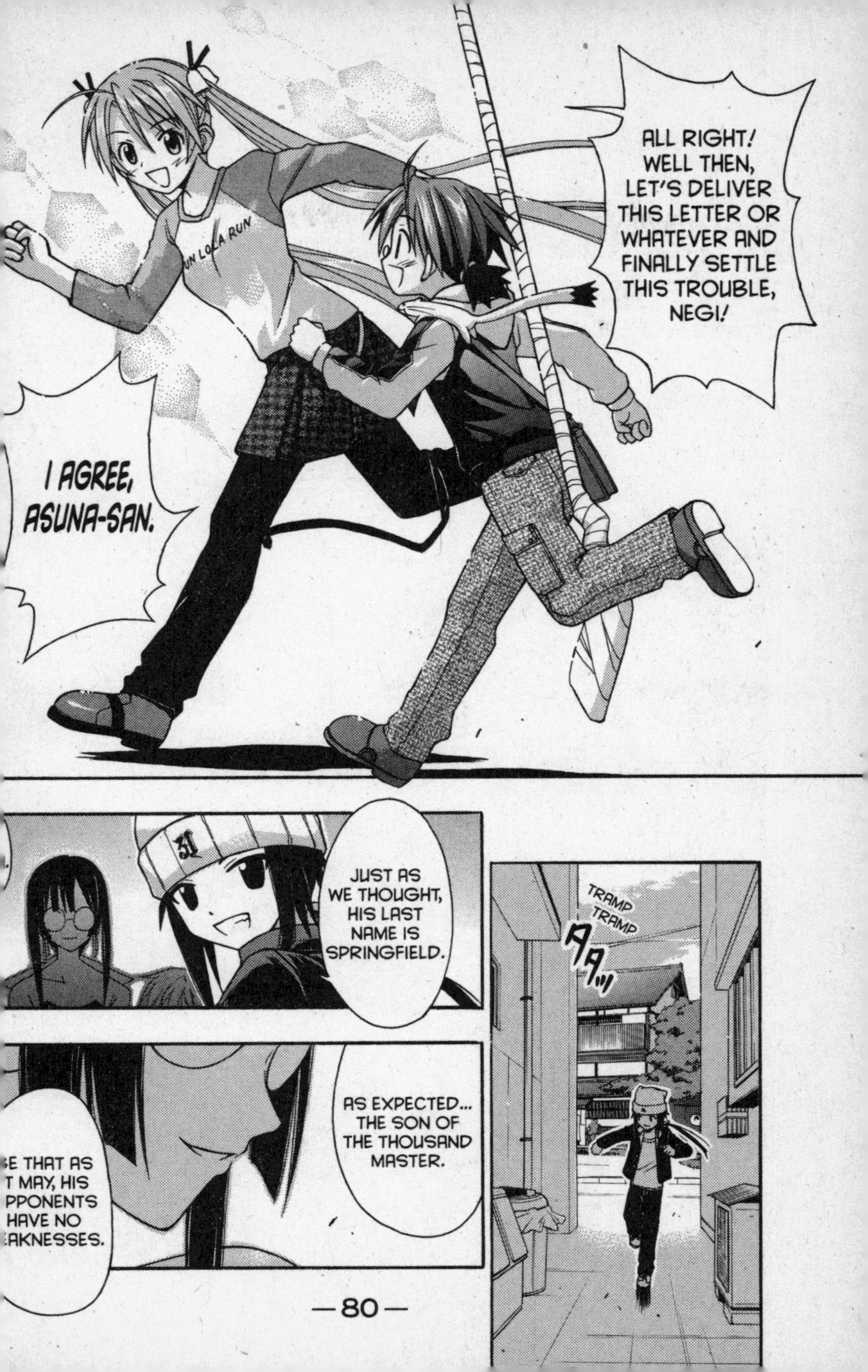
ALL RIGHT! WELL THEN, LET'S DELIVER THIS LETTER OR WHATEVER AND FINALLY SETTLE THIS TROUBLE, NEGI!
I AGREE, ASUNA-SAN.
TRAMP TRAMP
タタッ
JUST AS WE THOUGHT, HIS LAST NAME IS SPRINGFIELD.
AS EXPECTED... THE SON OF THE THOUSAND MASTER.
E THAT AS T MAY, HIS PPONENTS HAVE NO EAKNESSES.

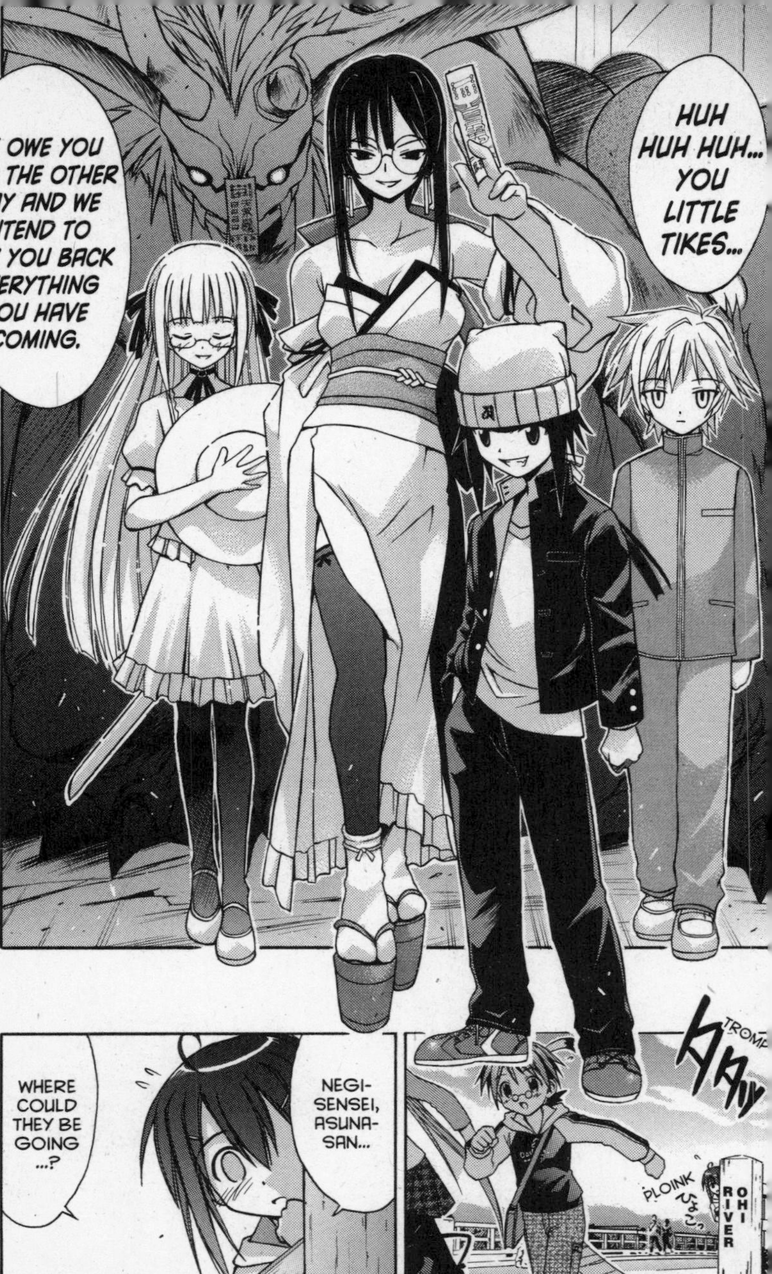
HUH HUH HUH... YOU LITTLE TIKES...
WE OWE YOU FOR THE OTHER DAY AND WE INTEND TO PAY YOU BACK EVERYTHING YOU HAVE COMING.
TROMP
PLOINK
OHI RIVER
NEGI-SENSEI, ASUNA-SAN...
WHERE COULD THEY BE GOING ...?

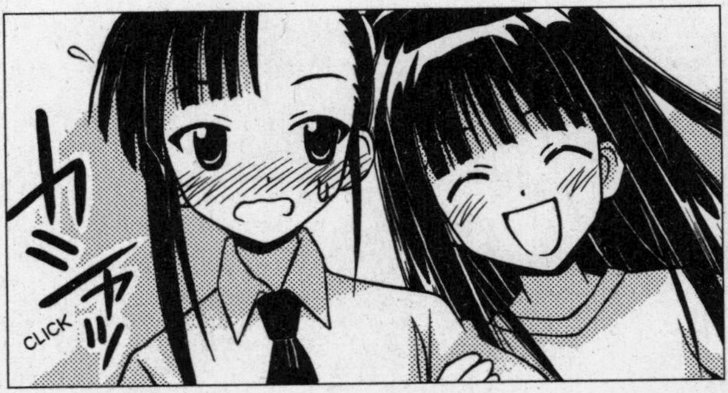
カシャッ
CLICK

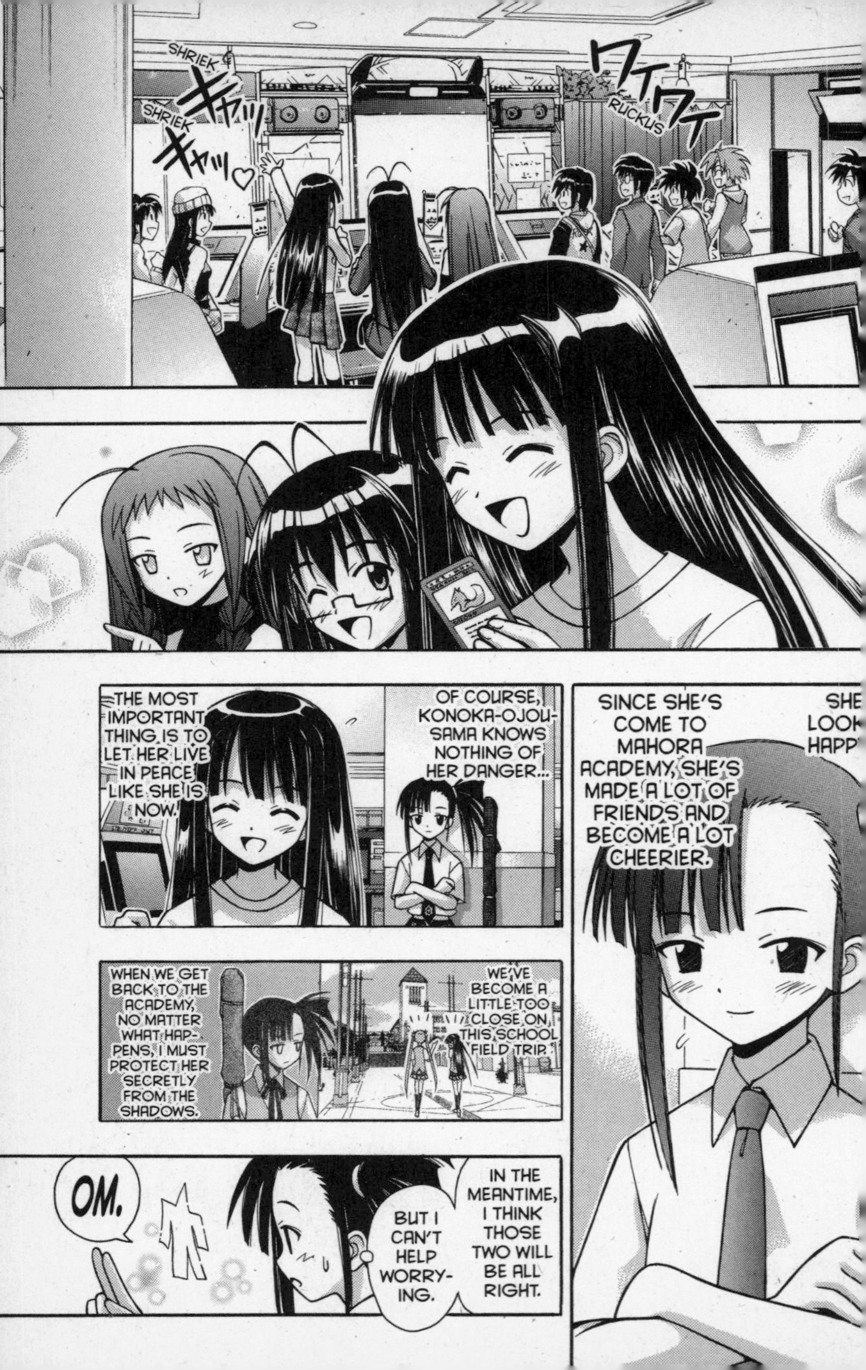
ワイワイ
RUCKUS
SHRIEK
キャッ
SHRIEK
キャッ♡
SHE LOOK HAPP
SINCE SHE'S COME TO MAHORA ACADEMY, SHE'S MADE A LOT OF FRIENDS AND BECOME A LOT CHEERIER.
OF COURSE, KONOKA-OJOUSAMA KNOWS NOTHING OF HER DANGER...
THE MOST IMPORTANT THING IS TO LET HER LIVE IN PEACE LIKE SHE IS NOW.
WE'VE BECOME A LITTLE TOO CLOSE ON THIS SCHOOL FIELD TRIP.
WHEN WE GET BACK TO THE ACADEMY, NO MATTER WHAT HAP-PENS, I MUST PROTECT HER SECRETLY FROM THE SHADOWS.
IN THE MEANTIME, I THINK THOSE TWO WILL BE ALL RIGHT.
BUT I CAN'T HELP WORRY-ING.
OM.

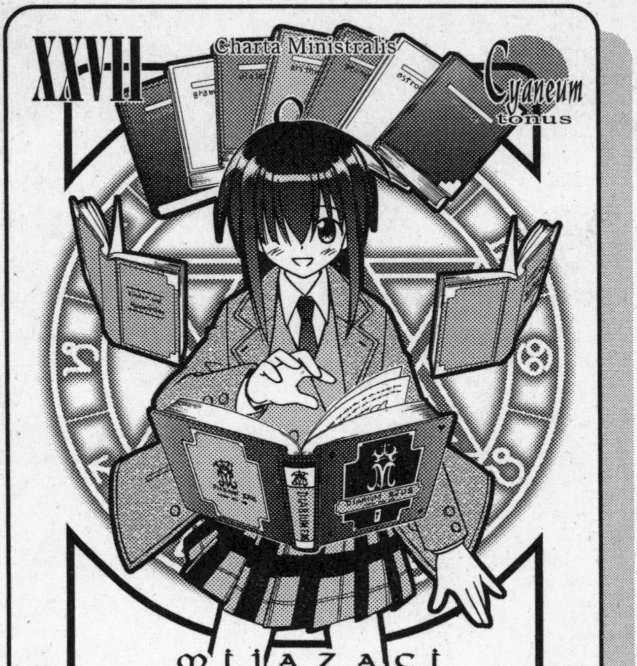
XXVII
Charta Ministralis
Cyaneum
tonus
MIJAZACI
NODOCA
PUDICA BIBLIOTHECARIA
virtus
audacia
astralitas
directio
occidens
Mercurius

NEGIMA!

MAGISTER NEGI MAGI

IRTY-NINTH PERIOD:
E DAZZLING WHIRLING LOOP SURVIVAL

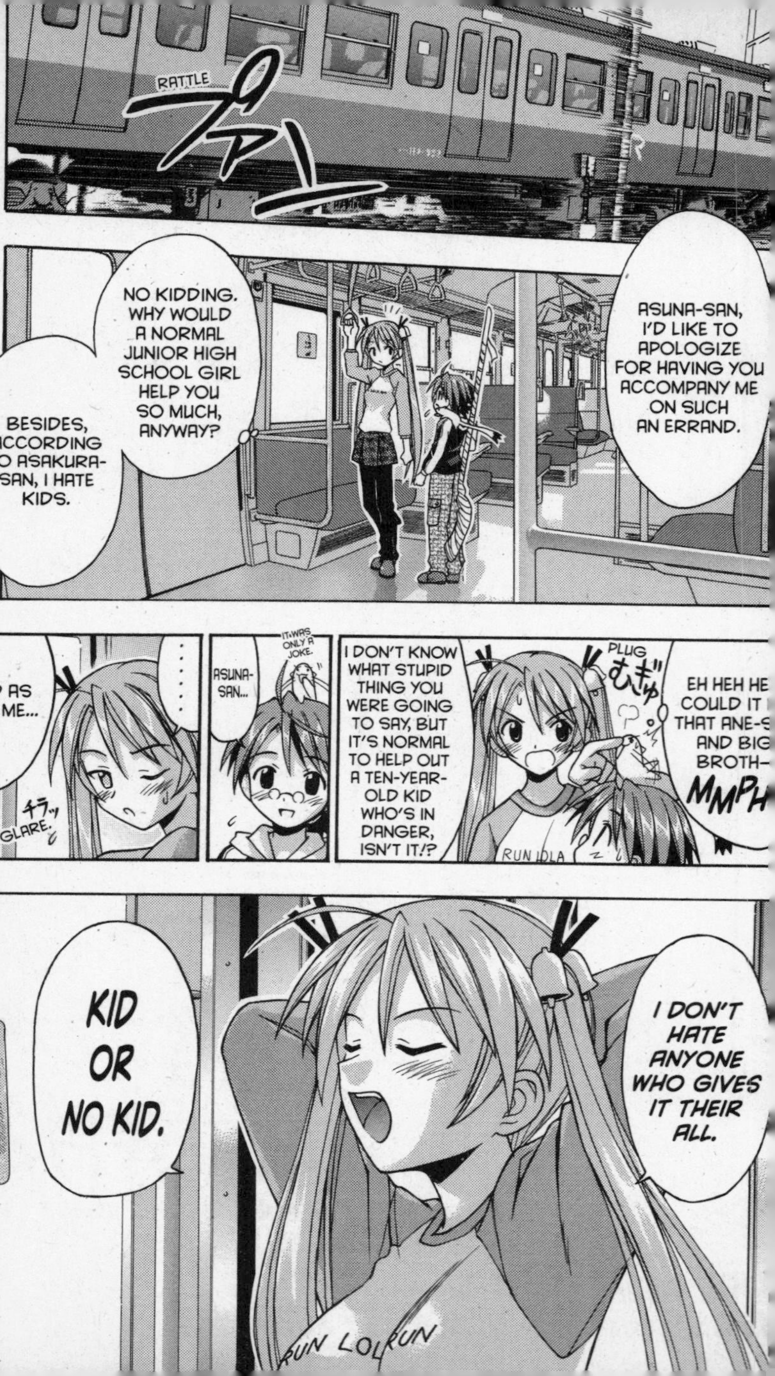
RATTLE
ASUNA-SAN, I'D LIKE TO APOLOGIZE FOR HAVING YOU ACCOMPANY ME ON SUCH AN ERRAND.
NO KIDDING. WHY WOULD A NORMAL JUNIOR HIGH SCHOOL GIRL HELP YOU SO MUCH, ANYWAY?
BESIDES, ACCORDING TO ASAKURA-SAN, I HATE KIDS.
EH HEH HE COULD IT THAT ANE- AND BIG BROTH—
MMPH
PLUG
I DON'T KNOW WHAT STUPID THING YOU WERE GOING TO SAY, BUT IT'S NORMAL TO HELP OUT A TEN-YEAR-OLD KID WHO'S IN DANGER, ISN'T IT!?
RUN IOLA
IT WAS ONLY A JOKE.
ASUNA-SAN...
......
AND AS FOR ME...
GLARE.
I DON'T HATE ANYONE WHO GIVES IT THEIR ALL.
KID OR NO KID.
RUN LOLRUN

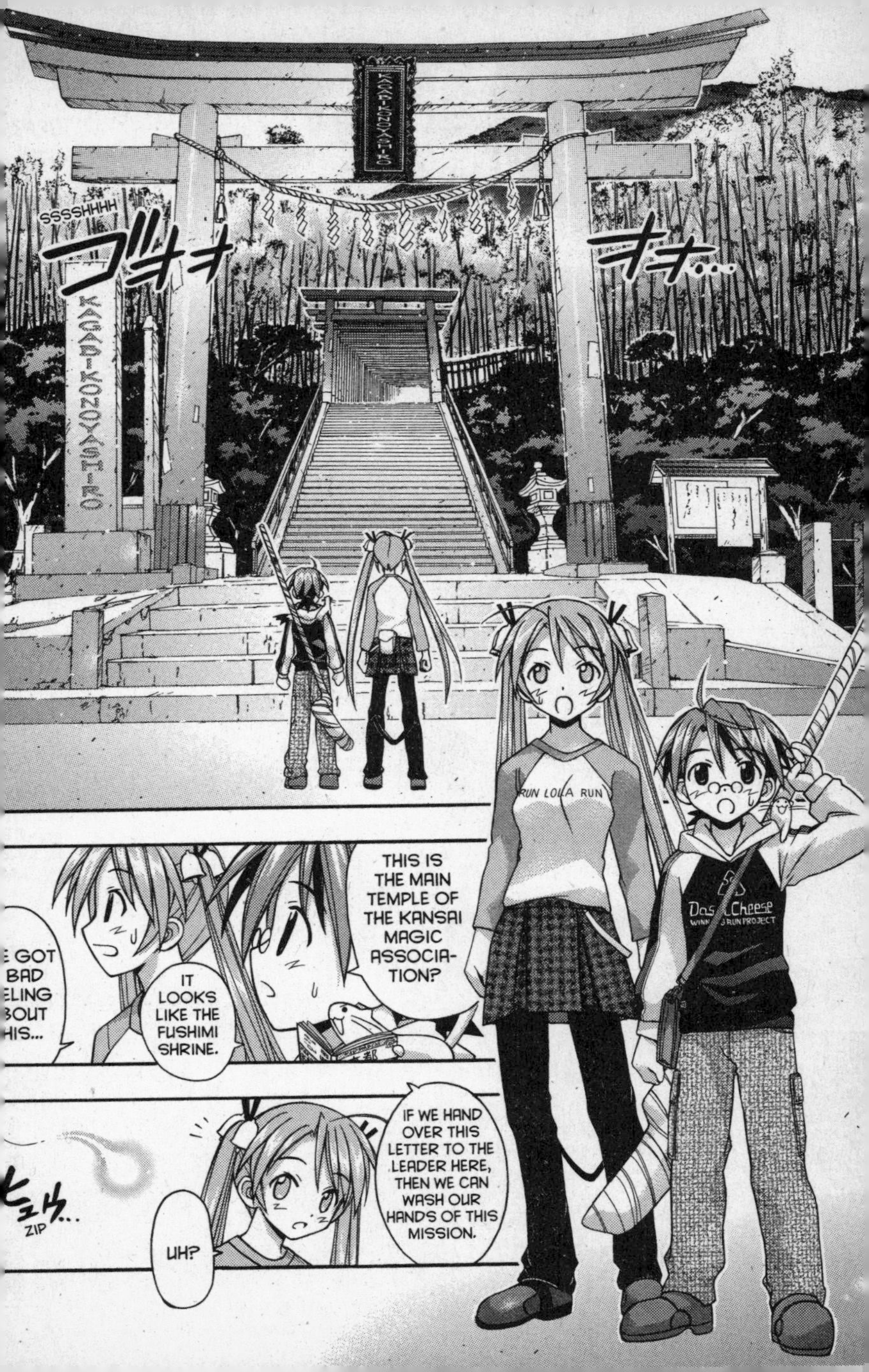
KAGABI-KONOYASHIRO
KAGABI-KONOYASHIRO
SSSSHHHH
RUN LOLA RUN
THIS IS THE MAIN TEMPLE OF THE KANSAI MAGIC ASSOCIA-TION?
IT LOOKS LIKE THE FUSHIMI SHRINE.
E GOT BAD ELING BOUT HIS...
IF WE HAND OVER THIS LETTER TO THE LEADER HERE, THEN WE CAN WASH OUR HANDS OF THIS MISSION.
UH?
ZIP

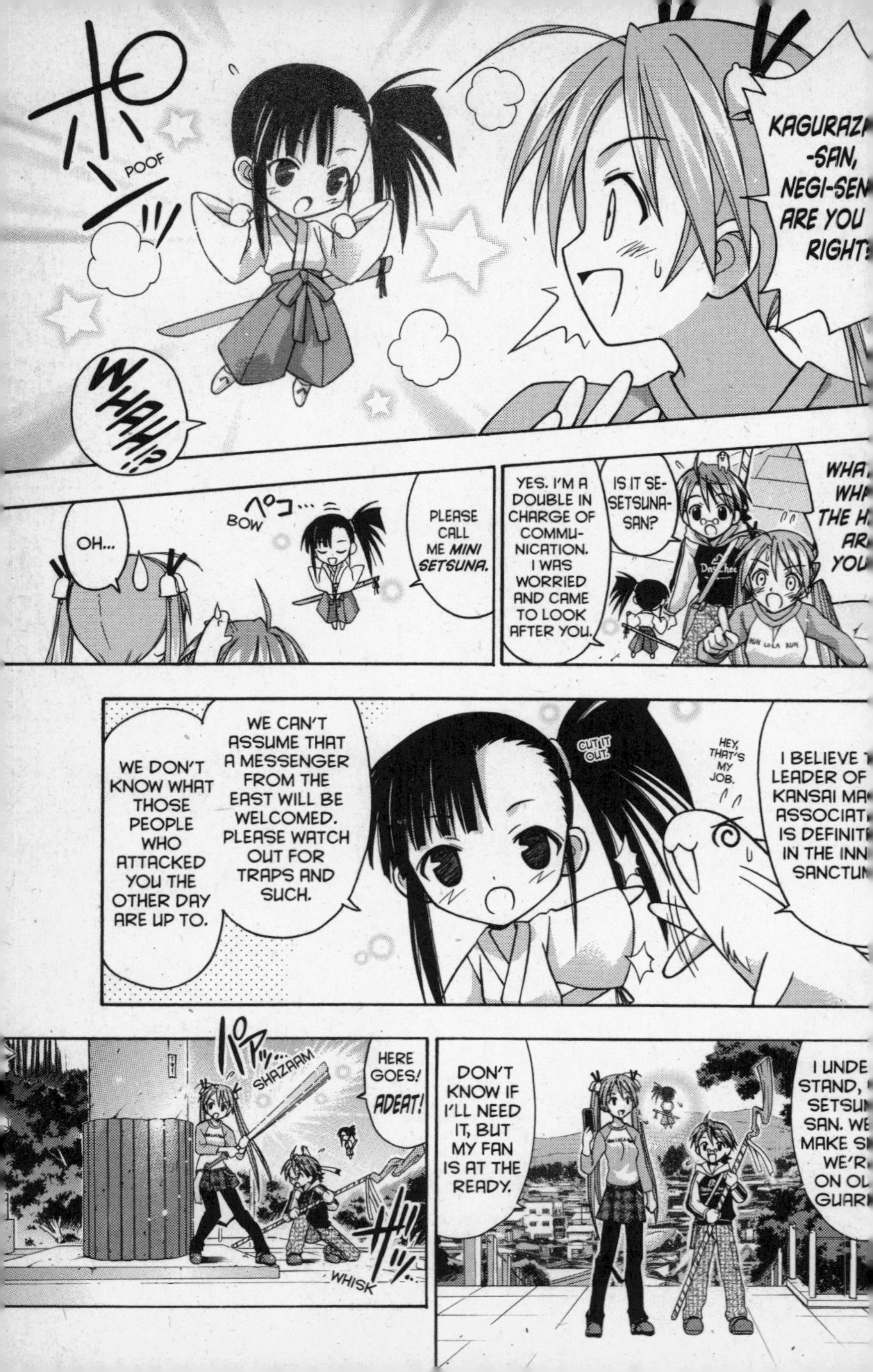
KAGURAZA -SAN, NEGI-SEN ARE YOU RIGHT!
ポン
POOF
WHAH!?
WHA WHA THE H ARE YOU
IS IT SE-SETSUNA-SAN?
YES. I'M A DOUBLE IN CHARGE OF COMMU-NICATION. I WAS WORRIED AND CAME TO LOOK AFTER YOU.
PLEASE CALL ME MINI SETSUNA.
ペコ…
BOW
OH...
I BELIEVE T LEADER OF KANSAI MA ASSOCIATI IS DEFINITE IN THE INN SANCTUM
HEY, THAT'S MY JOB.
CUT IT OUT.
WE CAN'T ASSUME THAT A MESSENGER FROM THE EAST WILL BE WELCOMED. PLEASE WATCH OUT FOR TRAPS AND SUCH.
WE DON'T KNOW WHAT THOSE PEOPLE WHO ATTACKED YOU THE OTHER DAY ARE UP TO.
I UNDE STAND, SETSUN SAN. WE MAKE S WE'R ON OU GUAR
DON'T KNOW IF I'LL NEED IT, BUT MY FAN IS AT THE READY.
HERE GOES! ADEAT!
パァッ…
SHAZAAM
WHISK

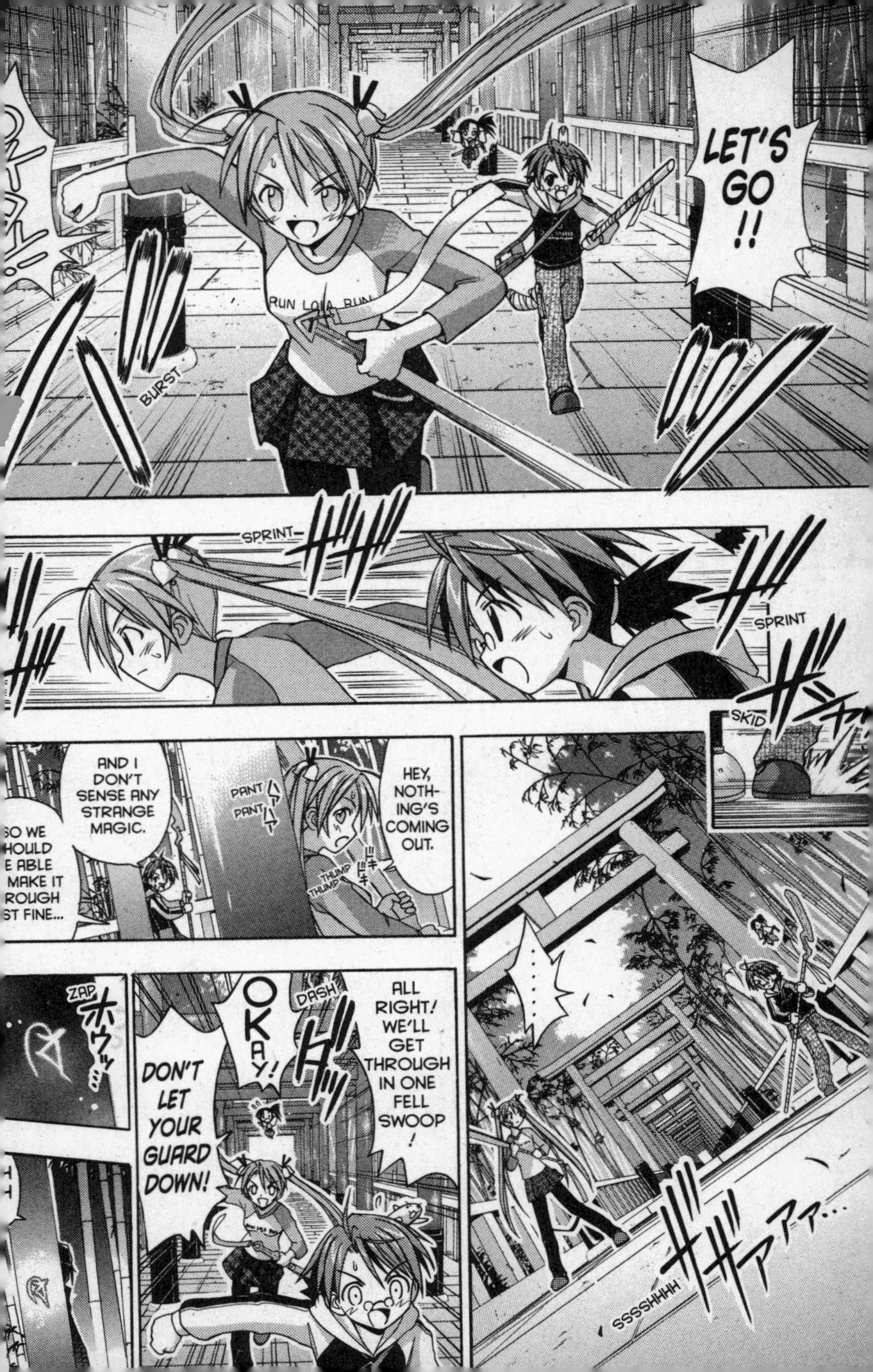
LET'S GO!!
BURST
SPRINT
SPRINT
SKID
...
SSSSHHHH
HEY, NOTHING'S COMING OUT.
PANT PANT
THUMP THUMP
AND I DON'T SENSE ANY STRANGE MAGIC.
SO WE HOULD E ABLE MAKE IT ROUGH ST FINE...
ALL RIGHT! WE'LL GET THROUGH IN ONE FELL SWOOP!
OKAY!
DASH
DON'T LET YOUR GUARD DOWN!
ZAP

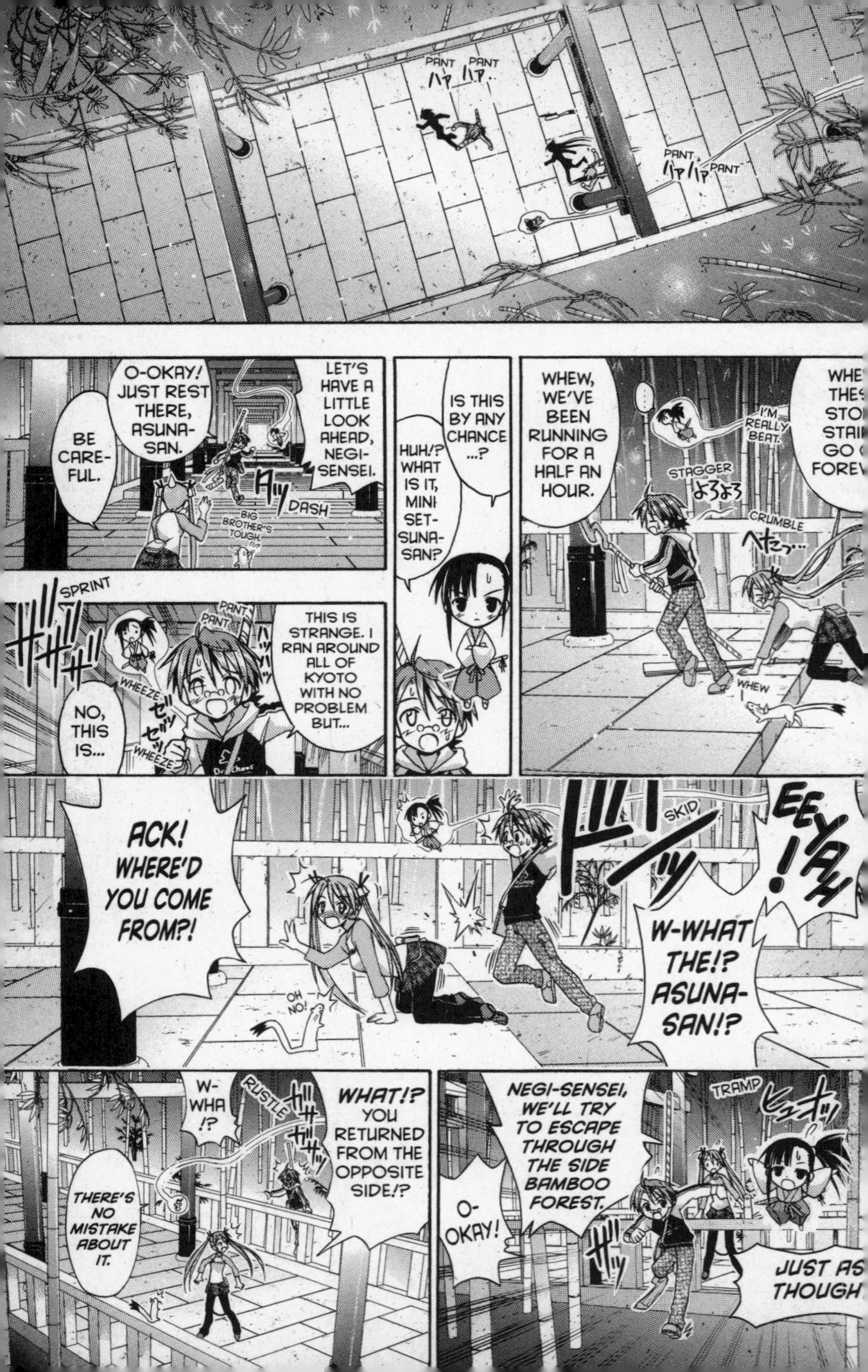
PANT ハァハァ PANT
PANT PANT ハァハァ..
WHE THES STO STAI GO FOREV
WHEW, WE'VE BEEN RUNNING FOR A HALF AN HOUR.
…
I'M REALLY BEAT.
STAGGER よろよろ
CRUMBLE へたっ…
WHEW
IS THIS BY ANY CHANCE ...?
HUH!? WHAT IS IT, MINI SET-SUNA-SAN?
LET'S HAVE A LITTLE LOOK AHEAD, NEGI-SENSEI.
O-OKAY! JUST REST THERE, ASUNA-SAN.
BE CARE-FUL.
ダッ DASH
BIG BROTHER'S TOUGH.
THIS IS STRANGE. I RAN AROUND ALL OF KYOTO WITH NO PROBLEM BUT...
PANT PANT ハッハッ
NO, THIS IS...
WHEEZE ゼッゼッ WHEEZE
SPRINT ザザザザ
EEYAAH!
W-WHAT THE!? ASUNA-SAN!?
SKID ドンッ
ACK! WHERE'D YOU COME FROM?!
OH NO!
JUST AS THOUGH
TRAMP ヒュオッ
NEGI-SENSEI, WE'LL TRY TO ESCAPE THROUGH THE SIDE BAMBOO FOREST.
O-OKAY!
ザッ
WHAT!? YOU RETURNED FROM THE OPPOSITE SIDE!?
RUSTLE ガサガサッ
W-WHA!?
THERE'S NO MISTAKE ABOUT IT.

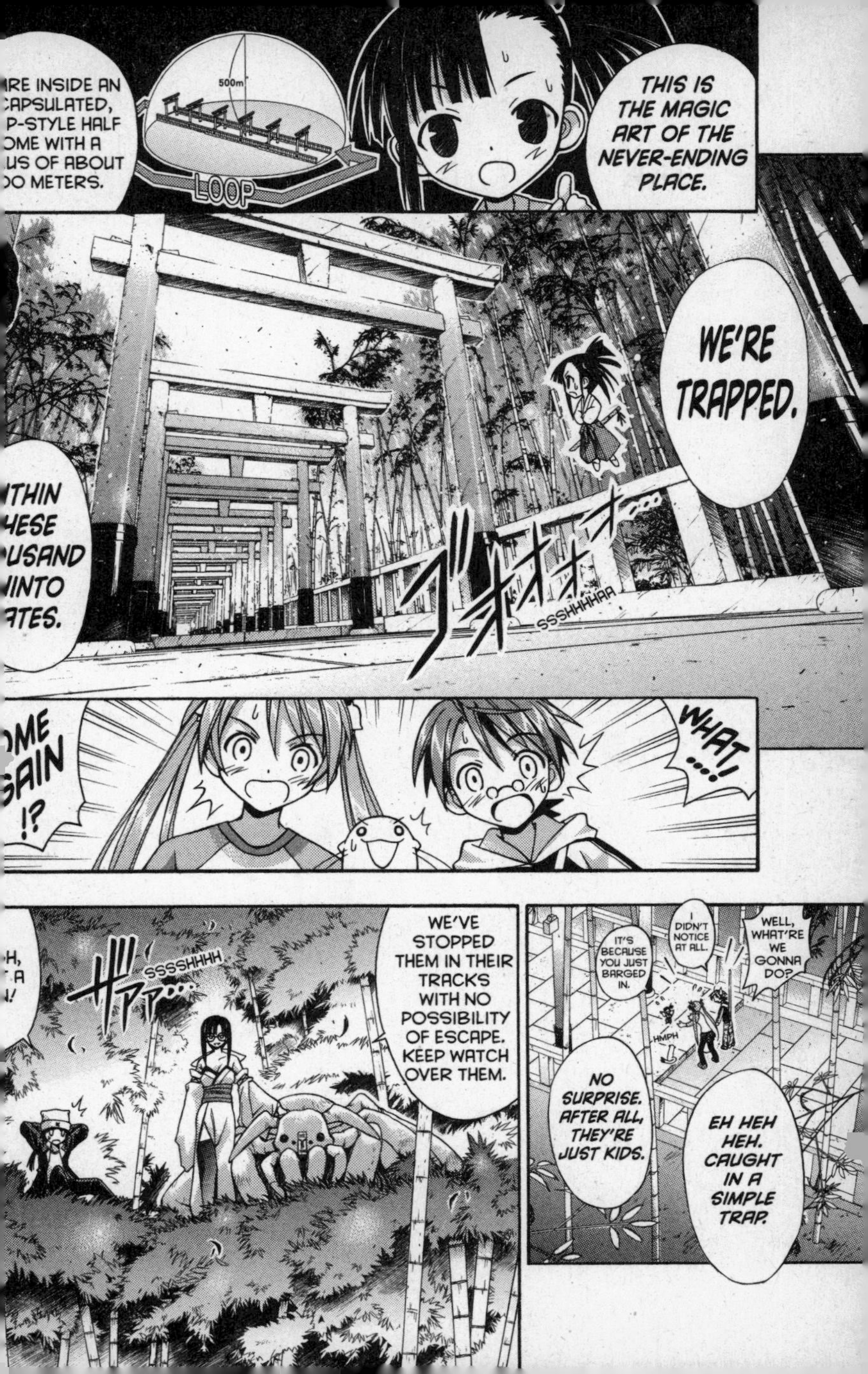
THIS IS THE MAGIC ART OF THE NEVER-ENDING PLACE.
RE INSIDE AN CAPSULATED, P-STYLE HALF OME WITH A IUS OF ABOUT OO METERS.
500m
LOOP
WE'RE TRAPPED.
SSSHHHHAA
ITHIN HESE USAND INTO ATES.
WHAT...!
OME GAIN !?
WELL, WHAT'RE WE GONNA DO?
I DIDN'T NOTICE AT ALL.
IT'S BECAUSE YOU JUST BARGED IN.
HMPH
EH HEH HEH. CAUGHT IN A SIMPLE TRAP.
NO SURPRISE. AFTER ALL, THEY'RE JUST KIDS.
WE'VE STOPPED THEM IN THEIR TRACKS WITH NO POSSIBILITY OF ESCAPE. KEEP WATCH OVER THEM.
SSSSHHHH
H, T A N!

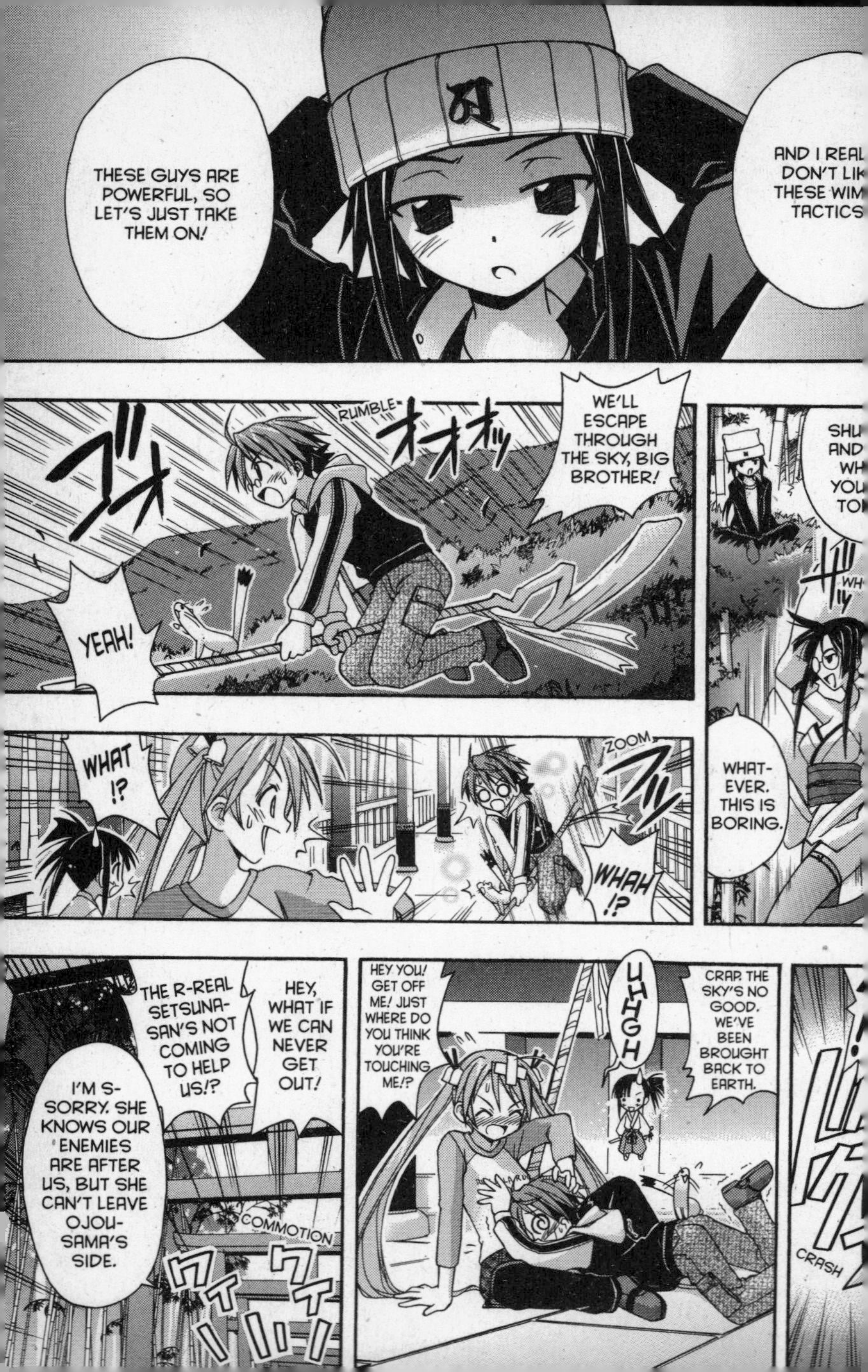
AND I REAL DON'T LIK THESE WIM TACTICS
THESE GUYS ARE POWERFUL, SO LET'S JUST TAKE THEM ON!
SHU AND WH YOU TO
WH
WHAT-EVER. THIS IS BORING.
RUMBLE
WE'LL ESCAPE THROUGH THE SKY, BIG BROTHER!
YEAH!
ZOOM
WHAH !?
WHAT !?
CRASH
CRAP. THE SKY'S NO GOOD. WE'VE BEEN BROUGHT BACK TO EARTH.
UHHGH
HEY YOU! GET OFF ME! JUST WHERE DO YOU THINK YOU'RE TOUCHING ME!?
HEY, WHAT IF WE CAN NEVER GET OUT!
THE R-REAL SETSUNA-SAN'S NOT COMING TO HELP US!?
I'M S-SORRY. SHE KNOWS OUR ENEMIES ARE AFTER US, BUT SHE CAN'T LEAVE OJOU-SAMA'S SIDE.
COMMOTION

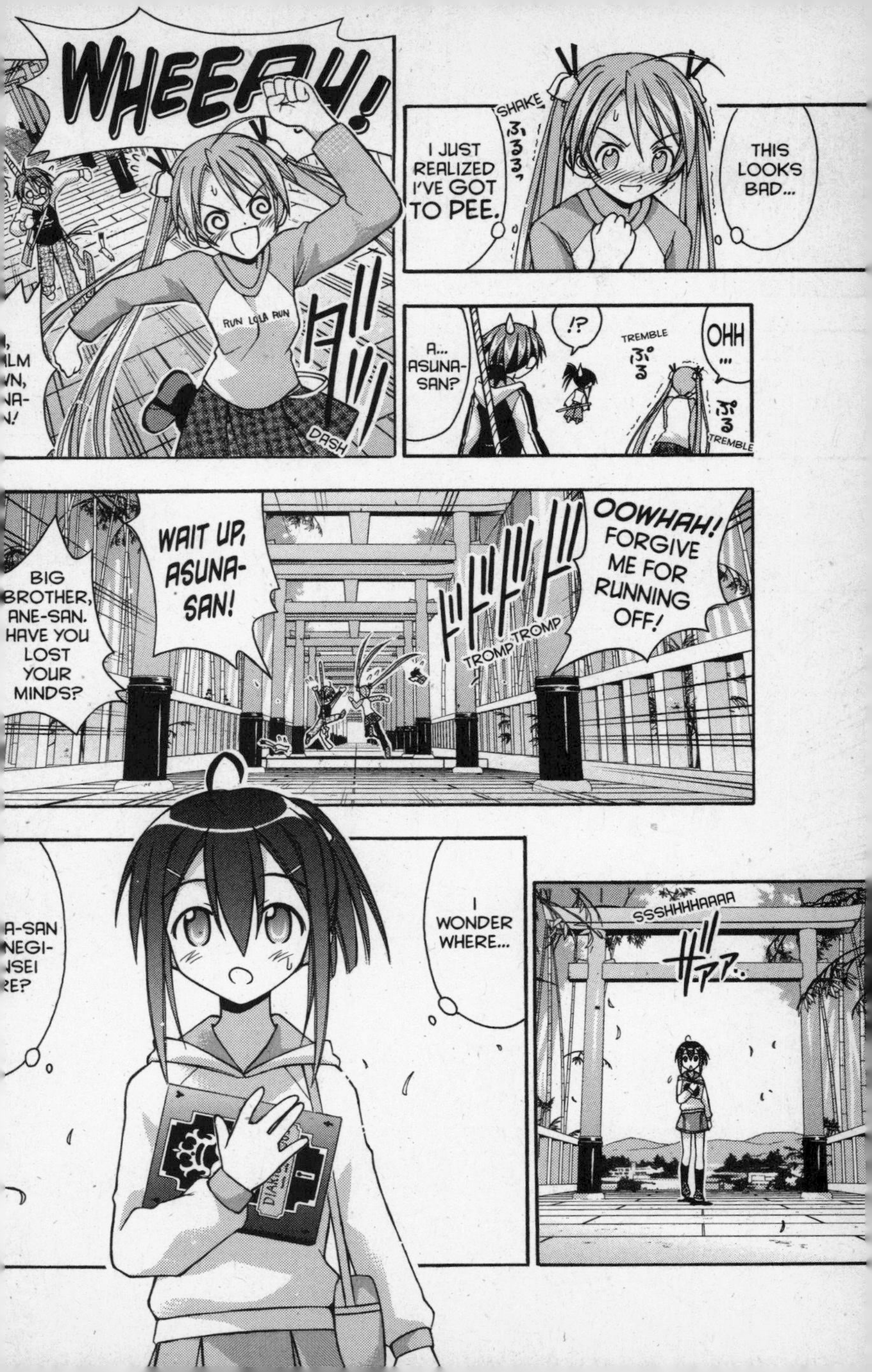
THIS LOOKS BAD...
SHAKE
I JUST REALIZED I'VE GOT TO PEE.
OHH ...
TREMBLE
TREMBLE
!?
A... ASUNA-SAN?
WHEEAAY!
RUN LOLA RUN
DASH
OOWHAH! FORGIVE ME FOR RUNNING OFF!
TROMP TROMP
WAIT UP, ASUNA-SAN!
BIG BROTHER, ANE-SAN. HAVE YOU LOST YOUR MINDS?
SSSHHHHAAAA
I WONDER WHERE...

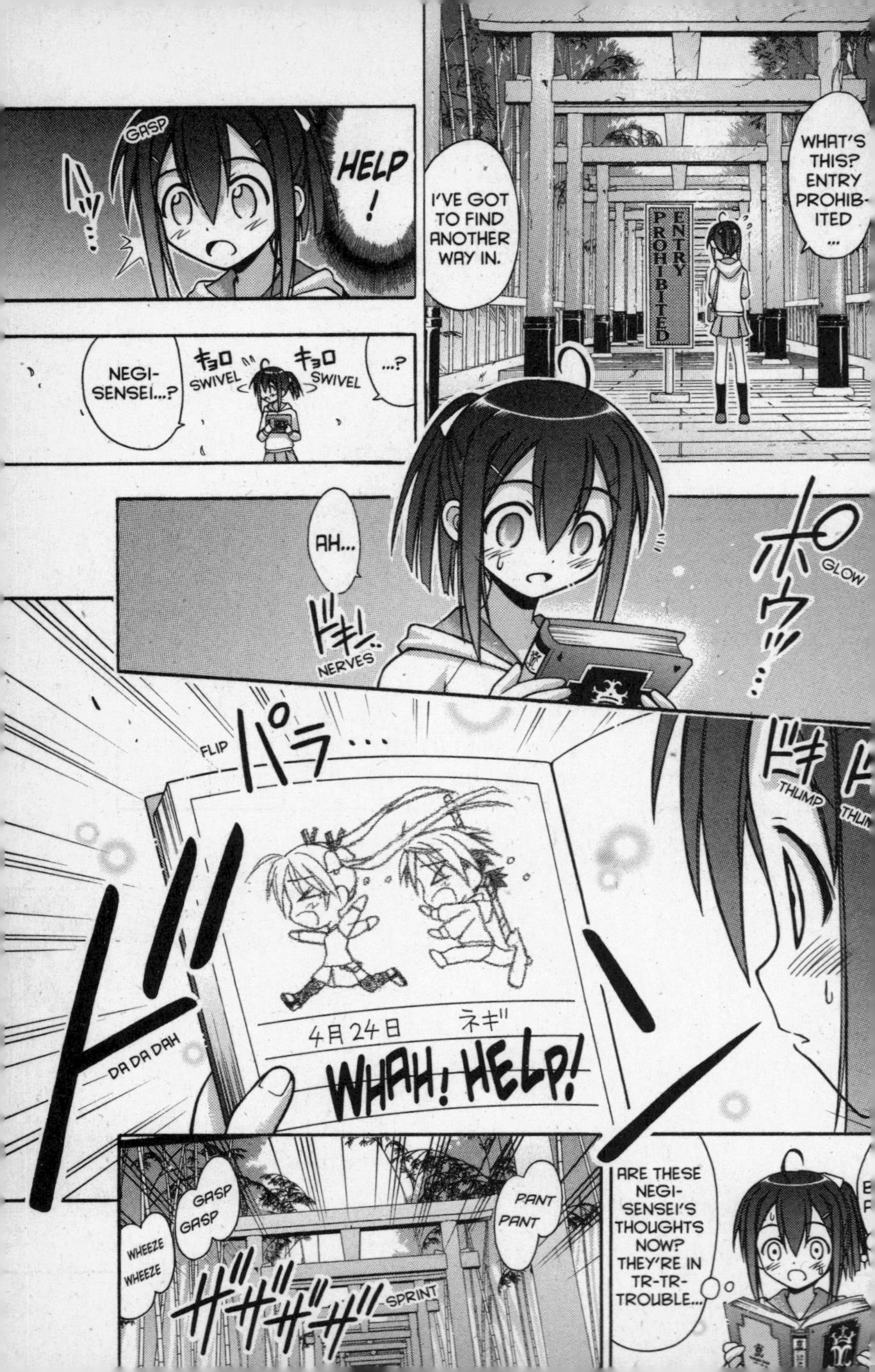
WHAT'S THIS? ENTRY PROHIBITED ...
ENTRY PROHIBITED
I'VE GOT TO FIND ANOTHER WAY IN.
GASP
HELP!
...?
キョロ SWIVEL
キョロ SWIVEL
NEGI-SENSEI...?
GLOW
AH...
NERVES
THUMP THUMP
FLIP
4月24日 ネギ
WHAH! HELP!
DA DA DAH
ARE THESE NEGI-SENSEI'S THOUGHTS NOW? THEY'RE IN TR-TR-TROUBLE...
PANT PANT
GASP GASP
WHEEZE WHEEZE
SPRINT

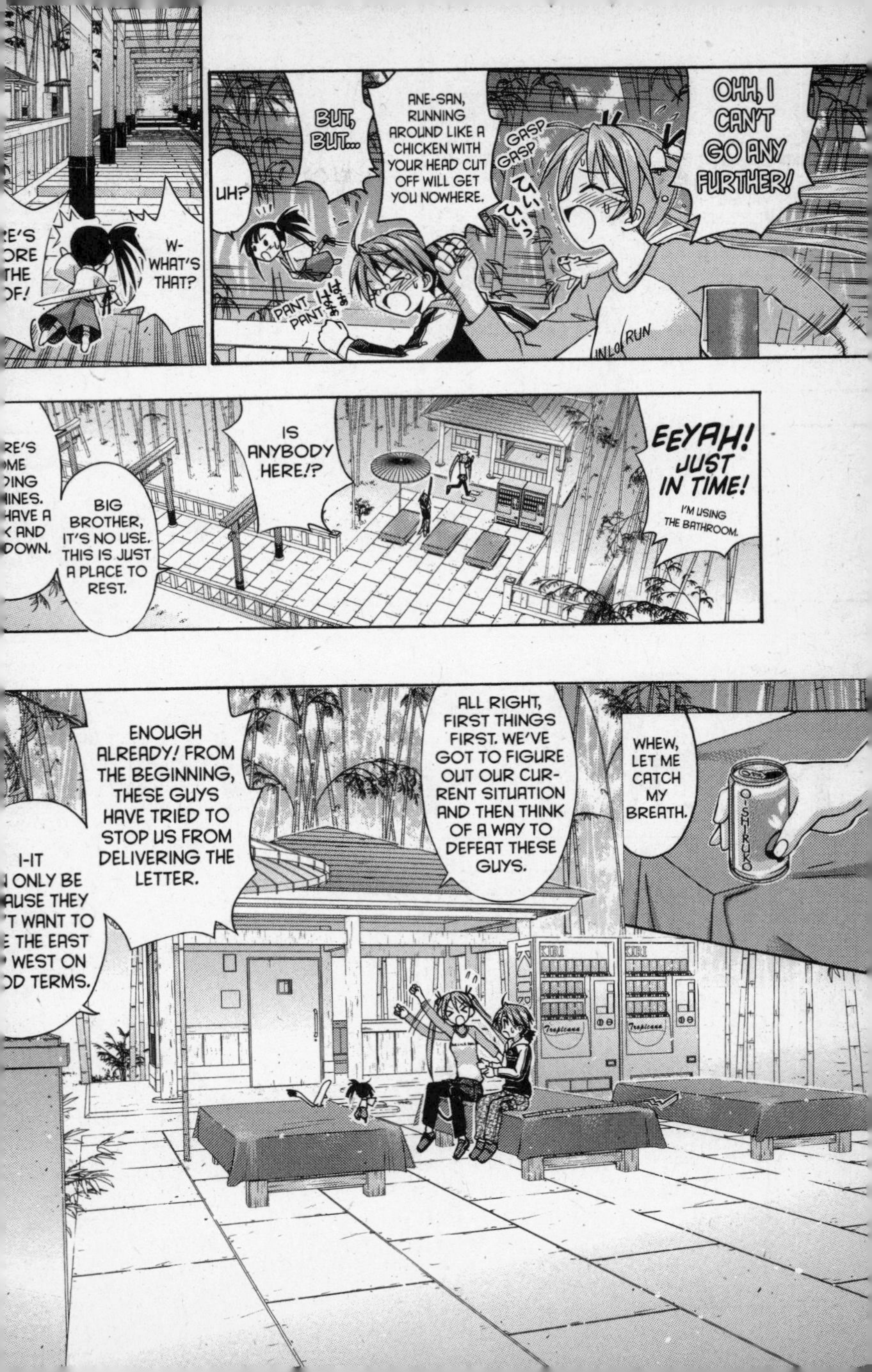

OHH, I CAN'T GO ANY FURTHER!
GASP GASP
ひいひいっ
BUT, BUT...
ANE-SAN, RUNNING AROUND LIKE A CHICKEN WITH YOUR HEAD CUT OFF WILL GET YOU NOWHERE.
UH?
PANT PANT
はぁはぁ
W-WHAT'S THAT?
EEYAH! JUST IN TIME!
I'M USING THE BATHROOM.
IS ANYBODY HERE!?
BIG BROTHER, IT'S NO USE. THIS IS JUST A PLACE TO REST.
WHEW, LET ME CATCH MY BREATH.
OISHIRUKO
ALL RIGHT, FIRST THINGS FIRST. WE'VE GOT TO FIGURE OUT OUR CURRENT SITUATION AND THEN THINK OF A WAY TO DEFEAT THESE GUYS.
ENOUGH ALREADY! FROM THE BEGINNING, THESE GUYS HAVE TRIED TO STOP US FROM DELIVERING THE LETTER.
KIRI
KIRI
Tropicana
Tropicana

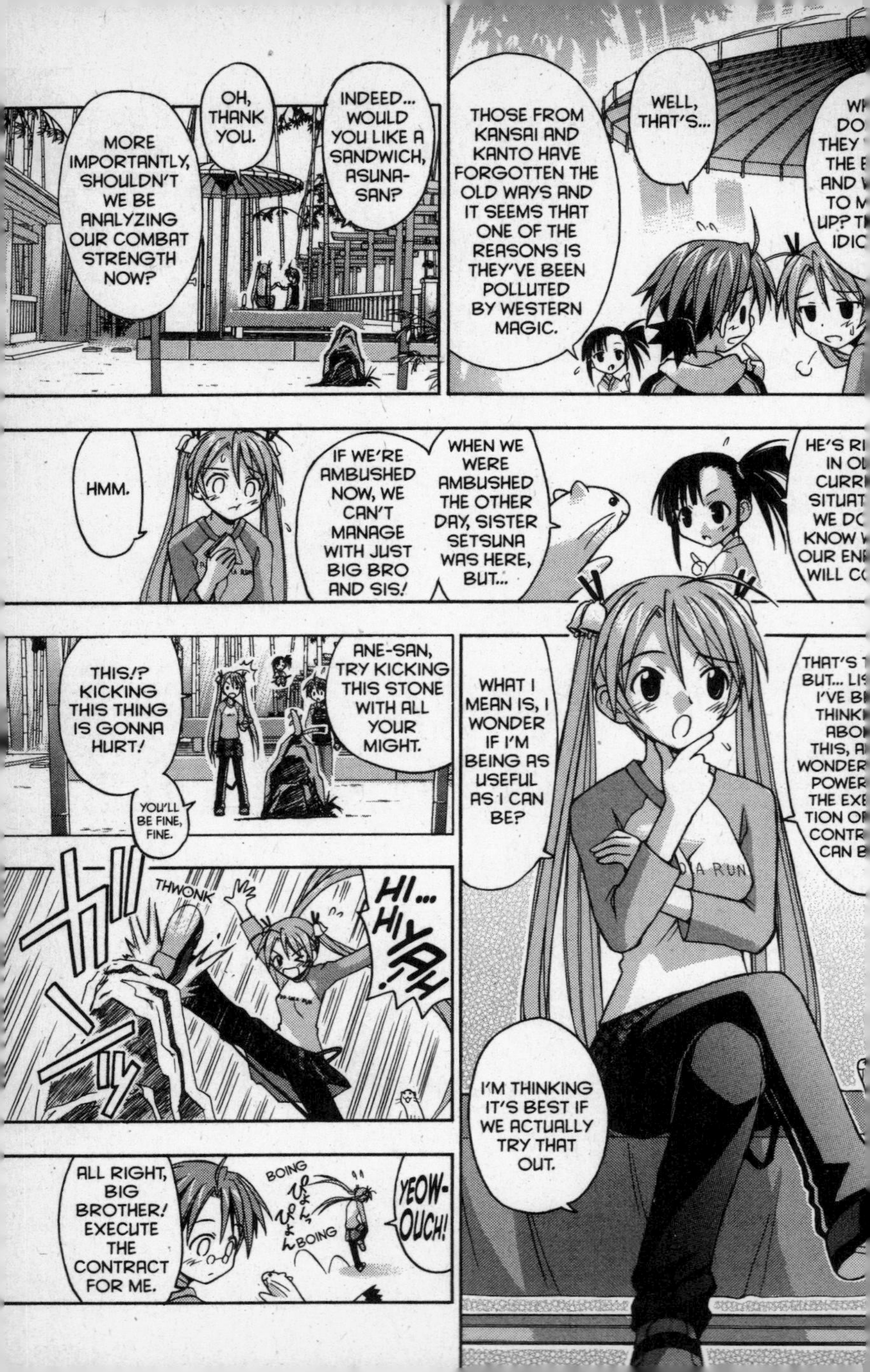
WELL, THAT'S...
THOSE FROM KANSAI AND KANTO HAVE FORGOTTEN THE OLD WAYS AND IT SEEMS THAT ONE OF THE REASONS IS THEY'VE BEEN POLLUTED BY WESTERN MAGIC.
INDEED... WOULD YOU LIKE A SANDWICH, ASUNA-SAN?
OH, THANK YOU.
MORE IMPORTANTLY, SHOULDN'T WE BE ANALYZING OUR COMBAT STRENGTH NOW?
WHEN WE WERE AMBUSHED THE OTHER DAY, SISTER SETSUNA WAS HERE, BUT...
IF WE'RE AMBUSHED NOW, WE CAN'T MANAGE WITH JUST BIG BRO AND SIS!
HMM.
WHAT I MEAN IS, I WONDER IF I'M BEING AS USEFUL AS I CAN BE?
I'M THINKING IT'S BEST IF WE ACTUALLY TRY THAT OUT.
ANE-SAN, TRY KICKING THIS STONE WITH ALL YOUR MIGHT.
THIS!? KICKING THIS THING IS GONNA HURT!
YOU'LL BE FINE, FINE.
HI... HIYAH!
THWONK
YEOW-OUCH!
BOING
BOING
ALL RIGHT, BIG BROTHER! EXECUTE THE CONTRACT FOR ME.

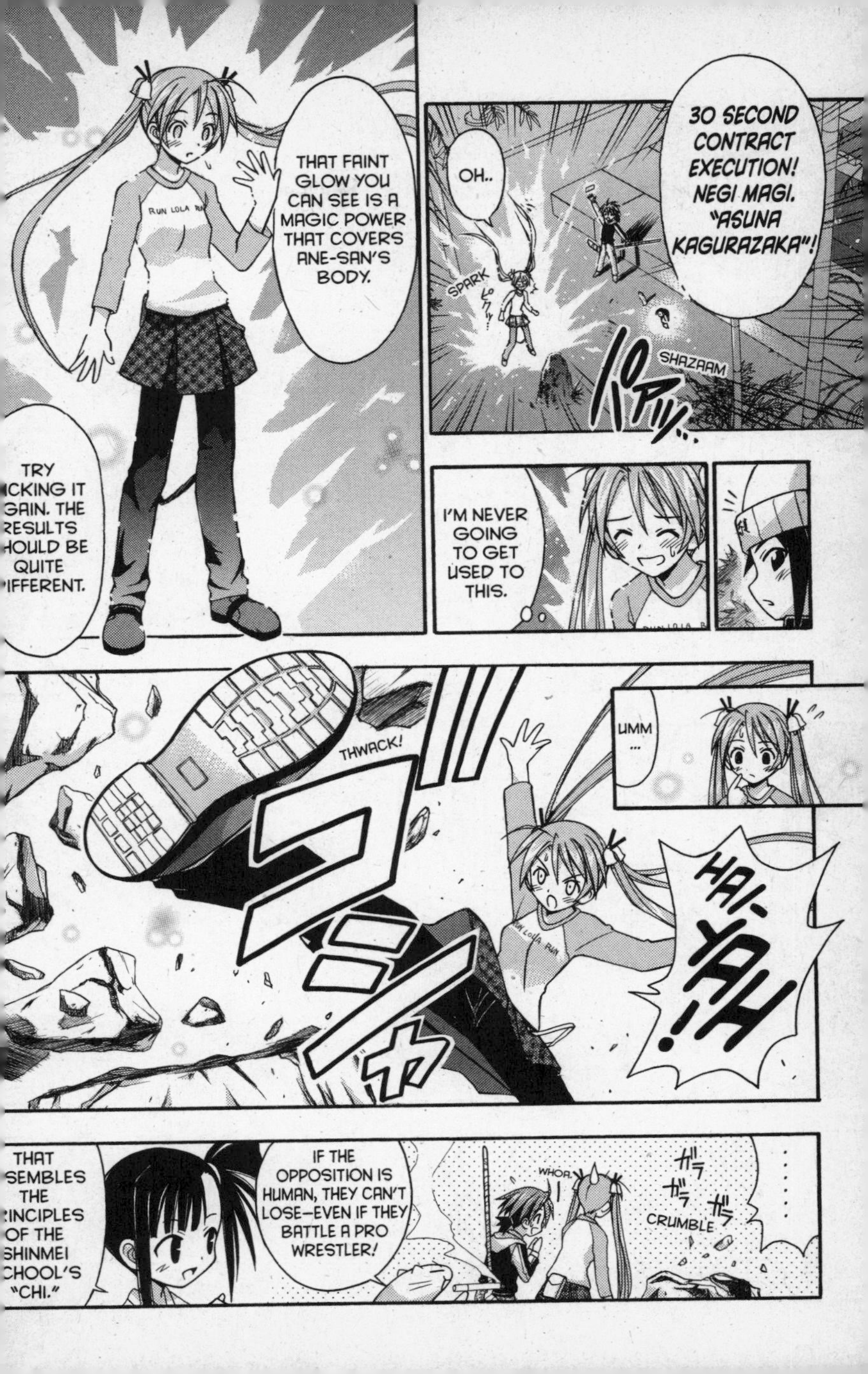
30 SECOND CONTRACT EXECUTION! NEGI MAGI. "ASUNA KAGURAZAKA"!
OH..
SPARK
SHAZAAM
I'M NEVER GOING TO GET USED TO THIS.
THAT FAINT GLOW YOU CAN SEE IS A MAGIC POWER THAT COVERS ANE-SAN'S BODY.
TRY ICKING IT GAIN. THE RESULTS HOULD BE QUITE IFFERENT.
UMM ...
HAI-YAH!!
THWACK!
.....
CRUMBLE
WHOA.
IF THE OPPOSITION IS HUMAN, THEY CAN'T LOSE—EVEN IF THEY BATTLE A PRO WRESTLER!
THAT SEMBLES THE INCIPLES OF THE SHINMEI CHOOL'S "CHI."

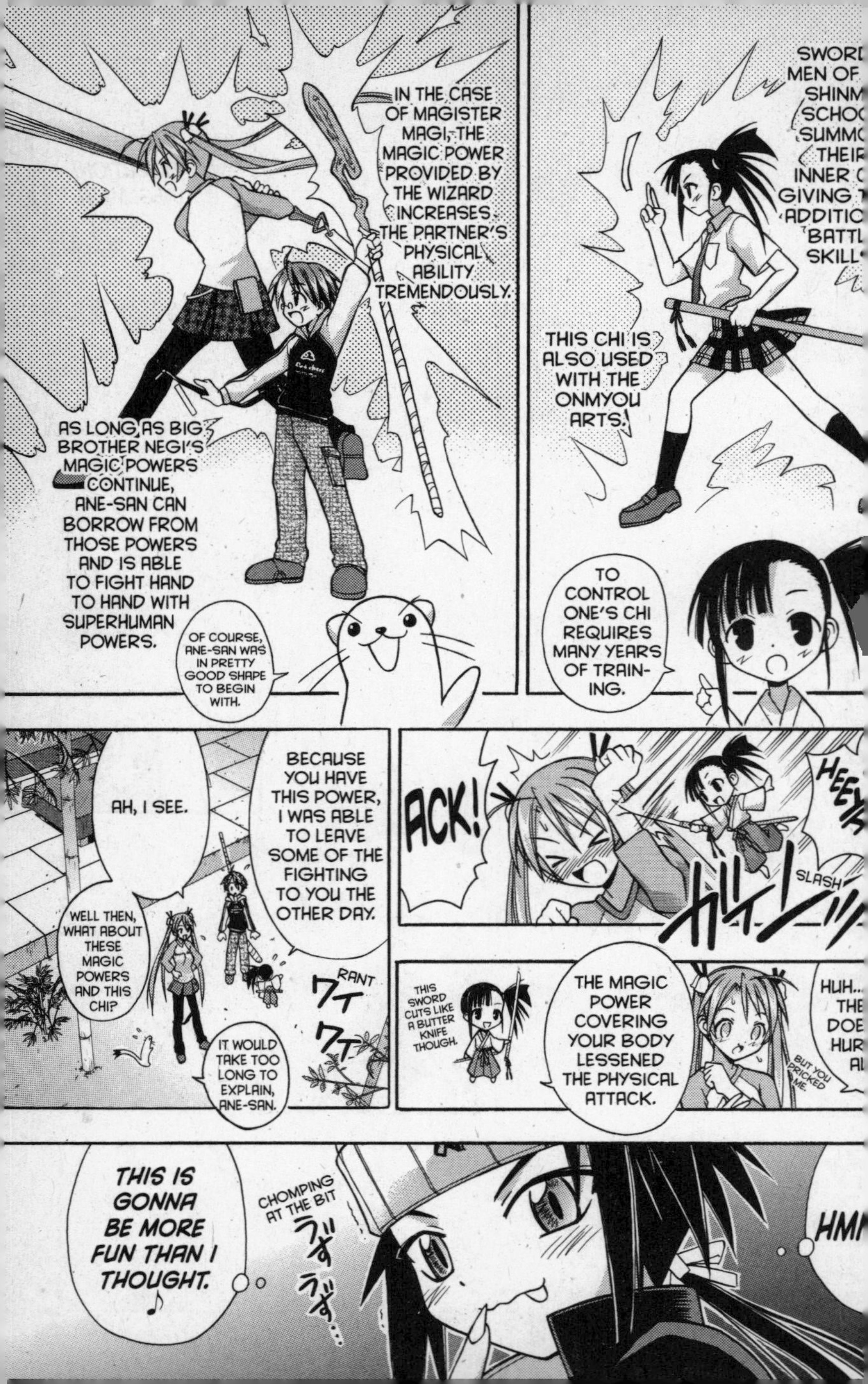
SWORD MEN OF SHINM SCHOO SUMMO THEIR INNER GIVING ADDITIO BATTL SKILL
THIS CHI IS ALSO USED WITH THE ONMYOU ARTS.
TO CONTROL ONE'S CHI REQUIRES MANY YEARS OF TRAIN-ING.
IN THE CASE OF MAGISTER MAGI, THE MAGIC POWER PROVIDED BY THE WIZARD INCREASES THE PARTNER'S PHYSICAL ABILITY TREMENDOUSLY.
AS LONG AS BIG BROTHER NEGI'S MAGIC POWERS CONTINUE, ANE-SAN CAN BORROW FROM THOSE POWERS AND IS ABLE TO FIGHT HAND TO HAND WITH SUPERHUMAN POWERS.
OF COURSE, ANE-SAN WAS IN PRETTY GOOD SHAPE TO BEGIN WITH.
ACK!
SLASH
ガイーン
HUH... THE DOE HUR
BUT YOU PRICKED ME.
THE MAGIC POWER COVERING YOUR BODY LESSENED THE PHYSICAL ATTACK.
THIS SWORD CUTS LIKE A BUTTER KNIFE THOUGH.
BECAUSE YOU HAVE THIS POWER, I WAS ABLE TO LEAVE SOME OF THE FIGHTING TO YOU THE OTHER DAY.
AH, I SEE.
WELL THEN, WHAT ABOUT THESE MAGIC POWERS AND THIS CHI?
RANT
ワイワイ
IT WOULD TAKE TOO LONG TO EXPLAIN, ANE-SAN.
HM
CHOMPING AT THE BIT
うずうず...
THIS IS GONNA BE MORE FUN THAN I THOUGHT. ♪

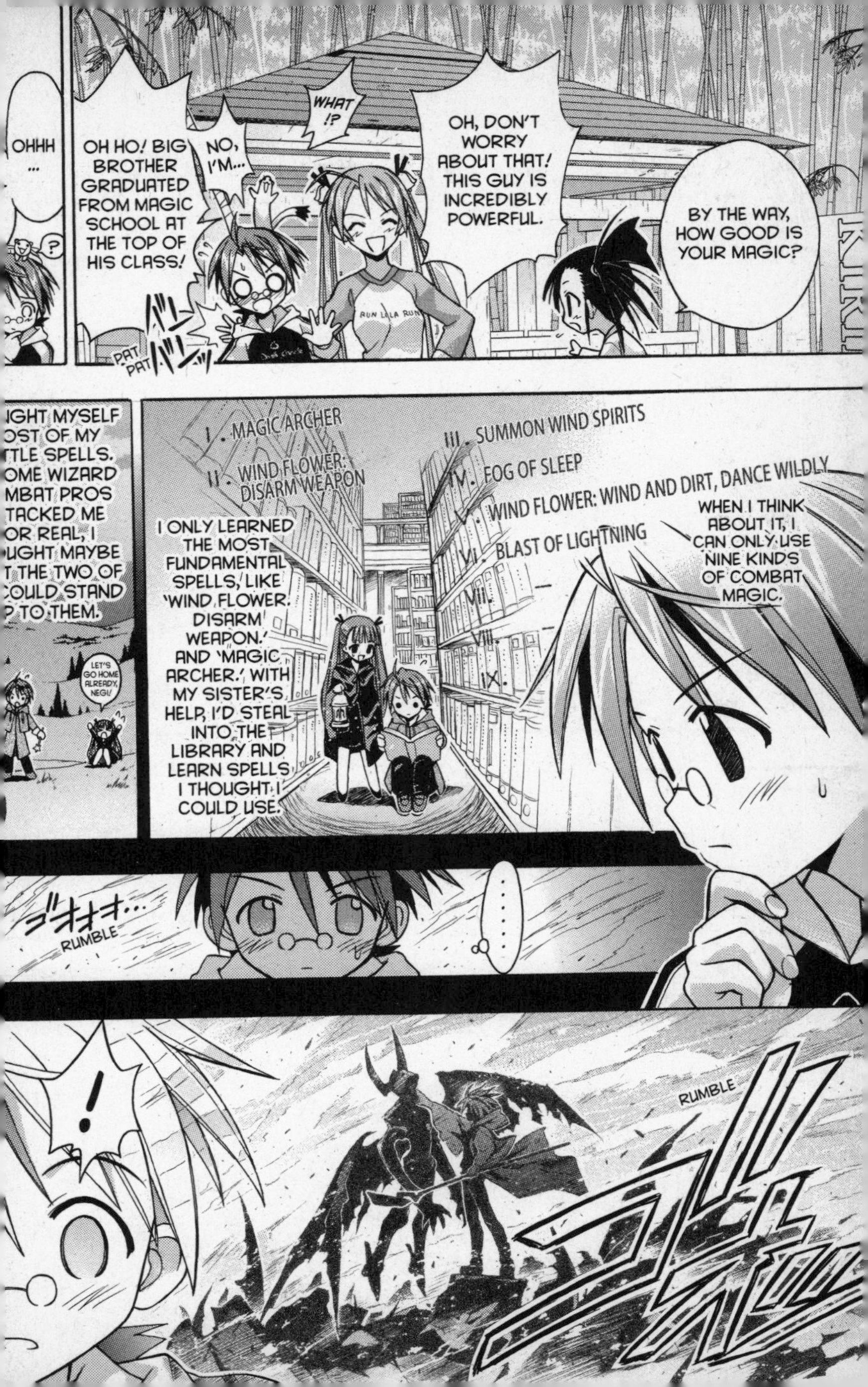

BY THE WAY, HOW GOOD IS YOUR MAGIC?
OH, DON'T WORRY ABOUT THAT! THIS GUY IS INCREDIBLY POWERFUL.
WHAT !?
NO, I'M...
OH HO! BIG BROTHER GRADUATED FROM MAGIC SCHOOL AT THE TOP OF HIS CLASS!
PAT PAT
OHHH ...
?
WHEN I THINK ABOUT IT, I CAN ONLY USE NINE KINDS OF COMBAT MAGIC.
I. MAGIC ARCHER
II. WIND FLOWER: DISARM WEAPON
III. SUMMON WIND SPIRITS
IV. FOG OF SLEEP
V. WIND FLOWER: WIND AND DIRT, DANCE WILDLY
VI. BLAST OF LIGHTNING
VII. —
VIII.
IX.
I ONLY LEARNED THE MOST FUNDAMENTAL SPELLS, LIKE 'WIND FLOWER. DISARM WEAPON.' AND 'MAGIC ARCHER.' WITH MY SISTER'S HELP, I'D STEAL INTO THE LIBRARY AND LEARN SPELLS I THOUGHT I COULD USE.
IGHT MYSELF OST OF MY TTLE SPELLS. OME WIZARD MBAT PROS TACKED ME OR REAL, I UGHT MAYBE T THE TWO OF COULD STAND P TO THEM.
LET'S GO HOME ALREADY, NEGI!
RUMBLE
......
!
RUMBLE

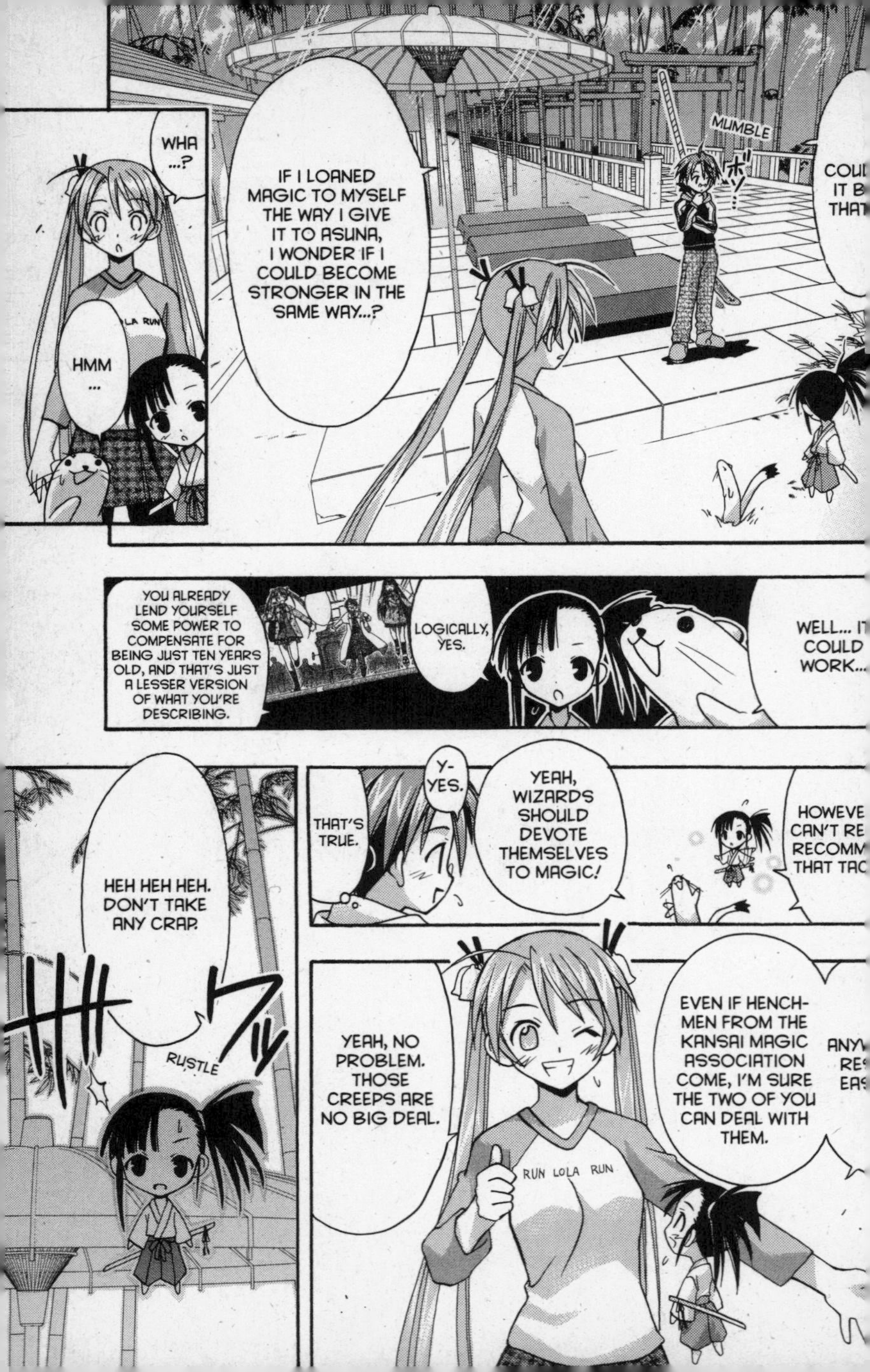
COUL
IT B
THAT
MUMBLE
IF I LOANED MAGIC TO MYSELF THE WAY I GIVE IT TO ASUNA, I WONDER IF I COULD BECOME STRONGER IN THE SAME WAY...?
WHA ...?
HMM ...
WELL... IT COULD WORK...
LOGICALLY, YES.
YOU ALREADY LEND YOURSELF SOME POWER TO COMPENSATE FOR BEING JUST TEN YEARS OLD, AND THAT'S JUST A LESSER VERSION OF WHAT YOU'RE DESCRIBING.
HOWEVE CAN'T RE RECOMM THAT TAC
YEAH, WIZARDS SHOULD DEVOTE THEMSELVES TO MAGIC!
Y-YES.
THAT'S TRUE.
ANYW RE EAS
EVEN IF HENCH-MEN FROM THE KANSAI MAGIC ASSOCIATION COME, I'M SURE THE TWO OF YOU CAN DEAL WITH THEM.
YEAH, NO PROBLEM. THOSE CREEPS ARE NO BIG DEAL.
HEH HEH HEH. DON'T TAKE ANY CRAP.
RUSTLE

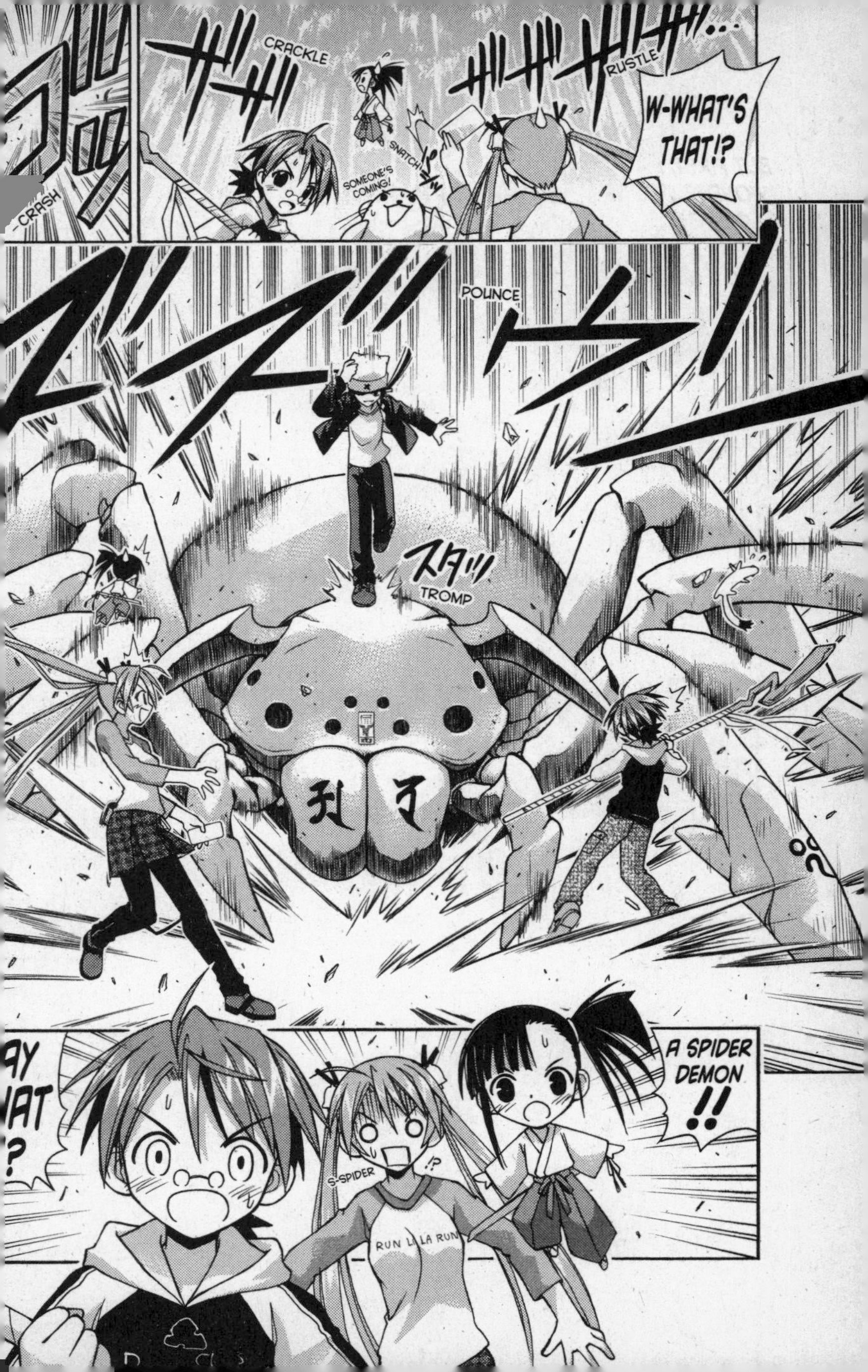
W-WHAT'S THAT!?
RUSTLE
SNATCH!
SOMEONE'S COMING!
CRACKLE
-CRASH
POUNCE
TROMP
A SPIDER DEMON!!
!?
S-SPIDER
RUN LALA RUN

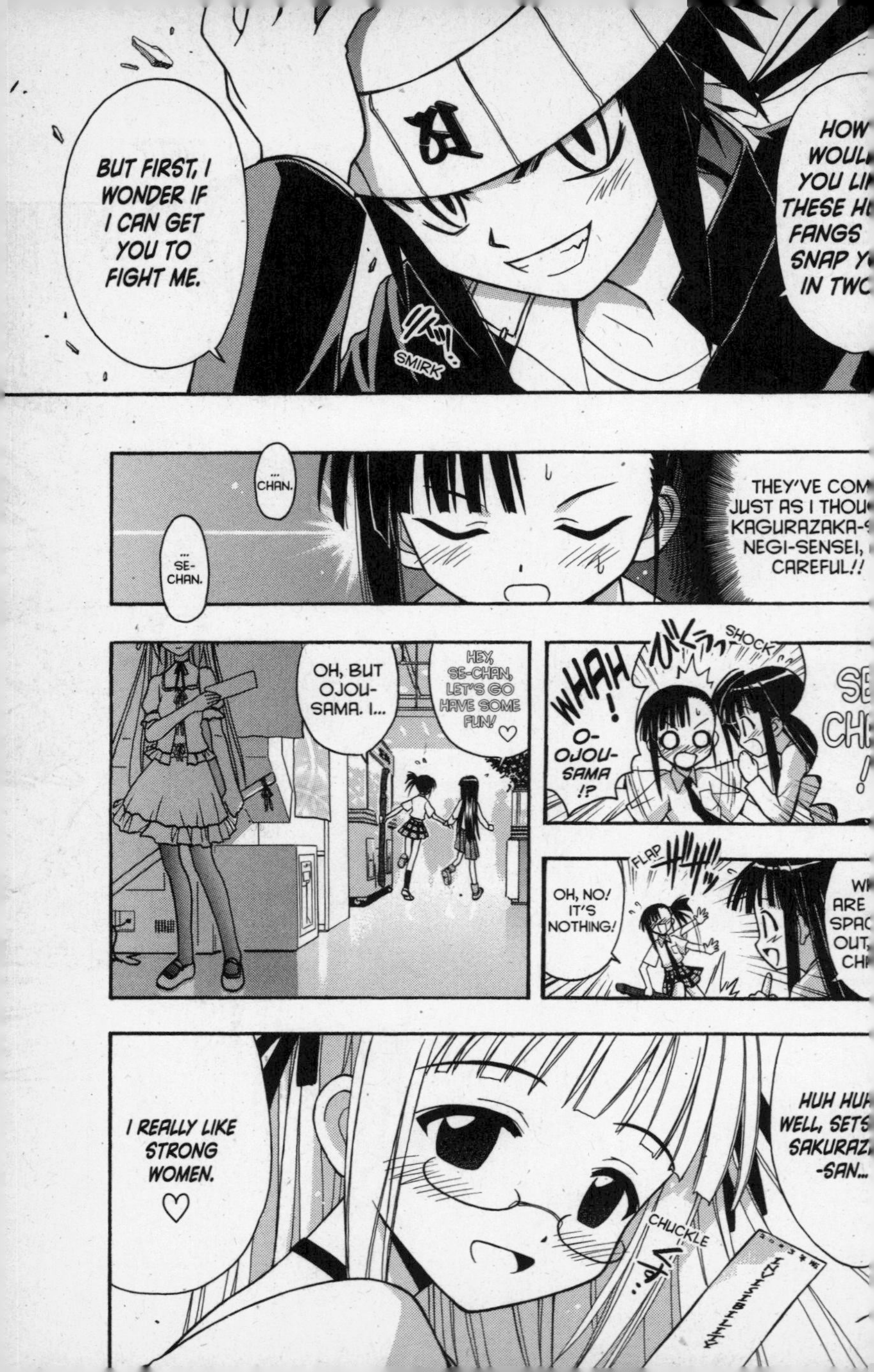
HOW WOULI YOU LI THESE H FANGS SNAP Y IN TWO
SMIRK
BUT FIRST, I WONDER IF I CAN GET YOU TO FIGHT ME.
THEY'VE COM JUST AS I THOU KAGURAZAKA-S NEGI-SENSEI, CAREFUL!!
...CHAN.
...SE-CHAN.
SHOCK
SE CH !
WHAH!
O-OJOU-SAMA!?
WH ARE SPAC OUT, CH
FLAP
OH, NO! IT'S NOTHING!
HEY, SE-CHAN, LET'S GO HAVE SOME FUN! ♡
OH, BUT OJOU-SAMA. I...
HUH HUH WELL, SETS SAKURAZ -SAN...
CHUCKLE
I REALLY LIKE STRONG WOMEN. ♡

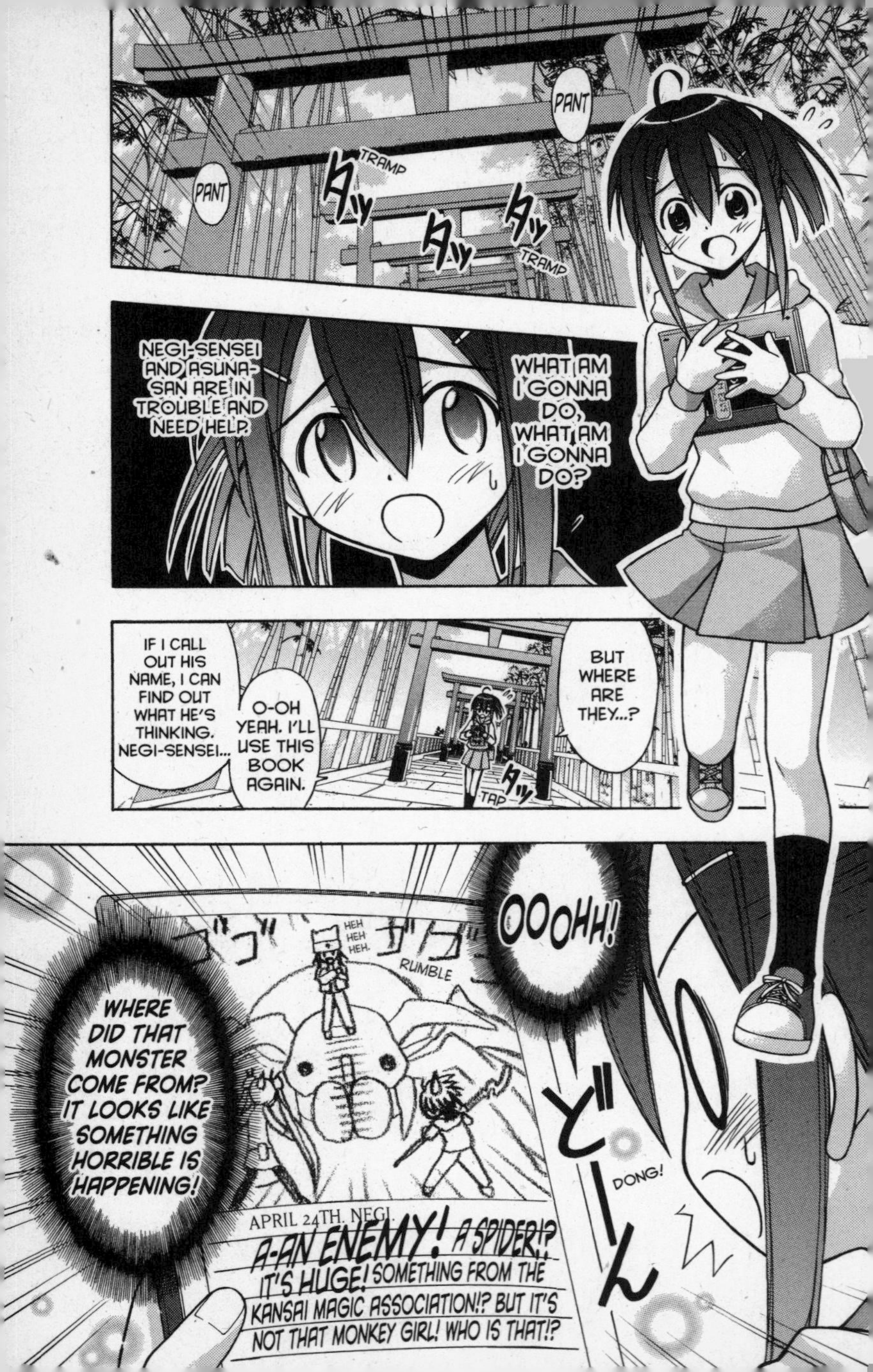
PANT
ダッ
TRAMP
ダッ
ダッ
TRAMP
PANT
WHAT AM I GONNA DO, WHAT AM I GONNA DO?
NEGI-SENSEI AND ASUNA-SAN ARE IN TROUBLE AND NEED HELP.
BUT WHERE ARE THEY...?
ダッ
TAP
O-OH YEAH. I'LL USE THIS BOOK AGAIN.
IF I CALL OUT HIS NAME, I CAN FIND OUT WHAT HE'S THINKING. NEGI-SENSEI...
OOOHH!
どーん
DONG!
RUMBLE
HEH HEH HEH.
WHERE DID THAT MONSTER COME FROM? IT LOOKS LIKE SOMETHING HORRIBLE IS HAPPENING!
APRIL 24TH. NEGI.
A-AN ENEMY! A SPIDER!? IT'S HUGE! SOMETHING FROM THE KANSAI MAGIC ASSOCIATION!? BUT IT'S NOT THAT MONKEY GIRL! WHO IS THAT!?

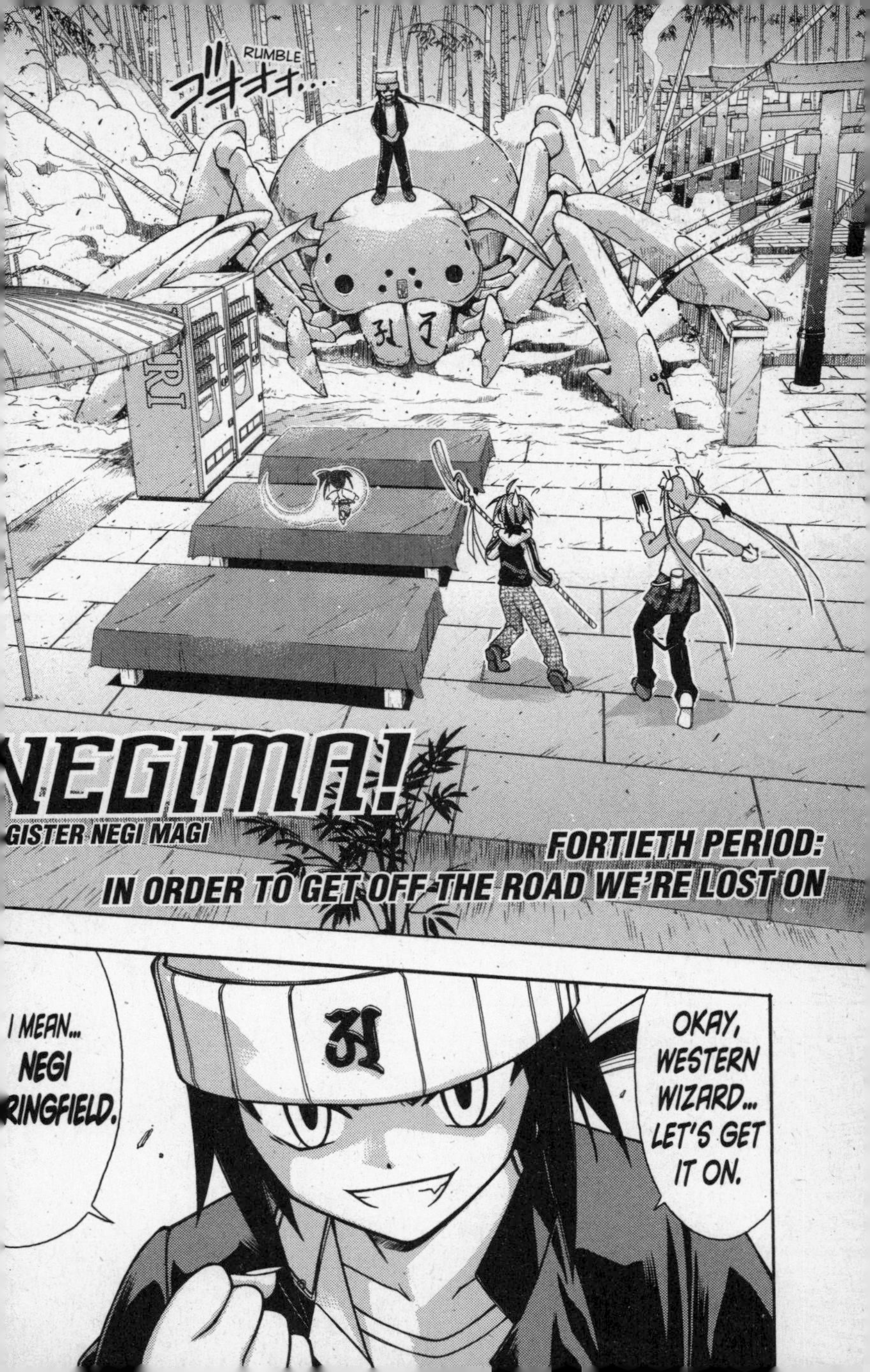
RUMBLE
ゴオオオ…
NEGIMA!
GISTER NEGI MAGI
FORTIETH PERIOD:
IN ORDER TO GET OFF THE ROAD WE'RE LOST ON
OKAY, WESTERN WIZARD... LET'S GET IT ON.
I MEAN... NEGI RINGFIELD.

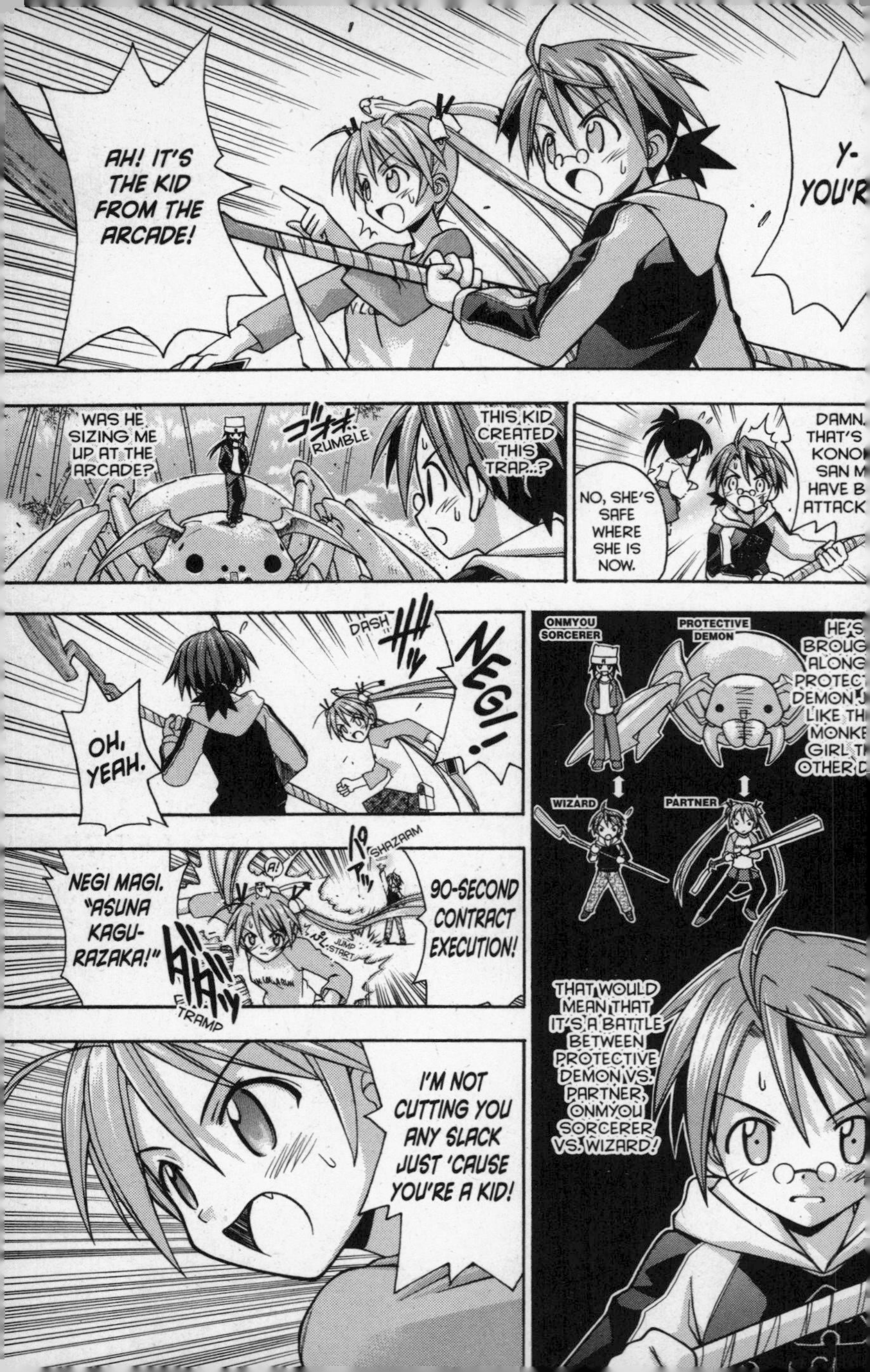
Y-
YOU'R
AH! IT'S THE KID FROM THE ARCADE!
DAMN. THAT'S KONO SAN M HAVE B ATTACK
NO, SHE'S SAFE WHERE SHE IS NOW.
THIS KID CREATED THIS TRAP...?
RUMBLE
WAS HE SIZING ME UP AT THE ARCADE?
HE'S BROUG ALONG PROTECT DEMON J LIKE TH MONKE GIRL T OTHER D
PROTECTIVE DEMON
ONMYOU SORCERER
PARTNER
WIZARD
THAT WOULD MEAN THAT IT'S A BATTLE BETWEEN PROTECTIVE DEMON VS. PARTNER, ONMYOU SORCERER VS. WIZARD!
NEGI!
DASH
OH, YEAH.
90-SECOND CONTRACT EXECUTION!
SHAZAAM
A!
JUMP START
NEGI MAGI. "ASUNA KAGURAZAKA!"
TRAMP
I'M NOT CUTTING YOU ANY SLACK JUST 'CAUSE YOU'RE A KID!

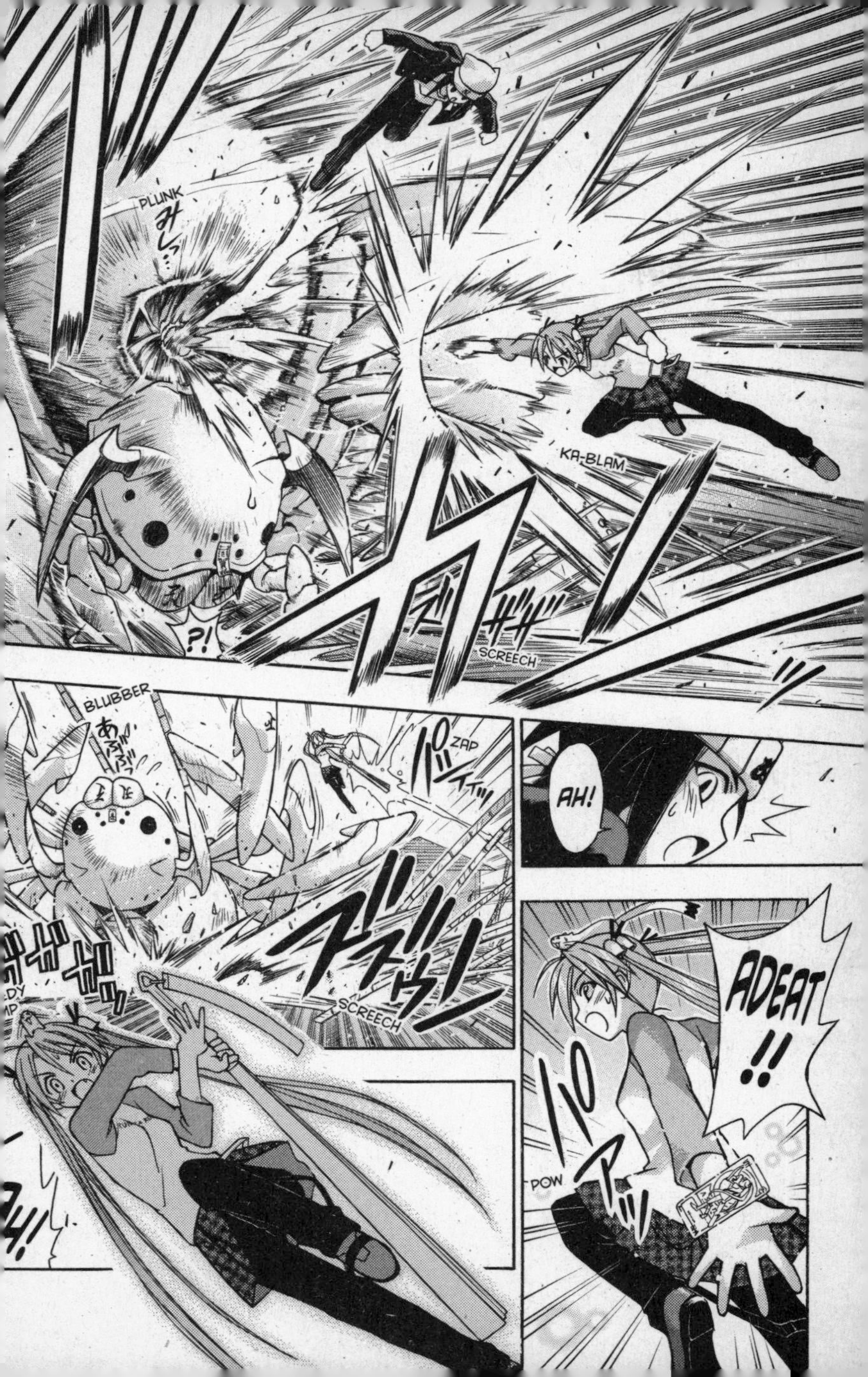
KA-BLAM
PLUNK
?!
SCREECH
AH!
ZAP
BLUBBER
SCREECH
ADEAT!!
POW

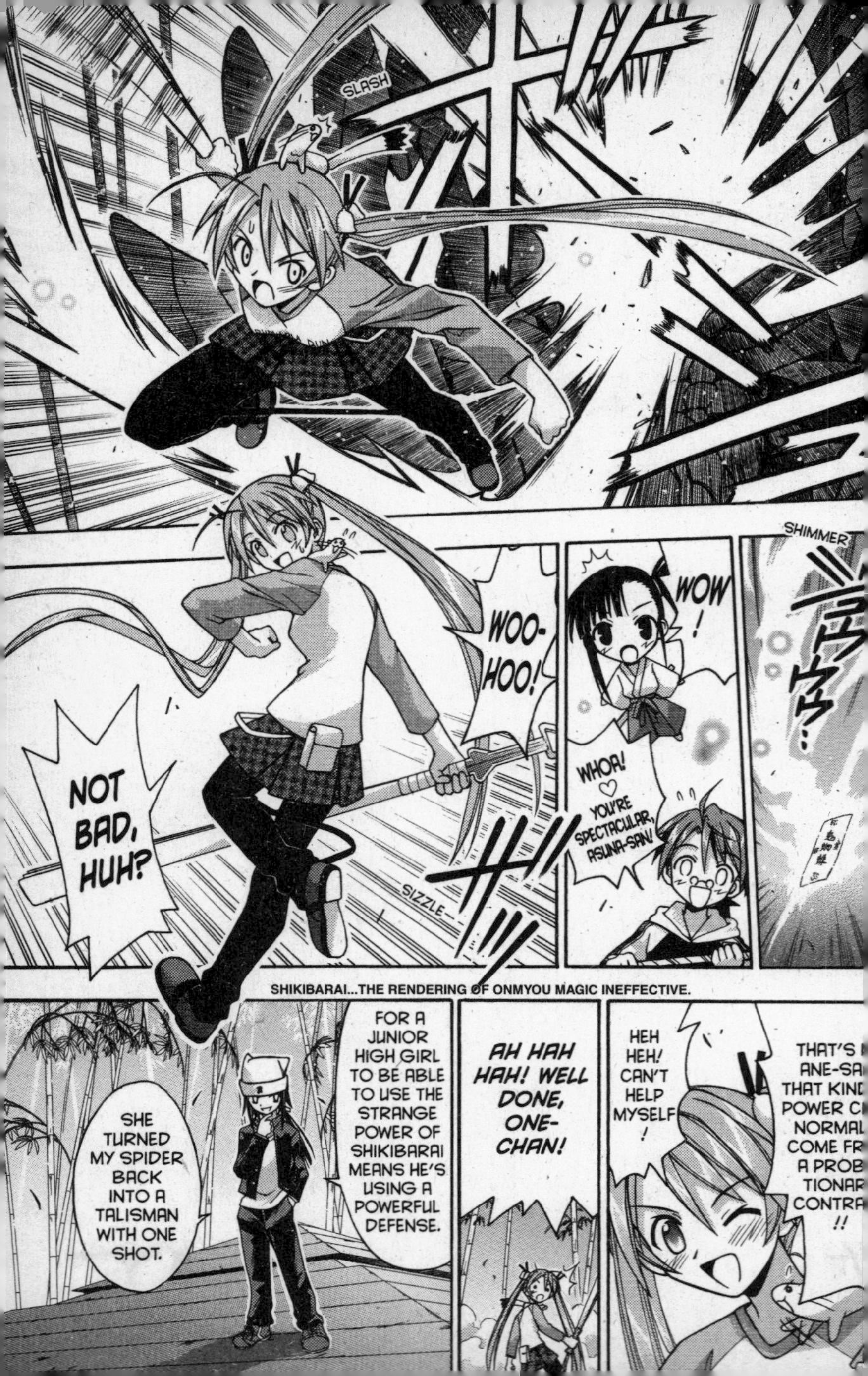
SLASH
SHIMMER
WOW!
WHOA! ♥ YOU'RE SPECTACULAR, ASUNA-SAN!
WOO-HOO!
NOT BAD, HUH?
SIZZLE
SHIKIBARAI...THE RENDERING OF ONMYOU MAGIC INEFFECTIVE.
THAT'S
ANE-SA
THAT KIND
POWER C
NORMAL
COME FR
A PROB
TIONAR
CONTRA
!!
HEH HEH! CAN'T HELP MYSELF!
AH HAH HAH! WELL DONE, ONE-CHAN!
FOR A JUNIOR HIGH GIRL TO BE ABLE TO USE THE STRANGE POWER OF SHIKIBARAI MEANS HE'S USING A POWERFUL DEFENSE.
SHE TURNED MY SPIDER BACK INTO A TALISMAN WITH ONE SHOT.

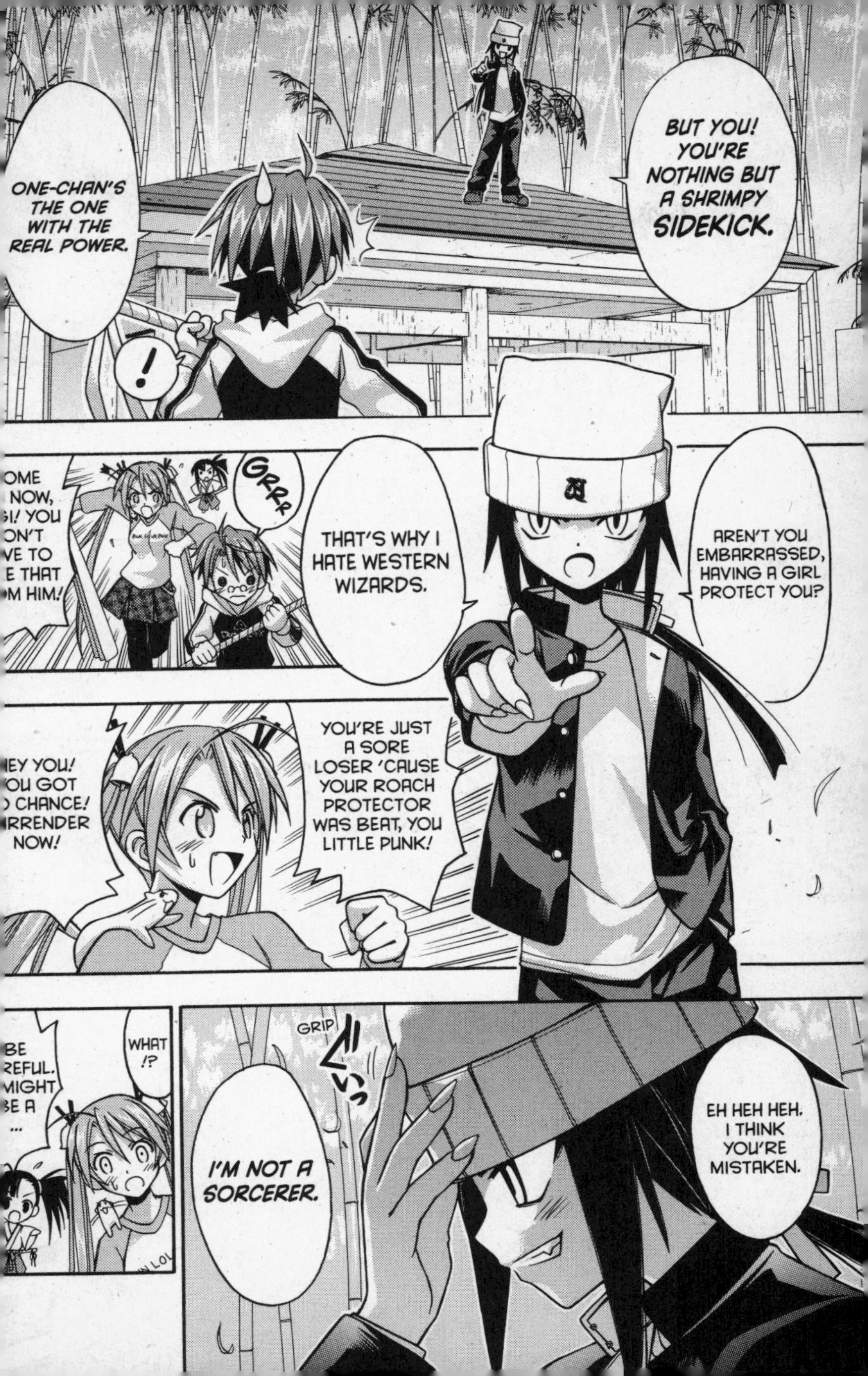
BUT YOU! YOU'RE NOTHING BUT A SHRIMPY SIDEKICK.
ONE-CHAN'S THE ONE WITH THE REAL POWER.
!
AREN'T YOU EMBARRASSED, HAVING A GIRL PROTECT YOU?
THAT'S WHY I HATE WESTERN WIZARDS.
GRRR
OME NOW, GI! YOU ON'T VE TO E THAT M HIM!
YOU'RE JUST A SORE LOSER 'CAUSE YOUR ROACH PROTECTOR WAS BEAT, YOU LITTLE PUNK!
EY YOU! OU GOT CHANCE! RRENDER NOW!
EH HEH HEH. I THINK YOU'RE MISTAKEN.
GRIP
I'M NOT A SORCERER.
WHAT !?
BE REFUL. MIGHT BE A ...

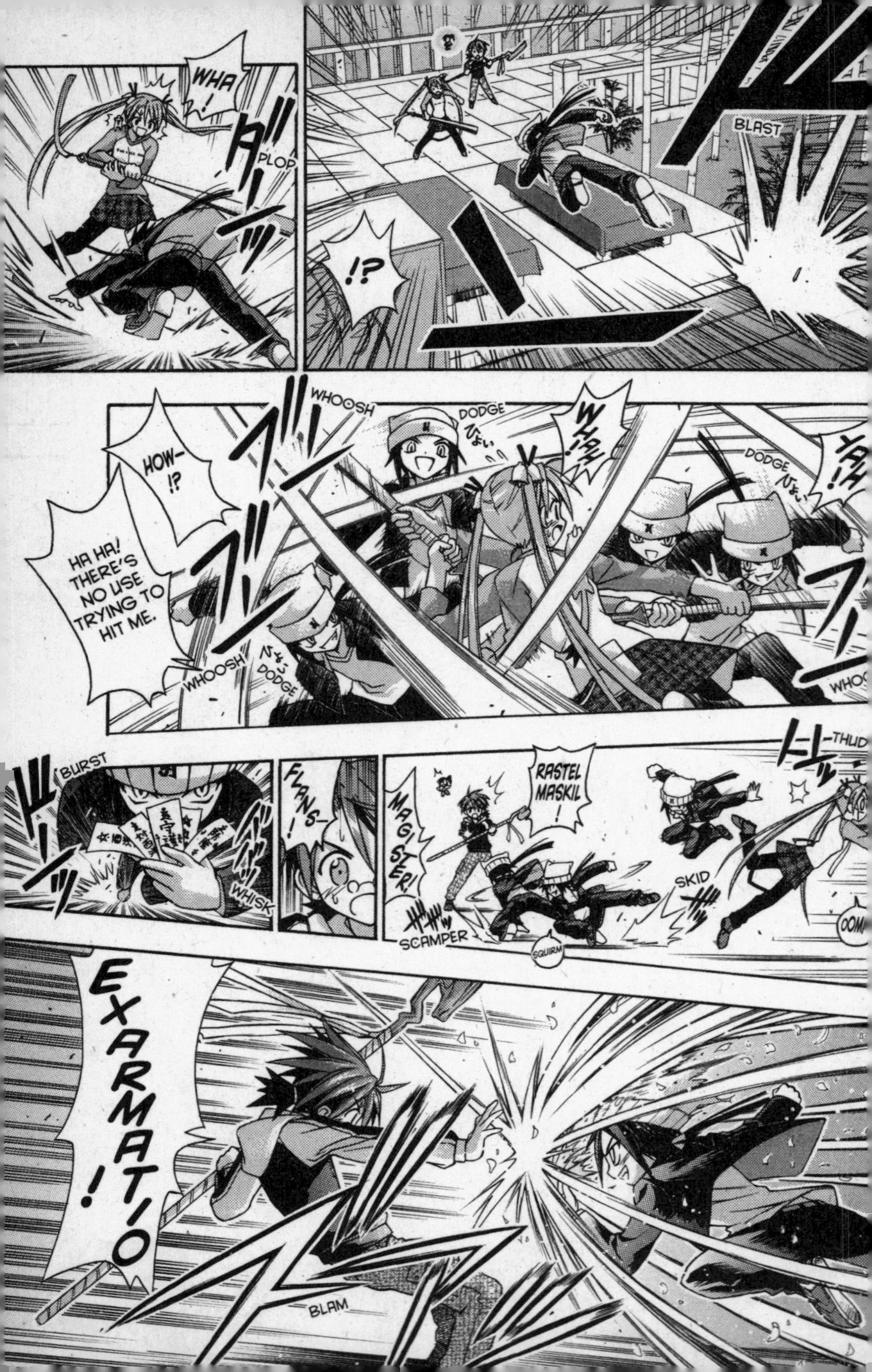

BLAST
!?
WHA!
PLOP
YAH!
DODGE
WHOOS
WHAH!?
DODGE
WHOOSH
HOW-!?
HA HA! THERE'S NO USE TRYING TO HIT ME.
WHOOSH
DODGE
THUD
RASTEL MASKIL!
OOM
SKID
MAGISTER!
SCAMPER
SQUIRM
FLANS-!
BURST
WHISK
EXARMATIO!
BLAM

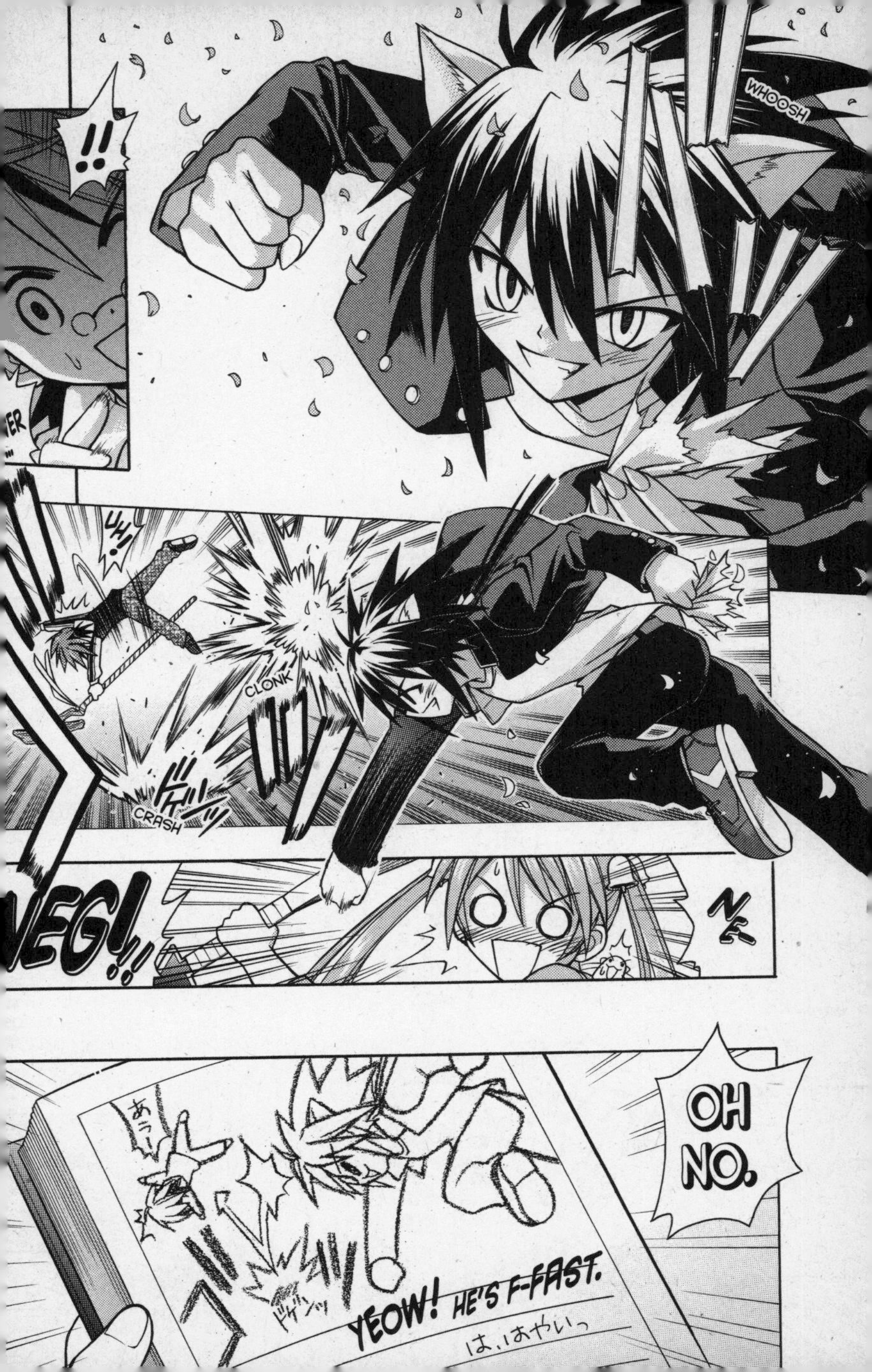
WHOOSH
!!
UH!!
CLONK
CRASH
NE-
NEG!!!
OH NO.
YEOW! HE'S F-FAST.
は、はやいっ

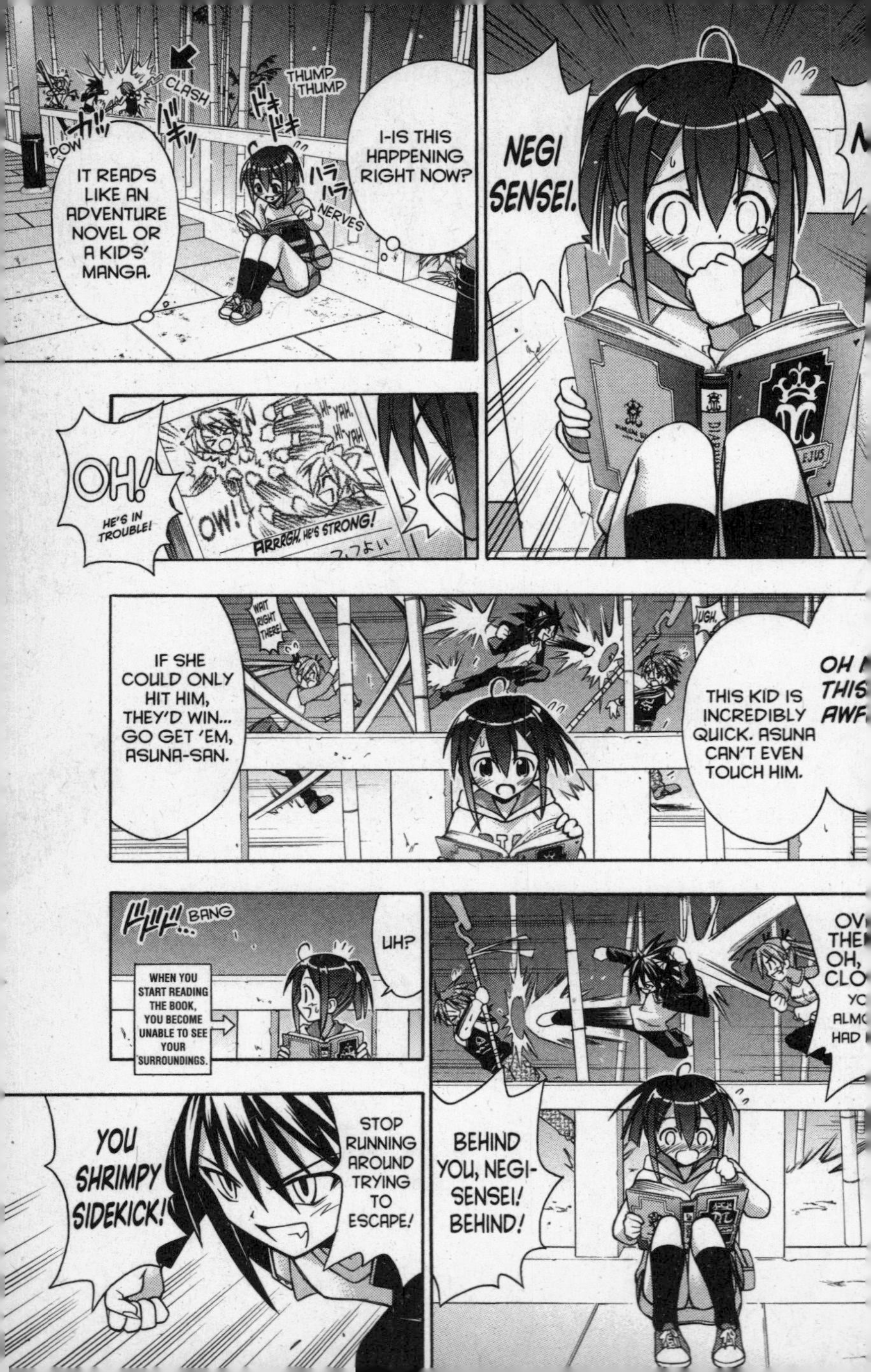
NEGI SENSEI.
I-IS THIS HAPPENING RIGHT NOW?
THUMP THUMP
CLASH
POW
NERVES
IT READS LIKE AN ADVENTURE NOVEL OR A KIDS' MANGA.
HI-YAH, HI-YAH
OW!
ARRRGH, HE'S STRONG!
OH!
HE'S IN TROUBLE!
OH
THIS
AWF
UGH.
THIS KID IS INCREDIBLY QUICK. ASUNA CAN'T EVEN TOUCH HIM.
WAIT RIGHT THERE!
IF SHE COULD ONLY HIT HIM, THEY'D WIN... GO GET 'EM, ASUNA-SAN.
OV
THE
OH,
CLO
YO
ALMO
HAD
UH?
BANG
WHEN YOU START READING THE BOOK, YOU BECOME UNABLE TO SEE YOUR SURROUNDINGS.
BEHIND YOU, NEGI-SENSEI! BEHIND!
STOP RUNNING AROUND TRYING TO ESCAPE!
YOU SHRIMPY SIDEKICK!

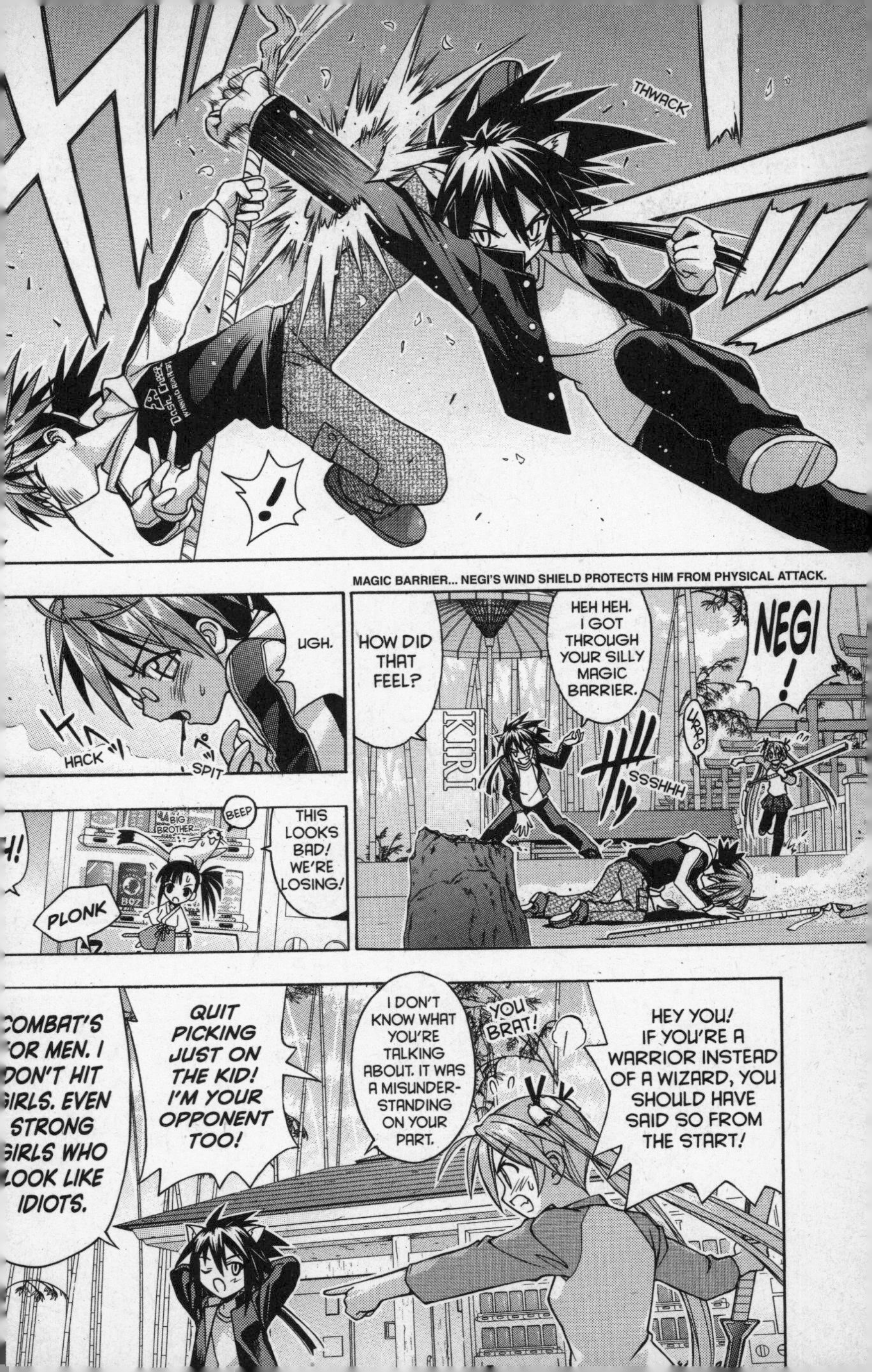
THWACK
!
MAGIC BARRIER... NEGI'S WIND SHIELD PROTECTS HIM FROM PHYSICAL ATTACK.
NEGI!
URRG
SSSHHH
HEH HEH. I GOT THROUGH YOUR SILLY MAGIC BARRIER.
HOW DID THAT FEEL?
KIRI
UGH.
HACK
SPIT
THIS LOOKS BAD! WE'RE LOSING!
BEEP
BIG BROTHER...
PLONK
HEY YOU! IF YOU'RE A WARRIOR INSTEAD OF A WIZARD, YOU SHOULD HAVE SAID SO FROM THE START!
YOU BRAT!
I DON'T KNOW WHAT YOU'RE TALKING ABOUT. IT WAS A MISUNDER-STANDING ON YOUR PART.
QUIT PICKING JUST ON THE KID! I'M YOUR OPPONENT TOO!
COMBAT'S FOR MEN. I DON'T HIT GIRLS. EVEN STRONG GIRLS WHO LOOK LIKE IDIOTS.

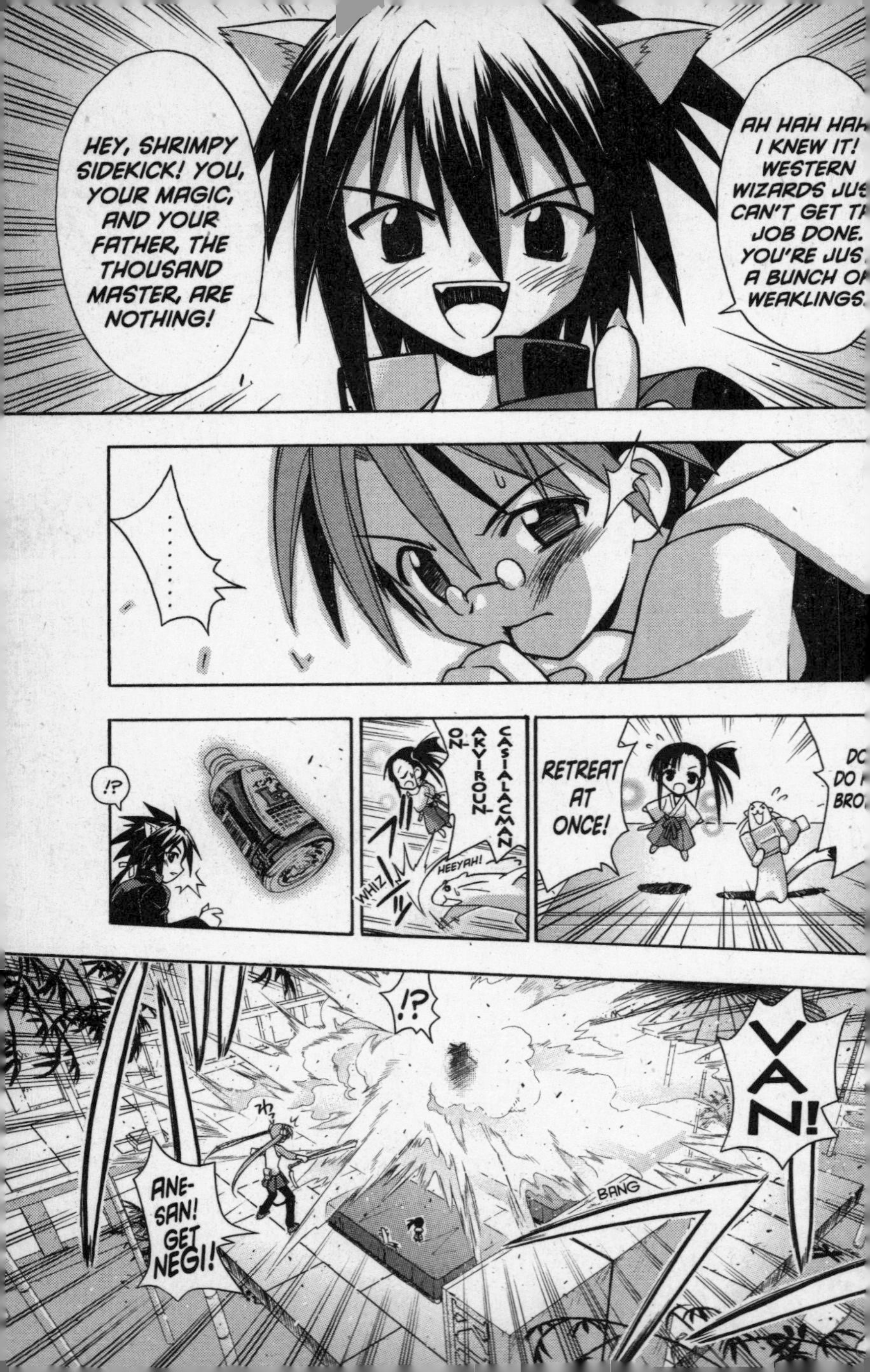
AH HAH HAH I KNEW IT! WESTERN WIZARDS JUS CAN'T GET T JOB DONE. YOU'RE JUS A BUNCH O WEAKLINGS
HEY, SHRIMPY SIDEKICK! YOU, YOUR MAGIC, AND YOUR FATHER, THE THOUSAND MASTER, ARE NOTHING!
......
DO DO BRO
RETREAT AT ONCE!
CASIALACMAN
AKVIROUN
ON
HEEYAH!
WHIZ
!?
VAN!
!?
BANG
ANE-SAN! GET NEGI!

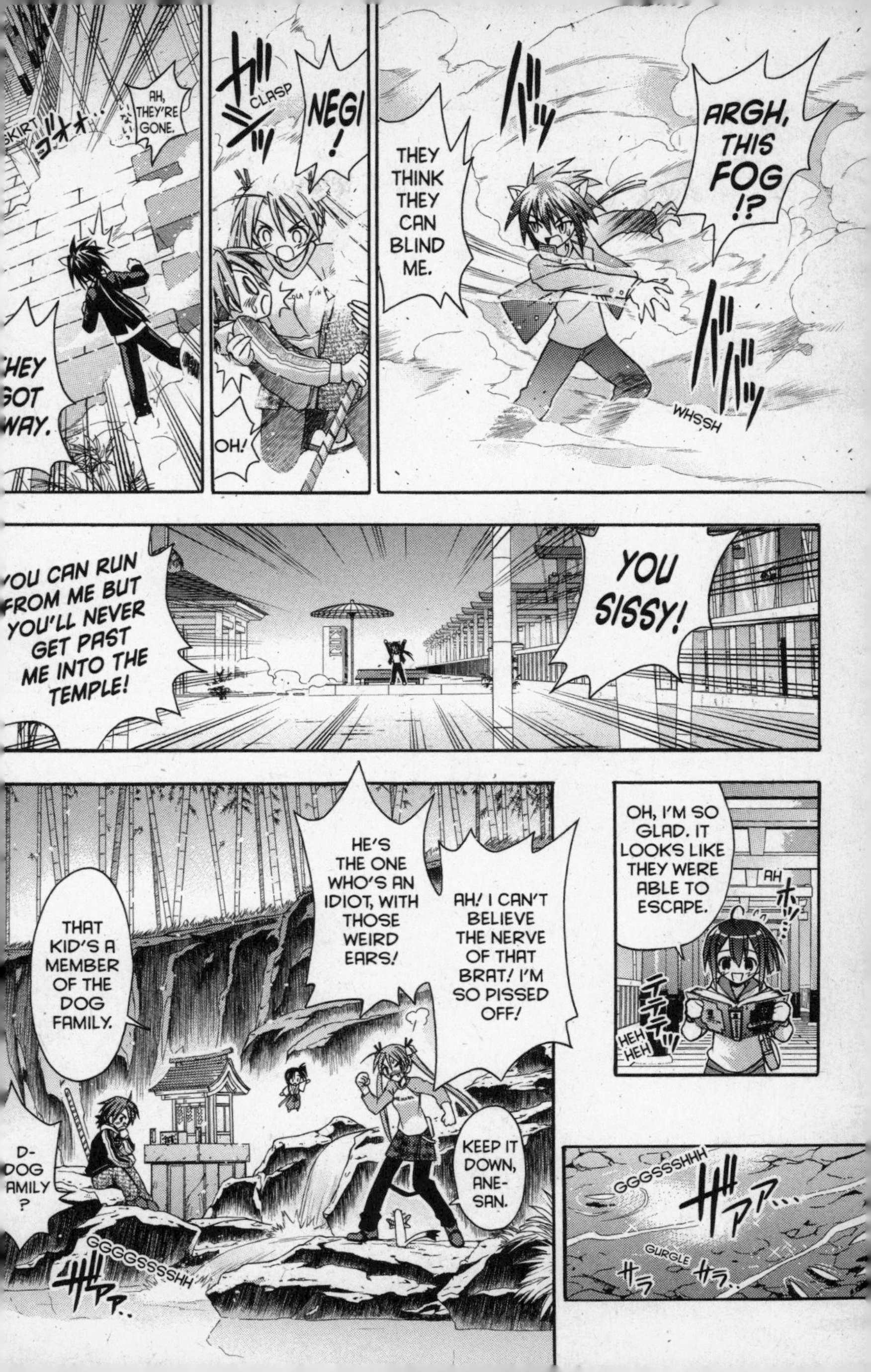
ARGH, THIS FOG!?
THEY THINK THEY CAN BLIND ME.
バッ
WHSSH
NEGI!
CLASP
OH!
AH, THEY'RE GONE.
いない…
SKIRT
HEY GOT WAY.
YOU SISSY!
OU CAN RUN FROM ME BUT YOU'LL NEVER GET PAST ME INTO THE TEMPLE!
OH, I'M SO GLAD. IT LOOKS LIKE THEY WERE ABLE TO ESCAPE.
AH
HEH HEH
GGGSSSHHH
GURGLE
AH! I CAN'T BELIEVE THE NERVE OF THAT BRAT! I'M SO PISSED OFF!
HE'S THE ONE WHO'S AN IDIOT, WITH THOSE WEIRD EARS!
THAT KID'S A MEMBER OF THE DOG FAMILY.
KEEP IT DOWN, ANE-SAN.
D-DOG AMILY?
GGGGSSSSHH

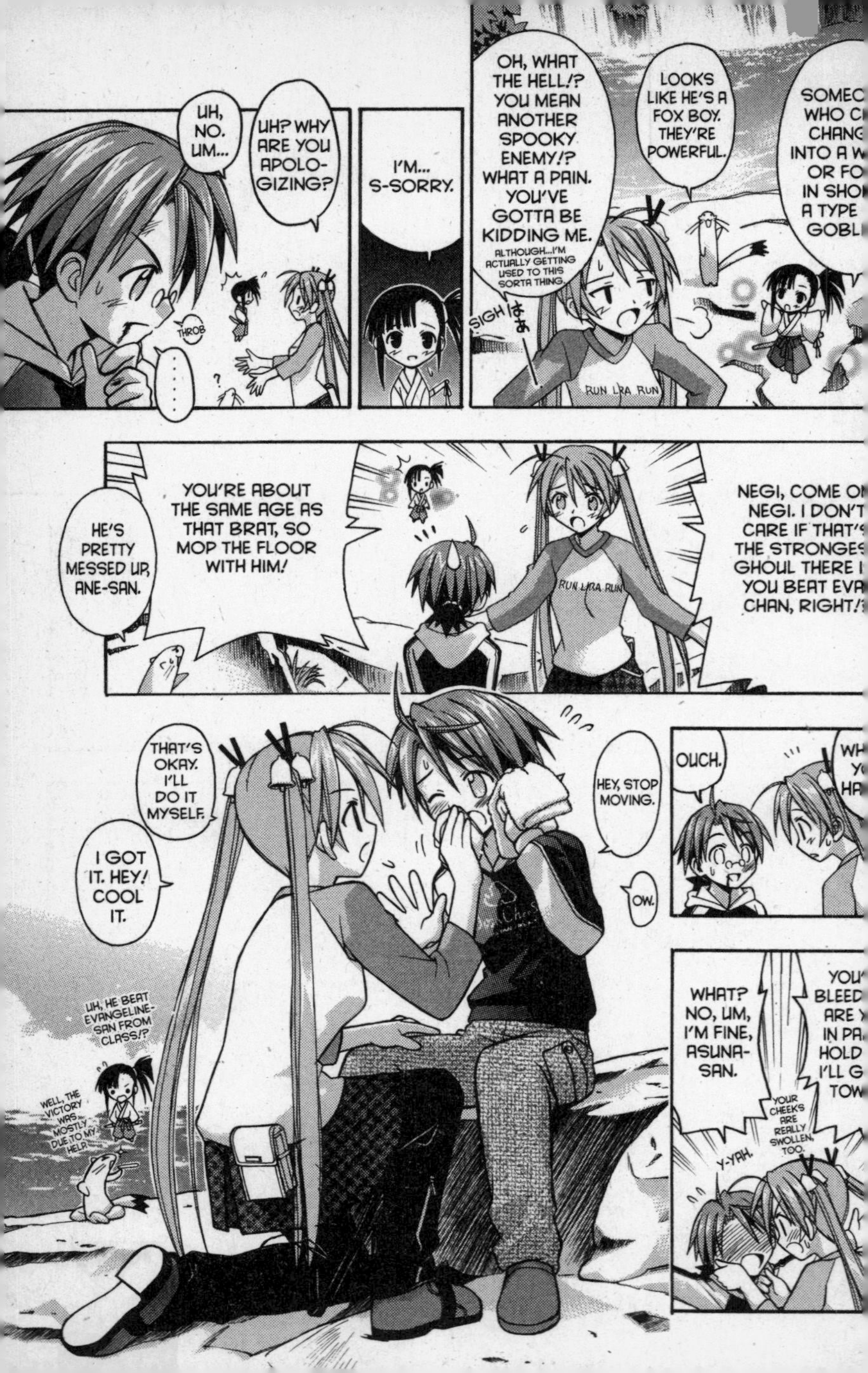

SOMEC WHO C CHANG INTO A W OR FO IN SHO A TYPE GOBL
LOOKS LIKE HE'S A FOX BOY. THEY'RE POWERFUL.
OH, WHAT THE HELL!? YOU MEAN ANOTHER SPOOKY ENEMY!? WHAT A PAIN. YOU'VE GOTTA BE KIDDING ME.
ALTHOUGH...I'M ACTUALLY GETTING USED TO THIS SORTA THING.
SIGH はぁ
I'M... S-SORRY.
UH? WHY ARE YOU APOLOGIZING?
UH, NO. UM...
THROB
......
?
NEGI, COME ON NEGI. I DON'T CARE IF THAT'S THE STRONGES GHOUL THERE I YOU BEAT EVA CHAN, RIGHT!?
YOU'RE ABOUT THE SAME AGE AS THAT BRAT, SO MOP THE FLOOR WITH HIM!
HE'S PRETTY MESSED UP, ANE-SAN.
WH Y HA
OUCH.
YOU' BLEED ARE Y IN PA HOLD I'LL G TOW
WHAT? NO, UM, I'M FINE, ASUNA-SAN.
YOUR CHEEKS ARE REALLY SWOLLEN, TOO.
Y-YAH.
HEY, STOP MOVING.
OW.
THAT'S OKAY. I'LL DO IT MYSELF.
I GOT IT. HEY! COOL IT.
UH, HE BEAT EVANGELINE-SAN FROM CLASS!?
WELL, THE VICTORY WAS MOSTLY DUE TO MY HELP.

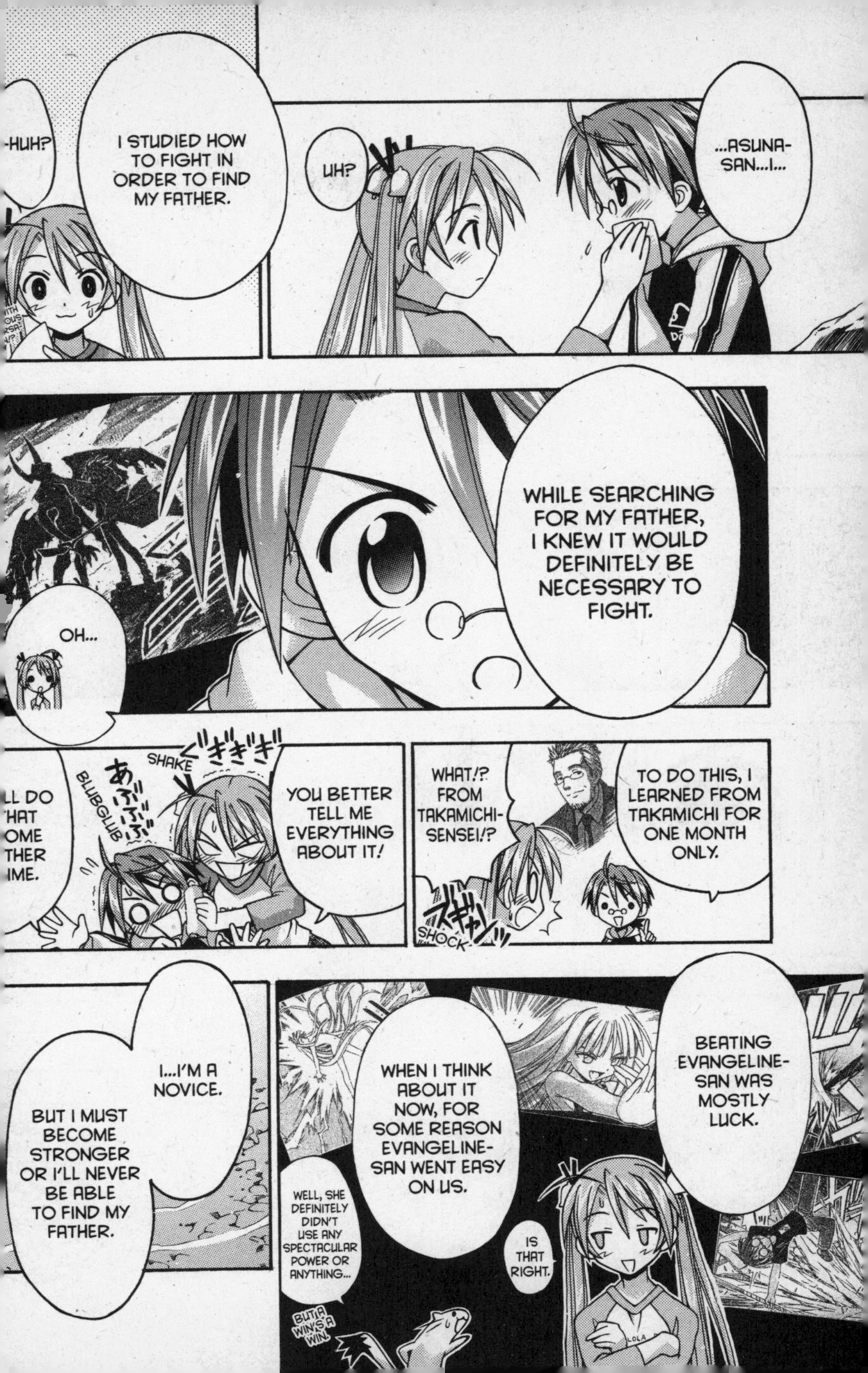
...ASUNA-SAN...I...
UH?
I STUDIED HOW TO FIGHT IN ORDER TO FIND MY FATHER.
-HUH?
WHILE SEARCHING FOR MY FATHER, I KNEW IT WOULD DEFINITELY BE NECESSARY TO FIGHT.
OH...
TO DO THIS, I LEARNED FROM TAKAMICHI FOR ONE MONTH ONLY.
WHAT!? FROM TAKAMICHI-SENSEI!?
SHOCK
YOU BETTER TELL ME EVERYTHING ABOUT IT!
SHAKE
BLUBBLUB
BEATING EVANGELINE-SAN WAS MOSTLY LUCK.
WHEN I THINK ABOUT IT NOW, FOR SOME REASON EVANGELINE-SAN WENT EASY ON US.
IS THAT RIGHT.
WELL, SHE DEFINITELY DIDN'T USE ANY SPECTACULAR POWER OR ANYTHING...
BUT A WIN'S A WIN.
I...I'M A NOVICE.
BUT I MUST BECOME STRONGER OR I'LL NEVER BE ABLE TO FIND MY FATHER.

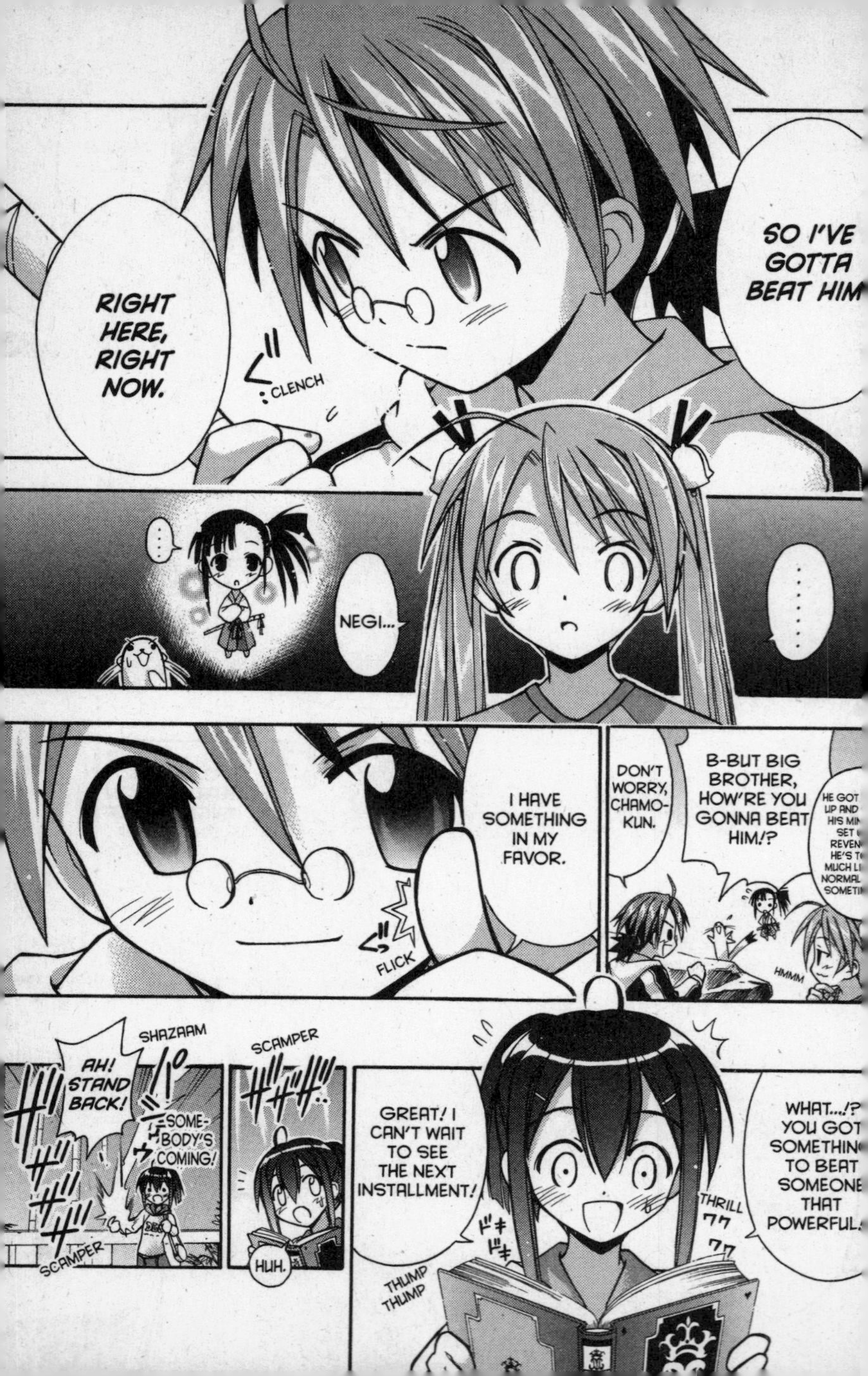
SO I'VE GOTTA BEAT HIM
RIGHT HERE, RIGHT NOW.
CLENCH
......
NEGI...
...
B-BUT BIG BROTHER, HOW'RE YOU GONNA BEAT HIM!?
DON'T WORRY, CHAMO-KUN.
HMMM
I HAVE SOMETHING IN MY FAVOR.
FLICK
WHAT...!? YOU GOT SOMETHING TO BEAT SOMEONE THAT POWERFUL!
THRILL
GREAT! I CAN'T WAIT TO SEE THE NEXT INSTALLMENT!
THUMP THUMP
SCAMPER
HUH.
SHAZAAM
AH! STAND BACK!
SOME-BODY'S COMING!
SCAMPER

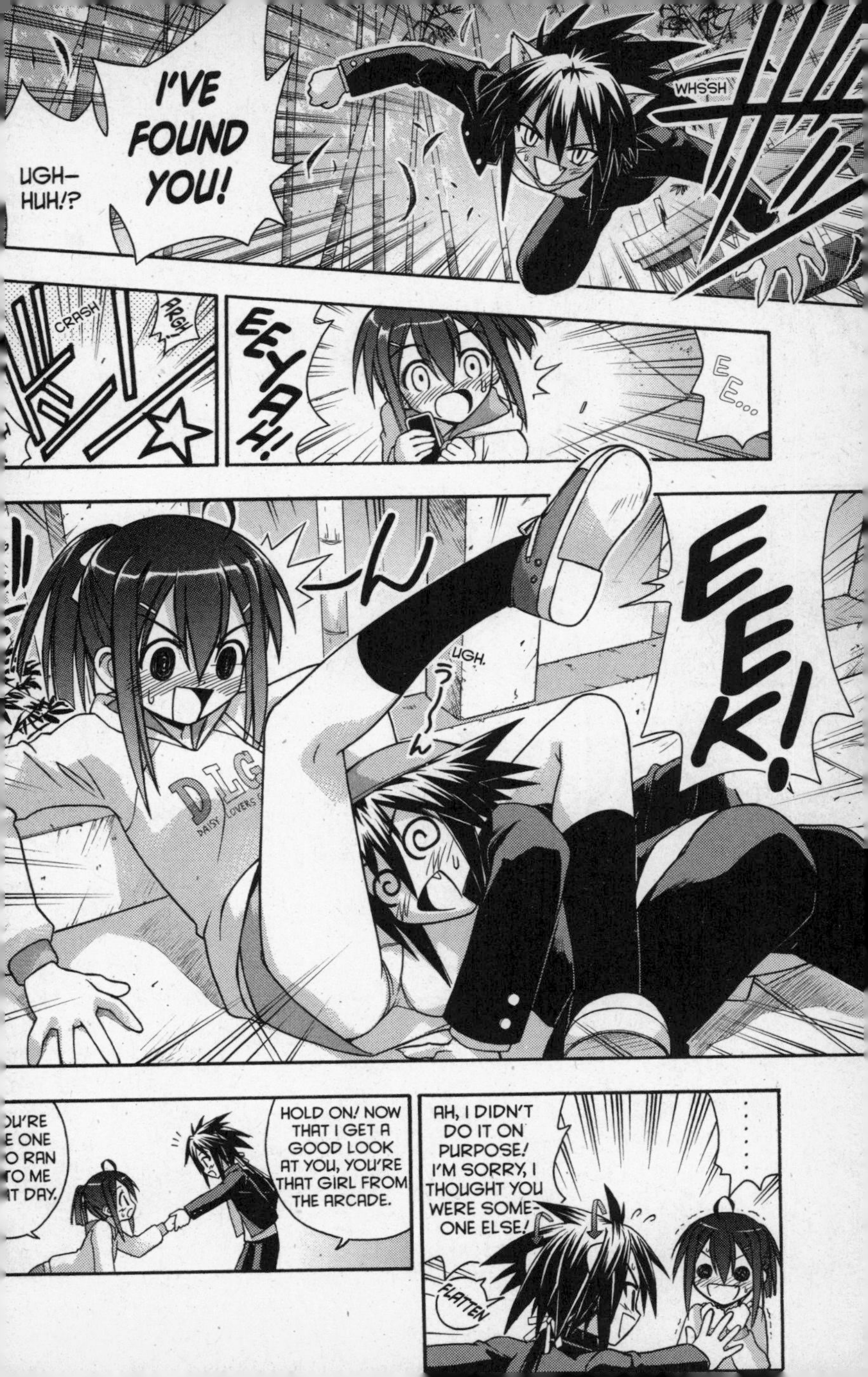
WHSSH
I'VE FOUND YOU!
UGH—HUH!?
E E...
EEYAAH!
ARGH
CRASH
EEEK!
UGH.
......
AH, I DIDN'T DO IT ON PURPOSE! I'M SORRY, I THOUGHT YOU WERE SOME-ONE ELSE!
FLATTEN
HOLD ON! NOW THAT I GET A GOOD LOOK AT YOU, YOU'RE THAT GIRL FROM THE ARCADE.
OU'RE E ONE O RAN TO ME AT DAY.

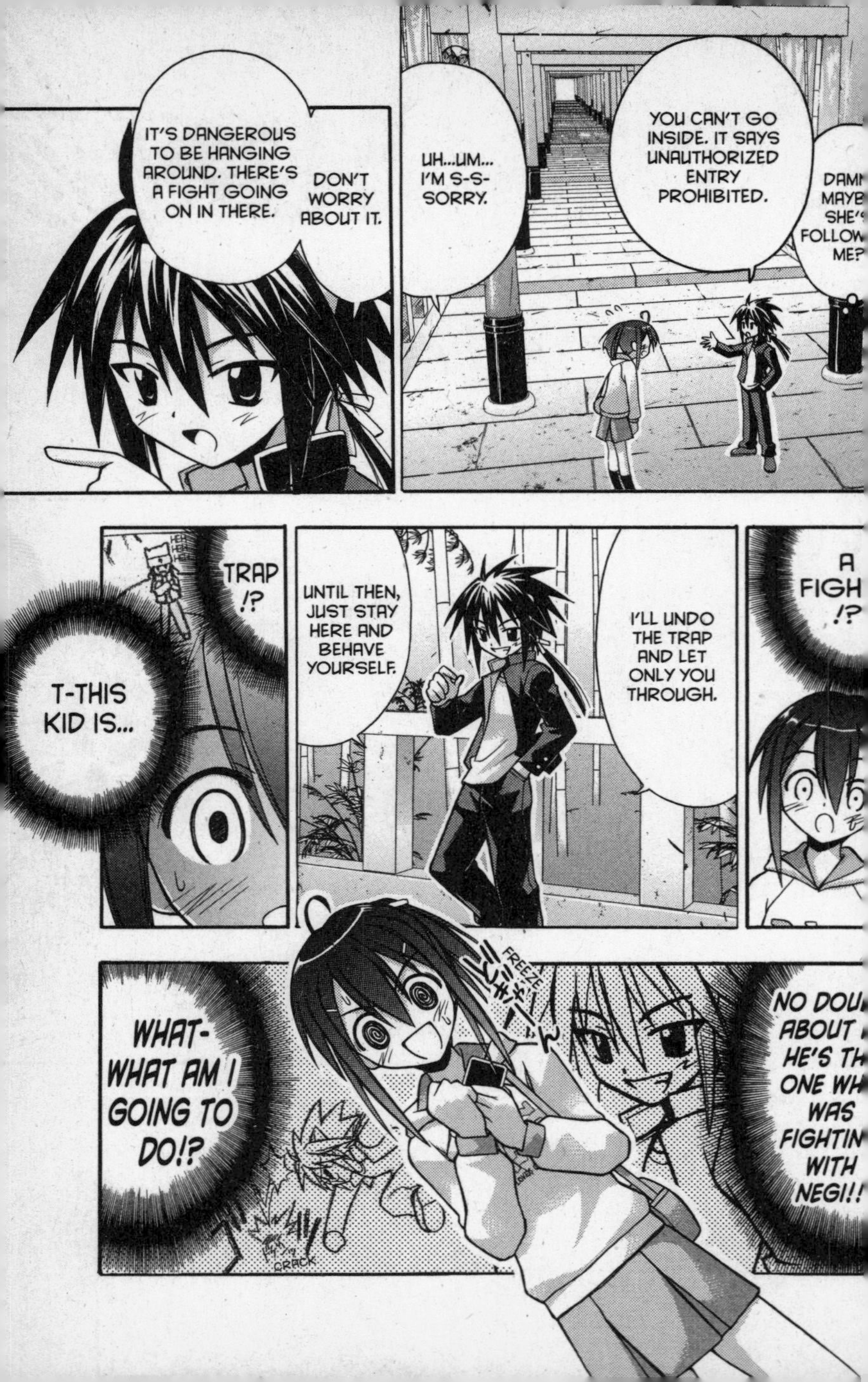
DAM MAYB SHE'S FOLLOW ME?
YOU CAN'T GO INSIDE. IT SAYS UNAUTHORIZED ENTRY PROHIBITED.
UH...UM... I'M S-S-SORRY.
DON'T WORRY ABOUT IT.
IT'S DANGEROUS TO BE HANGING AROUND. THERE'S A FIGHT GOING ON IN THERE.
A FIGH !?
I'LL UNDO THE TRAP AND LET ONLY YOU THROUGH.
UNTIL THEN, JUST STAY HERE AND BEHAVE YOURSELF.
TRAP !?
T-THIS KID IS...
NO DOU ABOUT HE'S TH ONE WH WAS FIGHTIN WITH NEGI!!
FREEZE
WHAT- WHAT AM I GOING TO DO!?
CRACK

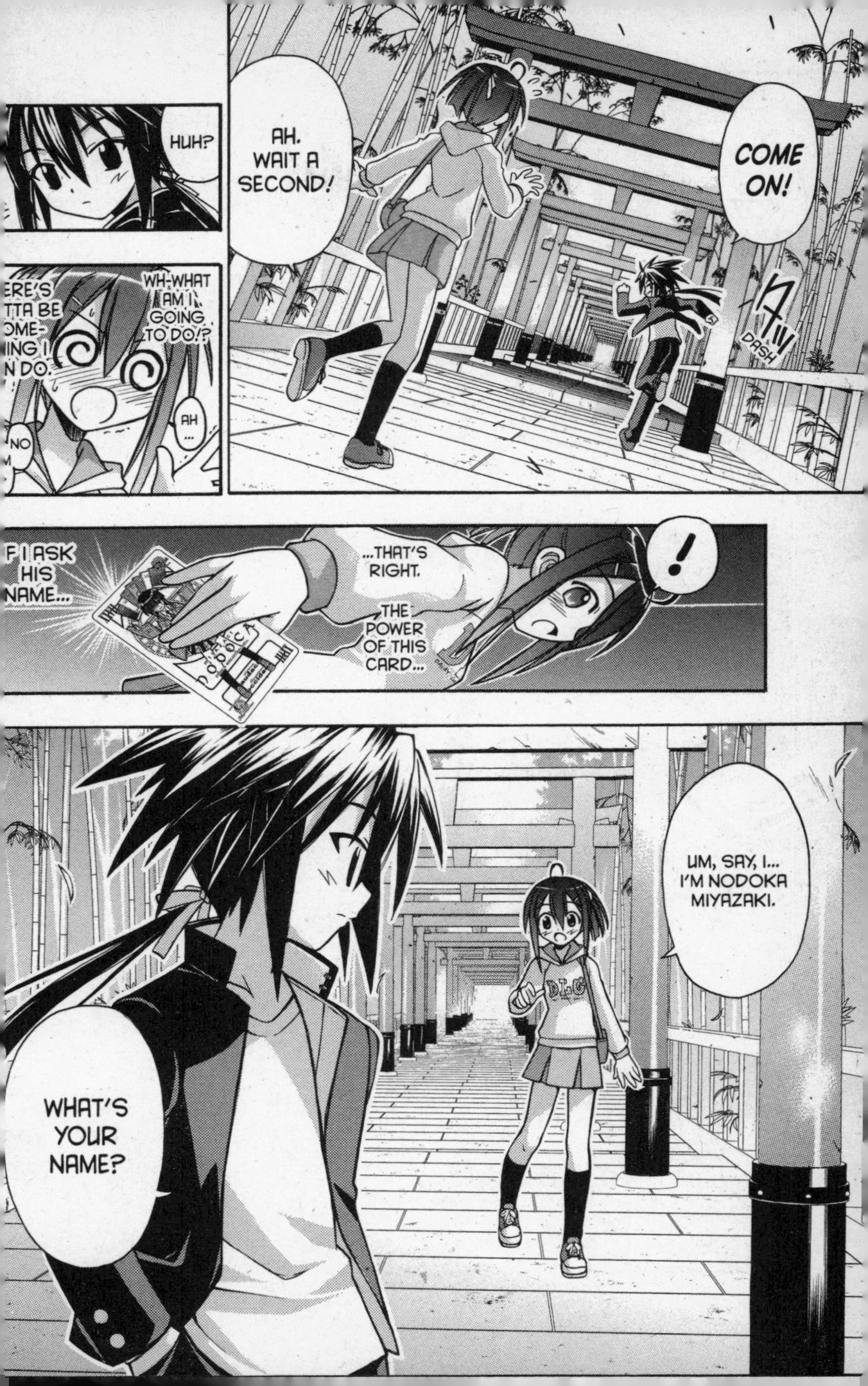
COME ON!
DASH
AH. WAIT A SECOND!
HUH?
WH-WHAT AM I GOING TO DO!?
ERE'S TTA BE OME- ING I N DO.
AH ...
NO M
!
...THAT'S RIGHT.
THE POWER OF THIS CARD...
F I ASK HIS NAME...
UM, SAY, I... I'M NODOKA MIYAZAKI.
WHAT'S YOUR NAME?

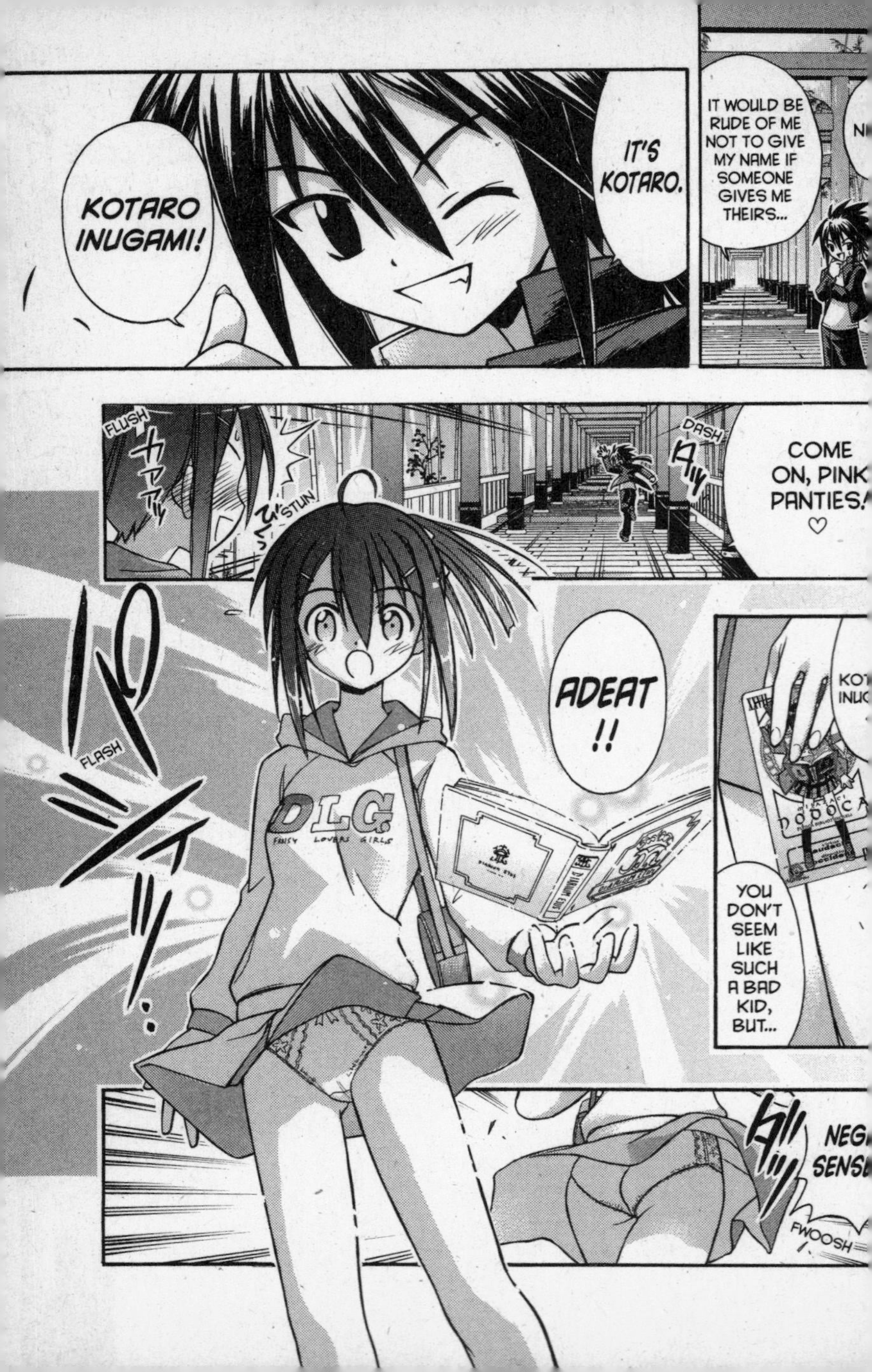
IT WOULD BE RUDE OF ME NOT TO GIVE MY NAME IF SOMEONE GIVES ME THEIRS...
IT'S KOTARO.
KOTARO INUGAMI!
COME ON, PINK PANTIES! ♡
DASH
STUN
FLUSH
YOU DON'T SEEM LIKE SUCH A BAD KID, BUT...
ADEAT !!
D.L.G.
FLASH
FWOOSH

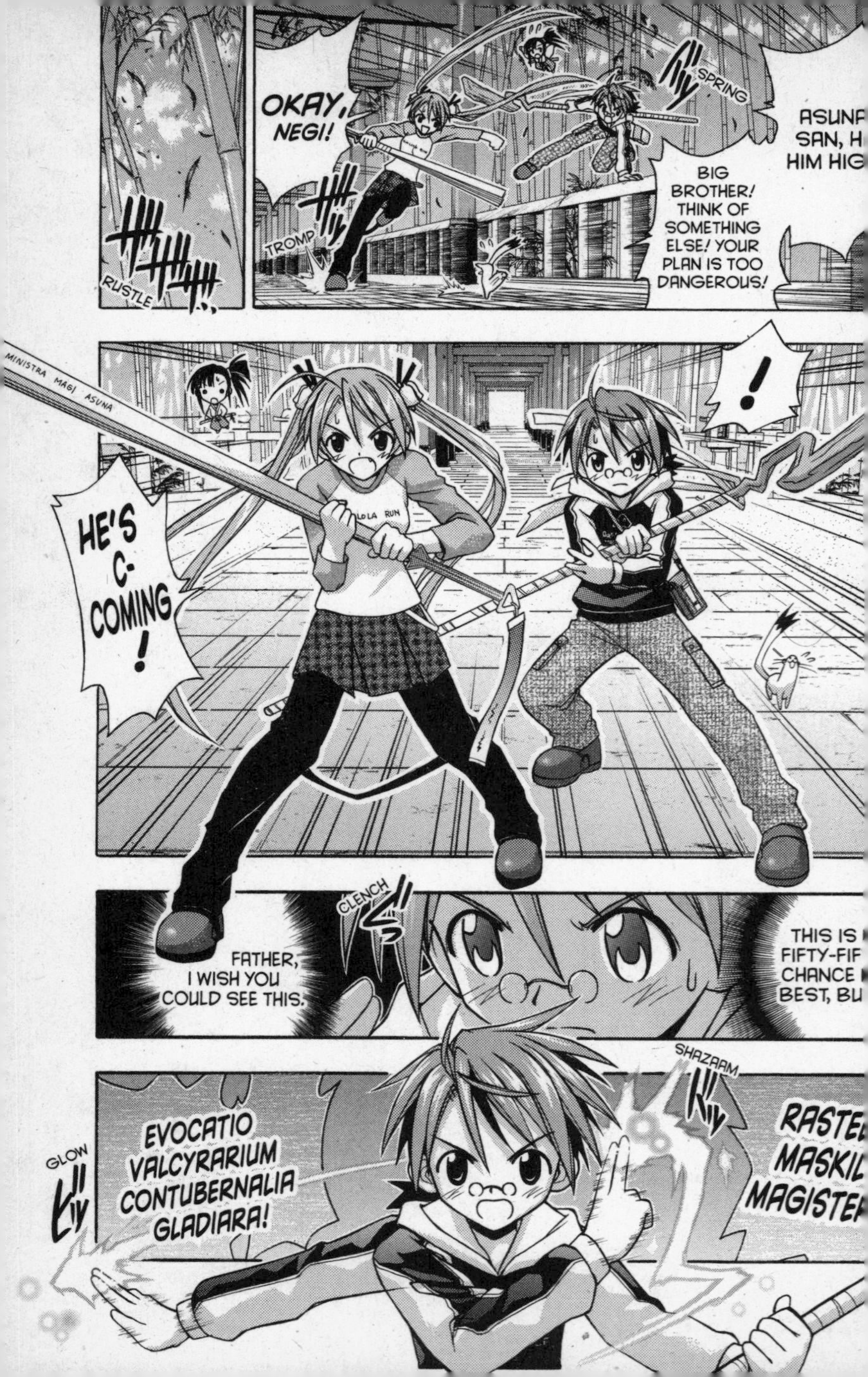

ASUNA SAN, H HIM HIG
SPRING
BIG BROTHER! THINK OF SOMETHING ELSE! YOUR PLAN IS TOO DANGEROUS!
OKAY, NEGI!
TROMP
RUSTLE
!
MINISTRA MAGI ASUNA
LOLA RUN
HE'S C-COMING!
THIS IS FIFTY-FIF CHANCE BEST, BU
CLENCH
FATHER, I WISH YOU COULD SEE THIS.
RASTE MASKIL MAGISTE
SHAZAAM
EVOCATIO VALCYRARIUM CONTUBERNALIA GLADIARA!
GLOW

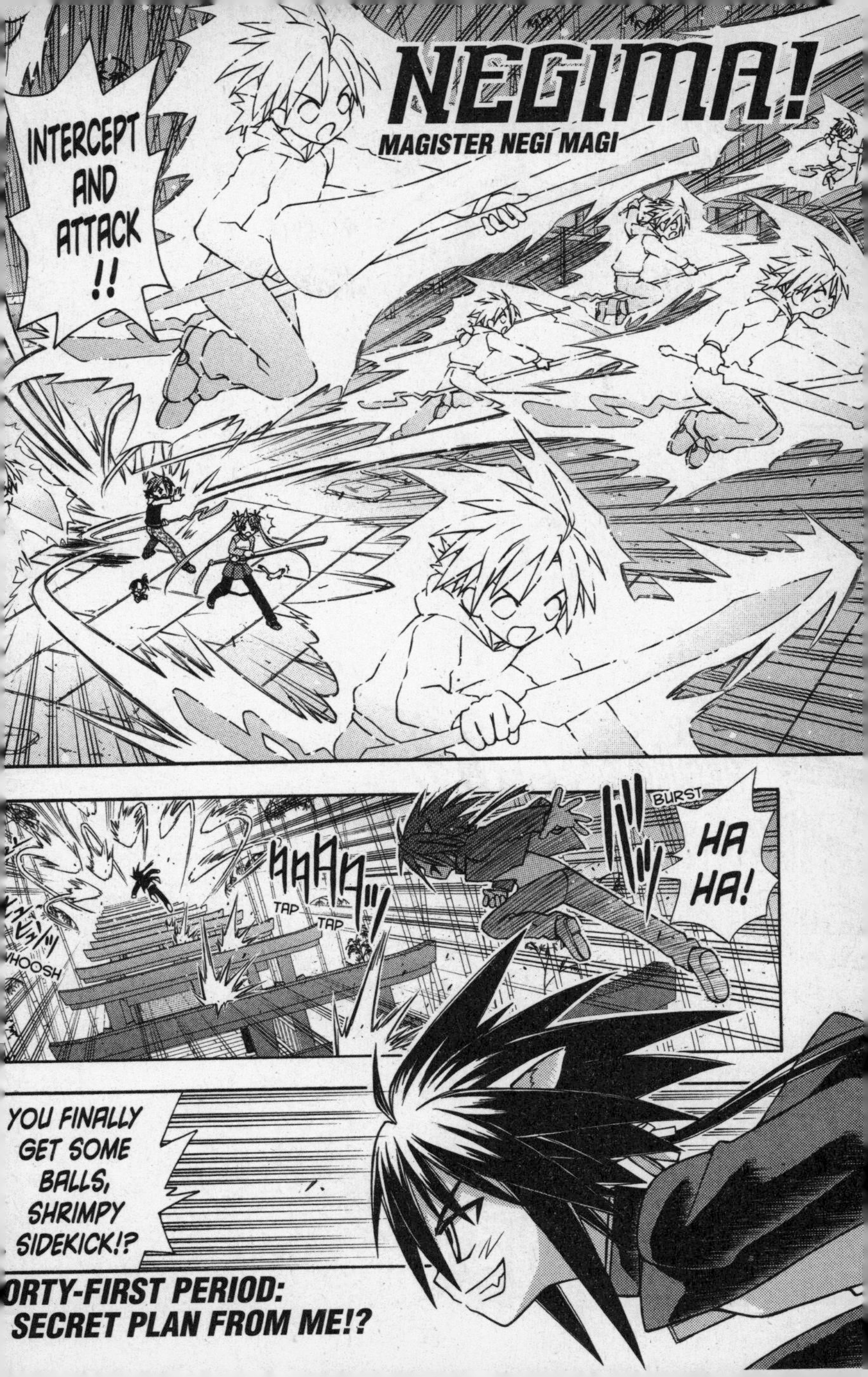
NEGIMA!
MAGISTER NEGI MAGI
INTERCEPT AND ATTACK !!
BURST
HA HA!
TAP
TAP
WHOOSH
YOU FINALLY GET SOME BALLS, SHRIMPY SIDEKICK!?
ORTY-FIRST PERIOD:
SECRET PLAN FROM ME!?

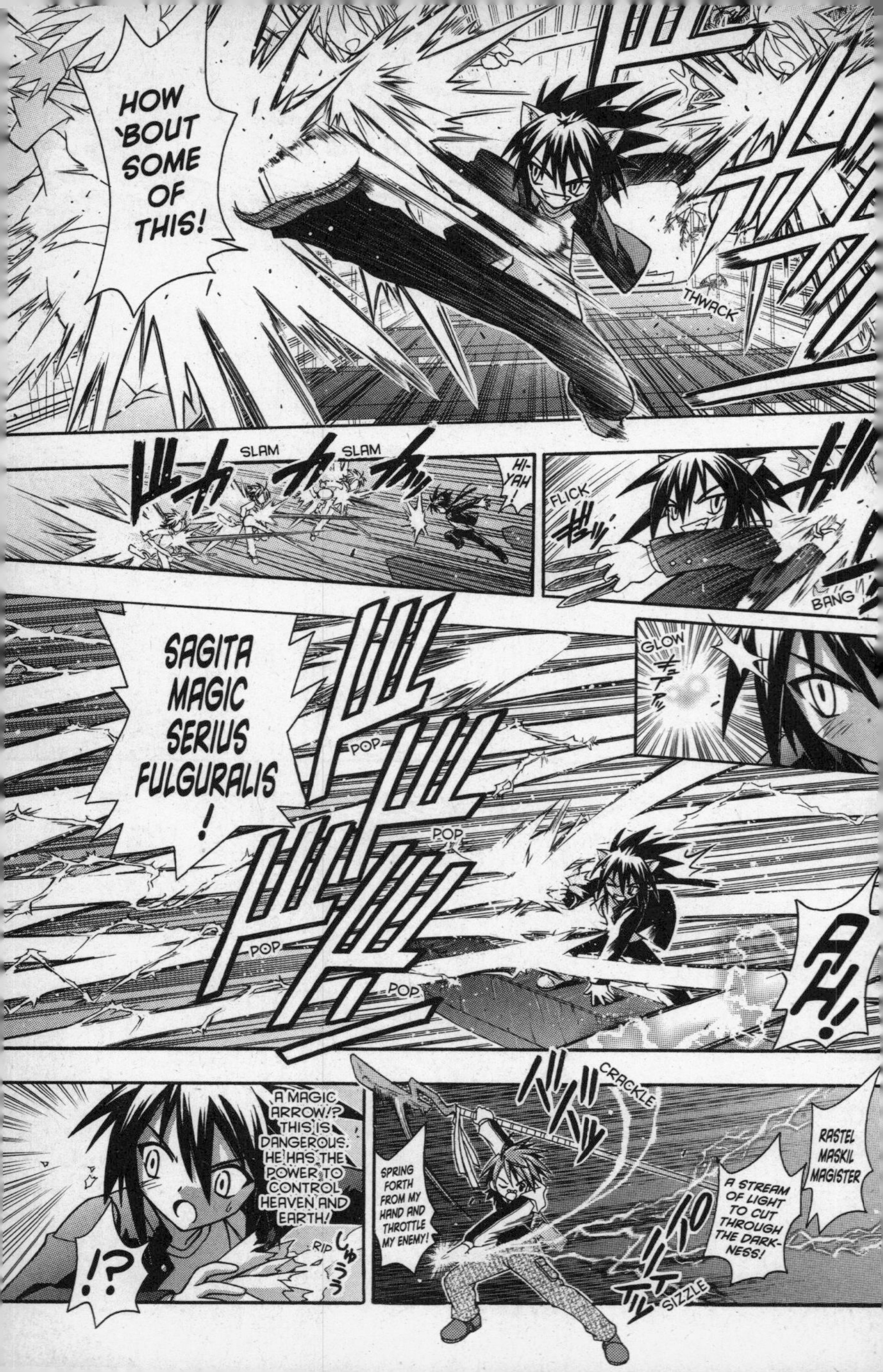
HOW 'BOUT SOME OF THIS!
THWACK
FLICK
BANG
SLAM
SLAM
HI-YAH!
GLOW
SAGITA MAGIC SERIUS FULGURALIS!
POP
POP
POP
POP
AH!
RASTEL MASKIL MAGISTER
A STREAM OF LIGHT TO CUT THROUGH THE DARKNESS!
CRACKLE
SPRING FORTH FROM MY HAND AND THROTTLE MY ENEMY!
SIZZLE
A MAGIC ARROW!? THIS IS DANGEROUS. HE HAS THE POWER TO CONTROL HEAVEN AND EARTH!
RIP
!?

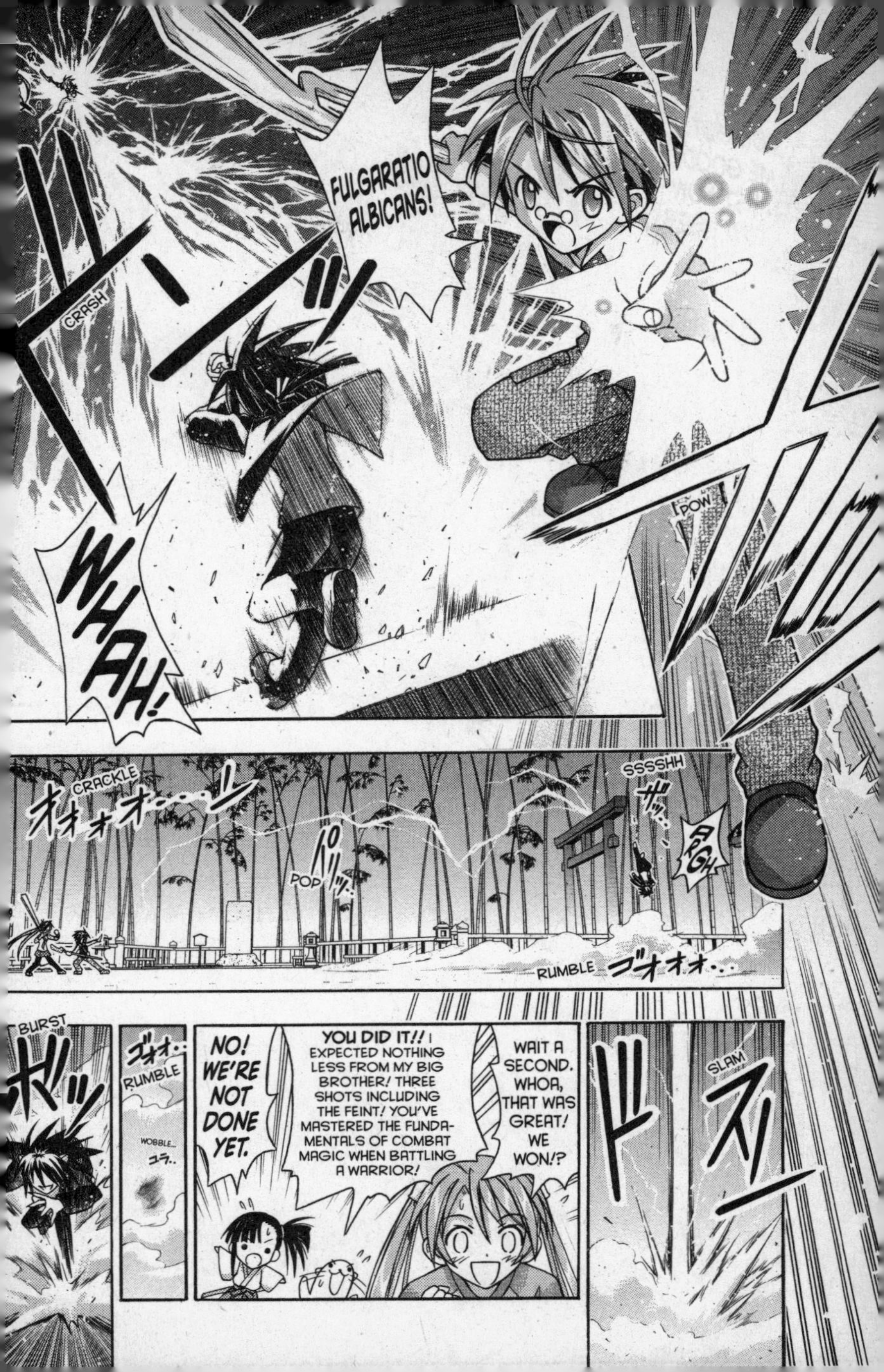
FULGARATIO ALBICANS!
CRASH
POW
WHAAH!
SSSSHH
ARGH
CRACKLE
POP
RUMBLE
SLAM
WAIT A SECOND. WHOA, THAT WAS GREAT! WE WON!?
YOU DID IT!! I EXPECTED NOTHING LESS FROM MY BIG BROTHER! THREE SHOTS INCLUDING THE FEINT! YOU'VE MASTERED THE FUNDAMENTALS OF COMBAT MAGIC WHEN BATTLING A WARRIOR!
NO! WE'RE NOT DONE YET.
RUMBLE
WOBBLE...
BURST

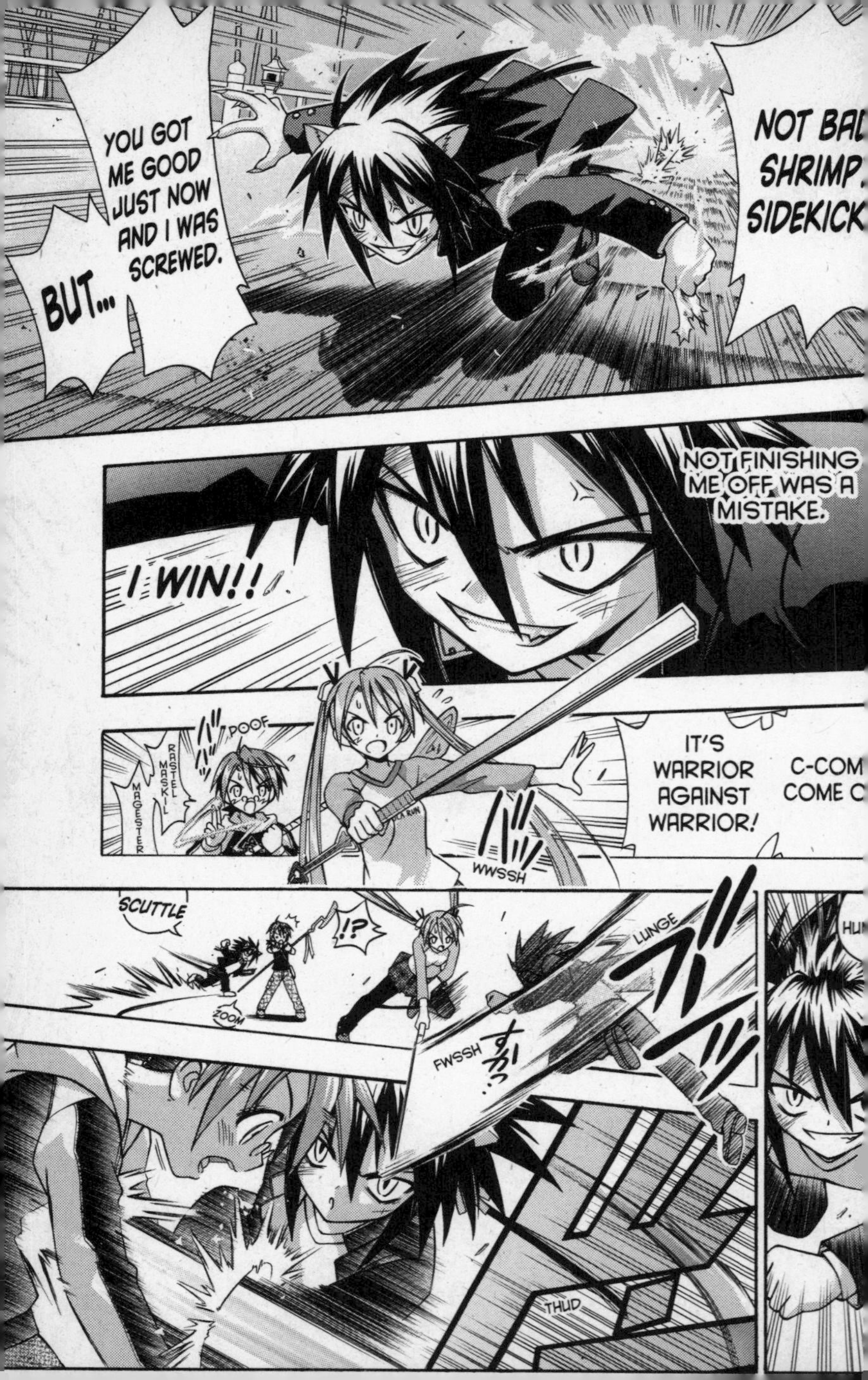
NOT BA
SHRIMP.
SIDEKICK
YOU GOT ME GOOD JUST NOW AND I WAS SCREWED.
BUT...
NOT FINISHING ME OFF WAS A MISTAKE.
I WIN!!
C-COM
COME C
IT'S WARRIOR AGAINST WARRIOR!
POOF
RASTEL MASKIL MAGESTER
WWSSH
HU
LUNGE
!?
SCUTTLE
ZOOM
FWSSH
THUD

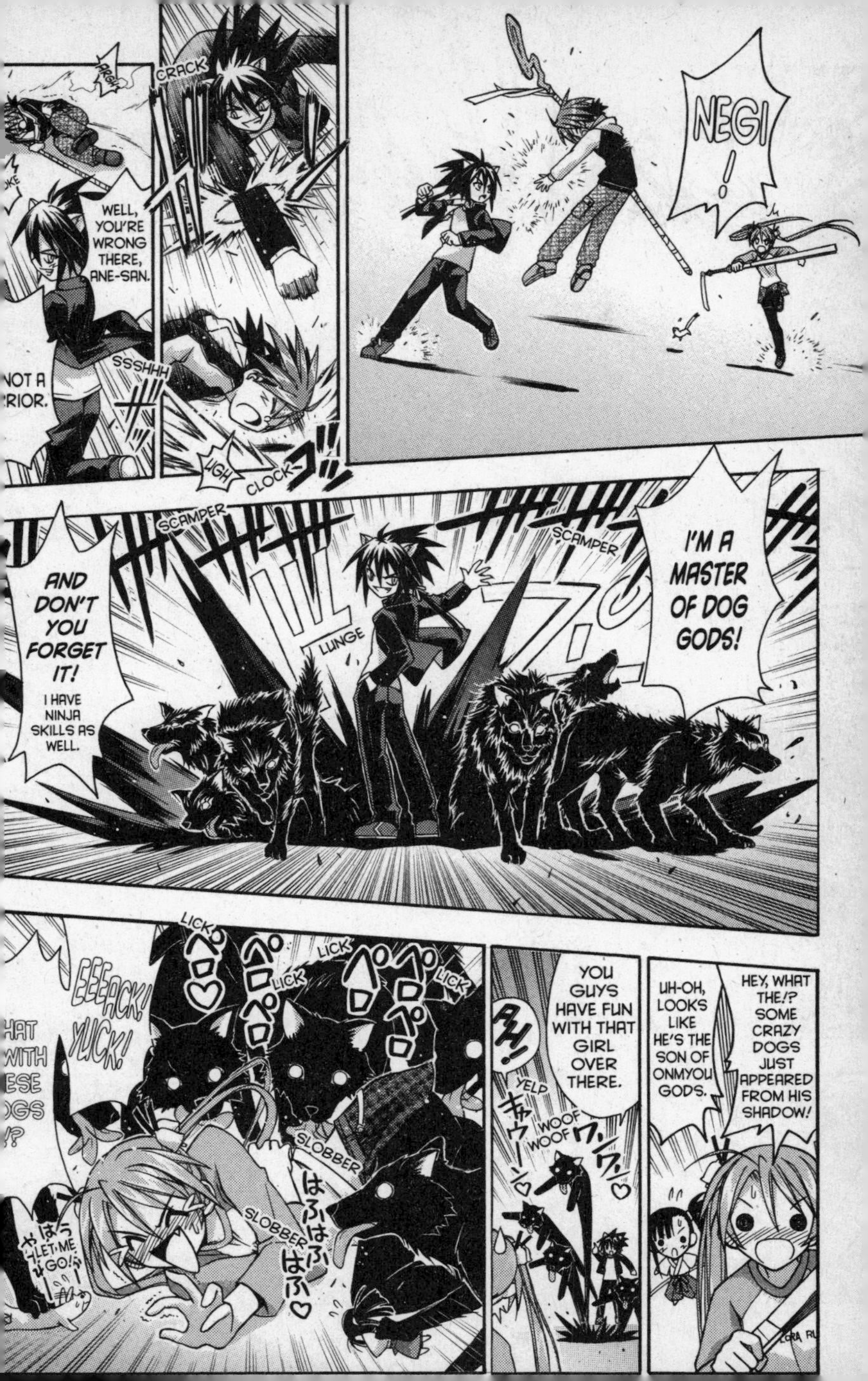
NEGI!
CRACK
ARGH
SSSHHH
UGH
CLOCK
WELL, YOU'RE WRONG THERE, ANE-SAN.
I'M A MASTER OF DOG GODS!
SCAMPER
SCAMPER
LUNGE
AND DON'T YOU FORGET IT!
I HAVE NINJA SKILLS AS WELL.
HEY, WHAT THE!? SOME CRAZY DOGS JUST APPEARED FROM HIS SHADOW!
UH-OH, LOOKS LIKE HE'S THE SON OF ONMYOU GODS.
YOU GUYS HAVE FUN WITH THAT GIRL OVER THERE.
AH!
YELP
WOOF WOOF
LICK
LICK
LICK
LICK
EEEEACK!
YUCK!
SLOBBER
SLOBBER
LET ME GO!

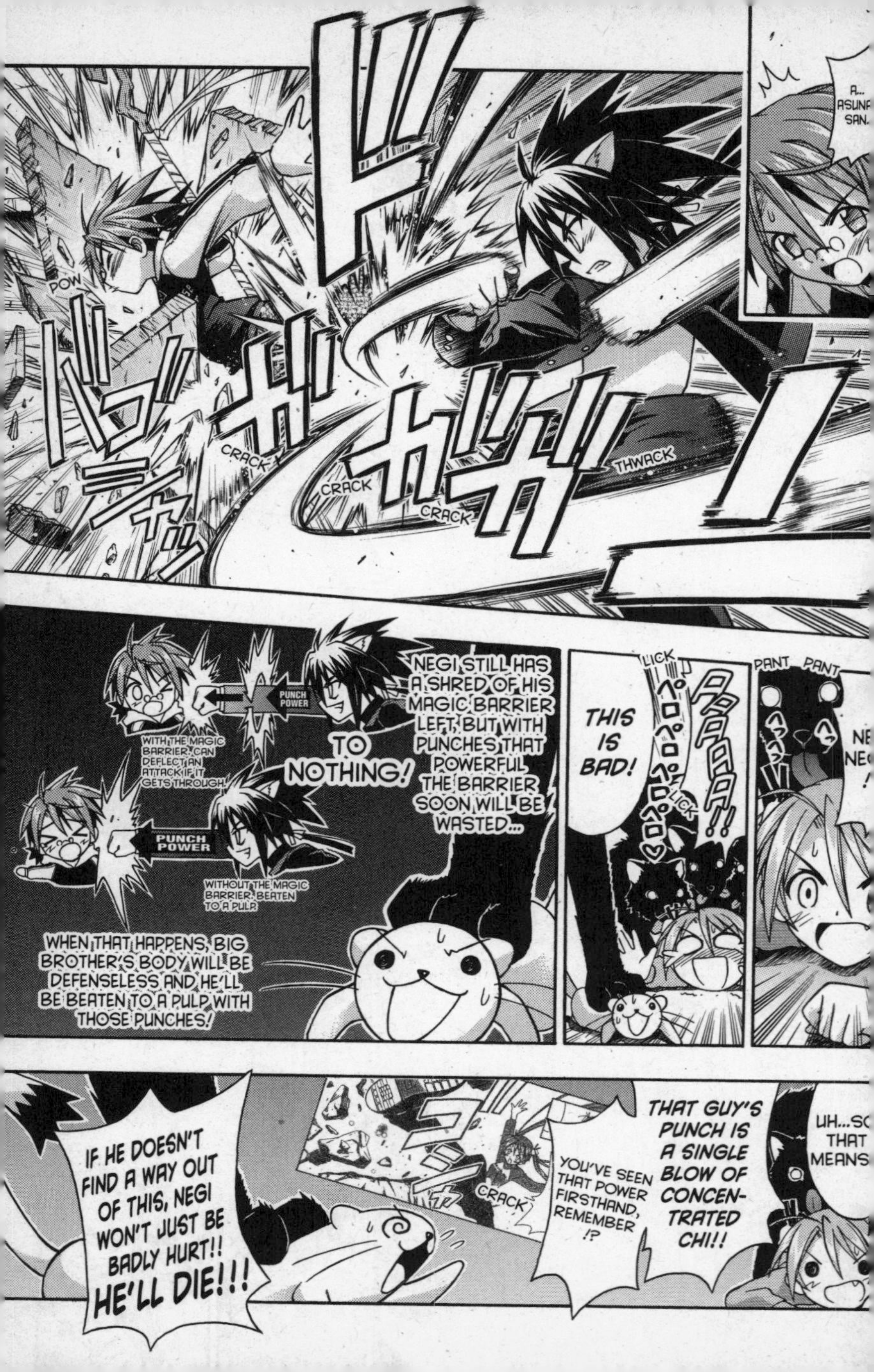
A... ASUNA-SAN.
THWACK
CRACK
CRACK
CRACK
POW
PANT PANT
NE NEG!
THIS IS BAD!
LICK
LICK
NEGI STILL HAS A SHRED OF HIS MAGIC BARRIER LEFT, BUT WITH PUNCHES THAT POWERFUL THE BARRIER SOON WILL BE WASTED...
TO NOTHING!
PUNCH POWER
WITH THE MAGIC BARRIER, CAN DEFLECT AN ATTACK IF IT GETS THROUGH.
PUNCH POWER
WITHOUT THE MAGIC BARRIER, BEATEN TO A PULP.
WHEN THAT HAPPENS, BIG BROTHER'S BODY WILL BE DEFENSELESS AND HE'LL BE BEATEN TO A PULP WITH THOSE PUNCHES!
UH...SO THAT MEANS
THAT GUY'S PUNCH IS A SINGLE BLOW OF CONCENTRATED CHI!!
YOU'VE SEEN THAT POWER FIRSTHAND, REMEMBER!?
CRACK
IF HE DOESN'T FIND A WAY OUT OF THIS, NEGI WON'T JUST BE BADLY HURT!! HE'LL DIE!!!

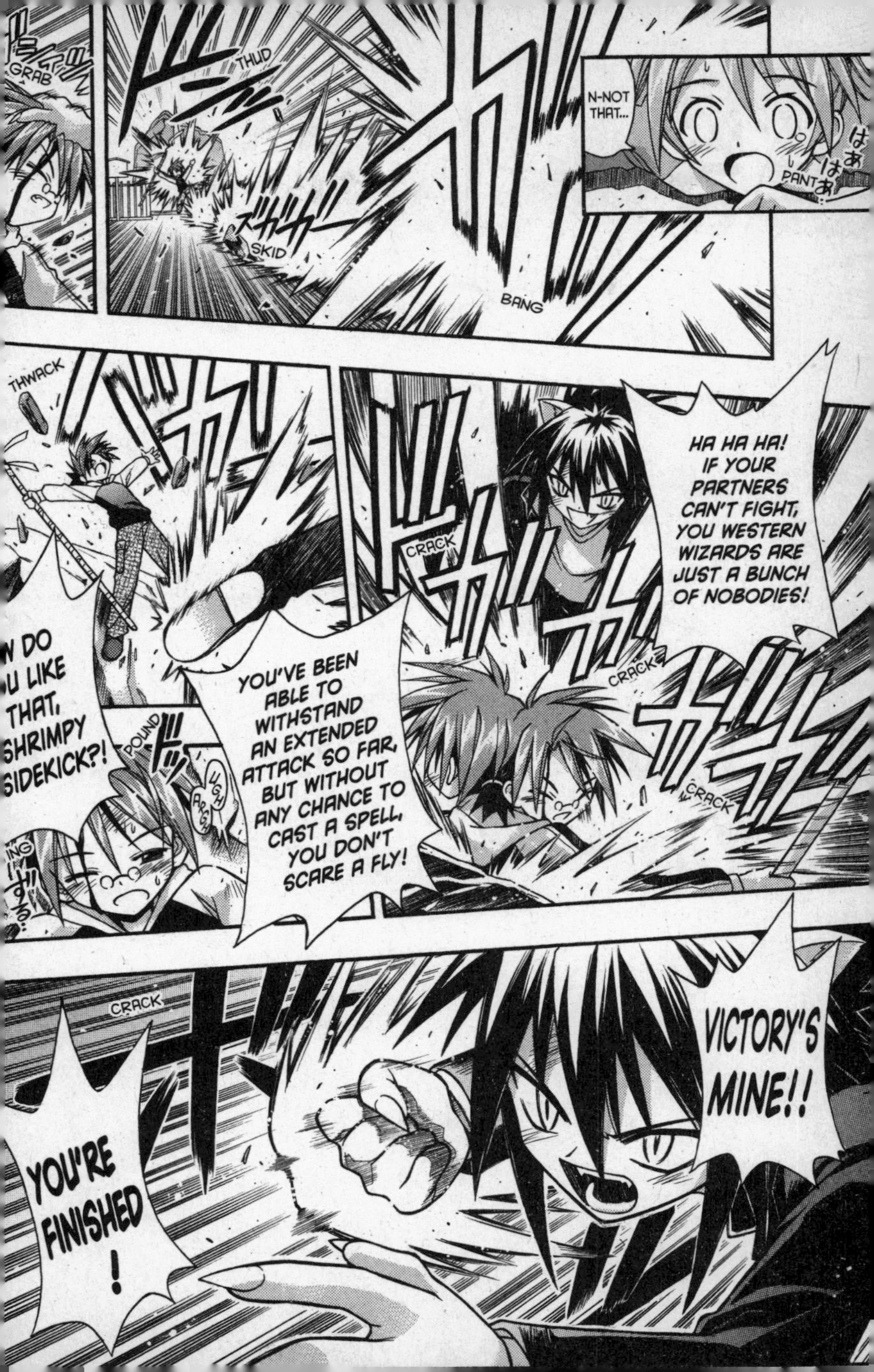
N-NOT THAT...
はあ はあ
PANT
THUD
SKID
BANG
GRAB
HA HA HA! IF YOUR PARTNERS CAN'T FIGHT, YOU WESTERN WIZARDS ARE JUST A BUNCH OF NOBODIES!
CRACK
CRACK
CRACK
YOU'VE BEEN ABLE TO WITHSTAND AN EXTENDED ATTACK SO FAR, BUT WITHOUT ANY CHANCE TO CAST A SPELL, YOU DON'T SCARE A FLY!
THWACK
POUND
UGH
ARGH
VICTORY'S MINE!!
YOU'RE FINISHED !
CRACK

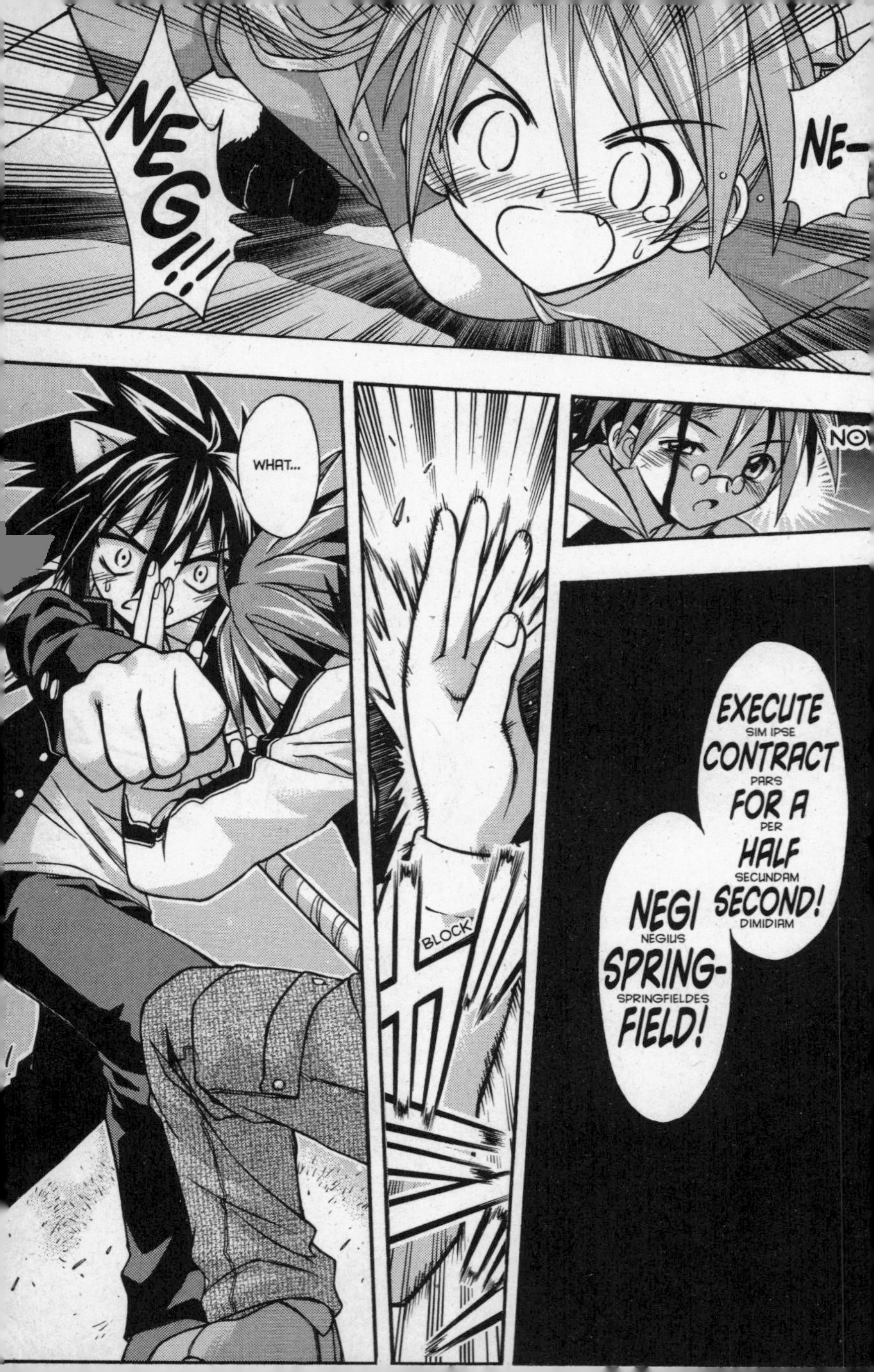
NE-
NEGI!!!
NOW
EXECUTE CONTRACT FOR A HALF SECOND!
SIM IPSE PARS PER SECUNDAM DIMIDIAM
NEGI SPRING-FIELD!
NEGIUS SPRINGFIELDES
BLOCK
WHAT...

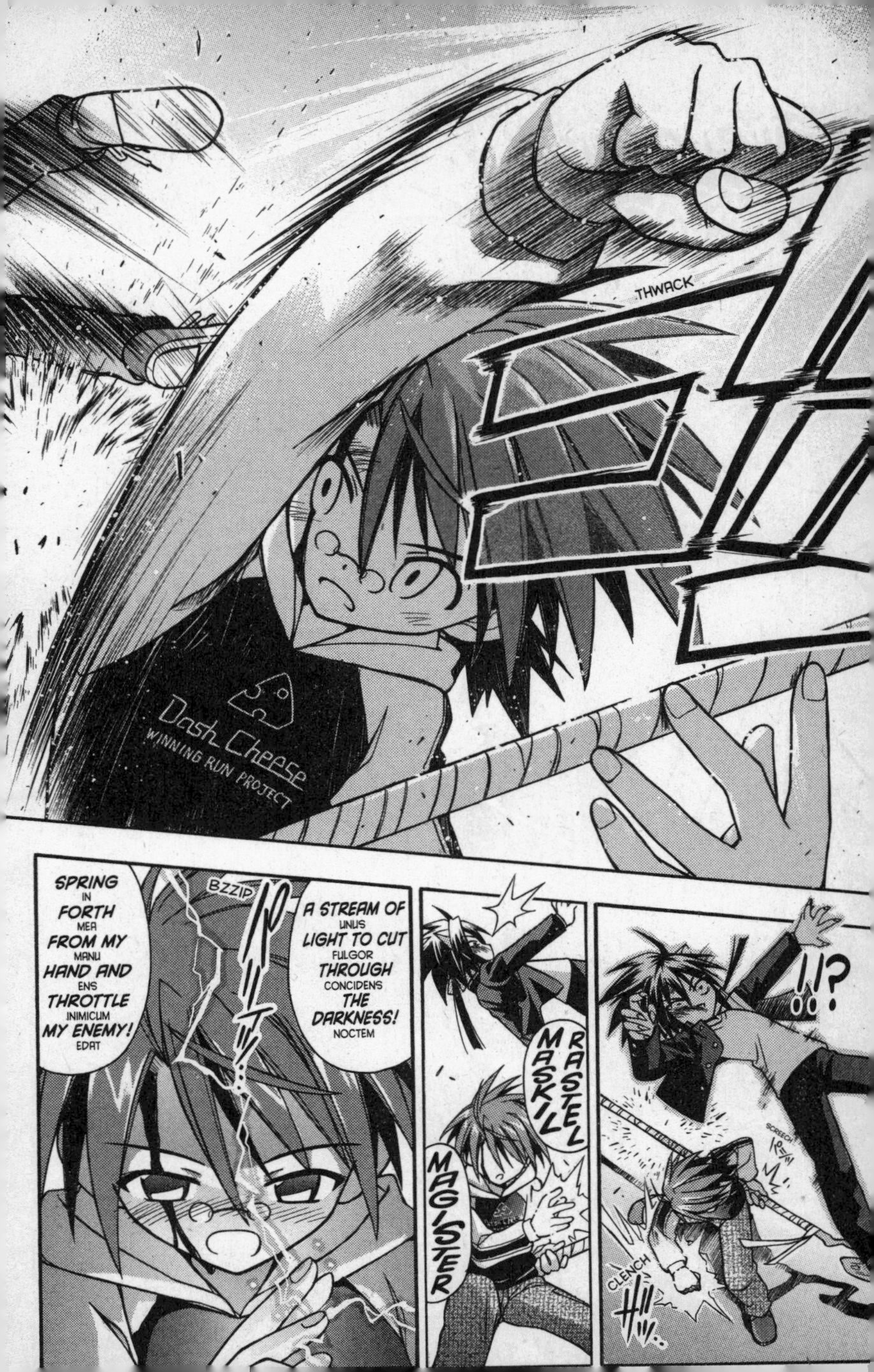
THWACK
!!?
SCREECH
CLENCH
RASTEL
MASKIL
MAGISTER
BZZIP
A STREAM OF UNUS LIGHT TO CUT FULGOR THROUGH CONCIDENS THE DARKNESS! NOCTEM
SPRING IN FORTH MEA FROM MY MANU HAND AND ENS THROTTLE INIMICUM MY ENEMY! EDAT
Dash Cheese WINNING RUN PROJECT

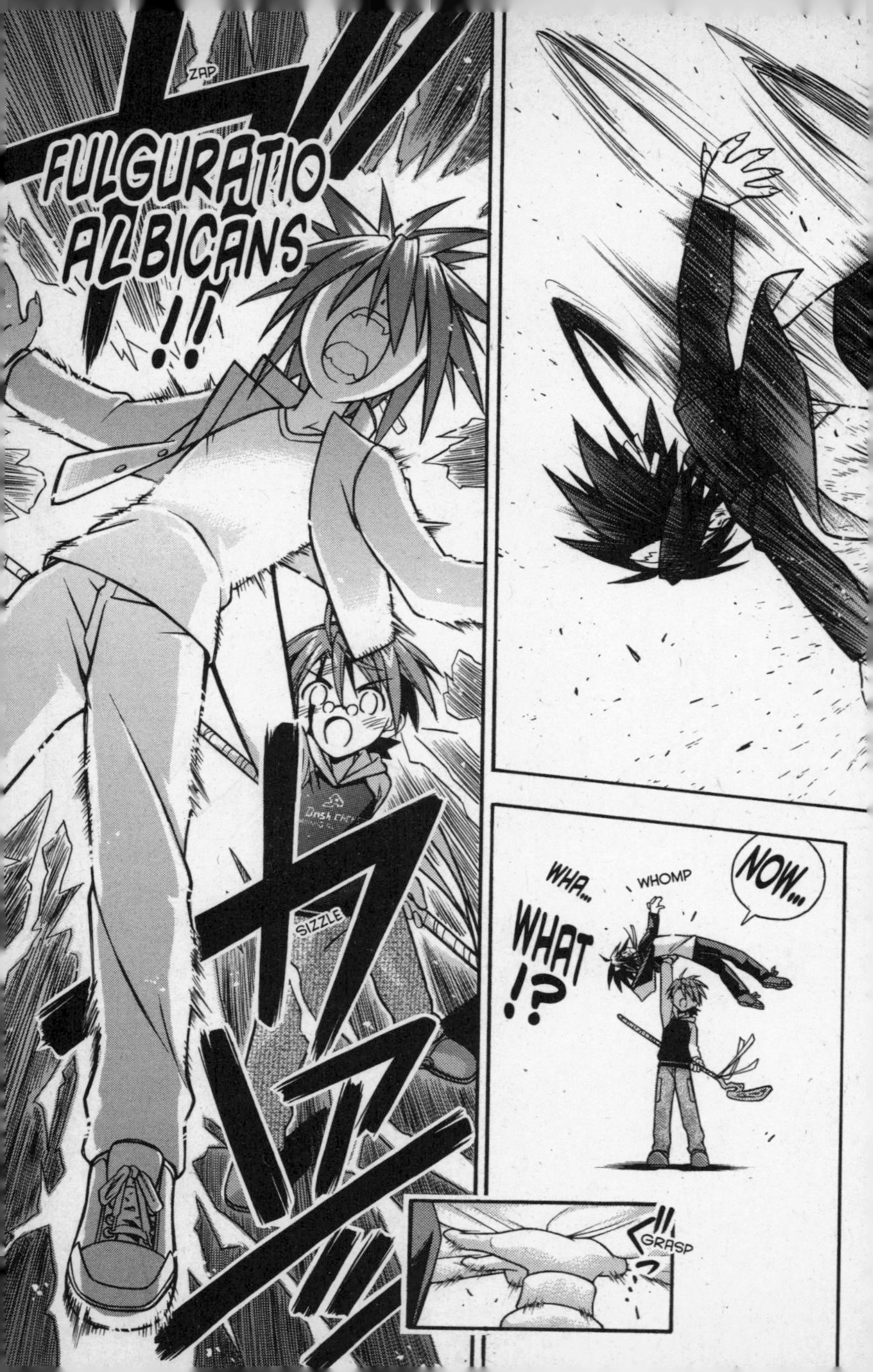
NOW...
WHOMP
WHA... WHAT!?
GRASP
ZAP
FULGURATIO ALBICANS!!
SIZZLE

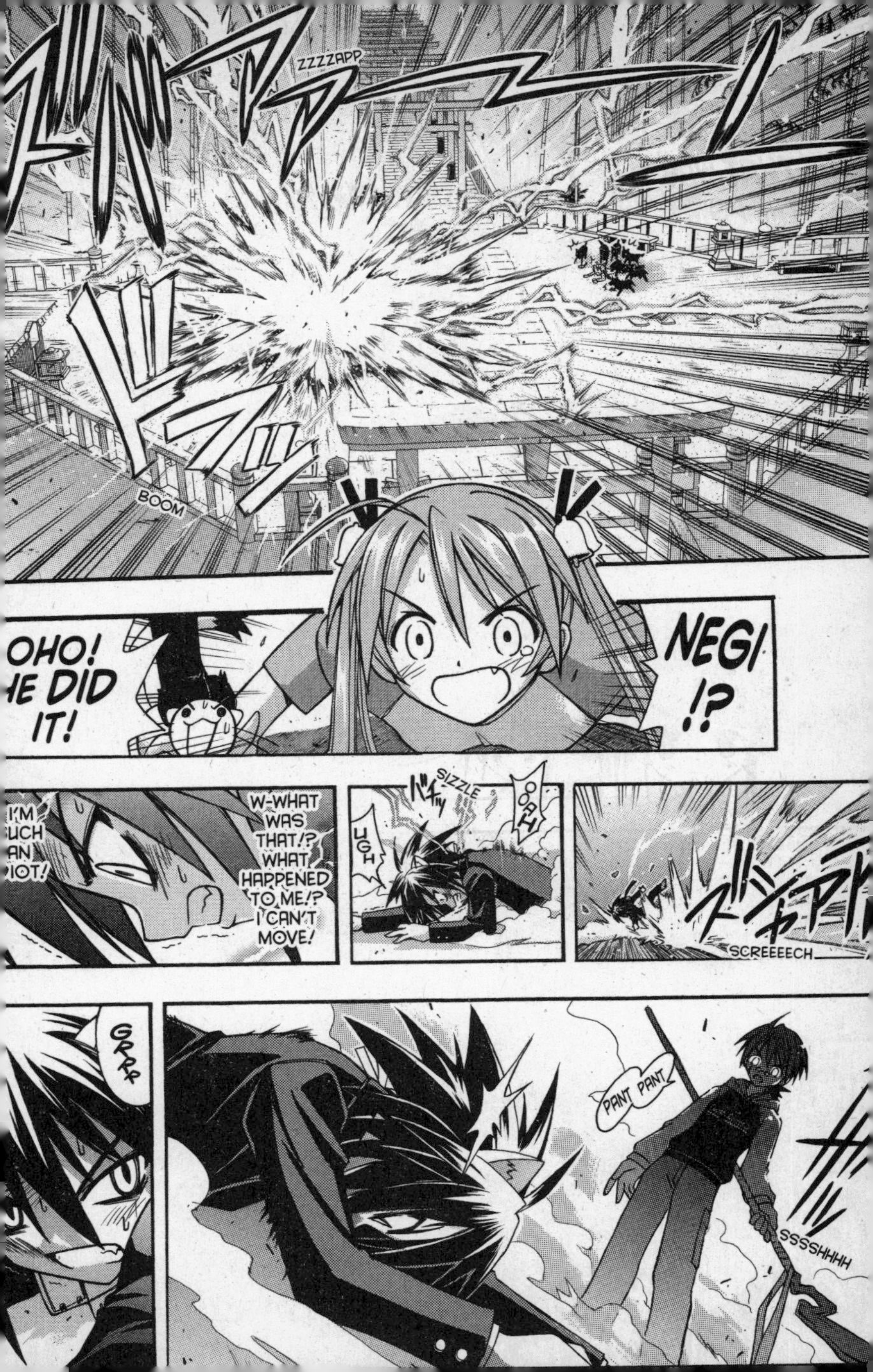
ZZZZAPP
BOOM
NEGI !?
OHO! HE DID IT!
SCREEEECH
SIZZLE
OOAH
UGH
W-WHAT WAS THAT!? WHAT HAPPENED TO ME!? I CAN'T MOVE!
I'M SUCH AN IDIOT!
PANT PANT
SSSSHHHH
GRRR

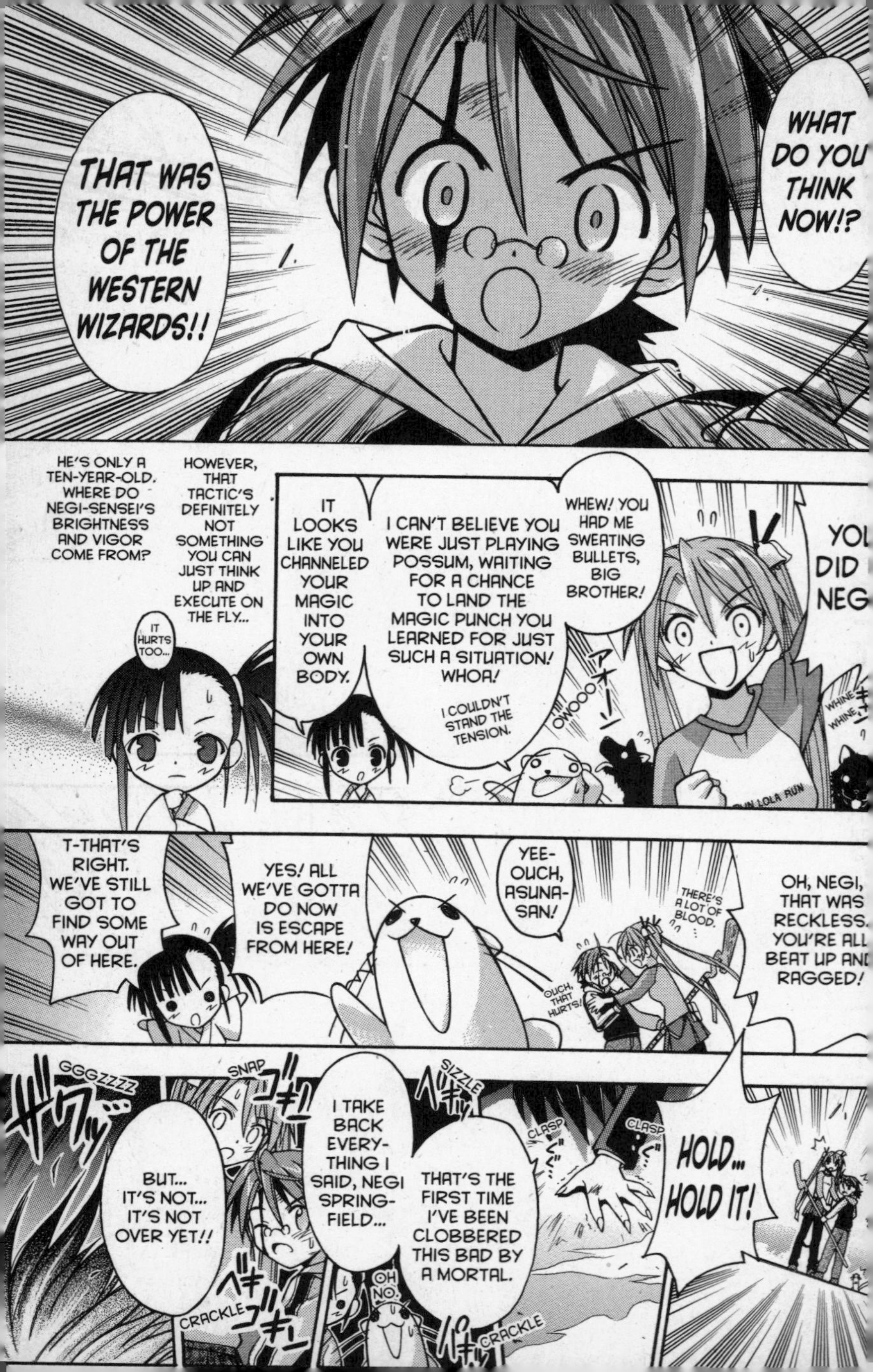
WHAT DO YOU THINK NOW!?
THAT WAS THE POWER OF THE WESTERN WIZARDS!!
YOU DID NEG
WHEW! YOU HAD ME SWEATING BULLETS, BIG BROTHER!
WHINE WHINE
OWOOO
I COULDN'T STAND THE TENSION.
I CAN'T BELIEVE YOU WERE JUST PLAYING POSSUM, WAITING FOR A CHANCE TO LAND THE MAGIC PUNCH YOU LEARNED FOR JUST SUCH A SITUATION! WHOA!
IT LOOKS LIKE YOU CHANNELED YOUR MAGIC INTO YOUR OWN BODY.
HOWEVER, THAT TACTIC'S DEFINITELY NOT SOMETHING YOU CAN JUST THINK UP AND EXECUTE ON THE FLY...
HE'S ONLY A TEN-YEAR-OLD. WHERE DO NEGI-SENSEI'S BRIGHTNESS AND VIGOR COME FROM?
IT HURTS TOO...
OH, NEGI, THAT WAS RECKLESS. YOU'RE ALL BEAT UP AND RAGGED!
THERE'S A LOT OF BLOOD.
YEE-OUCH, ASUNA-SAN!
OUCH, THAT HURTS!
YES! ALL WE'VE GOTTA DO NOW IS ESCAPE FROM HERE!
T-THAT'S RIGHT. WE'VE STILL GOT TO FIND SOME WAY OUT OF HERE.
HOLD... HOLD IT!
CLASP
CLASP
SIZZLE
THAT'S THE FIRST TIME I'VE BEEN CLOBBERED THIS BAD BY A MORTAL.
I TAKE BACK EVERY-THING I SAID, NEGI SPRING-FIELD...
SNAP
GGGZZZZ
BUT... IT'S NOT... IT'S NOT OVER YET!!
OH NO.
CRACKLE
CRACKLE

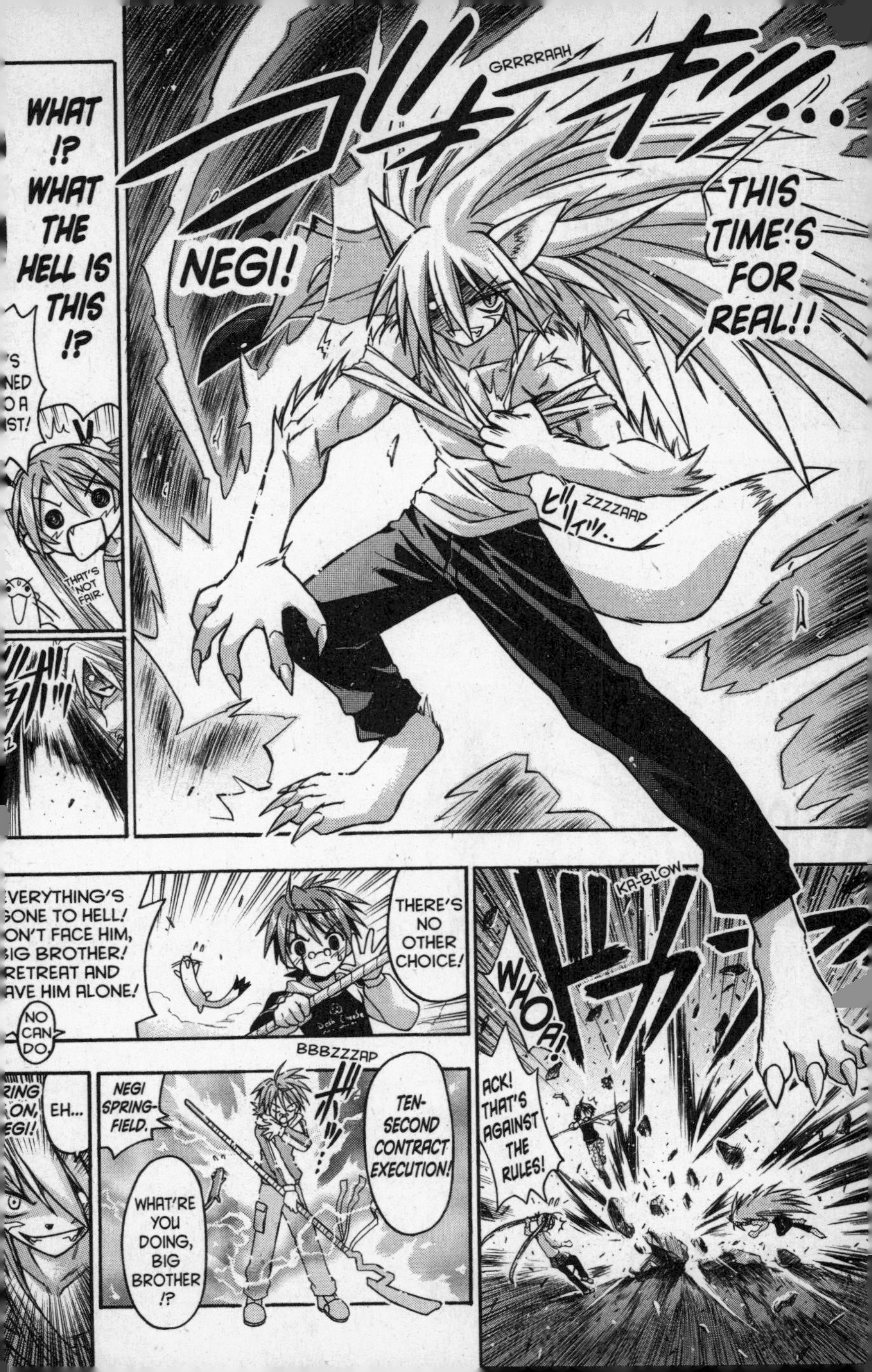
GRRRRAAH
THIS TIME'S FOR REAL!!
NEGI!
ZZZZZAAP
WHAT!? WHAT THE HELL IS THIS!?
THAT'S NOT FAIR.
KA-BLOW
WHOA!
ACK! THAT'S AGAINST THE RULES!
THERE'S NO OTHER CHOICE!
EVERYTHING'S GONE TO HELL! ON'T FACE HIM, BIG BROTHER! RETREAT AND AVE HIM ALONE!
NO CAN DO.
BBBZZZAP
TEN-SECOND CONTRACT EXECUTION!
NEGI SPRING-FIELD.
WHAT'RE YOU DOING, BIG BROTHER!?
EH...

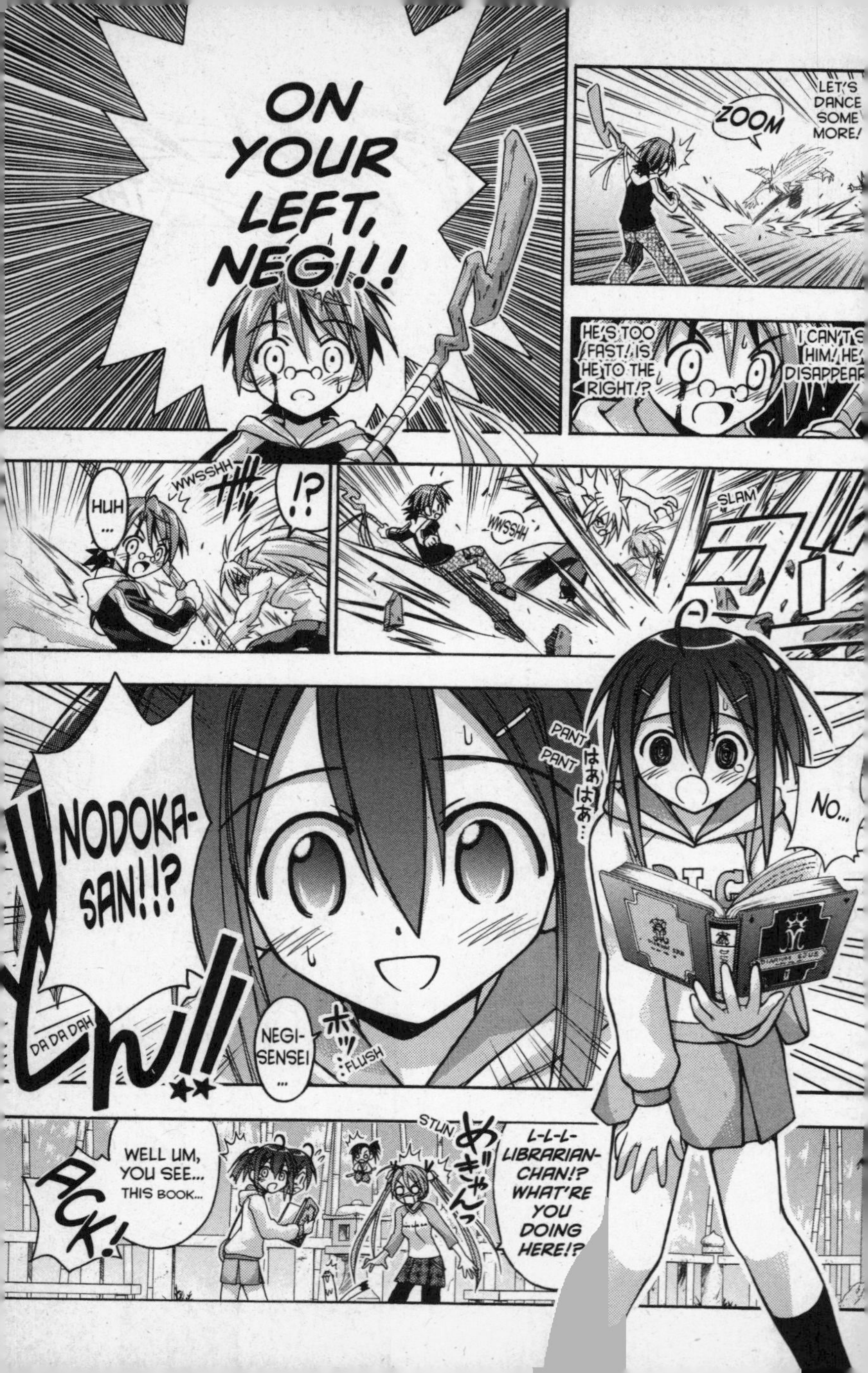

LET'S DANCE SOME MORE!
ZOOM
I CAN'T S HIM! HE' DISAPPEAR
HE'S TOO FAST! IS HE TO THE RIGHT!?
ON YOUR LEFT, NEGI!!
SLAM
WWSSHH
!?
WWSSHH
HUH ...
NO...
PANT PANT
はあはあ…
NEGI-SENSEI ...
ホッ FLUSH
NODOKA-SAN!!?
DA DA DAH
L-L-L-LIBRARIAN-CHAN!? WHAT'RE YOU DOING HERE!?
STUN めぎゃんっ
WELL UM, YOU SEE... THIS BOOK...
ACK!

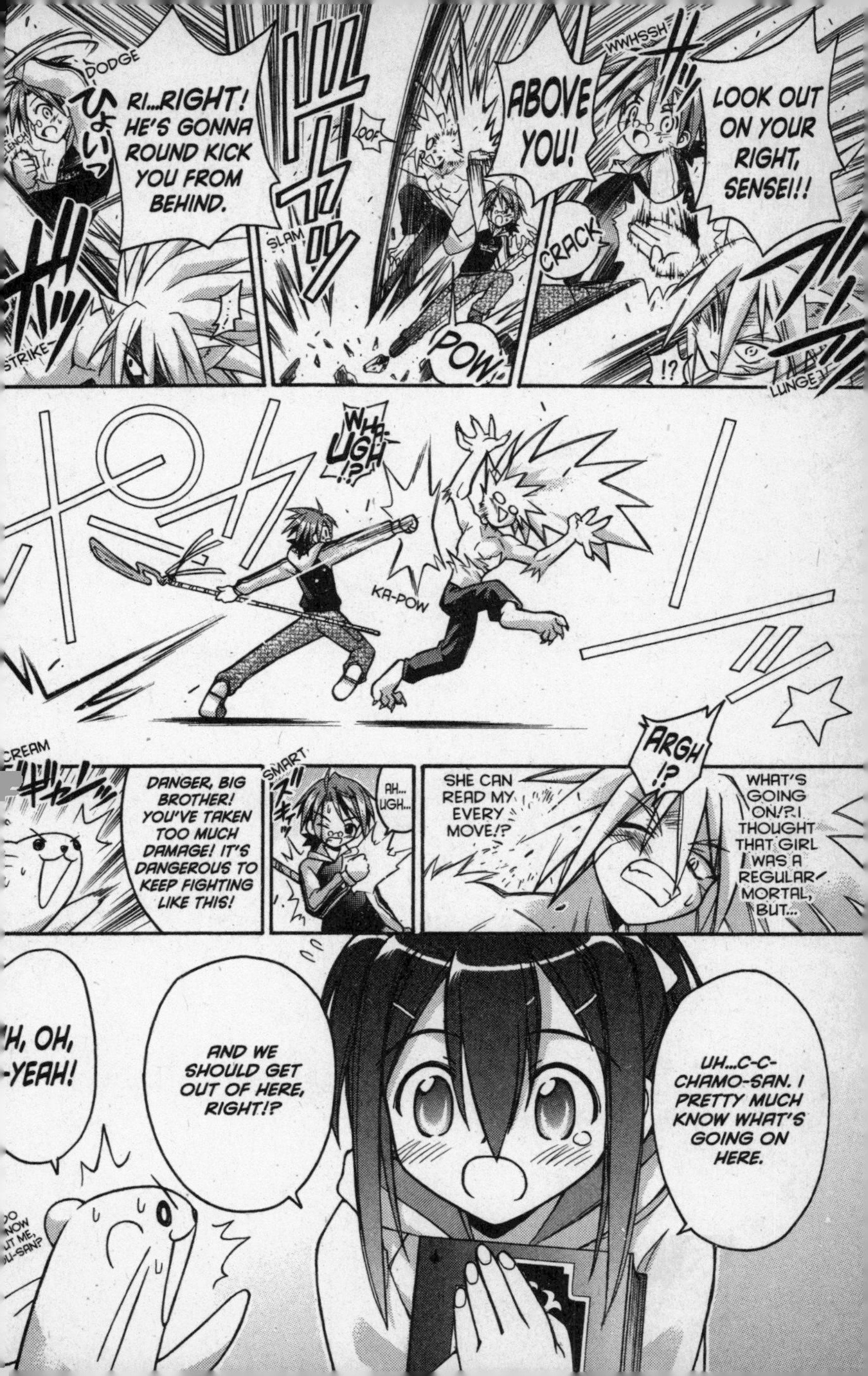
WWHSSH
LOOK OUT ON YOUR RIGHT, SENSEI!!
CRACK
!?
LUNGE
ABOVE YOU!
OOF
SLAM
POW
DODGE
ひょいっ
RI...RIGHT! HE'S GONNA ROUND KICK YOU FROM BEHIND.
STRIKE
WHA-UGH!?
KA-POW
WHAT'S GOING ON!? I THOUGHT THAT GIRL WAS A REGULAR MORTAL, BUT...
ARGH!?
SHE CAN READ MY EVERY MOVE!?
SMART
AH... UGH...
DANGER, BIG BROTHER! YOU'VE TAKEN TOO MUCH DAMAGE! IT'S DANGEROUS TO KEEP FIGHTING LIKE THIS!
UH...C-C-CHAMO-SAN. I PRETTY MUCH KNOW WHAT'S GOING ON HERE.
AND WE SHOULD GET OUT OF HERE, RIGHT!?

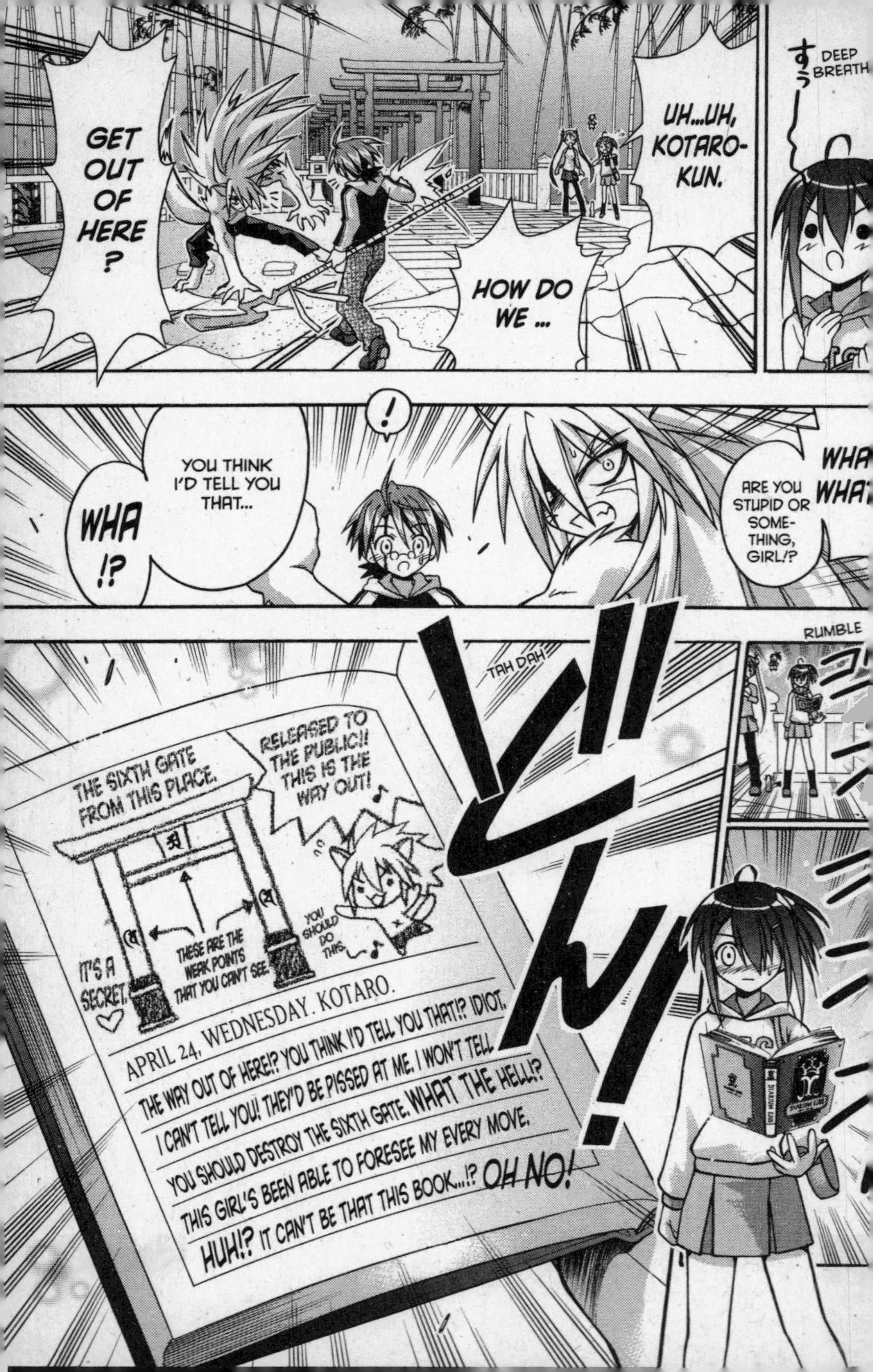
すぅ
DEEP BREATH
UH...UH, KOTARO-KUN.
HOW DO WE ...
GET OUT OF HERE?
WHA WHAT
ARE YOU STUPID OR SOME-THING, GIRL!?
!
YOU THINK I'D TELL YOU THAT...
WHA !?
RUMBLE
TAH DAH
ジャン!
THE SIXTH GATE FROM THIS PLACE.
RELEASED TO THE PUBLIC!! THIS IS THE WAY OUT!
YOU SHOULD DO THIS.
THESE ARE THE WEAK POINTS THAT YOU CAN'T SEE.
IT'S A SECRET.
APRIL 24, WEDNESDAY. KOTARO.
THE WAY OUT OF HERE!? YOU THINK I'D TELL YOU THAT!? IDIOT.
I CAN'T TELL YOU! THEY'D BE PISSED AT ME. I WON'T TELL
YOU SHOULD DESTROY THE SIXTH GATE. WHAT THE HELL!?
THIS GIRL'S BEEN ABLE TO FORESEE MY EVERY MOVE.
HUH!? IT CAN'T BE THAT THIS BOOK...!? OH NO!

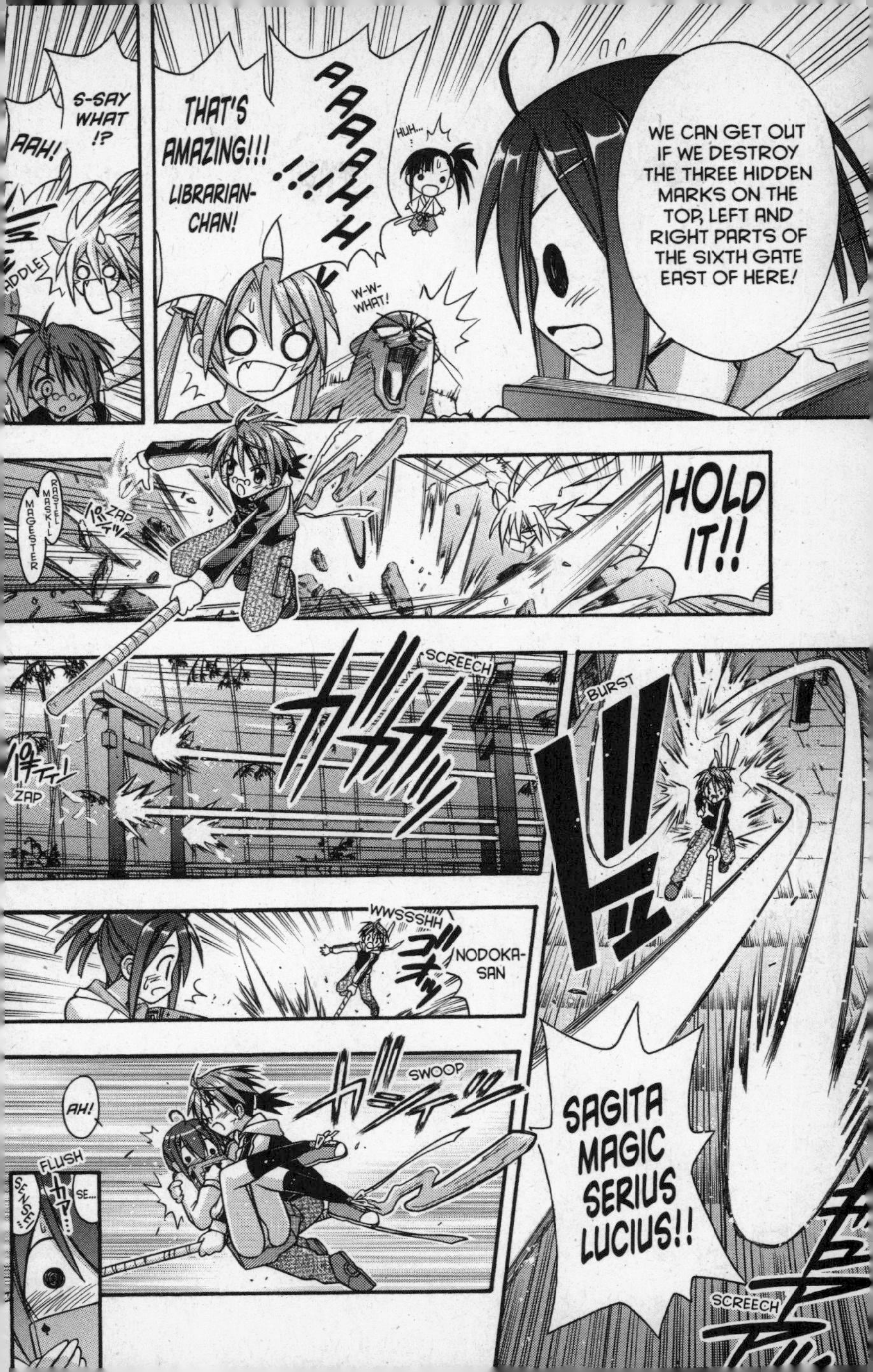
WE CAN GET OUT IF WE DESTROY THE THREE HIDDEN MARKS ON THE TOP, LEFT AND RIGHT PARTS OF THE SIXTH GATE EAST OF HERE!
AAAAHHH!!!!
HUH...
W-W-WHAT!
THAT'S AMAZING!!!
LIBRARIAN-CHAN!
S-SAY WHAT!?
AAH!
ADDLE
HOLD IT!!
RASTEL MASKIL MAGESTER
ZAP
BURST
SAGITA MAGIC SERIUS LUCIUS!!
SCREECH
SCREECH
ZAP
WWSSSHH
NODOKA-SAN
SWOOP
AH!
FLUSH
SE...
SENSEI...

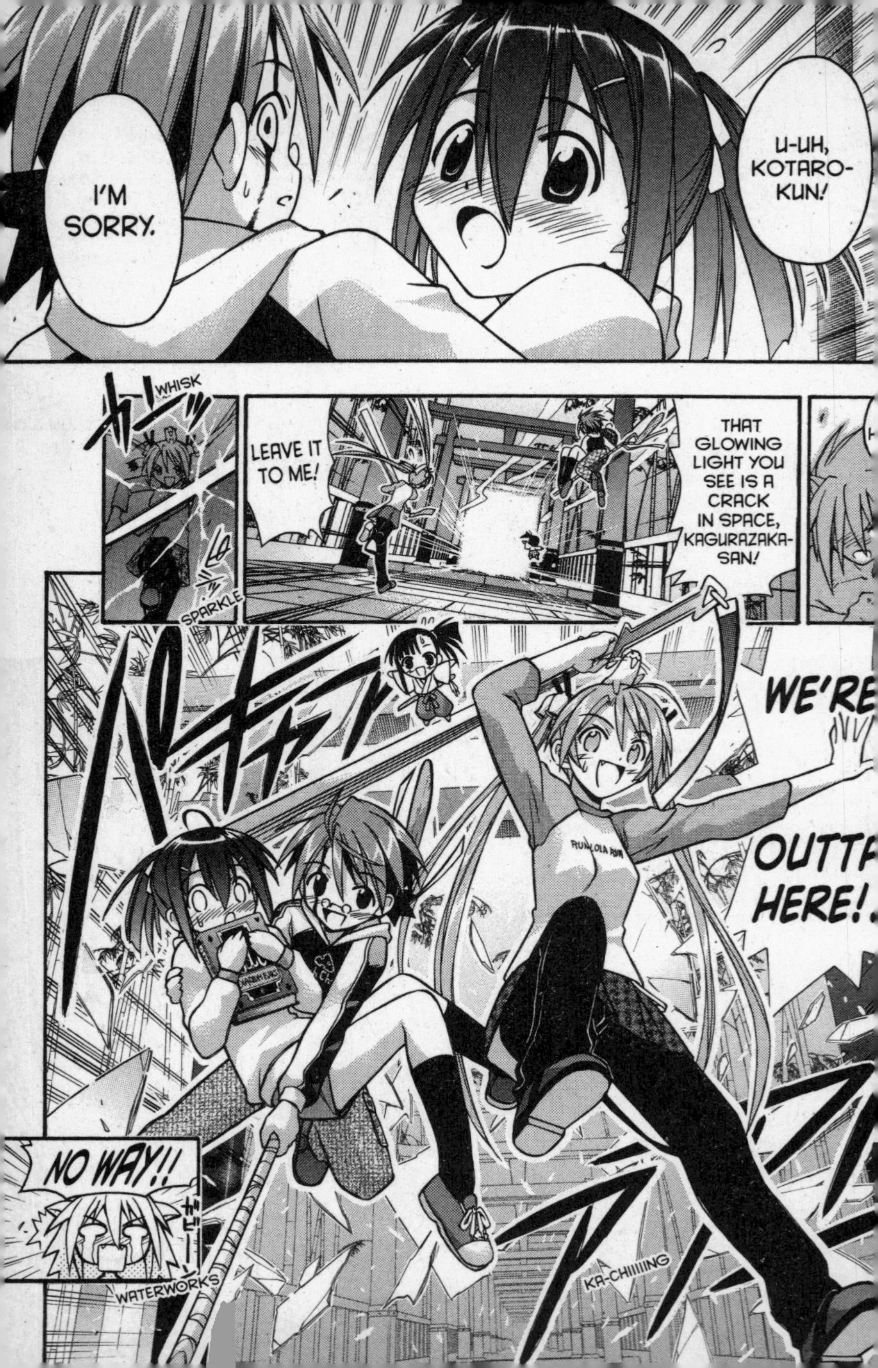
U-UH, KOTARO-KUN!
I'M SORRY.
THAT GLOWING LIGHT YOU SEE IS A CRACK IN SPACE, KAGURAZAKA-SAN!
LEAVE IT TO ME!
WHISK
SPARKLE
WE'RE OUTTA HERE!..
RUN LOLA RUN
KA-CHIIIIING
NO WAY!!
WATERWORKS

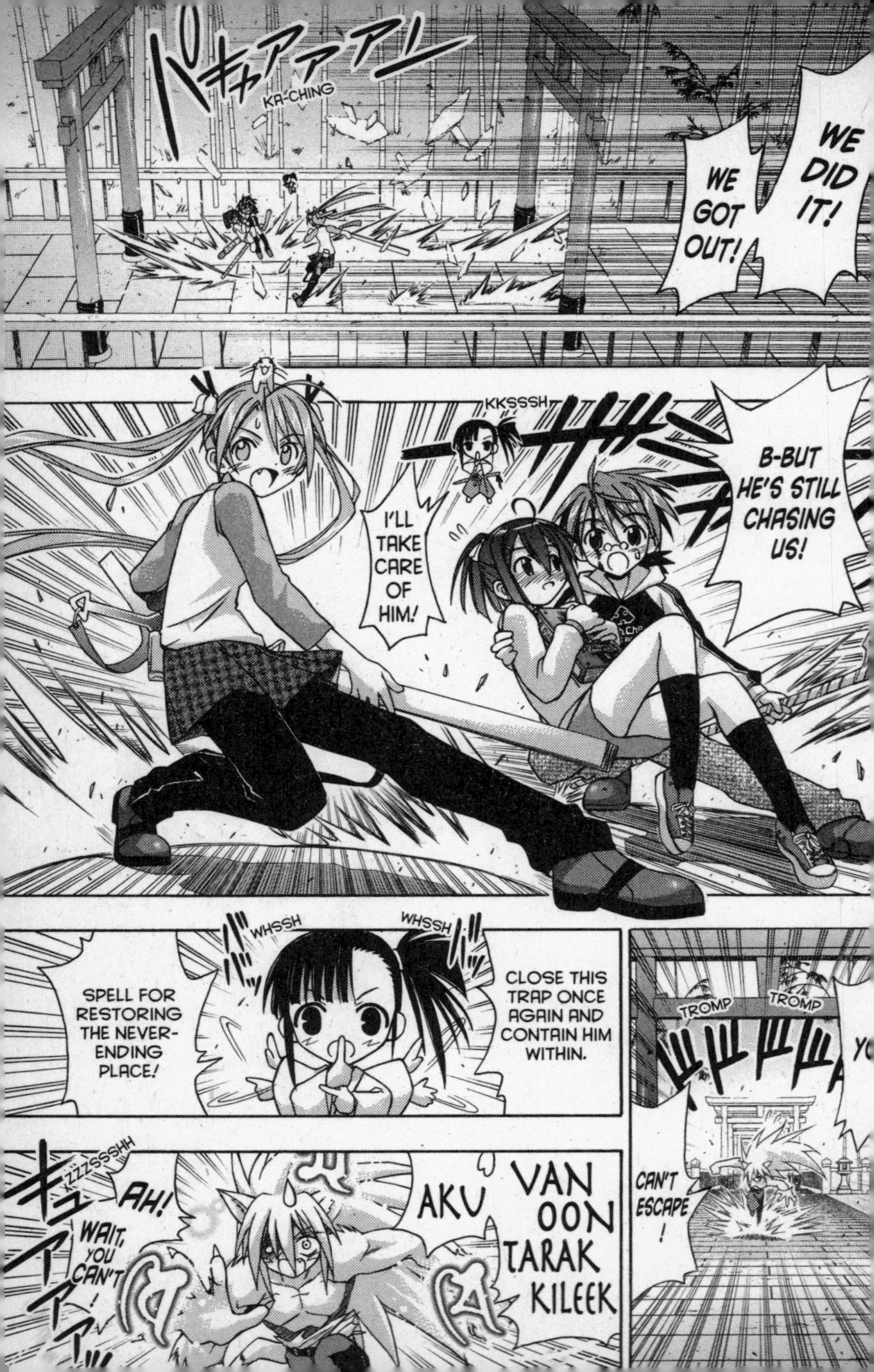
KA-CHING
WE DID IT!
WE GOT OUT!
KKSSSH
B-BUT HE'S STILL CHASING US!
I'LL TAKE CARE OF HIM!
TROMP
TROMP
CAN'T ESCAPE!
WHSSH
WHSSH
CLOSE THIS TRAP ONCE AGAIN AND CONTAIN HIM WITHIN.
SPELL FOR RESTORING THE NEVER-ENDING PLACE!
VAN OON TARAK KILEEK
AKU
ZZZSSSHH
AH!
WAIT, YOU CAN'T!

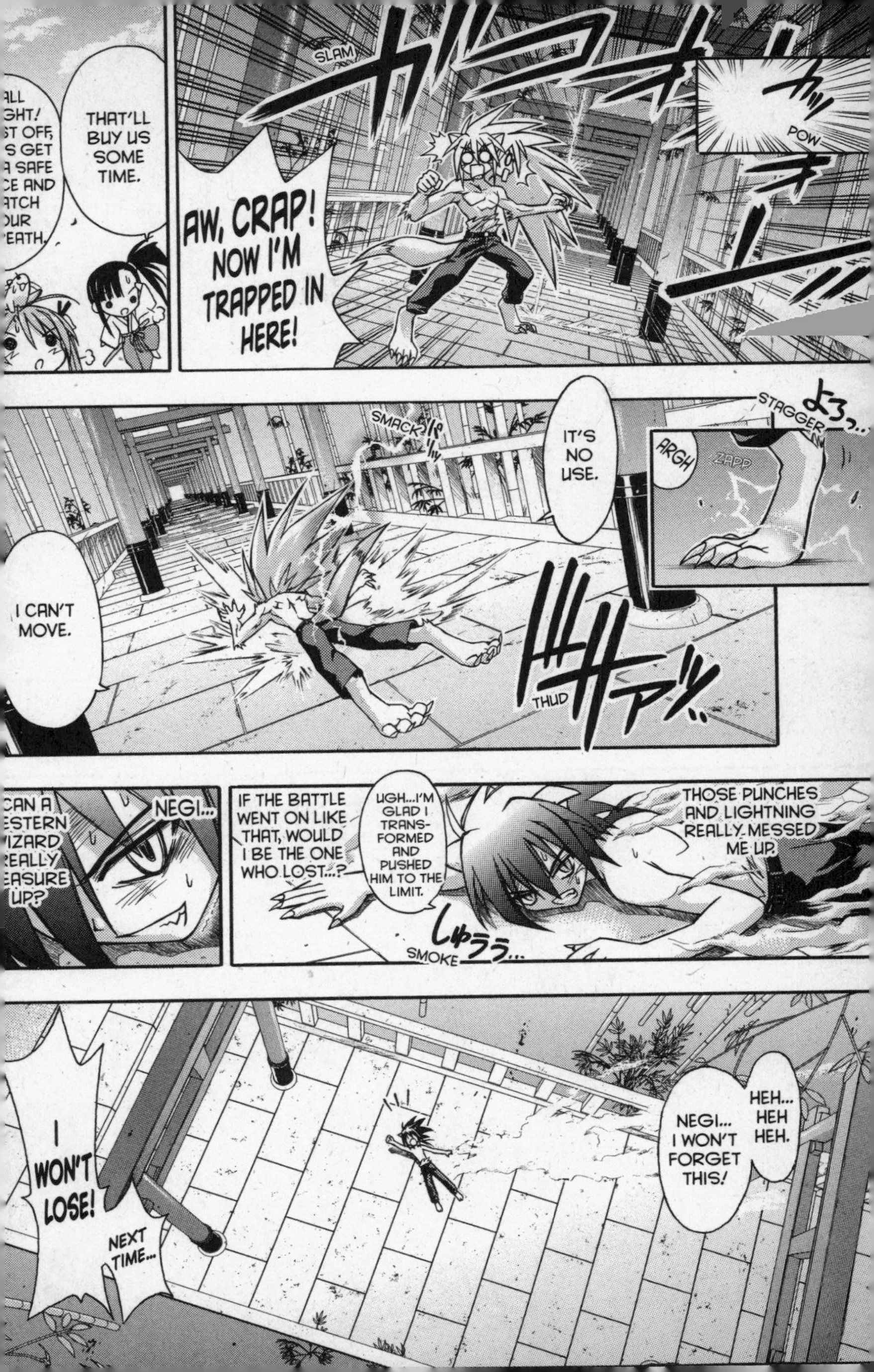
SLAM
POW
AW, CRAP! NOW I'M TRAPPED IN HERE!
THAT'LL BUY US SOME TIME.
ALL GHT! ST OFF, S GET A SAFE CE AND ATCH OUR EATH.
STAGGER
ARGH
ZAPP
IT'S NO USE.
SMACK
THUD
I CAN'T MOVE.
THOSE PUNCHES AND LIGHTNING REALLY MESSED ME UP.
UGH...I'M GLAD I TRANS-FORMED AND PUSHED HIM TO THE LIMIT.
IF THE BATTLE WENT ON LIKE THAT, WOULD I BE THE ONE WHO LOST...?
SMOKE
NEGI...
CAN A ESTERN IZARD REALLY EASURE UP?
HEH... HEH HEH.
NEGI... I WON'T FORGET THIS!
NEXT TIME...
I WON'T LOSE!

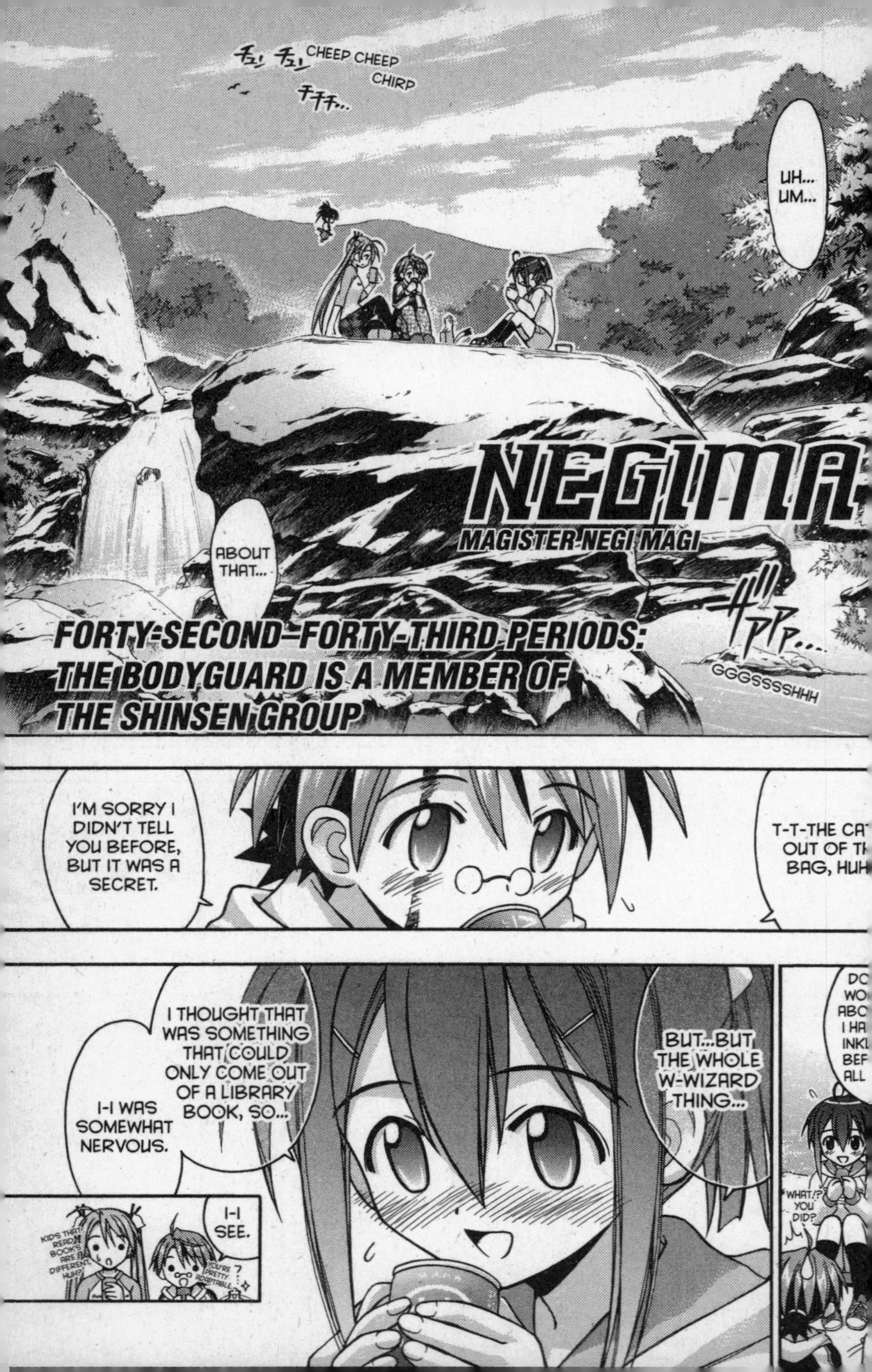
UH... UM...
チュン チュン CHEEP CHEEP
CHIRP
チチチ...
NEGIMA
MAGISTER NEGI MAGI
GGGSSSSHHH
ABOUT THAT...
FORTY-SECOND–FORTY-THIRD PERIODS: THE BODYGUARD IS A MEMBER OF THE SHINSEN GROUP
T-T-THE CA OUT OF TH BAG, HUH
I'M SORRY I DIDN'T TELL YOU BEFORE, BUT IT WAS A SECRET.
DO WO ABO I HA INKL BEF ALL
WHAT!? YOU DID?
BUT...BUT THE WHOLE W-WIZARD THING...
I THOUGHT THAT WAS SOMETHING THAT COULD ONLY COME OUT OF A LIBRARY BOOK, SO...
I-I WAS SOMEWHAT NERVOUS.
I-I SEE.
YOU'RE PRETTY ADAPTABLE.
KIDS THAT READ BOOKS ARE DIFFERENT, HUH?

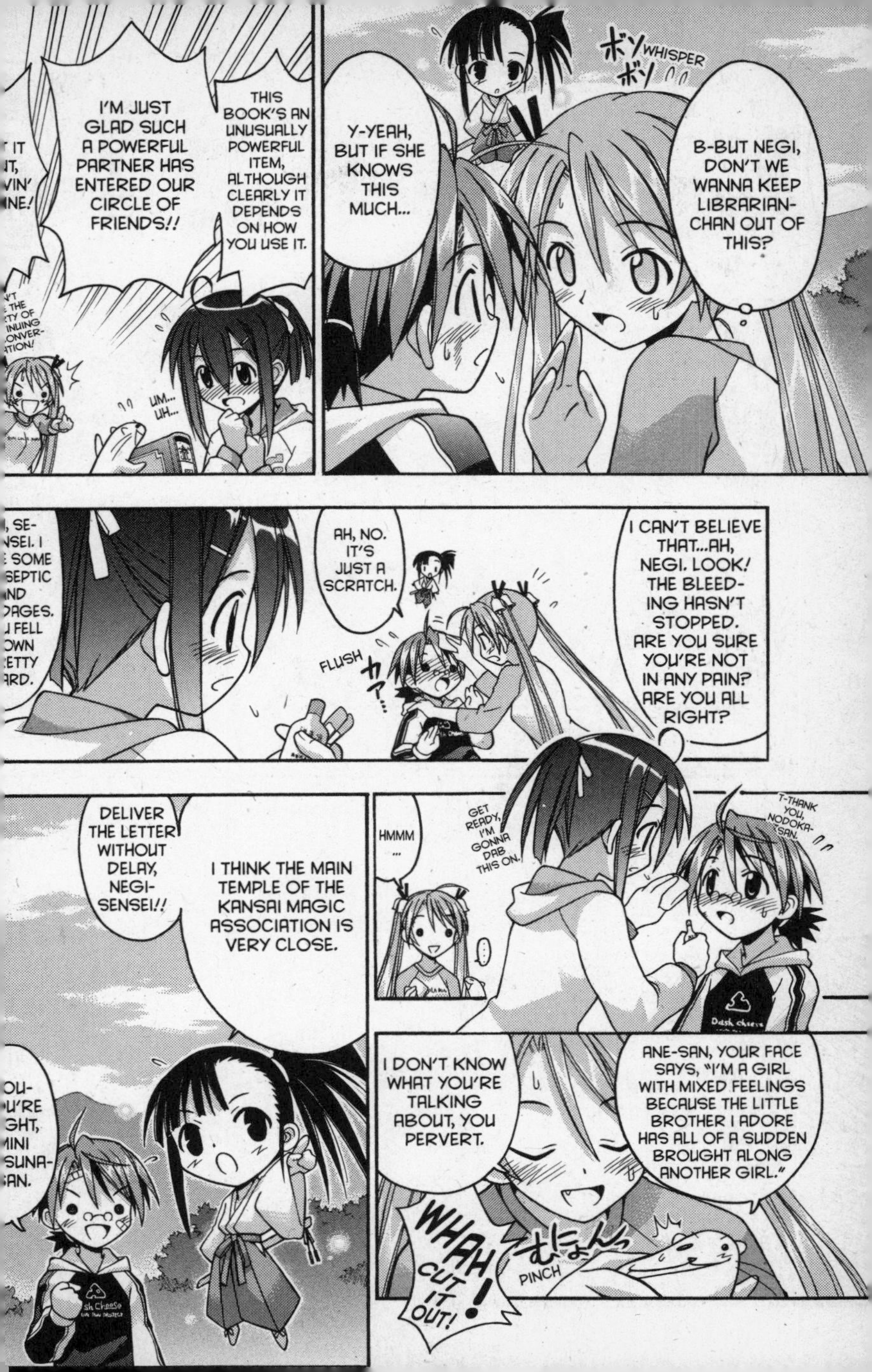
ボソ WHISPER ボソ
B-BUT NEGI, DON'T WE WANNA KEEP LIBRARIAN-CHAN OUT OF THIS?
Y-YEAH, BUT IF SHE KNOWS THIS MUCH...
THIS BOOK'S AN UNUSUALLY POWERFUL ITEM, ALTHOUGH CLEARLY IT DEPENDS ON HOW YOU USE IT.
I'M JUST GLAD SUCH A POWERFUL PARTNER HAS ENTERED OUR CIRCLE OF FRIENDS!!
UM... UH...
I CAN'T BELIEVE THAT...AH, NEGI. LOOK! THE BLEEDING HASN'T STOPPED. ARE YOU SURE YOU'RE NOT IN ANY PAIN? ARE YOU ALL RIGHT?
AH, NO. IT'S JUST A SCRATCH.
FLUSH カァ...
T-THANK YOU, NODOKA-SAN.
GET READY, I'M GONNA DAB THIS ON.
HMMM ...
I THINK THE MAIN TEMPLE OF THE KANSAI MAGIC ASSOCIATION IS VERY CLOSE.
DELIVER THE LETTER WITHOUT DELAY, NEGI-SENSEI!!
ANE-SAN, YOUR FACE SAYS, "I'M A GIRL WITH MIXED FEELINGS BECAUSE THE LITTLE BROTHER I ADORE HAS ALL OF A SUDDEN BROUGHT ALONG ANOTHER GIRL."
I DON'T KNOW WHAT YOU'RE TALKING ABOUT, YOU PERVERT.
むにょん PINCH
WHAH CUT IT OUT!

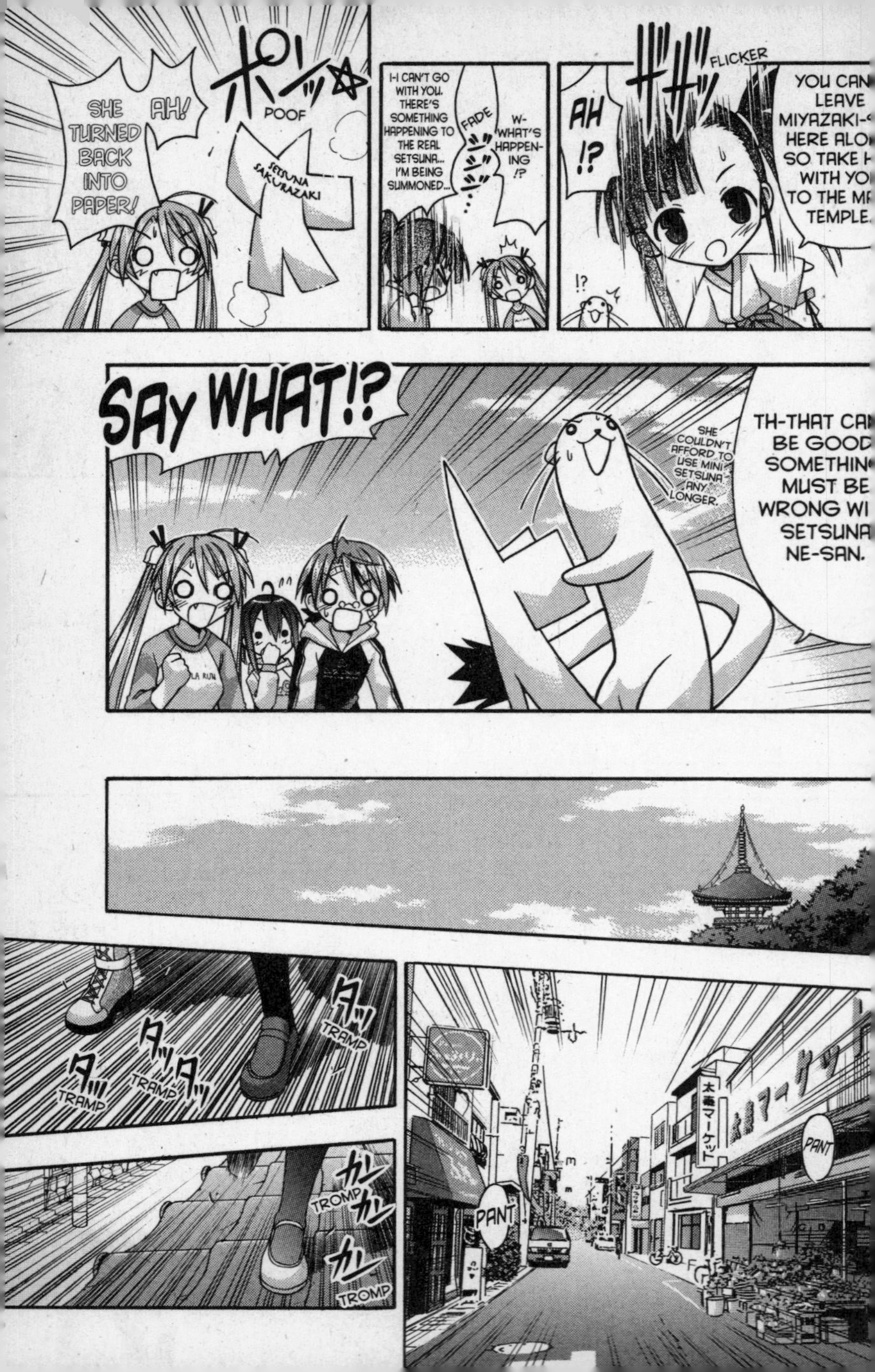
FLICKER
AH !?
YOU CAN LEAVE MIYAZAKI-S HERE ALO SO TAKE H WITH YO TO THE M TEMPLE.
!?
I-I CAN'T GO WITH YOU. THERE'S SOMETHING HAPPENING TO THE REAL SETSUNA... I'M BEING SUMMONED...
FADE
W-WHAT'S HAPPEN-ING !?
POOF
SETSUNA SAKURAZAKI
AH!
SHE TURNED BACK INTO PAPER!
TH-THAT CA BE GOOD SOMETHIN MUST BE WRONG WI SETSUNA NE-SAN.
SHE COULDN'T AFFORD TO USE MINI SETSUNA ANY LONGER.
SAY WHAT!?
PANT
PANT
TRAMP
TRAMP
TRAMP
TROMP
TROMP
TROMP

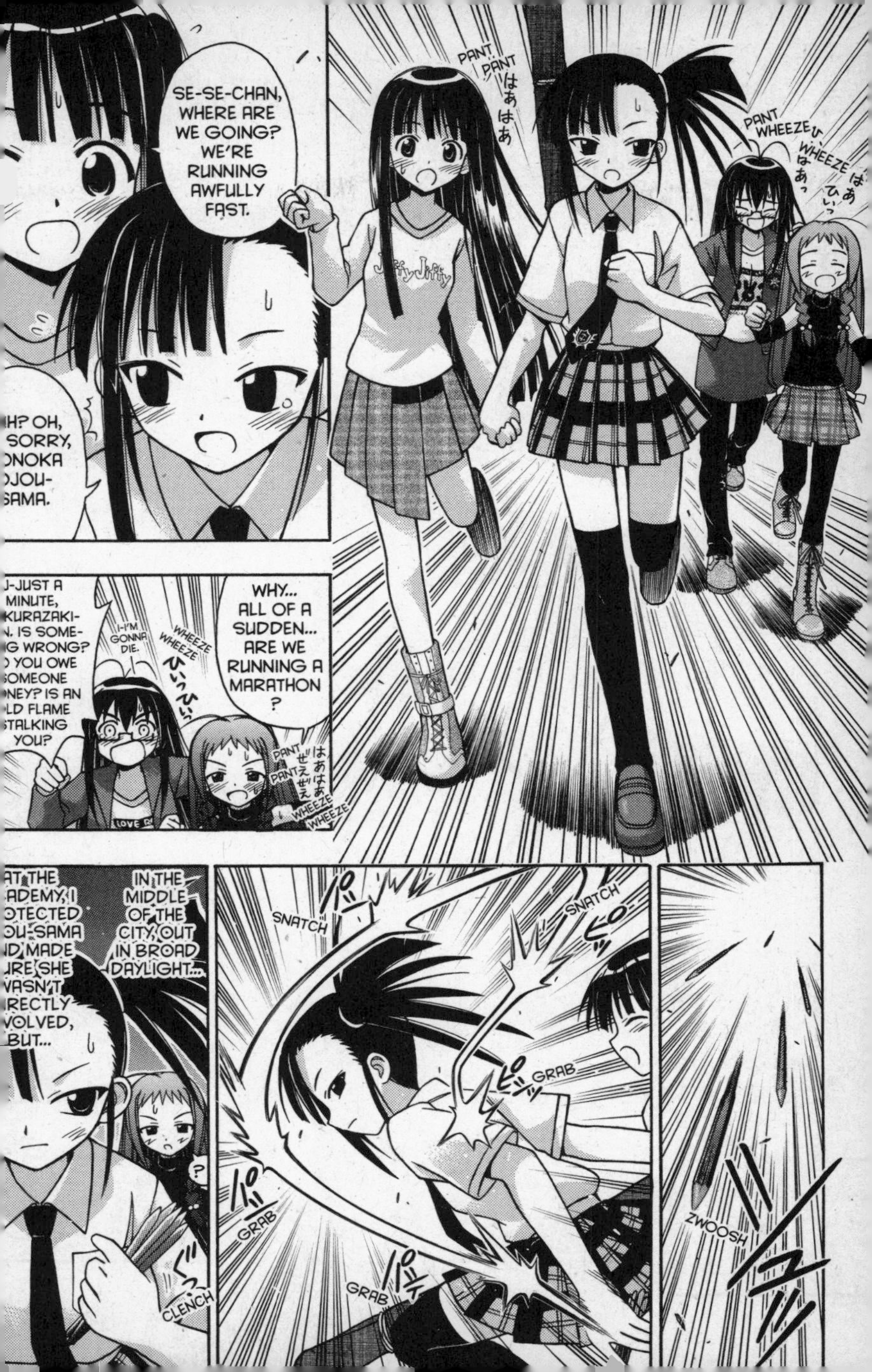
PANT PANT はあはあ
PANT WHEEZE ひ WHEEZE はあ ひいっ はあっ
SE-SE-CHAN, WHERE ARE WE GOING? WE'RE RUNNING AWFULLY FAST.
H? OH, SORRY, ONOKA OJOU-SAMA.
WHY... ALL OF A SUDDEN... ARE WE RUNNING A MARATHON?
I-I'M GONNA DIE.
WHEEZE WHEEZE ひいっひいっ
-JUST A MINUTE, KURAZAKI-N. IS SOME-G WRONG? O YOU OWE SOMEONE ONEY? IS AN LD FLAME STALKING YOU?
PANT PANT はあはあ ぜえぜえ WHEEZE WHEEZE
ZWOOSH
SNATCH
SNATCH
GRAB
GRAB
GRAB
IN THE MIDDLE OF THE CITY, OUT IN BROAD DAYLIGHT...
AT THE ADEMY, I OTECTED OU-SAMA ND MADE URE SHE WASN'T IRECTLY VOLVED, BUT...
?
CLENCH

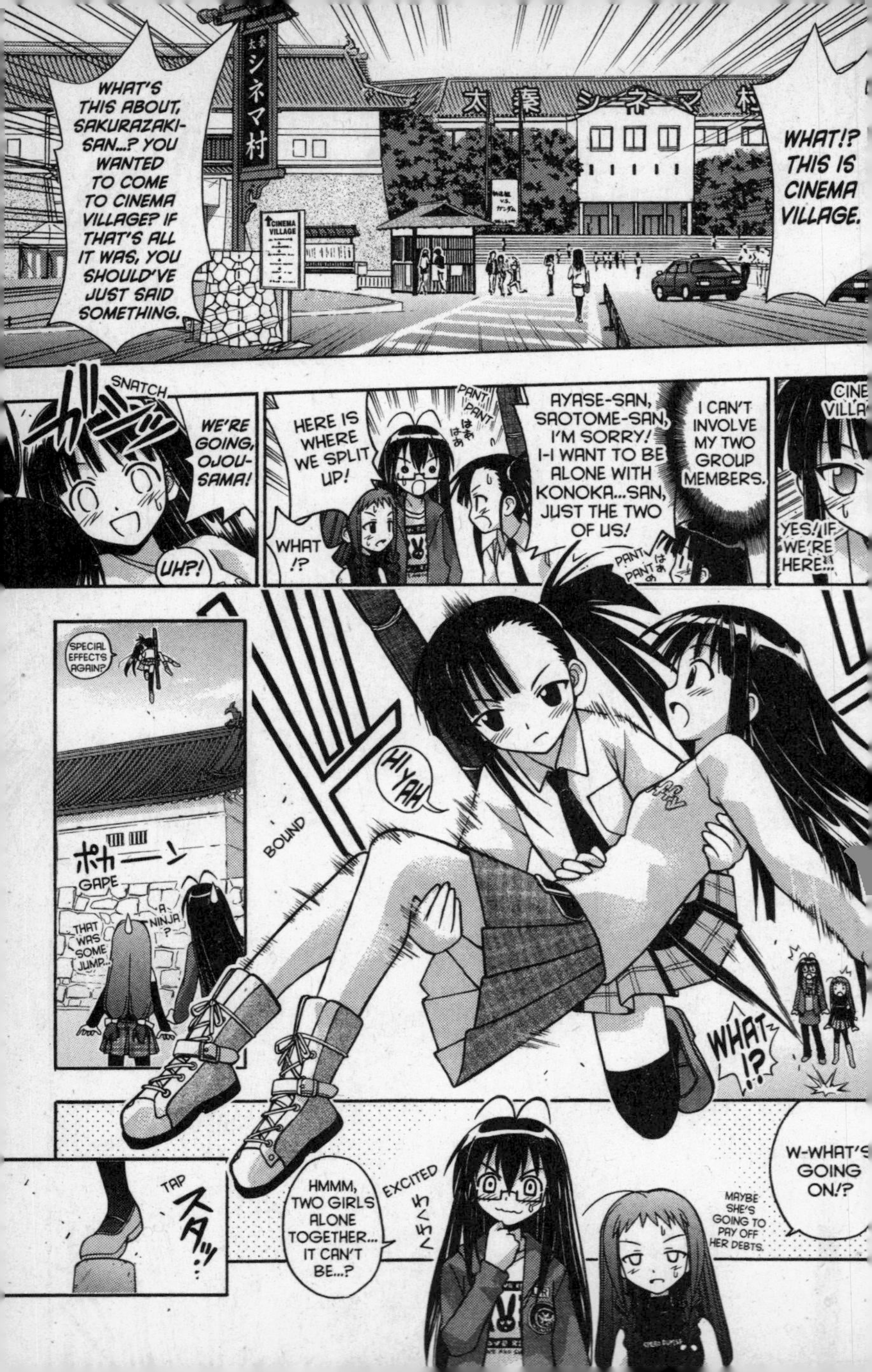

WHAT!? THIS IS CINEMA VILLAGE.
太秦シネマ村
WHAT'S THIS ABOUT, SAKURAZAKI-SAN...? YOU WANTED TO COME TO CINEMA VILLAGE? IF THAT'S ALL IT WAS, YOU SHOULD'VE JUST SAID SOMETHING.
CINEMA VILLAGE
CINE VILLA
YES! IF WE'RE HERE...
PANT PANT はあ はあ
I CAN'T INVOLVE MY TWO GROUP MEMBERS.
AYASE-SAN, SAOTOME-SAN, I'M SORRY! I-I WANT TO BE ALONE WITH KONOKA...SAN, JUST THE TWO OF US!
PANT PANT はあ はあ
HERE IS WHERE WE SPLIT UP!
WHAT!?
SNATCH
WE'RE GOING, OJOU-SAMA!
UH?!
HI YAH
BOUND
WHAT!?
SPECIAL EFFECTS AGAIN?
ポカーン
GAPE
A NINJA?
THAT WAS SOME JUMP...
W-WHAT'S GOING ON!?
MAYBE SHE'S GOING TO PAY OFF HER DEBTS.
わくわく
EXCITED
HMMM, TWO GIRLS ALONE TOGETHER... IT CAN'T BE...?
TAP
スタッ

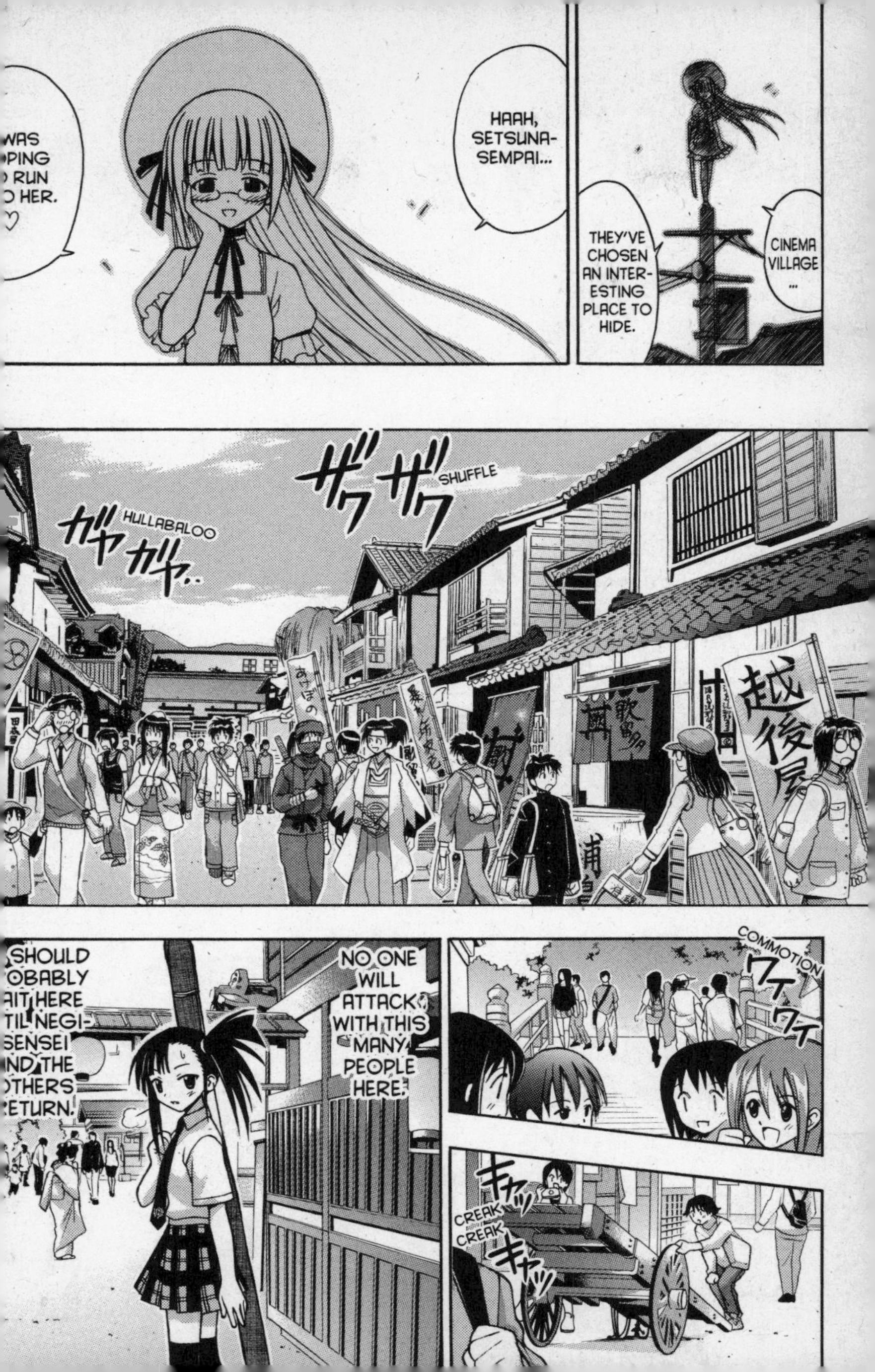

CINEMA VILLAGE ...
THEY'VE CHOSEN AN INTERESTING PLACE TO HIDE.
HAAH, SETSUNA-SEMPAI...
WAS PING RUN HER. ♡
ザワザワ
SHUFFLE
ガヤガヤ..
HULLABALOO
越後屋
COMMOTION
ワイワイ
キャッ
CREAK CREAK
キャッ
NO ONE WILL ATTACK WITH THIS MANY PEOPLE HERE.
SHOULD OBABLY AIT HERE TIL NEGI-SENSEI ND THE OTHERS ETURN.

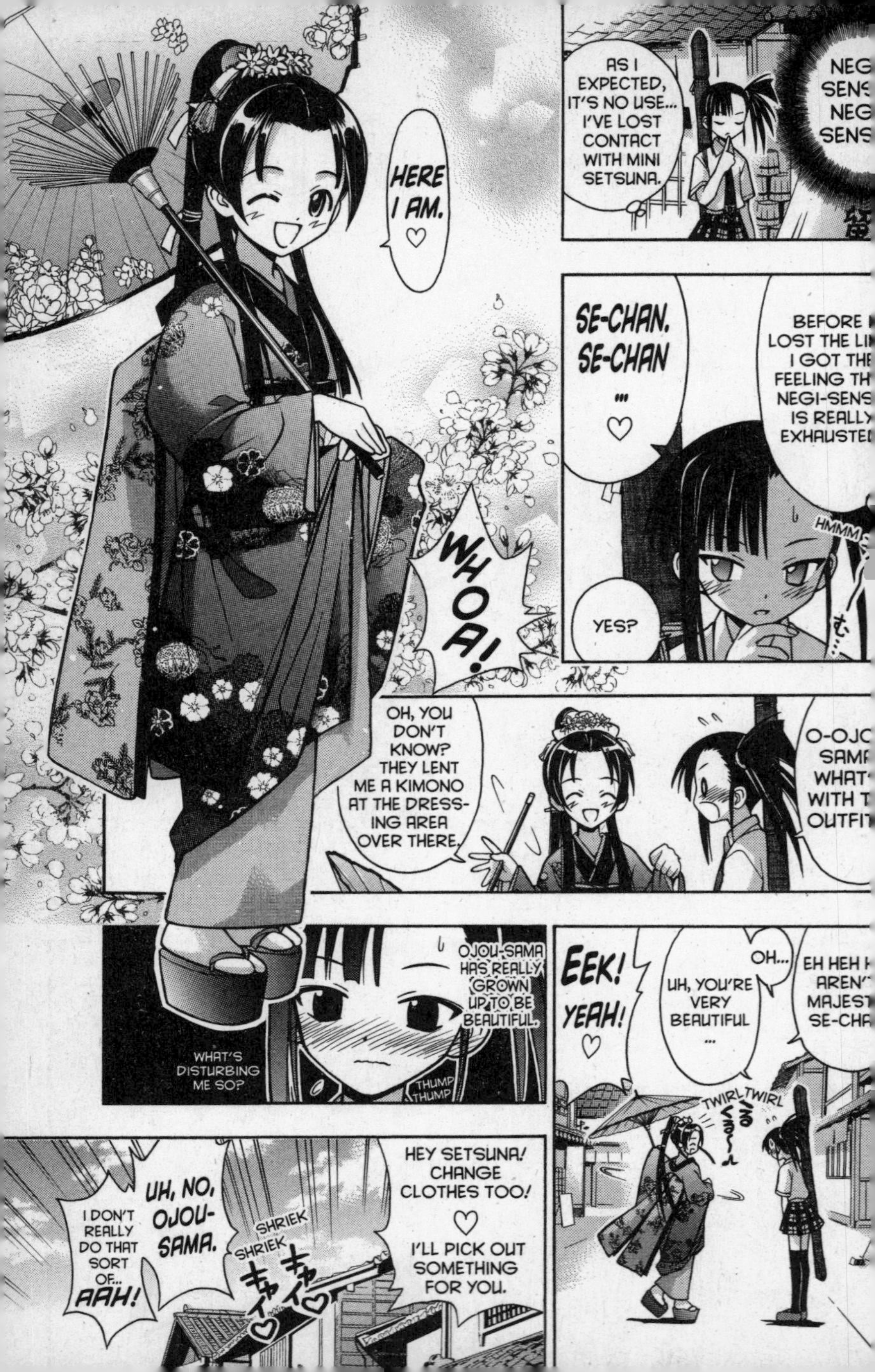

NEG SENS NEG SENS
AS I EXPECTED, IT'S NO USE... I'VE LOST CONTACT WITH MINI SETSUNA.
BEFORE I LOST THE LI I GOT THE FEELING TH NEGI-SENS IS REALLY EXHAUSTED
SE-CHAN. SE-CHAN ... ♡
HMMM
む…
YES?
O-OJO SAMA WHAT' WITH T OUTFIT
OH, YOU DON'T KNOW? THEY LENT ME A KIMONO AT THE DRESSING AREA OVER THERE.
HERE I AM. ♡
WHOA!
EH HEH H AREN'T MAJEST SE-CHA
OH...
UH, YOU'RE VERY BEAUTIFUL ...
EEK! YEAH! ♡
OJOU-SAMA HAS REALLY GROWN UP TO BE BEAUTIFUL.
WHAT'S DISTURBING ME SO?
THUMP THUMP
TWIRL TWIRL
くるっ くるっ~♪
HEY SETSUNA! CHANGE CLOTHES TOO! ♡ I'LL PICK OUT SOMETHING FOR YOU.
UH, NO, OJOU-SAMA.
I DON'T REALLY DO THAT SORT OF... AAH!
SHRIEK SHRIEK
キャイキャイ♡

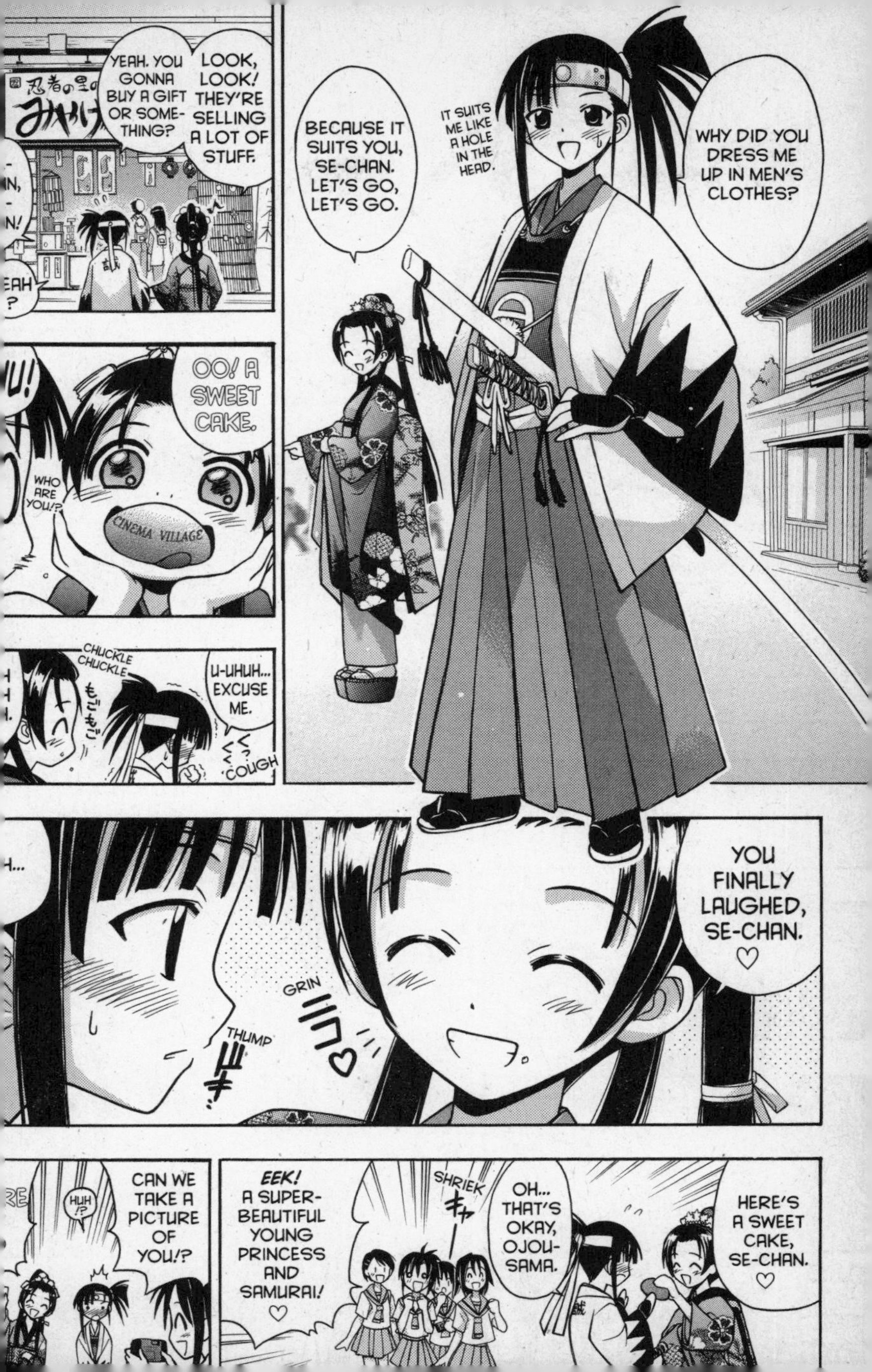

WHY DID YOU DRESS ME UP IN MEN'S CLOTHES?
IT SUITS ME LIKE A HOLE IN THE HEAD.
BECAUSE IT SUITS YOU, SE-CHAN. LET'S GO, LET'S GO.
LOOK, LOOK! THEY'RE SELLING A LOT OF STUFF.
YEAH. YOU GONNA BUY A GIFT OR SOME-THING?
OO! A SWEET CAKE.
CINEMA VILLAGE
WHO ARE YOU!?
U-UHUH... EXCUSE ME.
COUGH
CHUCKLE CHUCKLE
YOU FINALLY LAUGHED, SE-CHAN. ♡
GRIN
THUMP
HERE'S A SWEET CAKE, SE-CHAN. ♡
OH... THAT'S OKAY, OJOU-SAMA.
SHRIEK
EEK! A SUPER-BEAUTIFUL YOUNG PRINCESS AND SAMURAI! ♡
CAN WE TAKE A PICTURE OF YOU!?
HUH!?

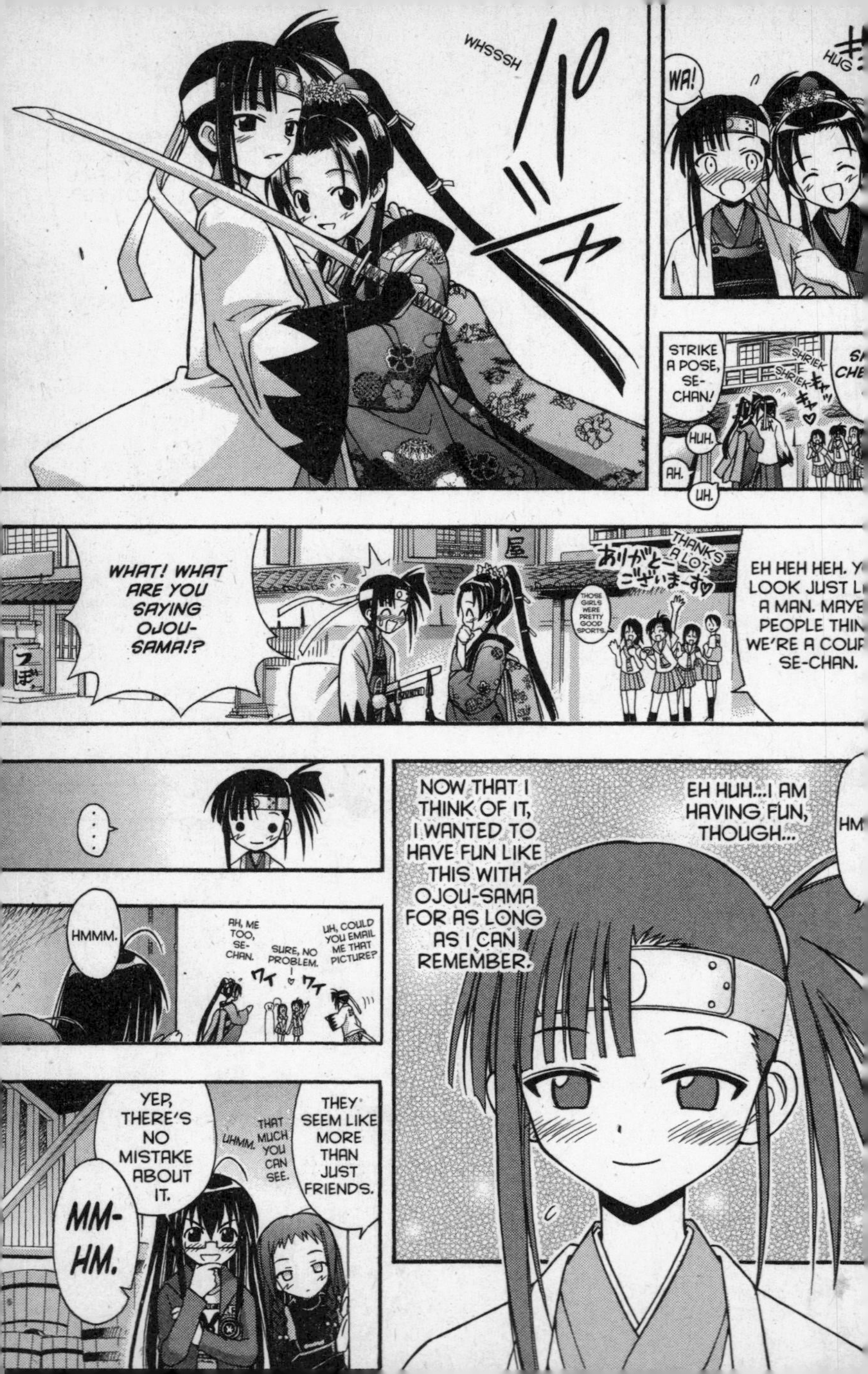

WA!
HUG
ギュ
STRIKE A POSE, SE-CHAN!
SHRIEK SHRIEK
キャッ キャ♥
HUH.
AH.
UH.
WHSSSH
EH HEH HEH. Y
LOOK JUST L
A MAN. MAYE
PEOPLE THIN
WE'RE A COUP
SE-CHAN.
THANKS A LOT.
ありがとーございまーす♥
THOSE GIRLS WERE PRETTY GOOD SPORTS.
WHAT! WHAT ARE YOU SAYING OJOU-SAMA!?
HM
EH HUH...I AM HAVING FUN, THOUGH...
NOW THAT I THINK OF IT, I WANTED TO HAVE FUN LIKE THIS WITH OJOU-SAMA FOR AS LONG AS I CAN REMEMBER.
...
HMMM.
UH, COULD YOU EMAIL ME THAT PICTURE?
SURE, NO PROBLEM.
AH, ME TOO, SE-CHAN.
ワイ ワイ
THEY SEEM LIKE MORE THAN JUST FRIENDS.
THAT MUCH YOU CAN SEE.
UHMM.
YEP, THERE'S NO MISTAKE ABOUT IT.
MM-HM.

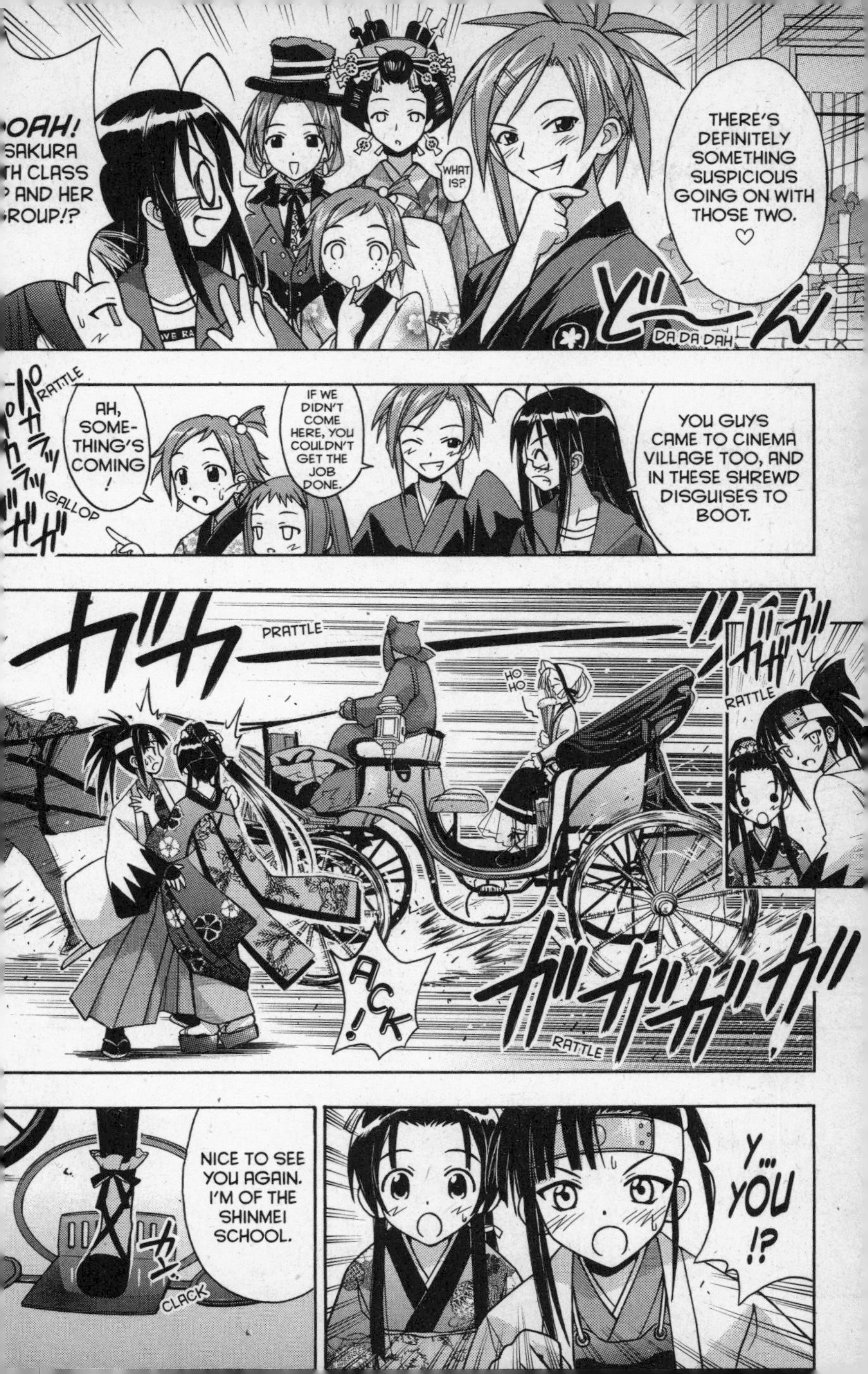
THERE'S DEFINITELY SOMETHING SUSPICIOUS GOING ON WITH THOSE TWO. ♡
DA DA DAH
WHAT IS?
OAH! SAKURA TH CLASS P AND HER ROUP!?
YOU GUYS CAME TO CINEMA VILLAGE TOO, AND IN THESE SHREWD DISGUISES TO BOOT.
IF WE DIDN'T COME HERE, YOU COULDN'T GET THE JOB DONE.
AH, SOME-THING'S COMING!
RATTLE
GALLOP
RATTLE
PRATTLE
HO HO
ACK!
RATTLE
Y... YOU !?
NICE TO SEE YOU AGAIN. I'M OF THE SHINMEI SCHOOL.
CLACK

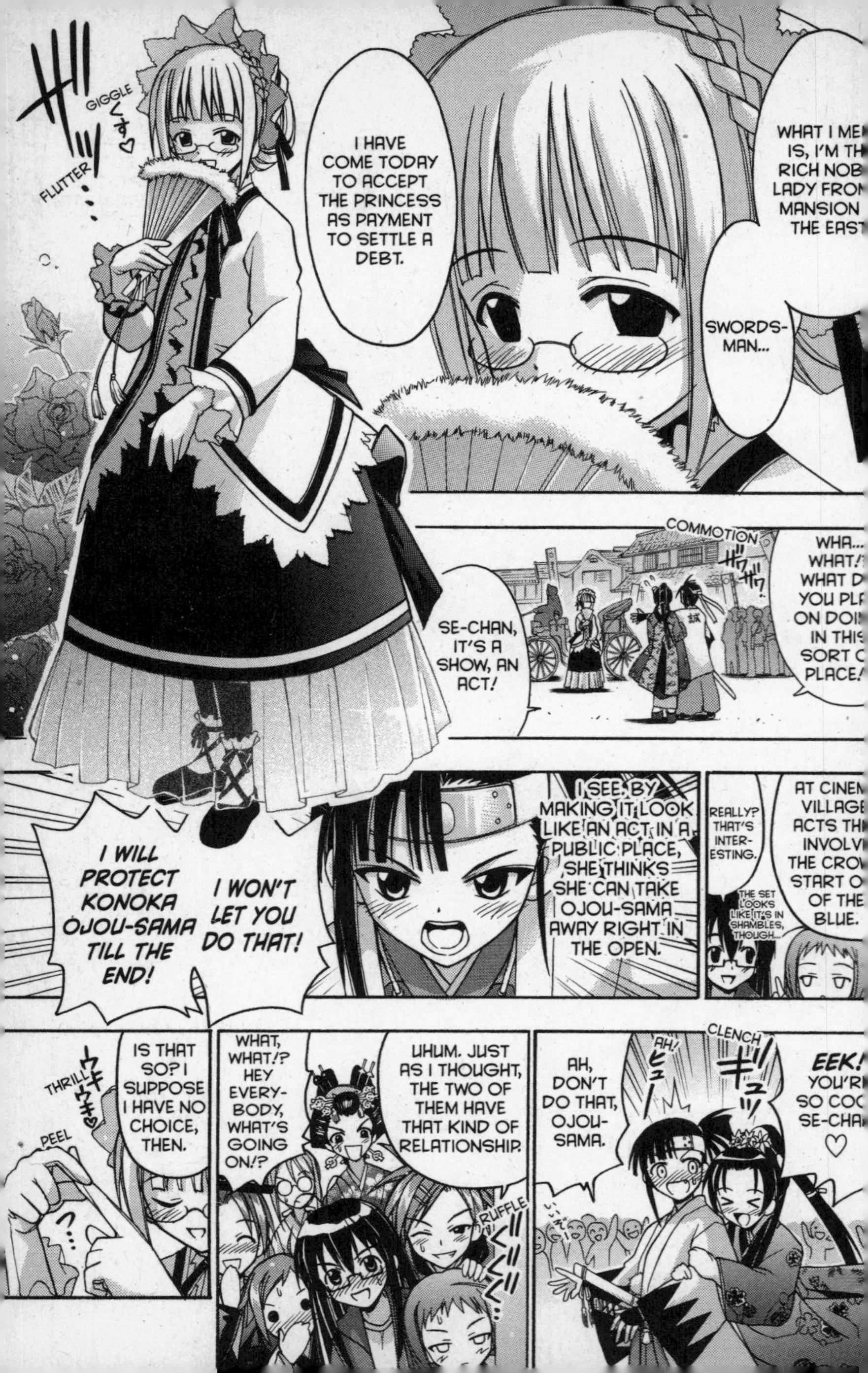

WHAT I ME IS, I'M TH RICH NOB LADY FROM MANSION THE EAST
SWORDS-MAN...
I HAVE COME TODAY TO ACCEPT THE PRINCESS AS PAYMENT TO SETTLE A DEBT.
COMMOTION
WHA... WHAT!? WHAT D YOU PLA ON DOI IN THIS SORT O PLACE!
SE-CHAN, IT'S A SHOW, AN ACT!
GIGGLE
くす♡
FLUTTER
AT CINEM VILLAGE ACTS TH INVOLV THE CROW START O OF THE BLUE.
REALLY? THAT'S INTER-ESTING.
THE SET LOOKS LIKE IT'S IN SHAMBLES, THOUGH...
I SEE. BY MAKING IT LOOK LIKE AN ACT IN A PUBLIC PLACE, SHE THINKS SHE CAN TAKE OJOU-SAMA AWAY RIGHT IN THE OPEN.
I WON'T LET YOU DO THAT!
I WILL PROTECT KONOKA OJOU-SAMA TILL THE END!
EEK! YOU'R SO COO SE-CHA ♡
CLENCH
AH!
AH, DON'T DO THAT, OJOU-SAMA.
UHUM. JUST AS I THOUGHT, THE TWO OF THEM HAVE THAT KIND OF RELATIONSHIP.
WHAT, WHAT!? HEY EVERY-BODY, WHAT'S GOING ON!?
RUFFLE
IS THAT SO? I SUPPOSE I HAVE NO CHOICE, THEN.
THRILL
ウキウキ♡
PEEL

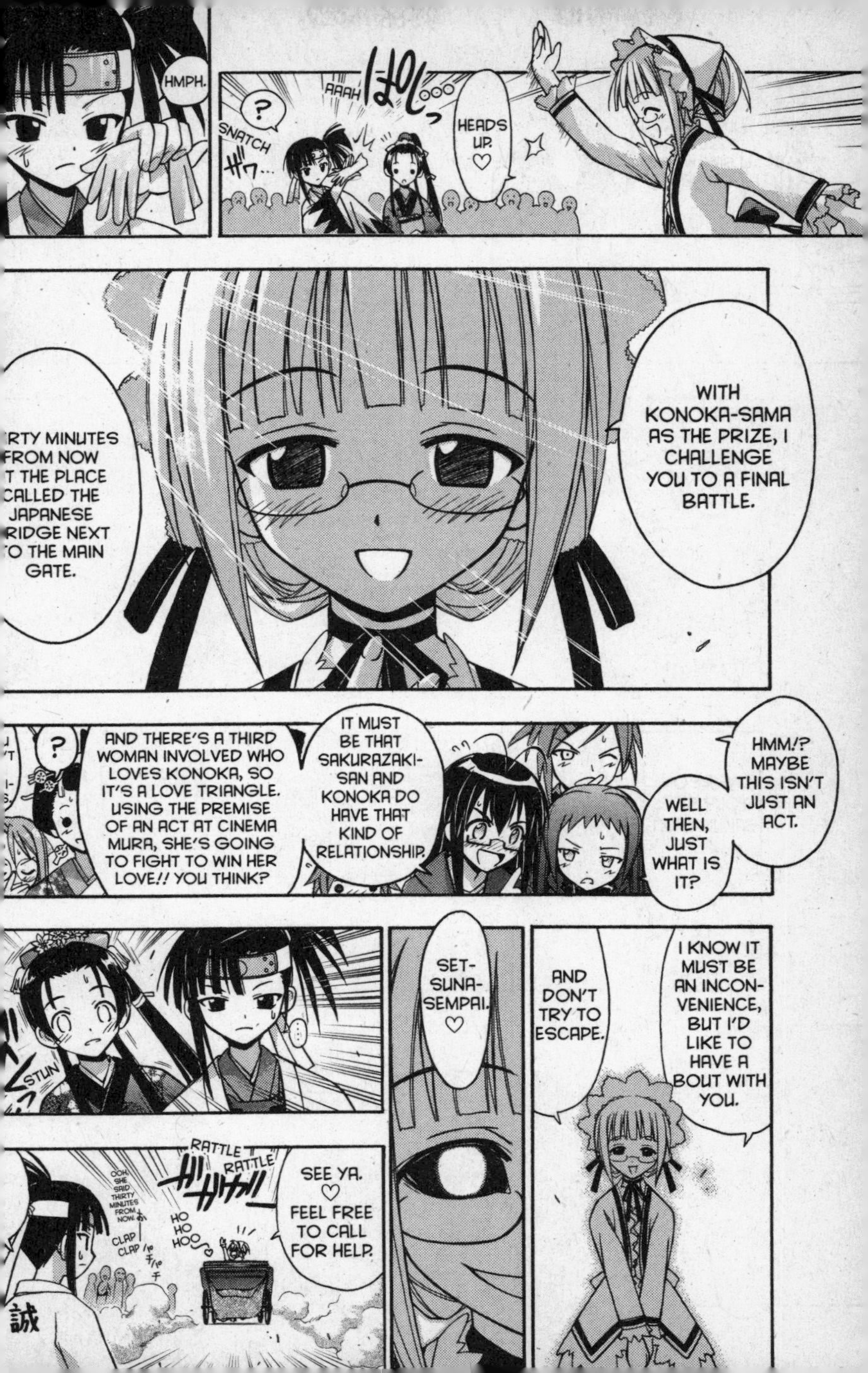

HEADS UP. ♡
AAAH
?
SNATCH
HMPH.
WITH KONOKA-SAMA AS THE PRIZE, I CHALLENGE YOU TO A FINAL BATTLE.
RTY MINUTES FROM NOW T THE PLACE CALLED THE JAPANESE RIDGE NEXT O THE MAIN GATE.
HMM!? MAYBE THIS ISN'T JUST AN ACT.
WELL THEN, JUST WHAT IS IT?
IT MUST BE THAT SAKURAZAKI-SAN AND KONOKA DO HAVE THAT KIND OF RELATIONSHIP.
AND THERE'S A THIRD WOMAN INVOLVED WHO LOVES KONOKA, SO IT'S A LOVE TRIANGLE. USING THE PREMISE OF AN ACT AT CINEMA MURA, SHE'S GOING TO FIGHT TO WIN HER LOVE!! YOU THINK?
?
I KNOW IT MUST BE AN INCONVENIENCE, BUT I'D LIKE TO HAVE A BOUT WITH YOU.
AND DON'T TRY TO ESCAPE.
SET-SUNA-SEMPAI. ♡
STUN
...
RATTLE RATTLE
SEE YA. ♡ FEEL FREE TO CALL FOR HELP.
HO HO HOO
OOH, SHE SAID THIRTY MINUTES FROM NOW.
CLAP CLAP

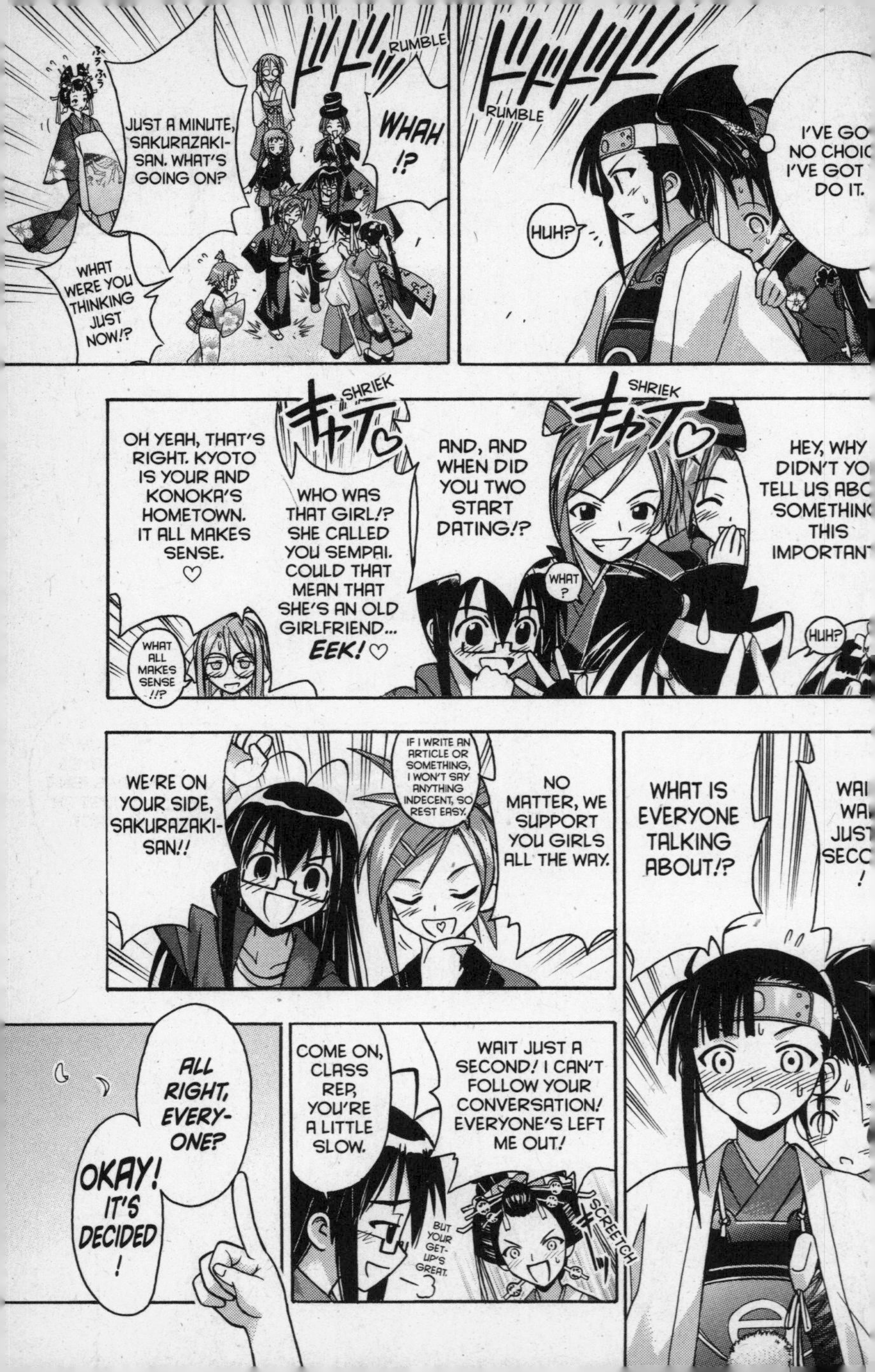
RUMBLE
I'VE GO NO CHOIC I'VE GOT DO IT.
HUH?
RUMBLE
WHAH!?
JUST A MINUTE, SAKURAZAKI-SAN. WHAT'S GOING ON?
WHAT WERE YOU THINKING JUST NOW!?
HEY, WHY DIDN'T YO TELL US ABO SOMETHIN THIS IMPORTANT
HUH?
SHRIEK
AND, AND WHEN DID YOU TWO START DATING!?
WHAT?
SHRIEK
WHO WAS THAT GIRL!? SHE CALLED YOU SEMPAI. COULD THAT MEAN THAT SHE'S AN OLD GIRLFRIEND... EEK! ♡
OH YEAH, THAT'S RIGHT. KYOTO IS YOUR AND KONOKA'S HOMETOWN. IT ALL MAKES SENSE. ♡
WHAT ALL MAKES SENSE!?
WAI WAI JUST SECO!
WHAT IS EVERYONE TALKING ABOUT!?
NO MATTER, WE SUPPORT YOU GIRLS ALL THE WAY.
IF I WRITE AN ARTICLE OR SOMETHING, I WON'T SAY ANYTHING INDECENT, SO REST EASY.
WE'RE ON YOUR SIDE, SAKURAZAKI-SAN!!
WAIT JUST A SECOND! I CAN'T FOLLOW YOUR CONVERSATION! EVERYONE'S LEFT ME OUT!
COME ON, CLASS REP, YOU'RE A LITTLE SLOW.
SCREECH
BUT YOUR GET-UP'S GREAT.
ALL RIGHT, EVERY-ONE?
OKAY! IT'S DECIDED!

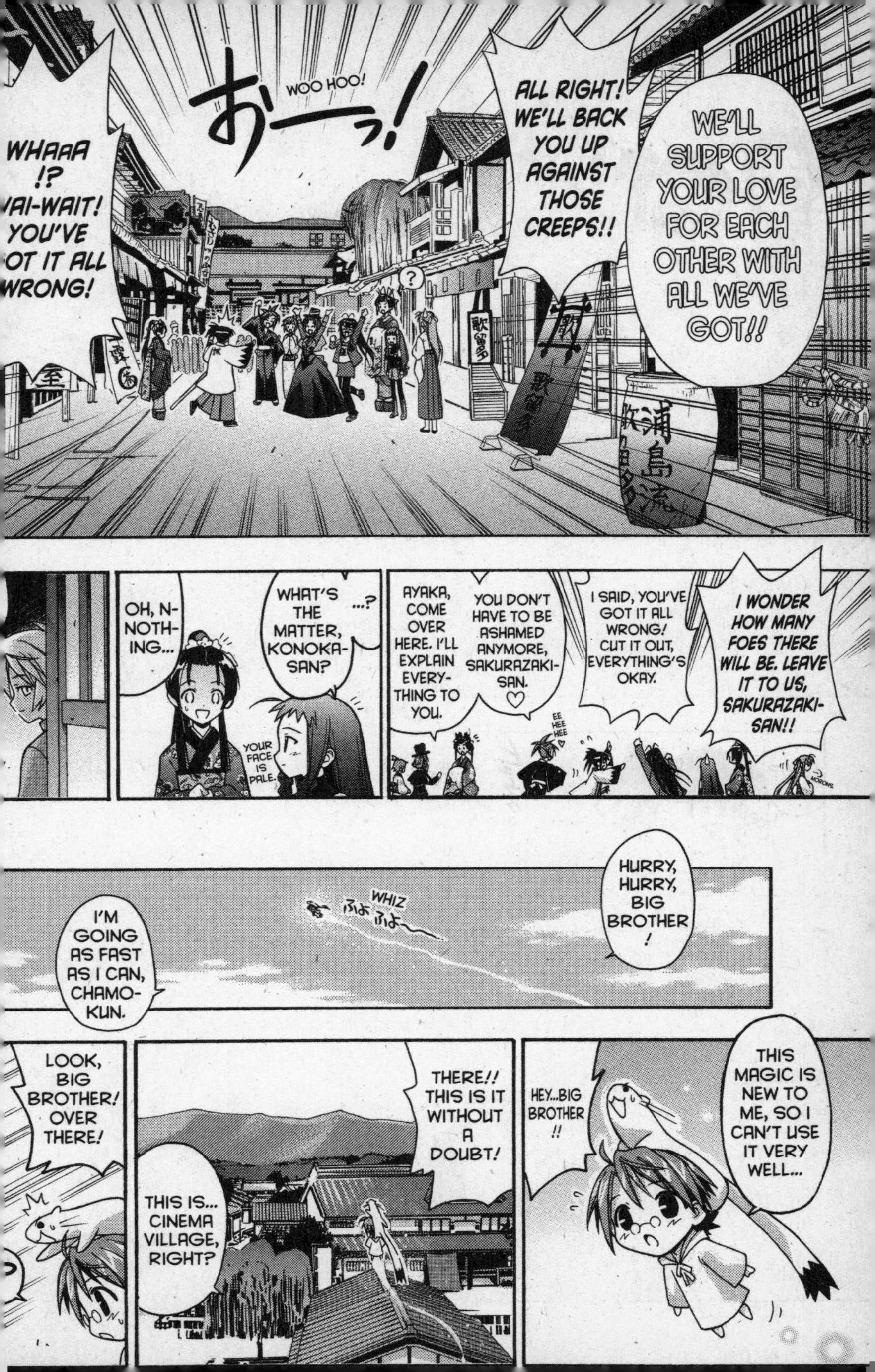
WE'LL SUPPORT YOUR LOVE FOR EACH OTHER WITH ALL WE'VE GOT!!
ALL RIGHT! WE'LL BACK YOU UP AGAINST THOSE CREEPS!!
おーっ!
WOO HOO!
?
WHAAA !? AI-WAIT! YOU'VE OT IT ALL WRONG!
浦島流
I WONDER HOW MANY FOES THERE WILL BE. LEAVE IT TO US, SAKURAZAKI-SAN!!
I SAID, YOU'VE GOT IT ALL WRONG! CUT IT OUT, EVERYTHING'S OKAY.
YOU DON'T HAVE TO BE ASHAMED ANYMORE, SAKURAZAKI-SAN. ♡
AYAKA, COME OVER HERE. I'LL EXPLAIN EVERYTHING TO YOU.
EE HEE HEE
MORONS.
...?
WHAT'S THE MATTER, KONOKA-SAN?
YOUR FACE IS PALE.
OH, N-NOTHING...
HURRY, HURRY, BIG BROTHER!
WHIZ
ふよふよ〜
I'M GOING AS FAST AS I CAN, CHAMO-KUN.
THIS MAGIC IS NEW TO ME, SO I CAN'T USE IT VERY WELL...
HEY...BIG BROTHER!!
THERE!! THIS IS IT WITHOUT A DOUBT!
THIS IS... CINEMA VILLAGE, RIGHT?
LOOK, BIG BROTHER! OVER THERE!

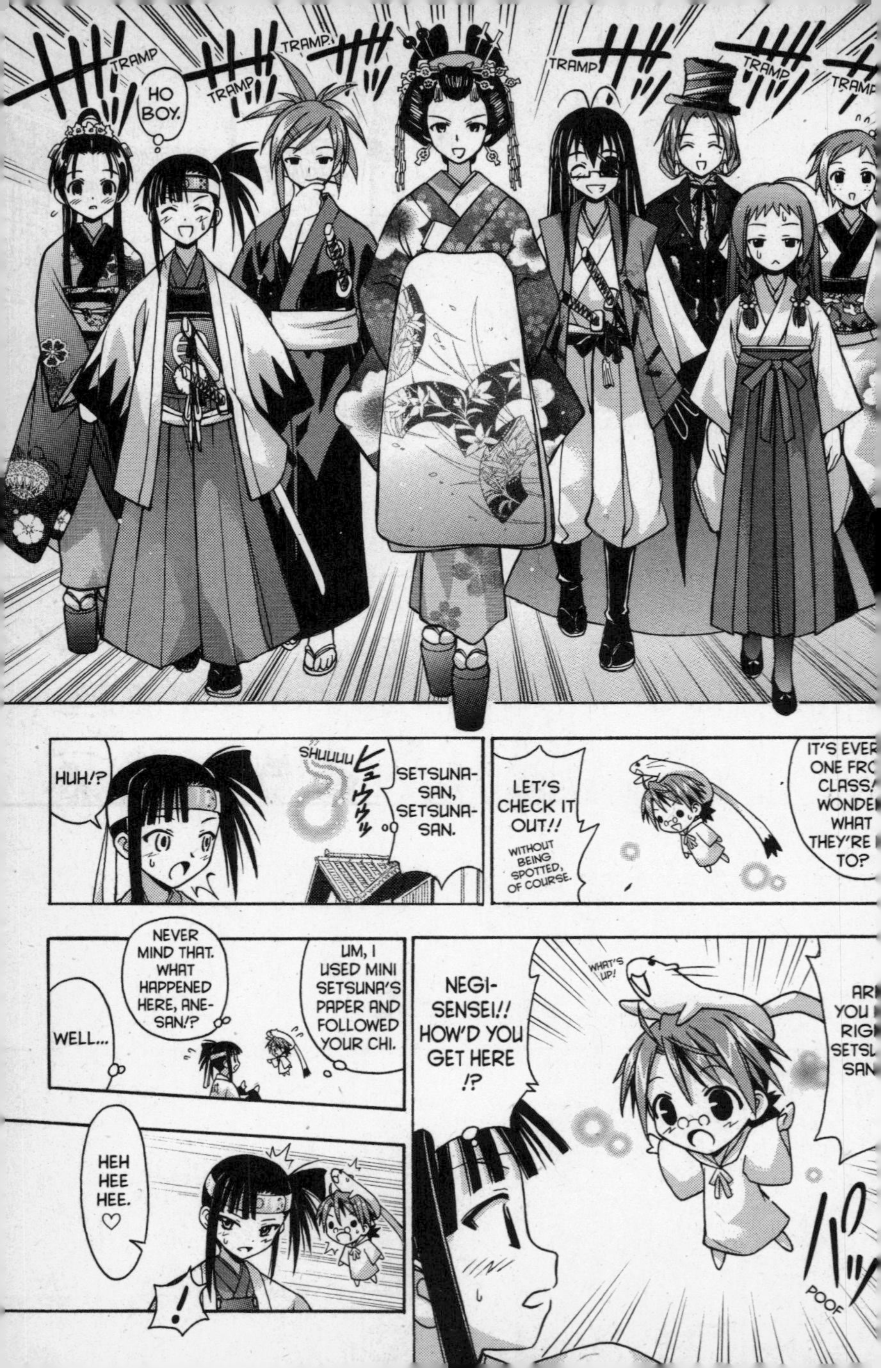
TRAMP
TRAMP
TRAMP
TRAMP.
TRAMP
HO BOY.
TRAMP
IT'S EVER ONE FRO CLASS! WONDE WHAT THEY'RE TO?
LET'S CHECK IT OUT!!
WITHOUT BEING SPOTTED, OF COURSE.
SETSUNA-SAN, SETSUNA-SAN.
SHUUUU
HUH!?
AR YOU RIG SETSU SAN
WHAT'S UP!
NEGI-SENSEI!! HOW'D YOU GET HERE !?
UM, I USED MINI SETSUNA'S PAPER AND FOLLOWED YOUR CHI.
NEVER MIND THAT. WHAT HAPPENED HERE, ANE-SAN!?
WELL...
POOF
HEH HEE HEE. ♡
!

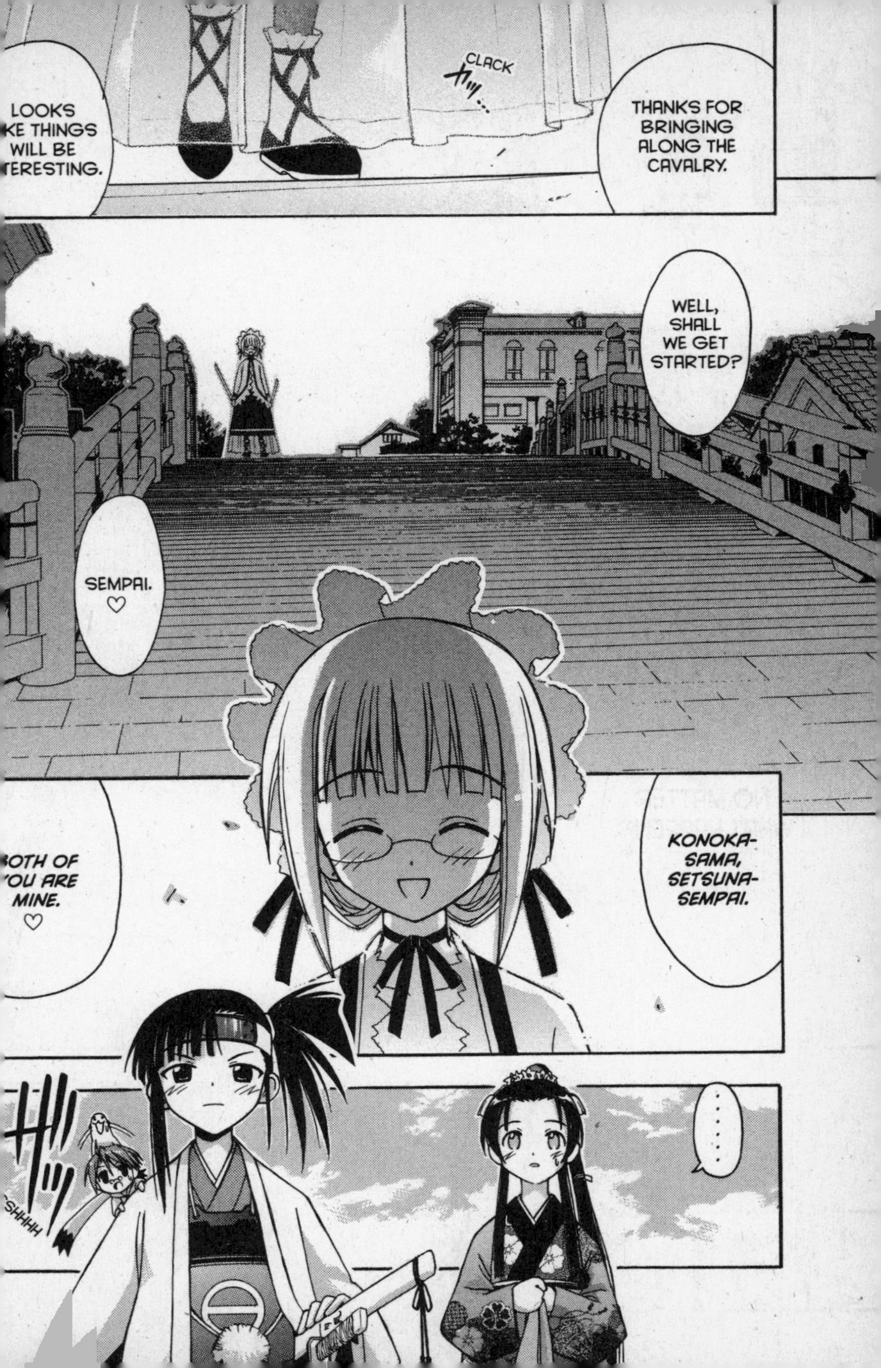
THANKS FOR BRINGING ALONG THE CAVALRY.
CLACK
LOOKS KE THINGS WILL BE TERESTING.
WELL, SHALL WE GET STARTED?
SEMPAI. ♡
KONOKA-SAMA, SETSUNA-SEMPAI.
OTH OF OU ARE MINE. ♡
......
SHHHH

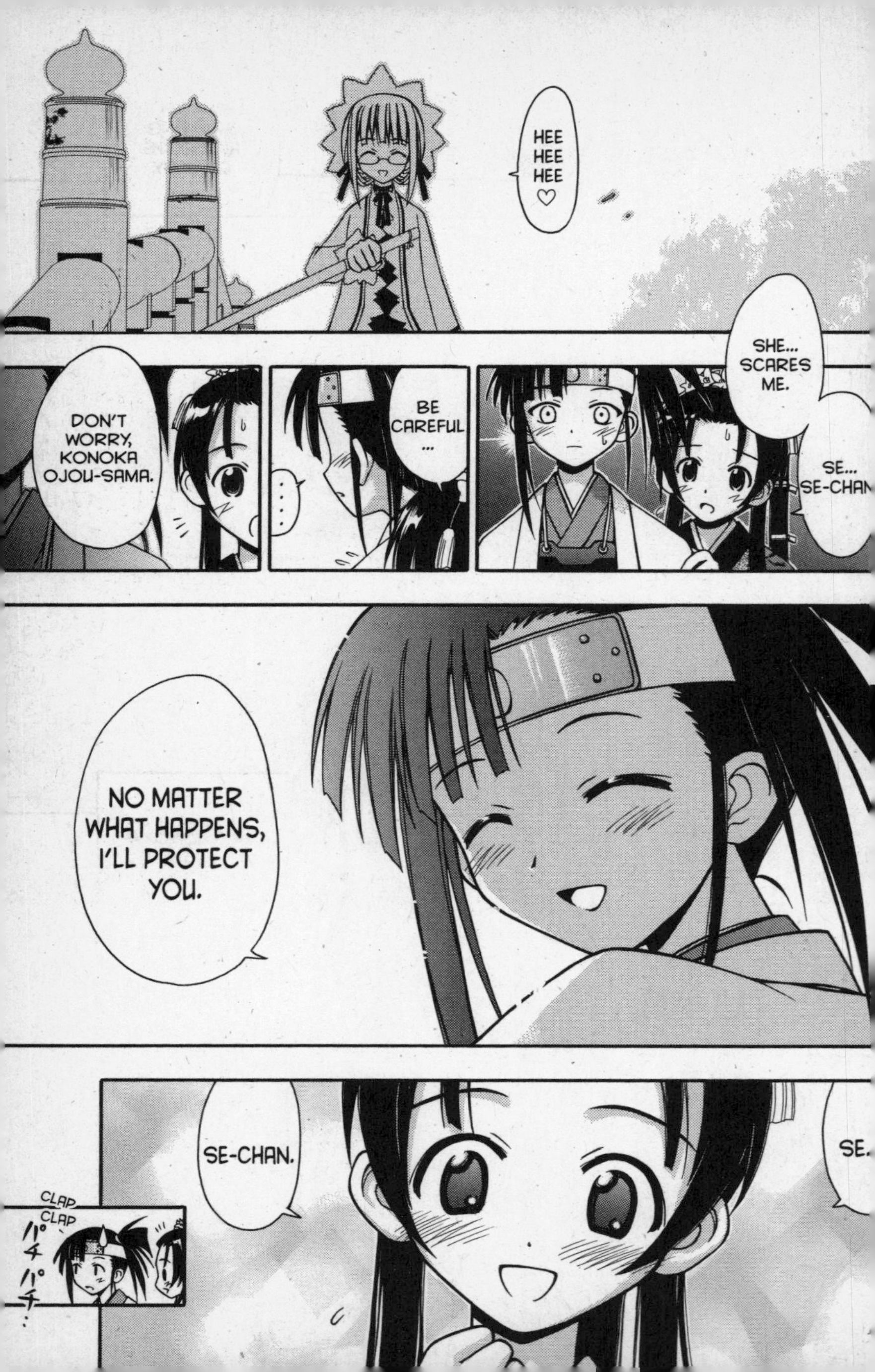
HEE HEE HEE ♡
SHE... SCARES ME.
SE... SE-CHAN
BE CAREFUL ...
...
DON'T WORRY, KONOKA OJOU-SAMA.
NO MATTER WHAT HAPPENS, I'LL PROTECT YOU.
SE.
SE-CHAN.
CLAP CLAP
パチパチ…

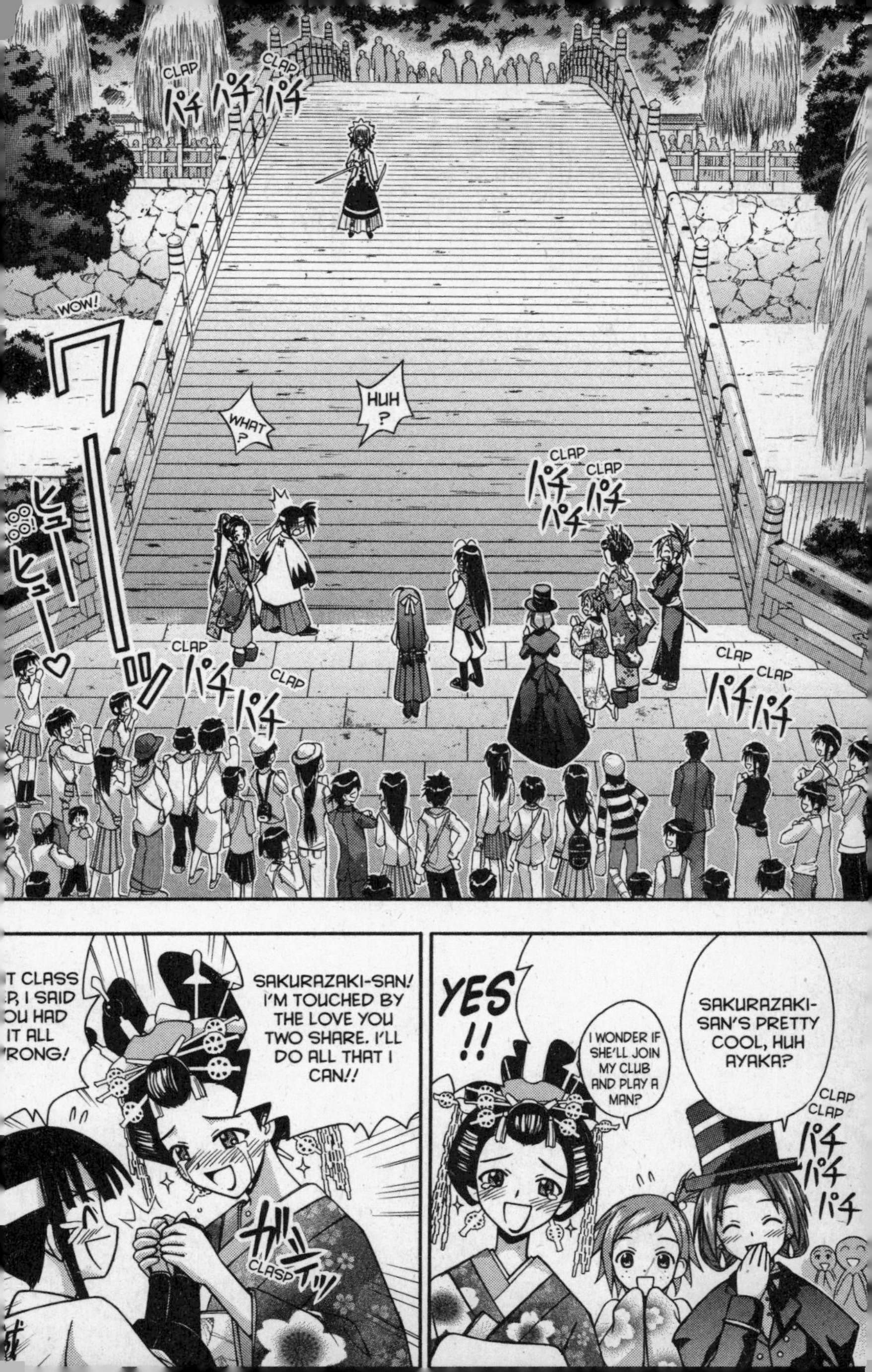

CLAP
CLAP
パチ パチ パチ
WOW!
HUH ?
WHAT ?
CLAP
CLAP
パチ パチ パチ
ヒューヒュー♥
ooo!
CLAP
CLAP
パチ パチ
CLAP
CLAP
パチ パチ
SAKURAZAKI-SAN'S PRETTY COOL, HUH AYAKA?
I WONDER IF SHE'LL JOIN MY CLUB AND PLAY A MAN?
YES !!
CLAP
CLAP
パチ パチ パチ
SAKURAZAKI-SAN! I'M TOUCHED BY THE LOVE YOU TWO SHARE. I'LL DO ALL THAT I CAN!!
T CLASS P, I SAID OU HAD IT ALL RONG!
CLASP

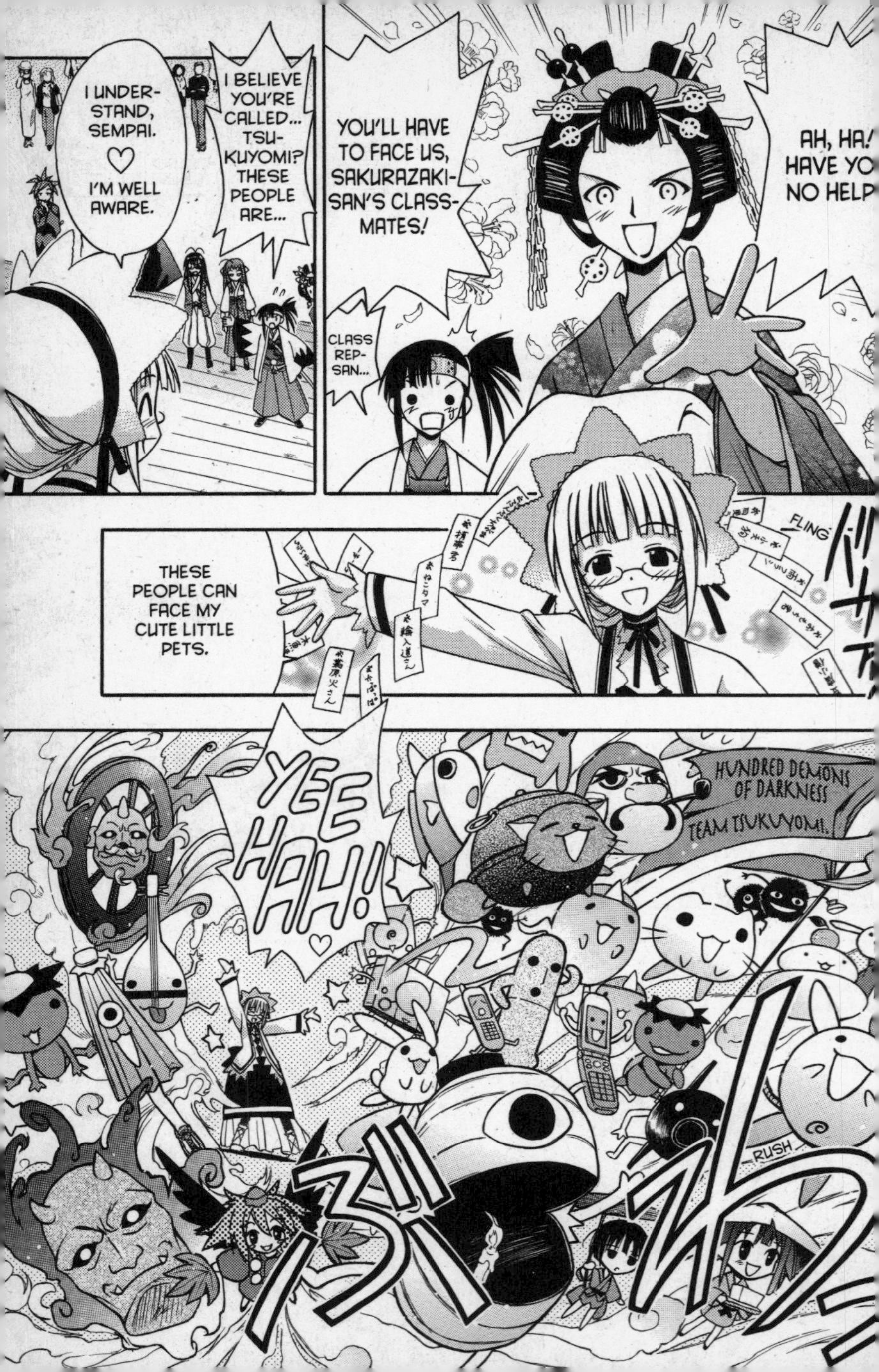
AH, HA! HAVE YO NO HELP
YOU'LL HAVE TO FACE US, SAKURAZAKI-SAN'S CLASS-MATES!
CLASS REP-SAN...
I BELIEVE YOU'RE CALLED... TSU-KUYOMI? THESE PEOPLE ARE...
I UNDER-STAND, SEMPAI. ♡ I'M WELL AWARE.
FLING
THESE PEOPLE CAN FACE MY CUTE LITTLE PETS.
HUNDRED DEMONS OF DARKNESS
TEAM TSUKUYOMI
YEE HAH!
RUSH

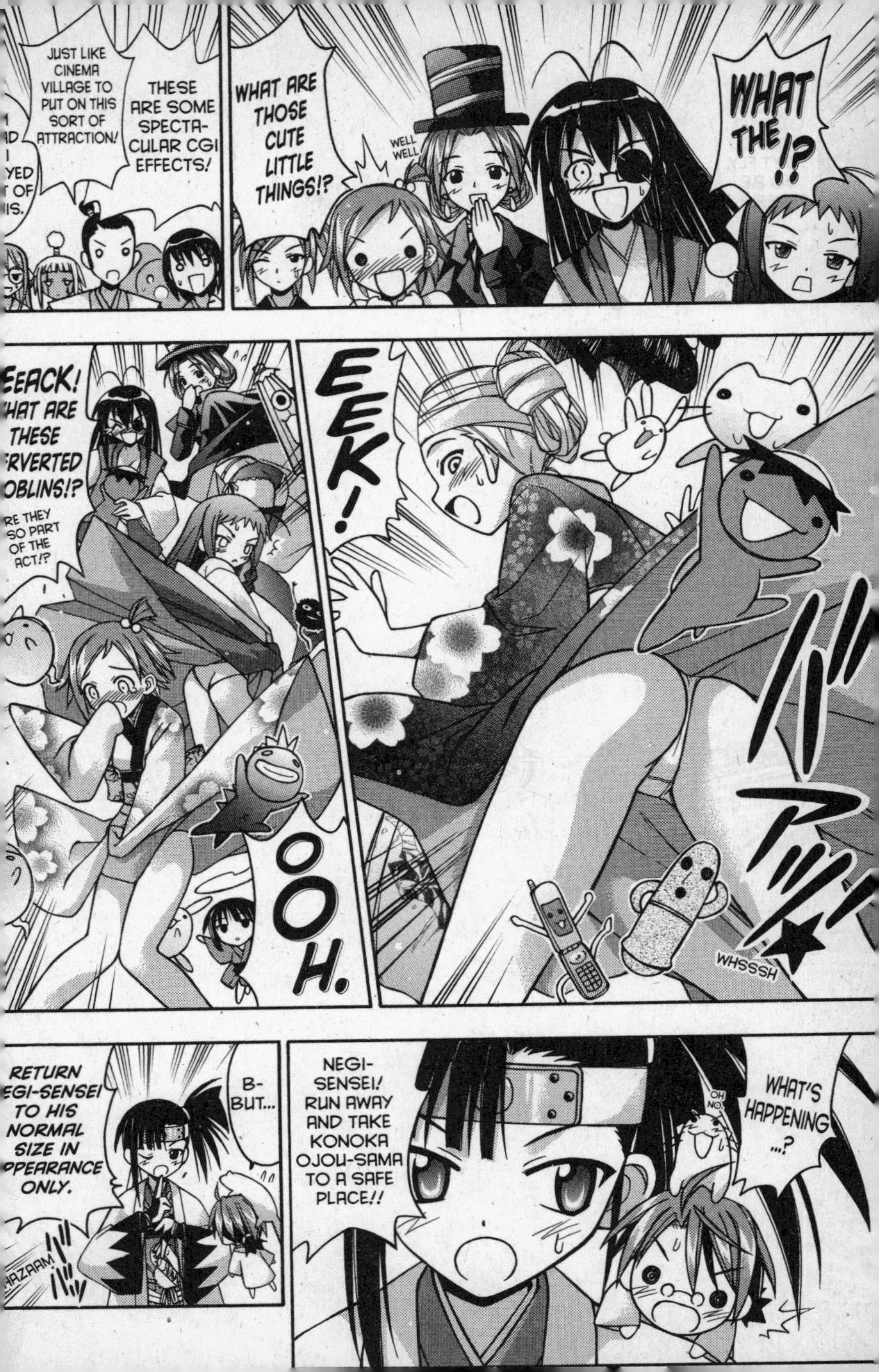
WHAT THE!?
WELL WELL
WHAT ARE THOSE CUTE LITTLE THINGS!?
THESE ARE SOME SPECTACULAR CGI EFFECTS!
JUST LIKE CINEMA VILLAGE TO PUT ON THIS SORT OF ATTRACTION!
EEK!
WHSSSH
OOOH.
EEACK! HAT ARE THESE ERVERTED OBLINS!?
RE THEY SO PART OF THE ACT!?
WHAT'S HAPPENING...?
OH NO.
NEGI-SENSEI! RUN AWAY AND TAKE KONOKA OJOU-SAMA TO A SAFE PLACE!!
B-BUT...
RETURN EGI-SENSEI TO HIS NORMAL SIZE IN PPEARANCE ONLY.
AZAAM

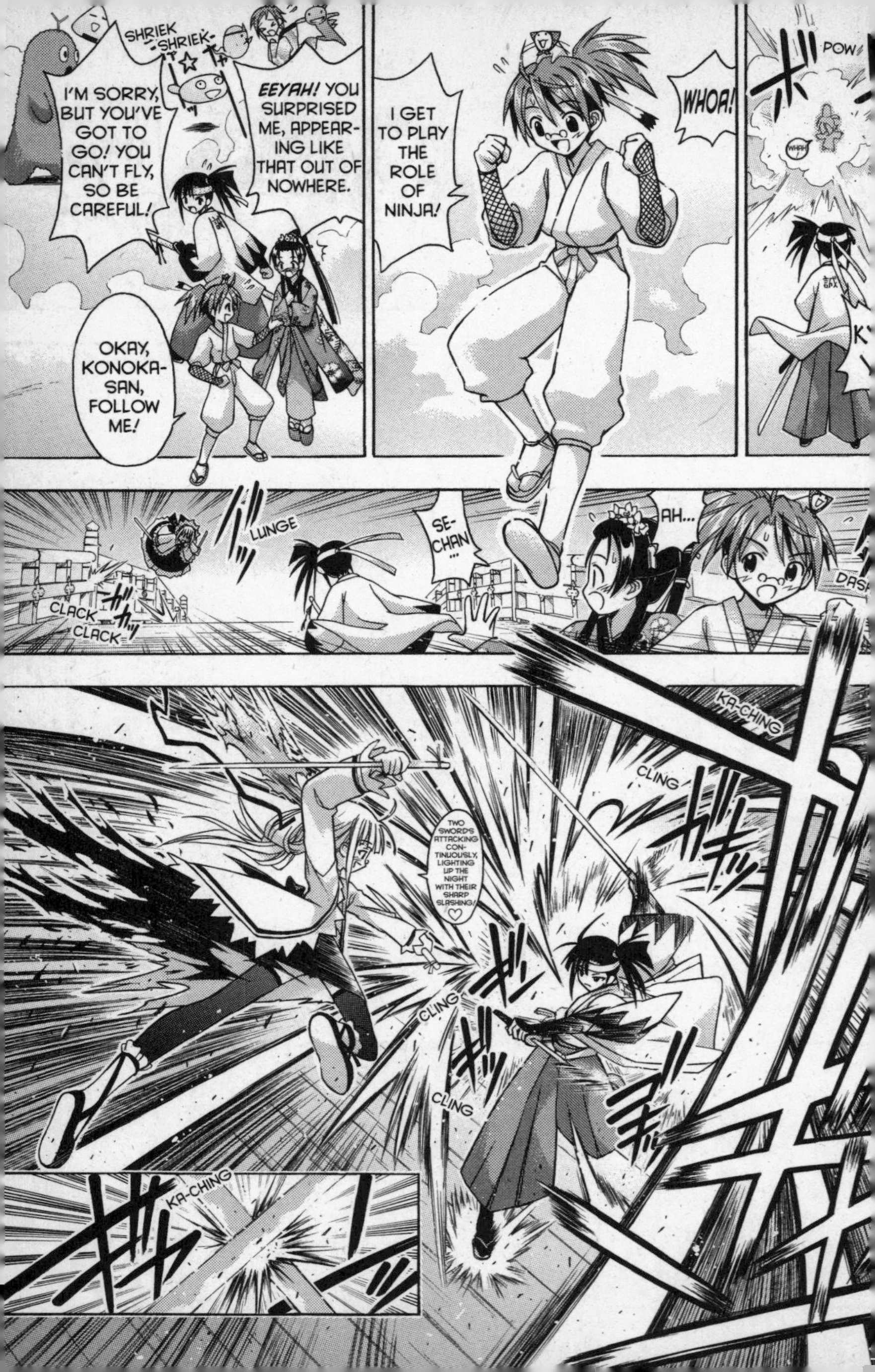
POW
WHOA!
I GET TO PLAY THE ROLE OF NINJA!
SHRIEK SHRIEK
EEYAH! YOU SURPRISED ME, APPEARING LIKE THAT OUT OF NOWHERE.
I'M SORRY, BUT YOU'VE GOT TO GO! YOU CAN'T FLY, SO BE CAREFUL!
OKAY, KONOKA-SAN, FOLLOW ME!
DASH
AH...
SE-CHAN...
LUNGE
CLACK
CLACK
KA-CHING
CLING
TWO SWORDS ATTACKING CONTINUOUSLY, LIGHTING UP THE NIGHT WITH THEIR SHARP SLASHING! ♡
CLING
CLING
KA-CHING

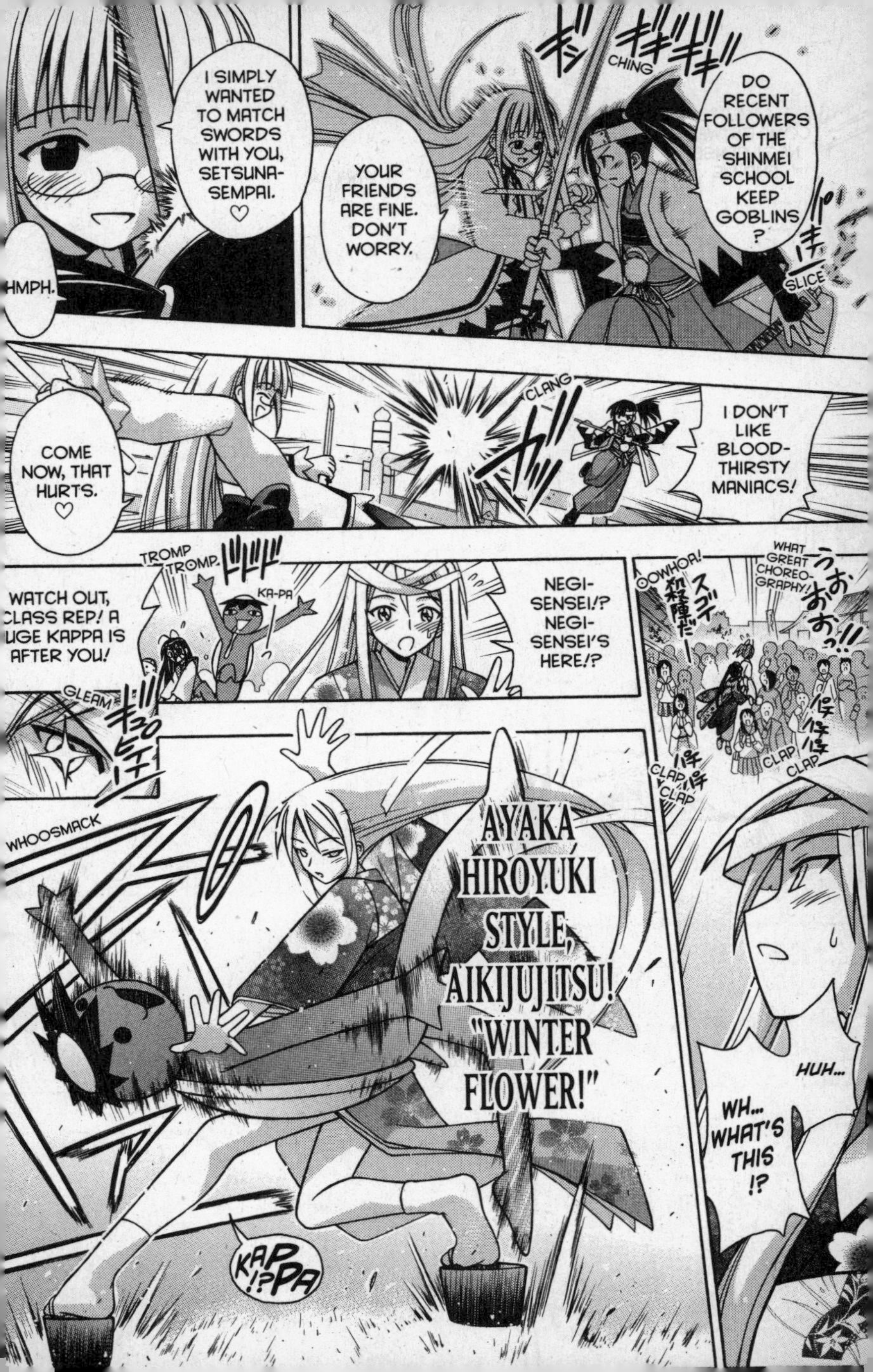
CHING
DO RECENT FOLLOWERS OF THE SHINMEI SCHOOL KEEP GOBLINS?
YOUR FRIENDS ARE FINE. DON'T WORRY.
SLICE
I SIMPLY WANTED TO MATCH SWORDS WITH YOU, SETSUNA-SEMPAI. ♡
HMPH.
I DON'T LIKE BLOOD-THIRSTY MANIACS!
CLANG
COME NOW, THAT HURTS. ♡
うおおおっ!!
WHAT GREAT CHOREOGRAPHY!
スゴイ殺陣だー
OOWHOA!
CLAP CLAP
CLAP CLAP
NEGI-SENSEI!? NEGI-SENSEI'S HERE!?
TROMP TROMP.
KA-PA
WATCH OUT, CLASS REP! A UGE KAPPA IS AFTER YOU!
HUH...
WH... WHAT'S THIS!?
GLEAM
WHOOSMACK
AYAKA HIROYUKI STYLE, AIKIJUJITSU! "WINTER FLOWER!"
KAPPA!?

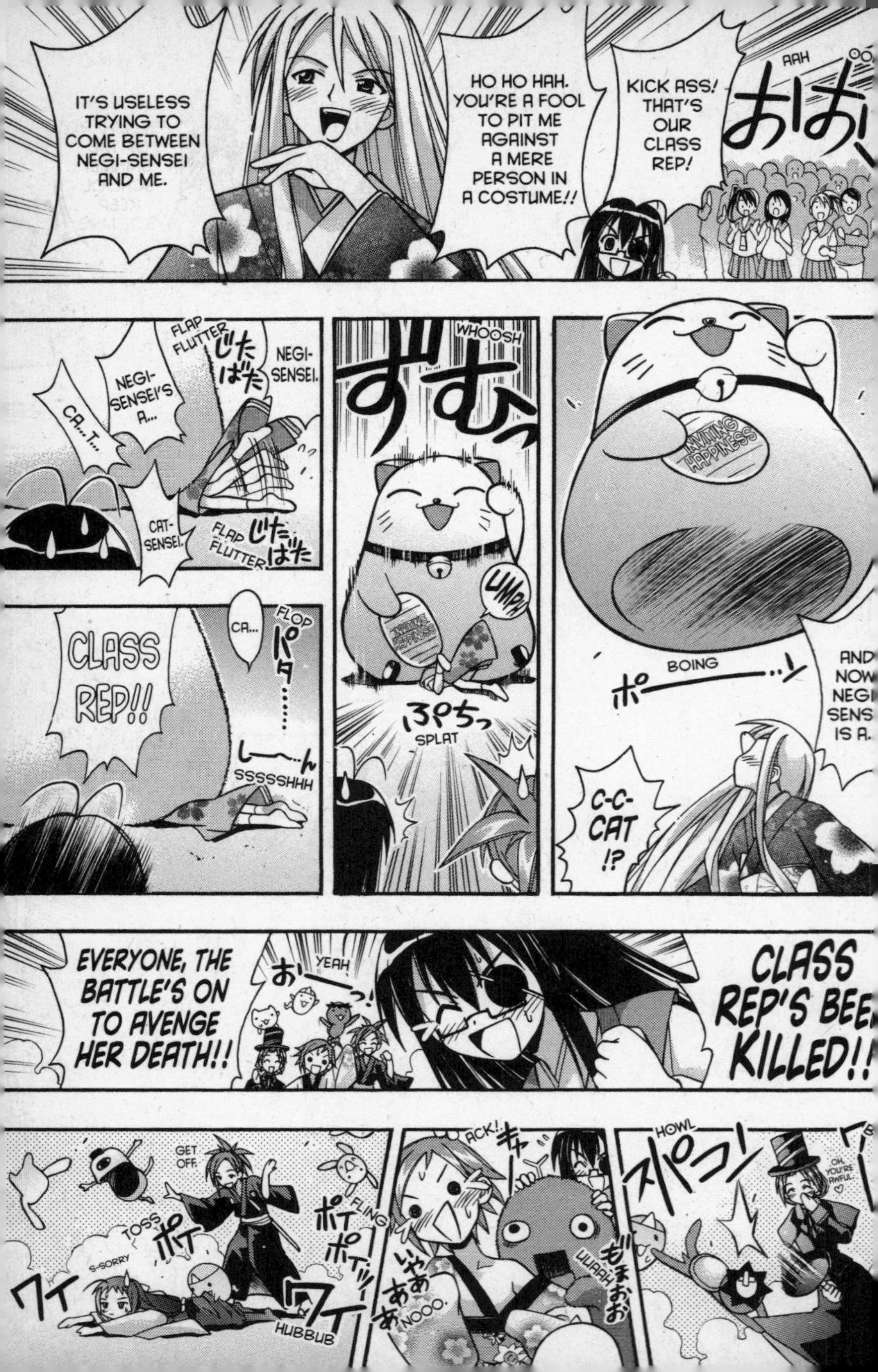

おぉ!
AAH
KICK ASS! THAT'S OUR CLASS REP!
HO HO HAH. YOU'RE A FOOL TO PIT ME AGAINST A MERE PERSON IN A COSTUME!!
IT'S USELESS TRYING TO COME BETWEEN NEGI-SENSEI AND ME.
INVITING HAPPINESS
ポー…ン
BOING
AND NOW NEGI SENS IS A.
C-C-CAT!?
ずむっ
WHOOSH
UMPH
INVITING HAPPINESS
ぷちっ
SPLAT
NEGI-SENSEI.
じたばた
FLAP FLUTTER
NEGI-SENSEI'S A...
CA...T...
CAT-SENSEI.
じたばた
FLAP FLUTTER
CA...
パタ……
FLOP
し〜…ん
SSSSSHHH
CLASS REP!!
CLASS REP'S BEE KILLED!!
お──っ!
YEAH
EVERYONE, THE BATTLE'S ON TO AVENGE HER DEATH!!
OH, YOU'RE AWFUL. ♡
スパコーン!
HOWL
キャー
ACK!
もぉぉ
UUAAH
いやああ
NOOO.
ポイポイッ
FLING
GET OFF.
ポイ
TOSS
S-SORRY
ワイワイ
HUBBUB

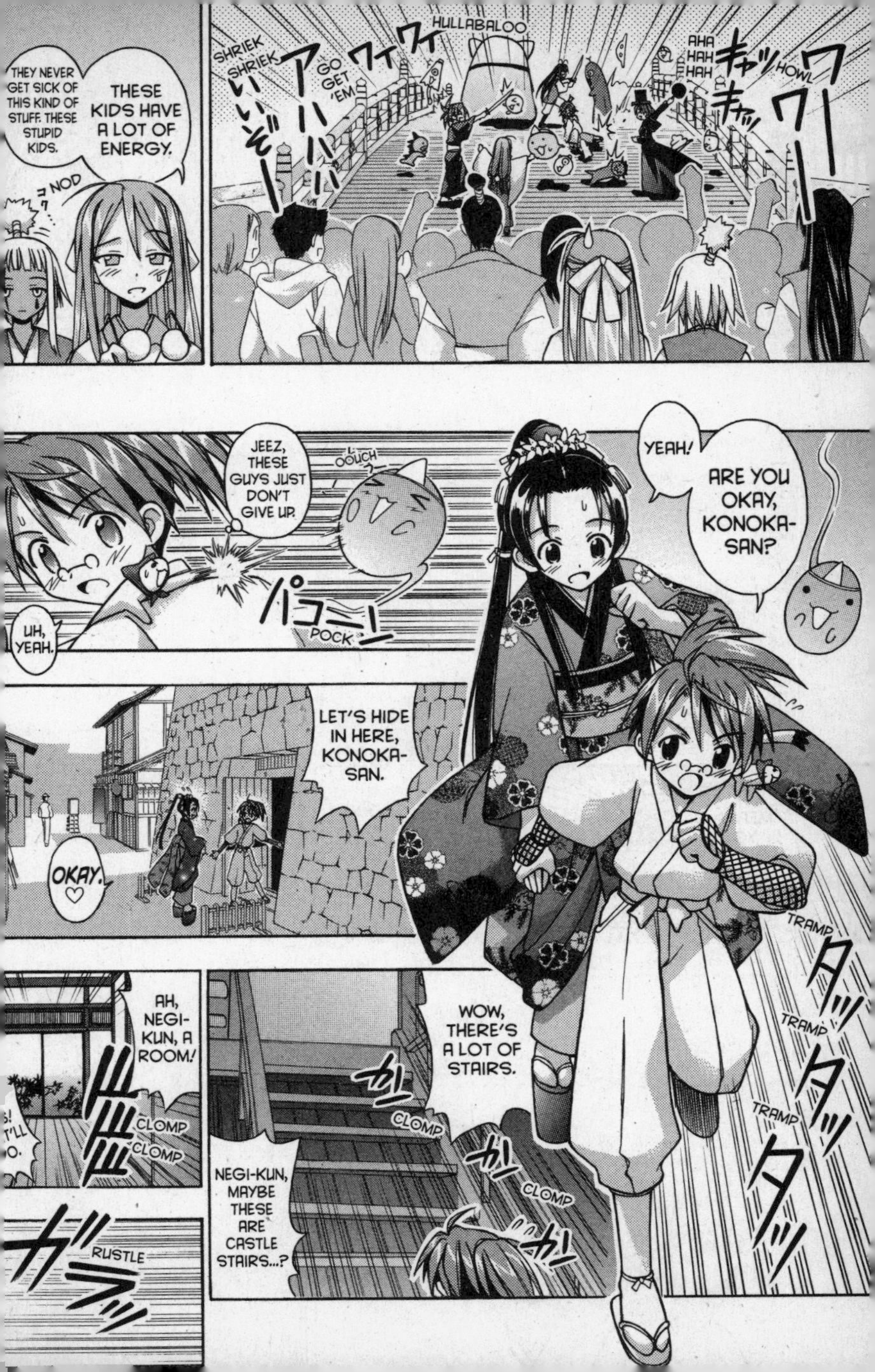
HULLABALOO
AHA HAH HAH
HOWL
GO GET 'EM
SHRIEK SHRIEK
THESE KIDS HAVE A LOT OF ENERGY.
THEY NEVER GET SICK OF THIS KIND OF STUFF. THESE STUPID KIDS.
NOD
ARE YOU OKAY, KONOKA-SAN?
YEAH!
TRAMP
TRAMP
TRAMP
JEEZ, THESE GUYS JUST DON'T GIVE UP.
OUCH
POCK
UH, YEAH.
LET'S HIDE IN HERE, KONOKA-SAN.
OKAY. ♡
WOW, THERE'S A LOT OF STAIRS.
CLOMP
CLOMP
NEGI-KUN, MAYBE THESE ARE CASTLE STAIRS...?
AH, NEGI-KUN, A ROOM!
CLOMP
CLOMP
RUSTLE

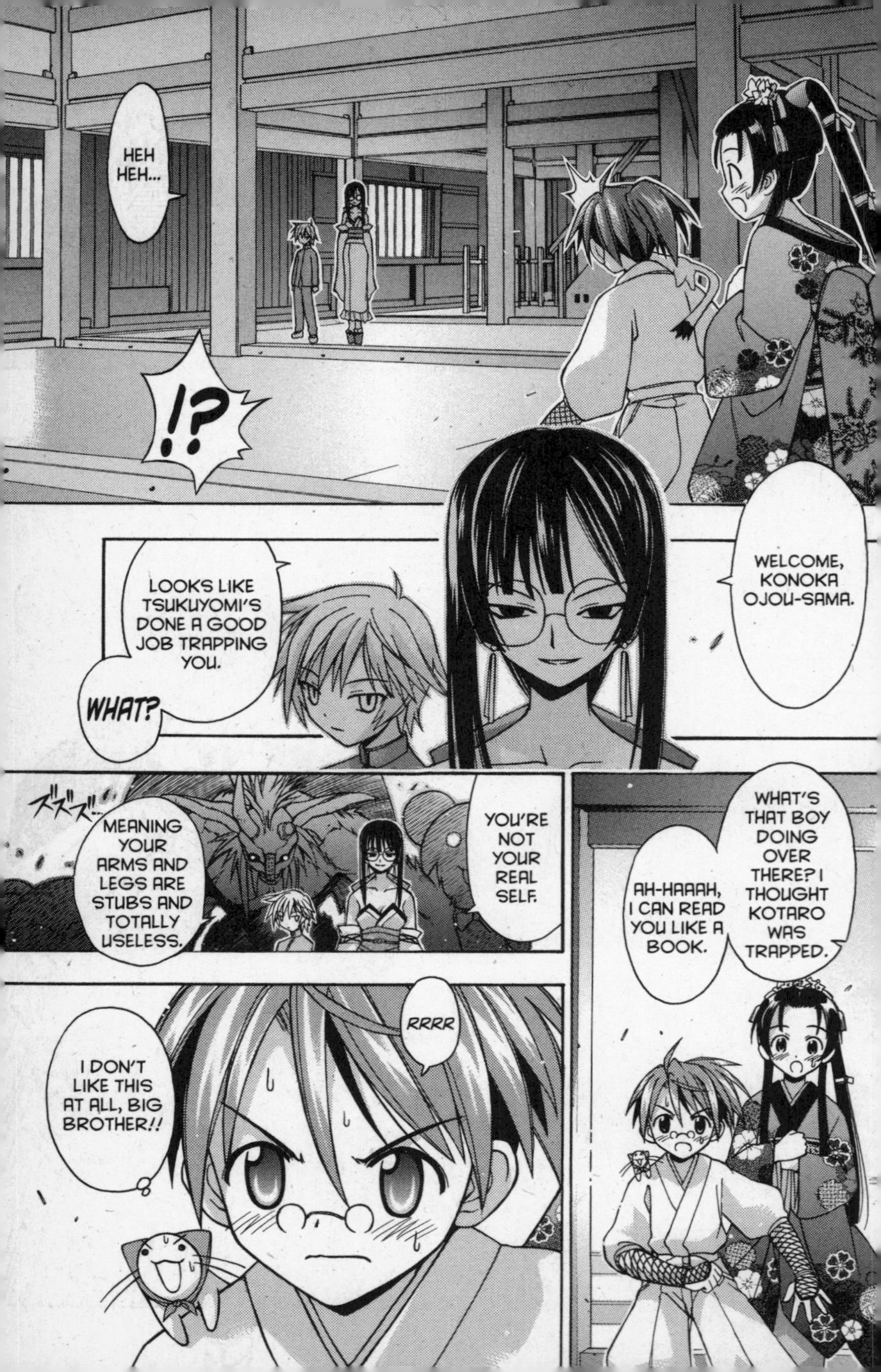
HEH HEH...
!?
WELCOME, KONOKA OJOU-SAMA.
LOOKS LIKE TSUKUYOMI'S DONE A GOOD JOB TRAPPING YOU.
WHAT?
WHAT'S THAT BOY DOING OVER THERE? I THOUGHT KOTARO WAS TRAPPED.
AH-HAAAH, I CAN READ YOU LIKE A BOOK.
YOU'RE NOT YOUR REAL SELF.
MEANING YOUR ARMS AND LEGS ARE STUBS AND TOTALLY USELESS.
ズズズ...
RRRR
I DON'T LIKE THIS AT ALL, BIG BROTHER!!

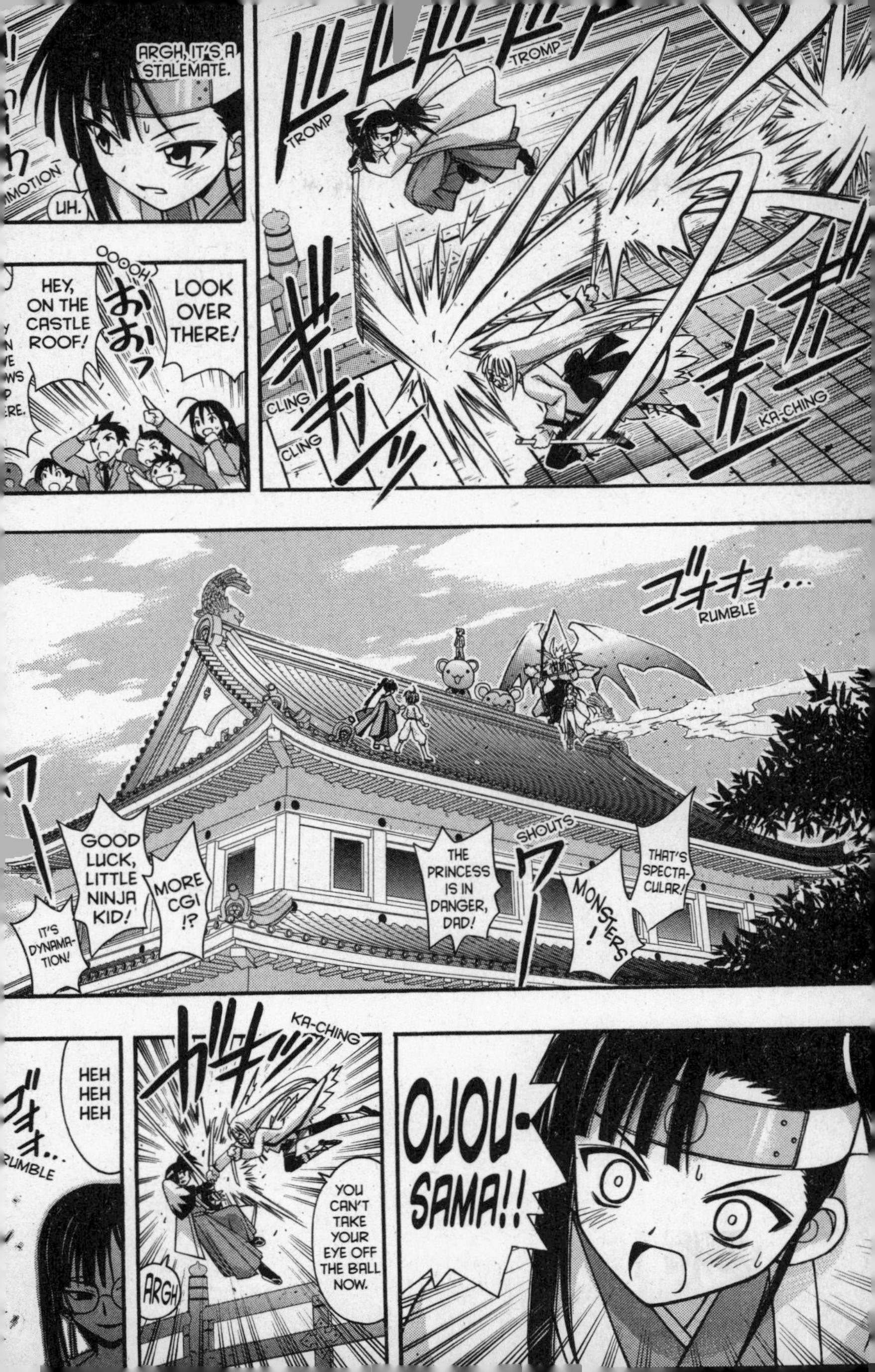
TROMP
TROMP
CLING
CLING
KA-CHING
ARGH, IT'S A STALEMATE.
UH.
LOOK OVER THERE!
OOOOH
HEY, ON THE CASTLE ROOF!
RUMBLE
THAT'S SPECTA-CULAR!
MONSTERS!
SHOUTS
THE PRINCESS IS IN DANGER, DAD!
MORE CGI!?
GOOD LUCK, LITTLE NINJA KID!
IT'S DYNAMA-TION!
OJOU-SAMA!!
KA-CHING
YOU CAN'T TAKE YOUR EYE OFF THE BALL NOW.
ARGH
HEH HEH HEH
RUMBLE

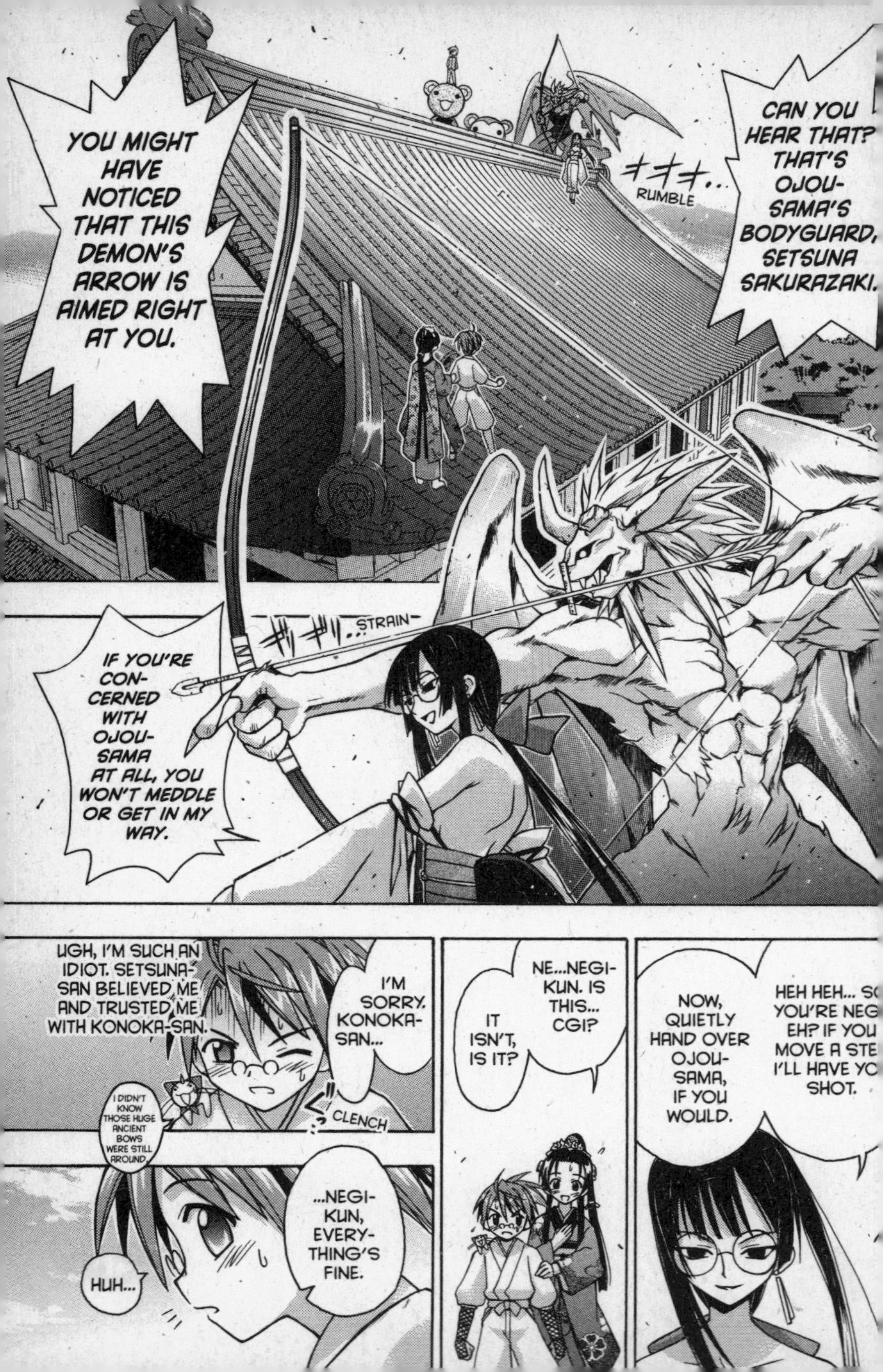
CAN YOU HEAR THAT? THAT'S OJOU-SAMA'S BODYGUARD, SETSUNA SAKURAZAKI.
RUMBLE
YOU MIGHT HAVE NOTICED THAT THIS DEMON'S ARROW IS AIMED RIGHT AT YOU.
STRAIN
IF YOU'RE CON-CERNED WITH OJOU-SAMA AT ALL, YOU WON'T MEDDLE OR GET IN MY WAY.
HEH HEH... S YOU'RE NEG EH? IF YOU MOVE A STE I'LL HAVE YO SHOT.
NOW, QUIETLY HAND OVER OJOU-SAMA, IF YOU WOULD.
NE...NEGI-KUN. IS THIS... CGI?
IT ISN'T, IS IT?
I'M SORRY. KONOKA-SAN...
UGH, I'M SUCH AN IDIOT. SETSUNA-SAN BELIEVED ME AND TRUSTED ME WITH KONOKA-SAN.
CLENCH
I DIDN'T KNOW THOSE HUGE ANCIENT BOWS WERE STILL AROUND.
...NEGI-KUN, EVERY-THING'S FINE.
HUH...

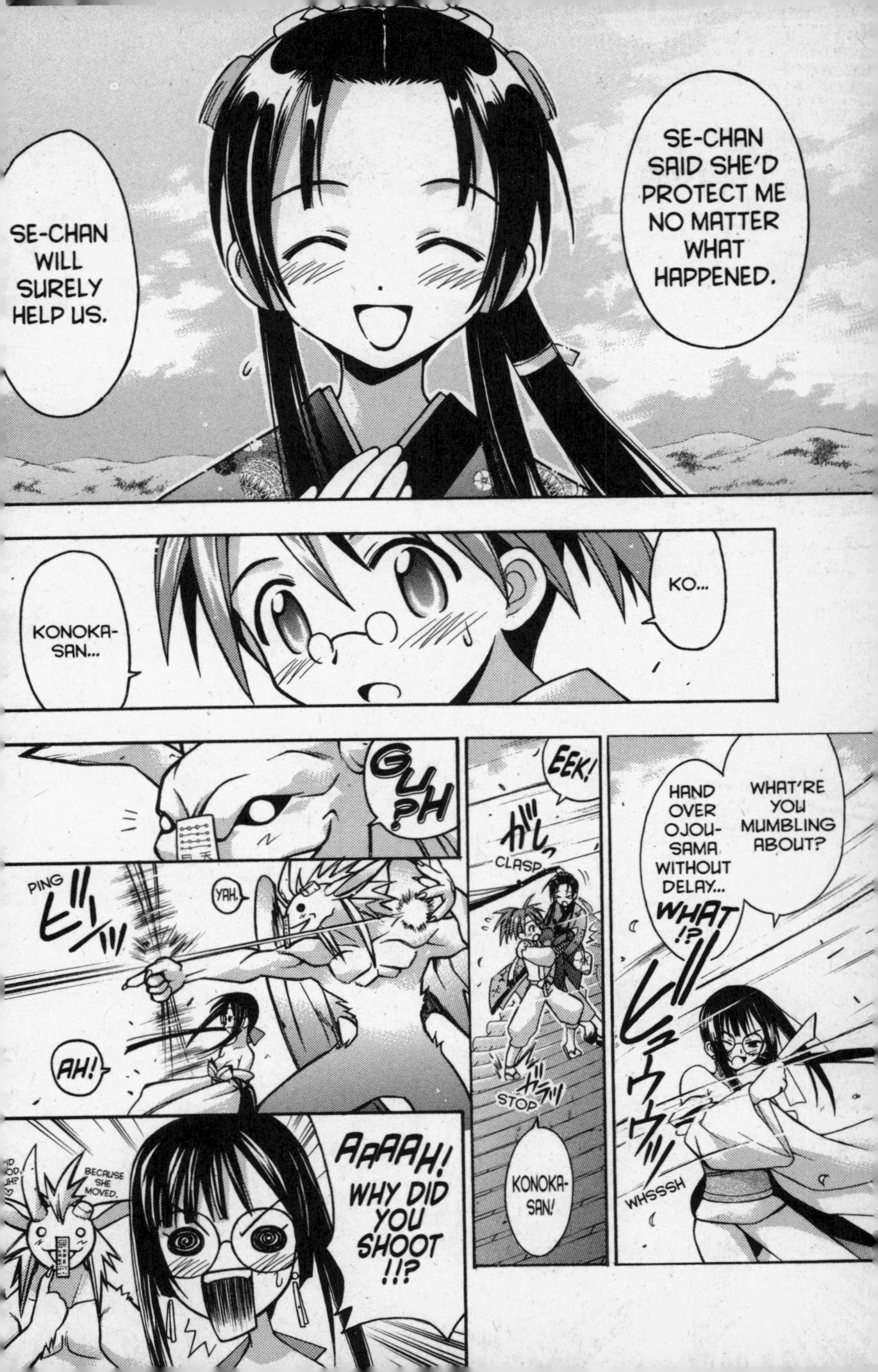
SE-CHAN SAID SHE'D PROTECT ME NO MATTER WHAT HAPPENED.
SE-CHAN WILL SURELY HELP US.
KO...
KONOKA-SAN...
WHAT'RE YOU MUMBLING ABOUT?
HAND OVER OJOU-SAMA WITHOUT DELAY... WHAT!?
WHSSSH
EEK!
CLASP
STOP
KONOKA-SAN!
GUH!?
YAH.
PING
AH!
AAAAH! WHY DID YOU SHOOT!!?
BECAUSE SHE MOVED.

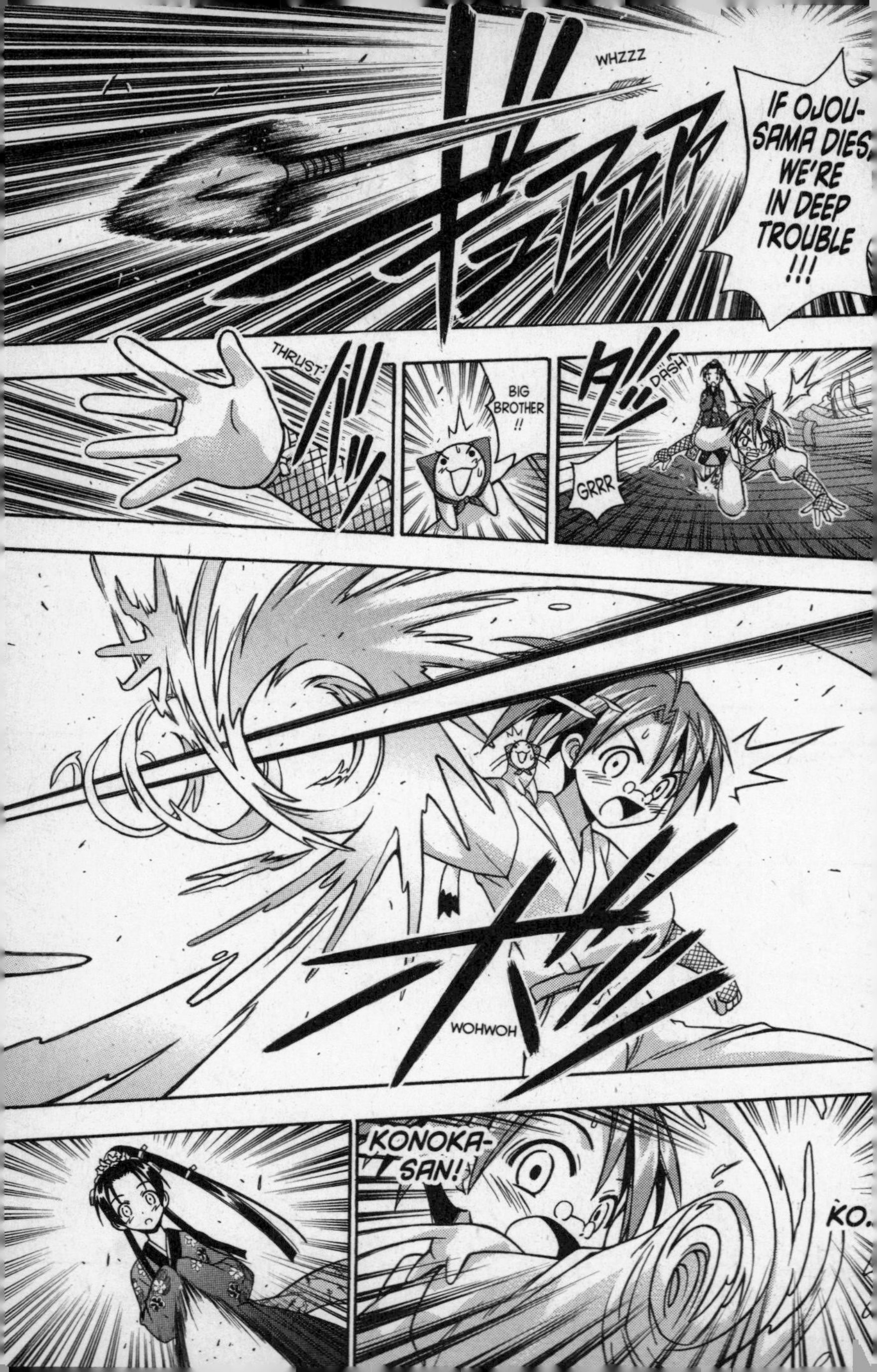
IF OJOU-SAMA DIES, WE'RE IN DEEP TROUBLE!!!
WHZZZ
DASH
GRRR
BIG BROTHER!!
THRUST
WOHWOH
KO...
KONOKA-SAN!

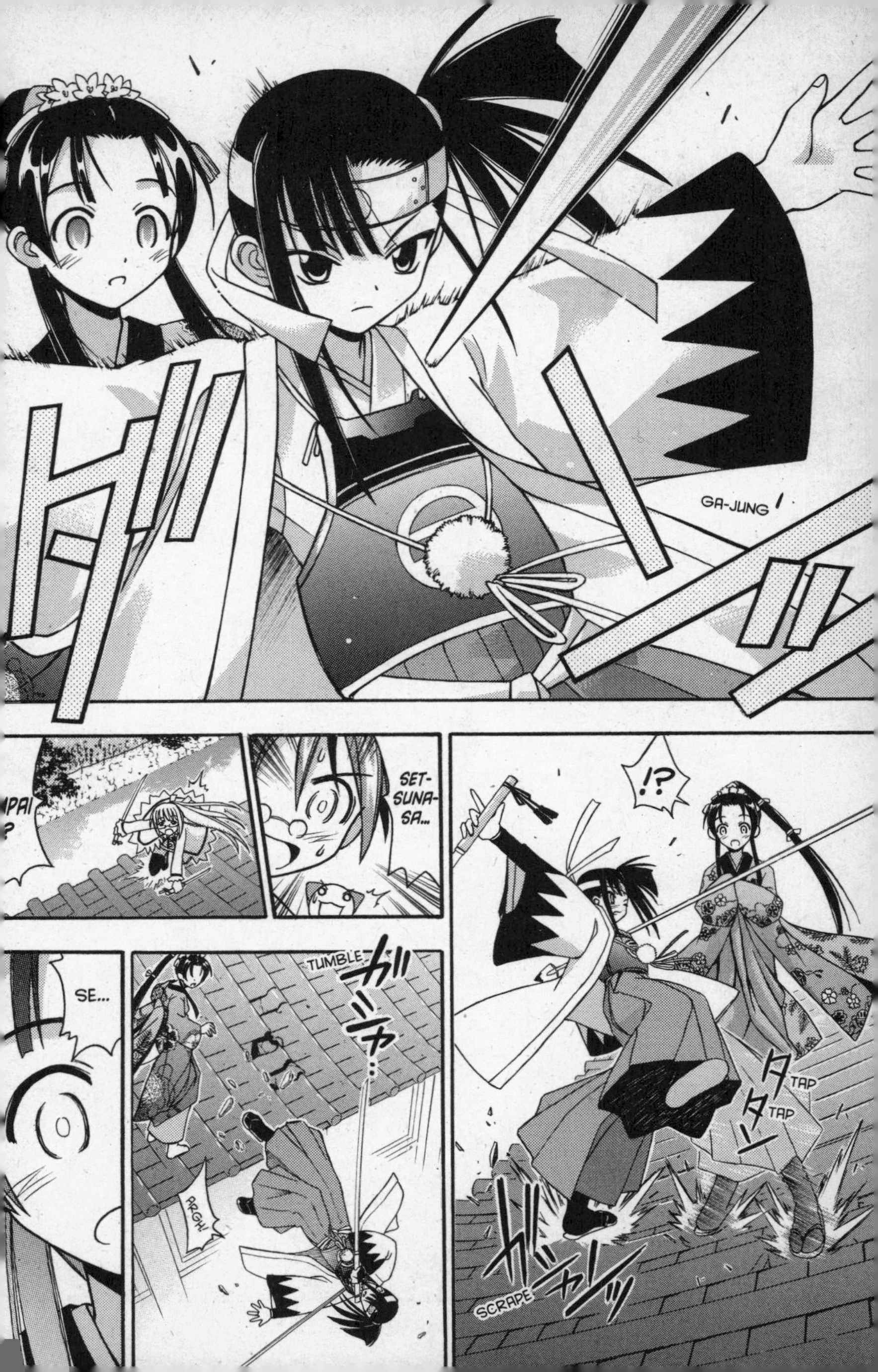
GA-JUNG
!?
TAP
TAP
SCRAPE
SET-
SUNA-
SA...
TUMBLE
ARGH!
SE...

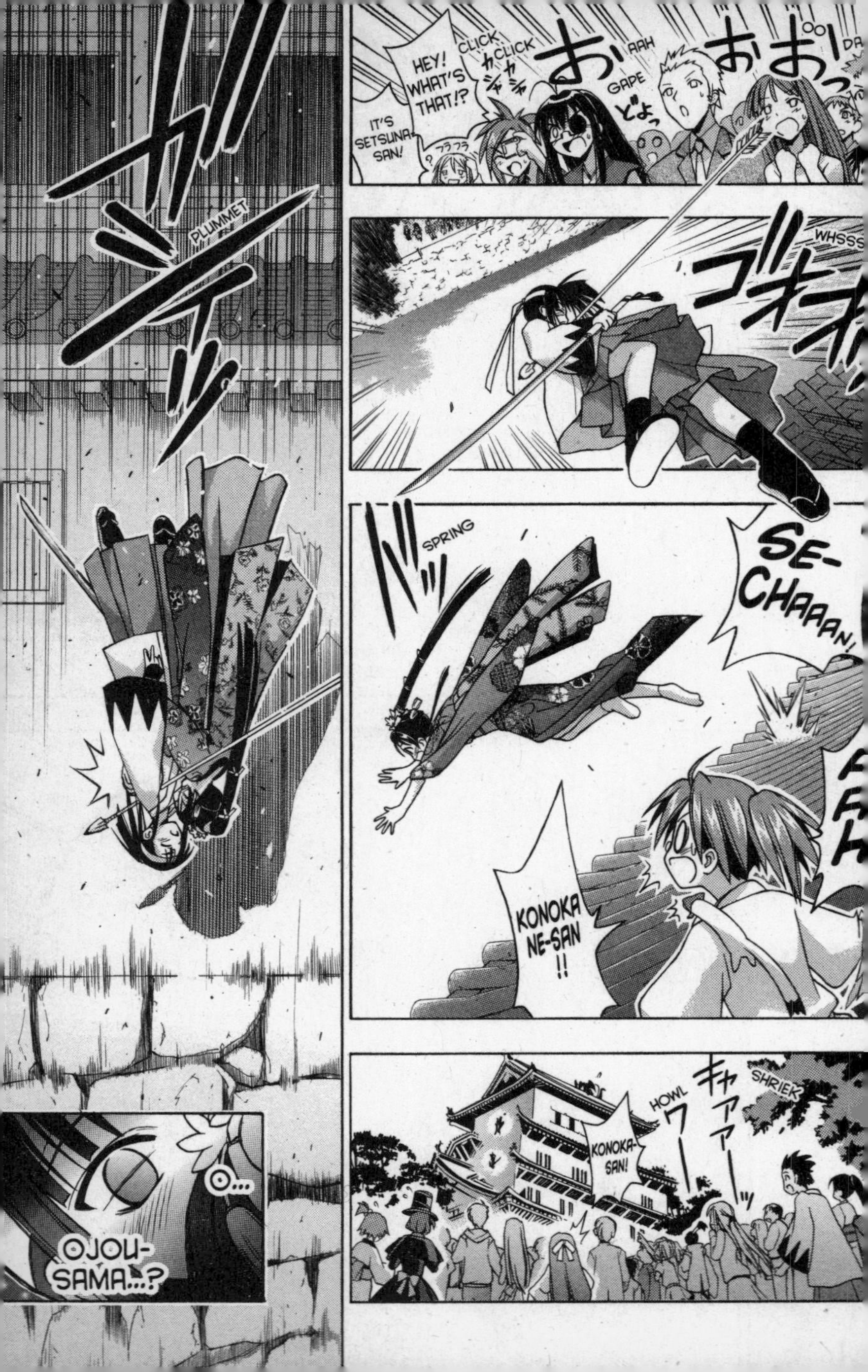
おおっ
OO
DA
おっ
AAH
どよっ
GAPE
カシャ カシャ
CLICK CLICK
HEY! WHAT'S THAT!?
IT'S SETSUNA-SAN!
フラフラ
?
ゴオオッ
WHSSS
SE-CHAAAAN!
ドッ
SPRING
AAAH
KONOKA NE-SAN !!
キャアアー
SHRIEK
ワー
HOWL
KONOKA-SAN!
ザンッ
PLUMMET
O...
OJOU-SAMA...?

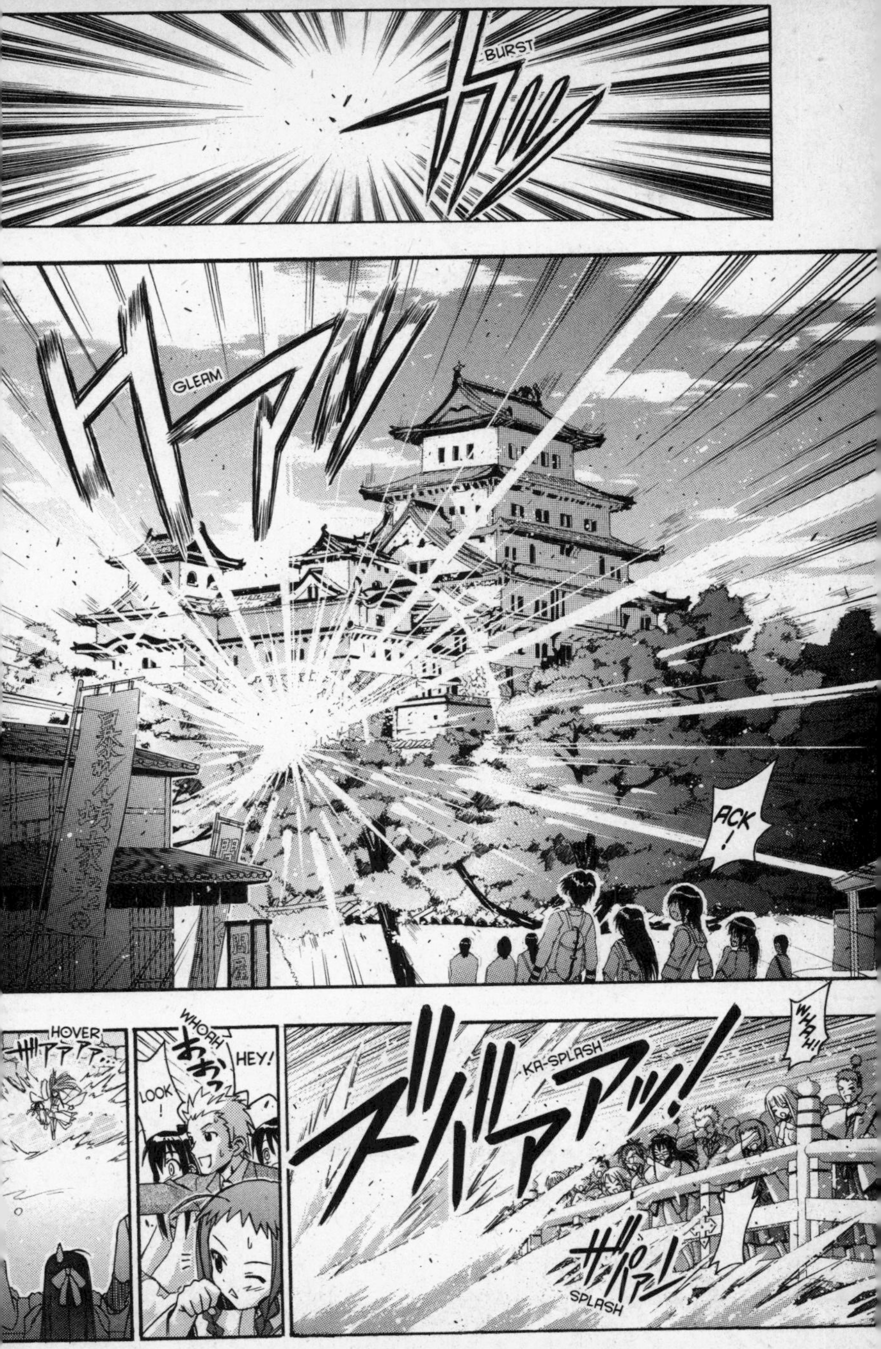
BURST
GLEAM
ACK!
WHAH!!
KA-SPLASH
SPLASH
WHOAH
HEY!
LOOK!
HOVER

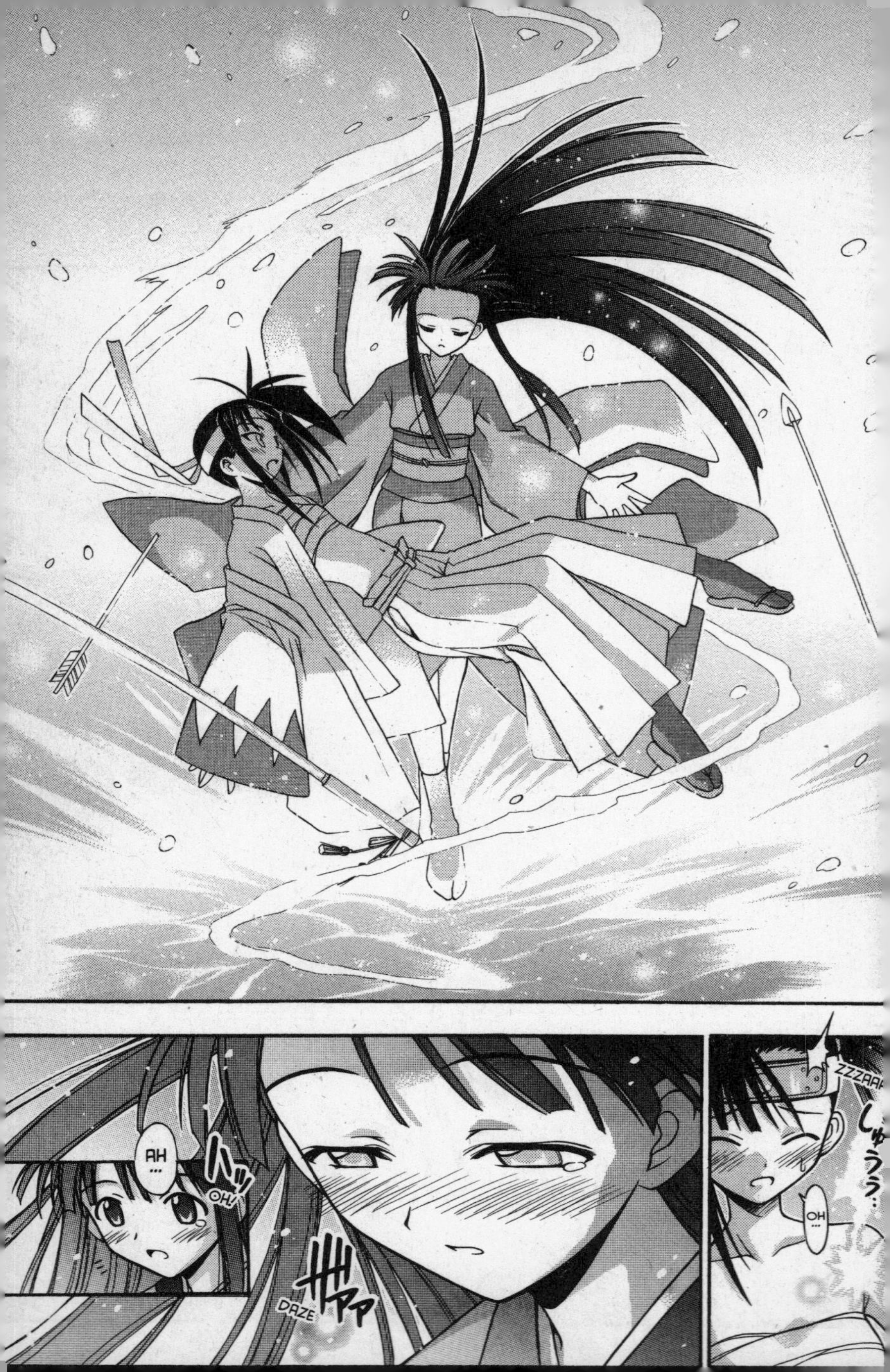
ZZZAA
しゅうう…
OH…
AH…
ハッ
OH!
DAZE

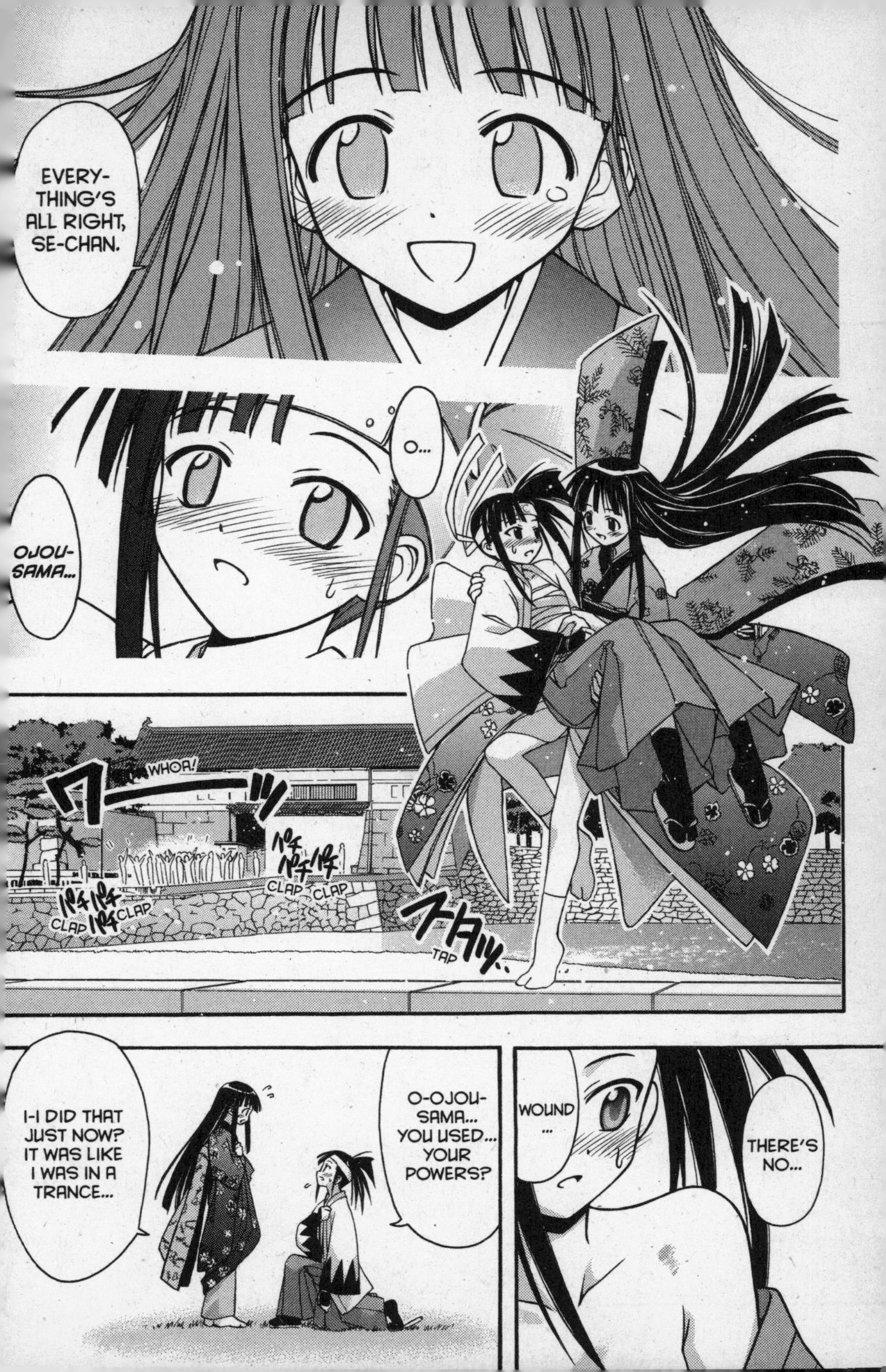
EVERY-THING'S ALL RIGHT, SE-CHAN.
O...
OJOU-SAMA...
TAP
CLAP CLAP
CLAP CLAP
WHOA!
THERE'S NO...
WOUND...
O-OJOU-SAMA... YOU USED... YOUR POWERS?
I-I DID THAT JUST NOW? IT WAS LIKE I WAS IN A TRANCE...

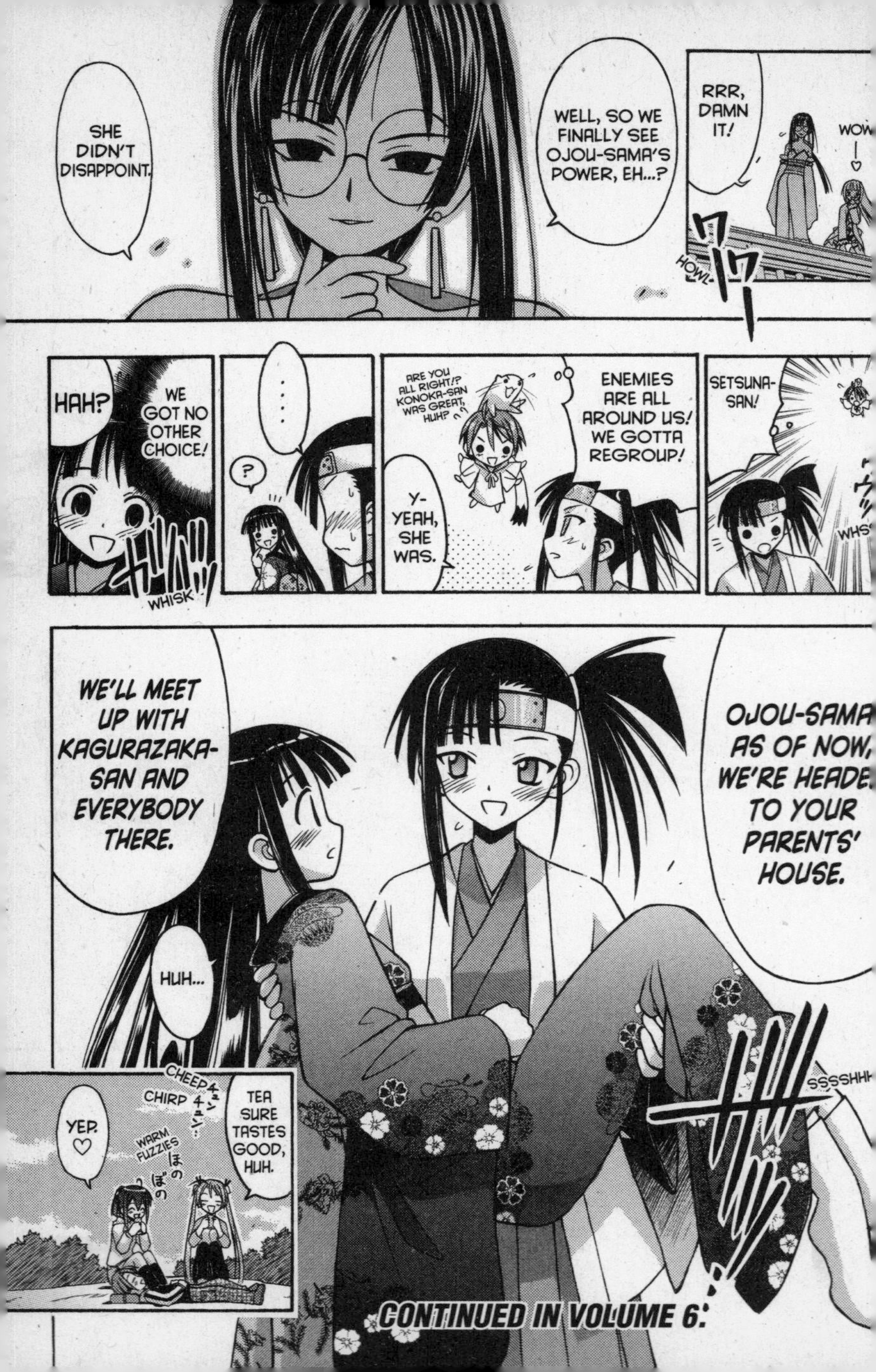
RRR, DAMN IT!
WOW —♡
HOWL
WELL, SO WE FINALLY SEE OJOU-SAMA'S POWER, EH...?
SHE DIDN'T DISAPPOINT.
SETSUNA-SAN!
WHS
ENEMIES ARE ALL AROUND US! WE GOTTA REGROUP!
ARE YOU ALL RIGHT!? KONOKA-SAN WAS GREAT, HUH?
Y-YEAH, SHE WAS.
....
?
WE GOT NO OTHER CHOICE!
HAH?
WHISK
OJOU-SAMA AS OF NOW, WE'RE HEADE TO YOUR PARENTS' HOUSE.
WE'LL MEET UP WITH KAGURAZAKA-SAN AND EVERYBODY THERE.
HUH...
SSSSHHH
TEA SURE TASTES GOOD, HUH.
CHEEP
CHIRP
WARM FUZZIES
YEP. ♡
CONTINUED IN VOLUME 6.

— STAFF —

Ken Akamatsu
Takashi Takemoto
Kenichi Nakamura
Masaki Ohyama
Keiichi Yamashita
Chigusa Amagasaki
Takaaki Miyahara

Thanks To

Ran Ayanaga

MAGISTER NEGI MAGI

NEGIMA! CHARACTER POPULARITY POLL—
CURRENT SHIFTS AND TRENDS

THESE ARE THE RESULTS FROM THE FIRST AND SECOND "3-A CLASSMATE POPULARITY POLL" CONDUCTED IN SHONEN MAGAZINE. FOR SOME REASON, MAKIE IS TOUGH TO BEAT (HA HA)! ALSO WATCH OUT FOR KAEDE AND THE LIBRARIAN! WHAT WILL THE RESULTS BE NEXT TIME!?
—AKAMATSU.

第1回人気投票結果	第2回人気投票結果
1. MAKIE SASAKI	1. MAKIE SASAKI
2. ASUNA KAGURAZAKA	2. ASUNA KAGURAZAKA
3. KONOKA KONOE	3. NODOKA MIYAZAKI
4. EVANGELINE A.K.M.	4. KONOKA KONOE
5. AYAKA HIROYUKI	5. KAEDE NAGASE
6. YUNA AKASHI	6. AKO IZUMI
7. SAKURAKO SHINA	7. SETSUNA SAKURAZAKI
8. KAZUMI ASAKURA	8. AYAKA HIROYUKI
9. CHITSURU NABA	9. YUNA AKASHI
10. NODOKA MIYAZAKI	10. EVANGELINE A.K.M.
11. CHACHAMARU KARAKURI	11. YUE AYASE
12. AKIRA OHKOUCHI	12. FEI KU
13. FEI KU	13. AKIRA OHKOUCHI
14. AKO IZUMI	14. CHISAME HASEGAWA
15. KAEDE NAGASE	15. SAKURAKO SHIINA
16. FUMIKA NARUTAKI	16. HARUNA SAOTOME
17. SAYO AZAKA	17. CHITSURU NABA
18. SETSUNA SAKURAZAKI	18. KAZUMI ASAKURA
19. FUKA NARUTAKI	19. CHACHAMARU KARAKURI
20. RINSHEN CHAO	20. ZAZIE RAINYDAY
21. SATOMI HAKASE	21. MISORA KASUGA
22. YUE AYASE	22. SATSUKI YOTSUBA
23. MISORA KASUGA	23. FUKA NARUTAKI
24. MADOKA KUGIMIYA	24. FUMIKA NARUTAKI
25. MISA KAKIZAKI	25. MADOKA KUGIMIYA
26. CHISAME HASEGAWA	26. RINSHEN CHAO
27. SATSUKI YOTSUBA	27. NATSUMI MURAGAMI
28. HARUNA SAOTOME	28. MANA TATSUMIYA
29. ZAZIE RAINYDAY	29. MISA KAKIZAKI
30. NATSUMI MURAGAMI	30. SATOMI HAKASE
31. MANA TATSUMIYA	31. SAYO AZAKA

COMPILATION OF MATERIAL FOR THE BEGINNING OF *NEGIMA!*

THE ORIGINAL CHARACTER SKETCHES

[YUE AYASE]

ONE ANTENNA STRAND.
SHE MIGHT LOOK GOOD WITH GLASSES AS WELL.
SLOPING SHOULDERS AND SMALL CHEST.
ATTACHED BELLS.
BEHIND.
WE'RE HOPING FOR HER IN THE THIRD EDITION. HOW ABOUT THIS?
SLANTED EYES.
SHE DOESN'T PARTICULARLY MIND IF SOMEONE SEES HER PANTIES OR UNDERWEAR BUT SHE'S EMBARRASSED BY OTHERS' STRANGE QUIRKS.
I'D BE GOOD TO GIVE HER A PERSONALITY LIKE HANAKO.
NAME: SUZUCHAN.

MY FORMER ASSISTANT, RAN AYANAGA, WAS IN CHARGE OF THE ORIGINAL CHARACTER SKETCHES FOR YUE. PERHAPS THEY LOOK LIKE RAN DID THEM? YUE ALWAYS DRINKS STRANGE BEVERAGES SO TRY LOOKING OUT FOR THIS. I WONDER IF THEY'RE ANY GOOD (HA HA).

MAGISTER NEGI MAGI

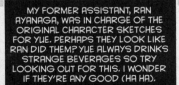

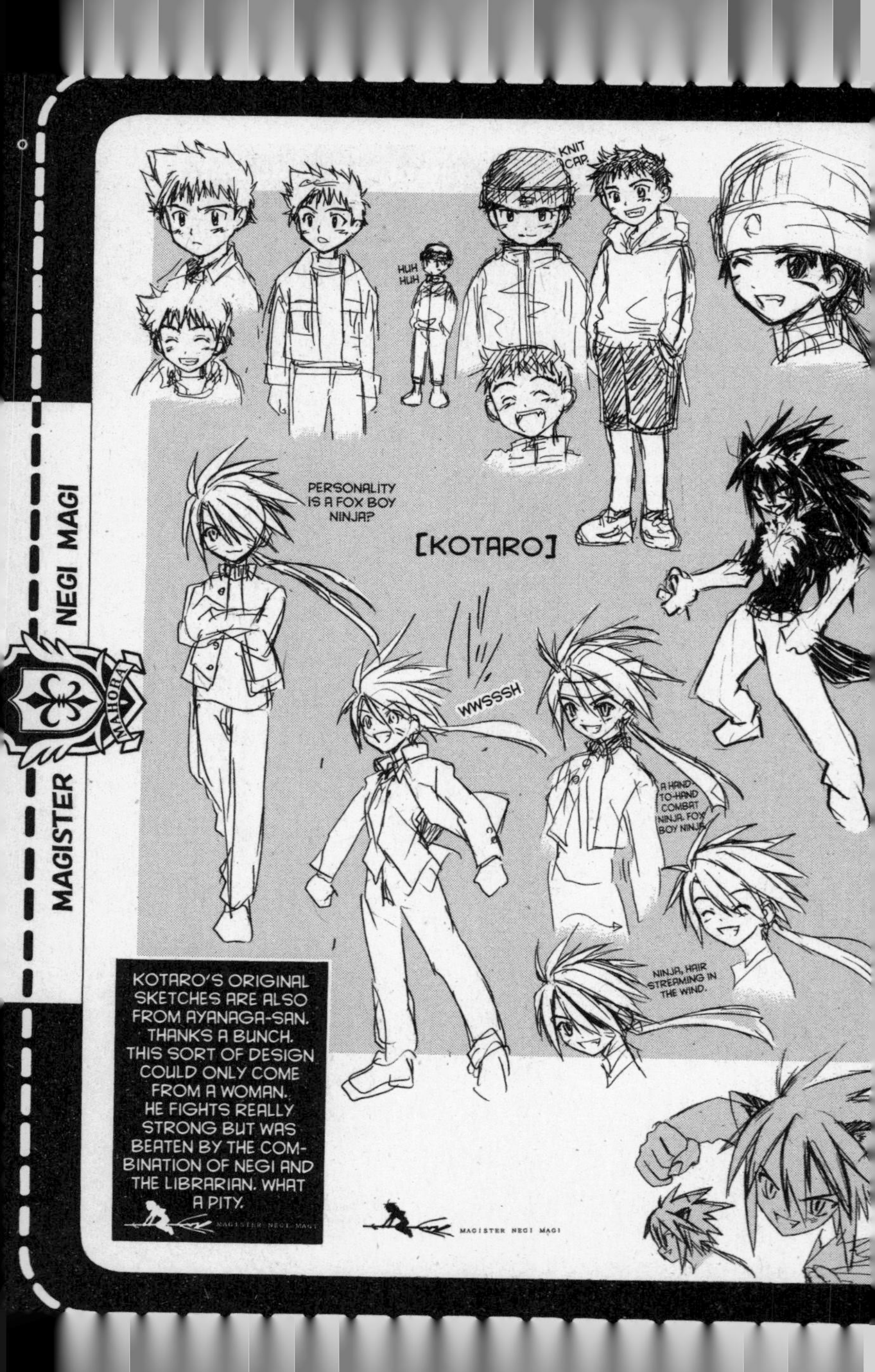
KNIT CAP.
HUH HUH
PERSONALITY IS A FOX BOY NINJA?
[KOTARO]
WWSSSH
A HAND-TO-HAND COMBAT NINJA. FOX BOY NINJA
NINJA, HAIR STREAMING IN THE WIND.
MAGISTER NEGI MAGI

KOTARO'S ORIGINAL SKETCHES ARE ALSO FROM AYANAGA-SAN. THANKS A BUNCH. THIS SORT OF DESIGN COULD ONLY COME FROM A WOMAN. HE FIGHTS REALLY STRONG BUT WAS BEATEN BY THE COMBINATION OF NEGI AND THE LIBRARIAN. WHAT A PITY.

MAGISTER NEGI MAGI

NEGIMA!

DICTIONARY OF VARIOUS TERMS OF BLACK MAGIC

"The island nation of Japan is a prosperous country with a mystical language so there is great joy."

— From the Manyoushu (an ancient collection of Japanese songs), Volume 13.

38th Period

Adeat/Abeat. A spell used by wizards' partners to summon the specially tailored weapons that have been given to them. *Adeat* means "Come!" and *abeat* means "Go away!" Because Asuna, who doesn't study magic, can use it, it doesn't appear that it's necessary to understand the meaning of the spell.

Diarium Ejus. The specially tailored weapon given to Negi's partner, Nodoka Miyazaki, according to the contract's power. *Diarium* derives from the English word *diary,* and means "everyday assignments," and from that gained the meaning of "a record of every day" or "journal." *Ejus* is the genitive case of the Latin pronoun *id* meaning "that thing" or "that person." This book gives one the ability to read a person's outward feelings, as well as what Freud called the subconscious, or the "id."

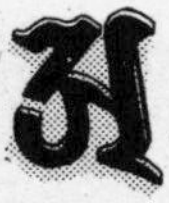

The Sanskrit character on Kotaro's cap. This character represents all Buddhas, with Tahagata, the Supreme Buddha of Sino-Japanese Esoteric Buddhism, at the top of the list. Tahagata's literal meaning is "the ultimate truth of nonexistence" or "the unobtainable." Esoteric Buddhism's take on the universe, which Tahagata revered and respected, incorporated many beliefs and magic arts from the people that practiced Shugendo, a kind of Japanese shamanism that encorporates Shinto and Buddhist concepts.

39th Period

Om. A word that's attached at the beginning of a mantra. The literal meaning is "the ultimate truth of nonexistence." Shingon is Sanskrit for "mantra" and can be translated as "spell." Originally they were magic spells used by the Brahman class in India, and those spells were recorded in the Veda (an ancient Indian religious text), In 1816, the

German Franz Bopp discovered that the grammatical structure of Greek and Latin closely resembled that of the European and Sanskrit classics, and he established the modern subject of comparative literature. In the same way, the structure of the spells of eastern magic and that of the western magic of Negi and company are distant relatives of each other.

Kagabikonoyashiro. A shrine with a thousand gates, like the Fushimi Grand Shrine. It's the main temple of the Kansai Magic Association not far from Arashiyama and Sagano, but details are unknown. *Kagabikonoyashiro* is, in the first volume of the Kojiki (a three-volume history of ancient Japan), a fire god also known as Obuto. When he was born, he burned his mother, Nami Iya, killing her. Because she also gave birth to the six gods corresponding to metal, earth, water, and wood in the process of dying, the *Kagabikonoyashiro* became connected to the five flows of the life force, also known as the five elements (wood, fire, earth, metal, and water) as the first important gods.

Ja/A/Ii/Da. The Sanskrit characters cut into the legs of the spider demon. *Ja* means "battle enemy," *Ii* means "disaster," and *Da* means "Hold a grudge." It's most likely a kind of magic for controlling Onmyou Gods.

Deflexio. (Wind Shield) Makes appear a magic shield that parries a physical attack. Wizards unleash a magic barrier in order to protect themselves from physical damage. In contrast to the extremely powerful barrier that's unleashed for an instant—the "Wind Flower! Wall of Wind" used in the 34th Period—this magic is comparatively weak but is constant. Negi's specialty is wind magic, so he broke out the "Wind Shield."

Om ak vi ra un kya sha rak man. This mantra is called the eight-character spell, and can be recited in various ways. It's called the eight-character spell even though it has nine characters because the first *Om* at the beginning of the mantra is a decorative attachment.

Van. A Sanskrit character that represents Tahagata of the Vajradhatu Mandala (the mandala is the Buddhist visual schema of the enlightened mind). But the character of *van* also represents water in the "earth, water, fire, wind, sky, knowledge" of the *Pillars of the Worship of Shugen* which states, "the character of *van* is water, everything and everyone in the universe obeys water." In order to unleash the fog from the drink bought at the vending machine, the character of *van* was recited.

41st Period

Contra Pugnent. ("Intercept and Attack") The call Negi used to summon the spirits. *Contra* means "confront" and *pugnent* means "fight."

Unus fulgor concidens noctem, in mea manu ens inimicum edat. FULGURATIO ALBICANS. (A stream of light to cut through the darkness! Spring forth from my hand and throttle my enemy! White Lightning!) Magic that wounds or kills the enemy with an intense electric shock that springs from the user's palm. It doesn't have the power

to completely destroy things, but it's a full-on battle spell with an extremely high offensive effectiveness with regards to people and animals.

Sim ipse pars per secundam dimidiam Negius Springfieldes. (Execute Contract For A Half Second! Negi Springfield!) A spell that turns back on themselves the magic powers received by the wizard according to the contract; in this case, on Negi himself. Normally, with *sis mea pars* ("thou art a part of me") two people's names are recited, but here it becomes a phrase with the strange meaning *sim ipse pars* ("I myself become a part"). Perhaps because it's an experimental technique, it takes a heavy toll on Negi's body.

A Vi Ci. The Sanskrit characters carved into the thousand gates. They mean "endless hell" and they establish the boundaries for the "never-ending place spell."

42nd Period

Van Oon Tarak Kileek Aku. An Onmyoudou spell known widely by the name of *Seman* and used in a variety of ways. Originally, they were the Sanskrit characters for esoteric Buddhism's Five Buddhas of the Vajradhatu and were not related to common Onmyoudou. However, in Volume 4 of the *Five Pages of the Earth God (Chijingoyou)* it says, "the present four Buddhas will increase to five Buddhas, changing to consist of the earth god of the five elements." In this way, the five Buddhas were arranged to correspond to the five elements. The five elements were the five life forces—wood, fire, earth, metal, and water—and the study of the flow of those life forces was the important task of the common Onmyou wizards. From the beginning, before the division of Shintoism and Buddhism in 1868 (the first year of the Meiji Era), Shintoism and Buddhism were jointly practiced everywhere. Before modern times, the Japanese openly incorporated a variety of religions and magic into their lives without concern. This single Onmyoudou spell that comes from the Sanskrit characters of Esoteric Buddhism gives us a glimpse of the history of those Japanese people.

43rd Period

Kya-ya. A word that means the "bodily actions" in the Bodily Actions, Speech, Thought of esoteric Buddhism. In short, it means the body and is a spell used, using the talisman arts, in order to give Negi the temporary, doll-like figure that he used.

References:
Iwanami Dictionary of Buddhism; "Examination of Shinto in the Middle Ages," *Compendium of Japanese Thought 19*, Iwanami Publishing; "Compendium of Shinto Articles," Volume 17, Shugendou (Shinto Compendium Editorial Foundation Society)

PARTNER CARDS EXPLAINED

Charta Ministralis
—PARTNER CARD—

Mysterious Roman numbers. There are various mysterious interpretations of numbers, especially numbers 1-13 where there are particular peculiarities in the prime numbers. For example, in contrast to the number 1, which means a unified complete whole, the number 2 means the fluctuation in activity brought on by the power of Onmyou. Lucky number 7 is a powerful number, being that it's the largest prime number in the decimal system. 13, which is not found in the duodecimal system, represents death in this world and rebirth in the next. It's very interesting that when you analyze the prime factor of the numbers written on Asuna and Nodoka's cards, you can see that they have the same logarithmic number of 3.

The contract's magic base. A simple thing made up of the 12 zodiac signs and a six pointed star. Pactio is a simple magic that even the ermine fairies can use, so the magic base is small.

Partner's title. The partner's ability and personality are frankly stated.

VIII
Charta Ministralis
Rubor
tonus
CAGURAZACA
ASUNA
BELLATRIX SAUCIATA
virtus
audacia
astralitas
Mars
directio
oriens
IIIA

virtus—VIRTUES

The virtue section of the partner's card mentions the seven virtues,

Knowledge *(sapientia)*
Bravery *(audacia)*
Temperance *(temterantia)*
Justice *(justitia)*
Faith *(fides)*
Hope *(spes)*
Love *(caritas)*

These are known as the seven European original virtues. The first four are found in Plato's Nation-State (427E, especially 441E-444A) and the next three are often written into marriage vows and found in Paulos' Corinthians I (13:13). Virtue is defined here as the virtue talked of in modern times. It means the advantages and usefulness of people and things and in the study of western classics, and it's often translated as "excellence." However, the principal meaning is the broad idea of "bravery" or "courageousness." The theme of "bravery is the real magic" is expounded here.

astralitas—ASTROLOGY

The various partners have astrological attributes, in short, an astrological sign that corresponds to their birth.

Moon *(Luna)*
Sun *(Sol)*
Mars *(Mars)*
Venus *(Venus)*
Mercury *(Mercurius)*
Jupiter *(Jupiter)*
Saturn *(Saturnus)*
Uranus *(Uranus)*
Neptune *(Neptunus)*
Pluto *(Pluto)*
Comet *(cometes)*
Falling Star *(fax)*
Fixed Star *(caelus sideralis)*
Black Hole *(nigrum foramen)*

The astrology relating to the seven astral bodies of the Moon, Sun, Mars, Venus, Mercury, Jupiter, and Saturn was established by the Sumerians and were inherited by the Sem peoples of Assyria and Babylonia. Later, through Alexander the Great's expeditions to the east, middle-eastern astronomy flowed through Greece and into Europe.

tonus—COLORS

In most modern natural sciences, color is nothing more than a uniform electromagnetic wave within a wavelength but, in premodern cultures, color ha important symbolism.

For example, in the Revelation of John (2:18), the son of God had eyes that were red like fire and, as you can see with the mother goddess, Cybele, of Asia Minor, black symbolizes the darkness that contrasts with light, death contrasting with life and also symbolizes rebirth fron that death.

The colors that are at the top of the partner card are known to be

Red *(rubor)*
Blue *(caerula)*
Green *(virude)*
Yellow *(flavum)*
Purple *(cyaneum)*
Violet *(viola)*
Orange *(luteum)*
Rose *(roseum)*
White *(album)*
Black *(nigror)*
Gold *(aurum)*
Silver *(argentums)*
Crimson *(prisma)*

The respective colors reflect th symbolism of the partner's birth development, and destiny. The gold, silver, and crimson cards are extremely rare and as their equally rare magic weapons are high in value, they are often traded on the black market.

directio—DIRECTIO

In astrology, back in the era of Ptolemy, it was known that the eart was a sphere. Therefore, the five directions on the top of the partner card—

East *(oriens)*
West *(occidens)*
South *(auster)*
North *(septentrio)*
Center *(centrum)*

—don't merely mean directions on a plane. For example, there was the widely held belief that paradise lies in a westerly direction, and in the north was the North Star, which symbolized the center of space. The east is the direction the sun rises and had the temporal meaning of the coming of a new day.

NEGI MA!

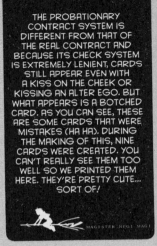

THE PROBATIONARY CONTRACT SYSTEM IS DIFFERENT FROM THAT OF THE REAL CONTRACT AND BECAUSE ITS CHECK SYSTEM IS EXTREMELY LENIENT, CARDS STILL APPEAR EVEN WITH A KISS ON THE CHEEK OR KISSING AN ALTER EGO. BUT WHAT APPEARS IS A BOTCHED CARD. AS YOU CAN SEE, THESE ARE SOME CARDS THAT WERE MISTAKES (HA HA). DURING THE MAKING OF THIS, NINE CARDS WERE CREATED. YOU CAN'T REALLY SEE THEM TOO WELL SO WE PRINTED THEM HERE. THEY'RE PRETTY CUTE... SORT OF!

MAGISTER NEGI MAGI

12
YELLOW
tonus
AI-YAH.
FEI KU
STOIC KUNGFU CHINA.
SPECIAL SKILL:
PONKEN KASHI-FU KICK!
astralitas
LIKES: IT'S TOO BAD THERE'S NO ONE STRONGER THAN ME!
HO-CHA.
12

8
RED
tonus
GRRR
ASUNA KAGURAZAKA
JUNIOR HIGH SCHOOL GIRL WITH THE FLYING KICK!
SPECIAL SKILL:
ASUNA PUNCH. ASUNA KICK.
astralitas
LIKES: MOVIES THAT HAVE DANDY OLD MEN
KEEYAH.
8

13
WHITE
tonus
HAH
KONOE KONOKA
EASYGOING WIZARD.
SPECIAL SKILL:
HAMMERTHRUST
astralitas
LIKES: CAKE, THE SWEET KIND
CONK.
13

NEGI MA!

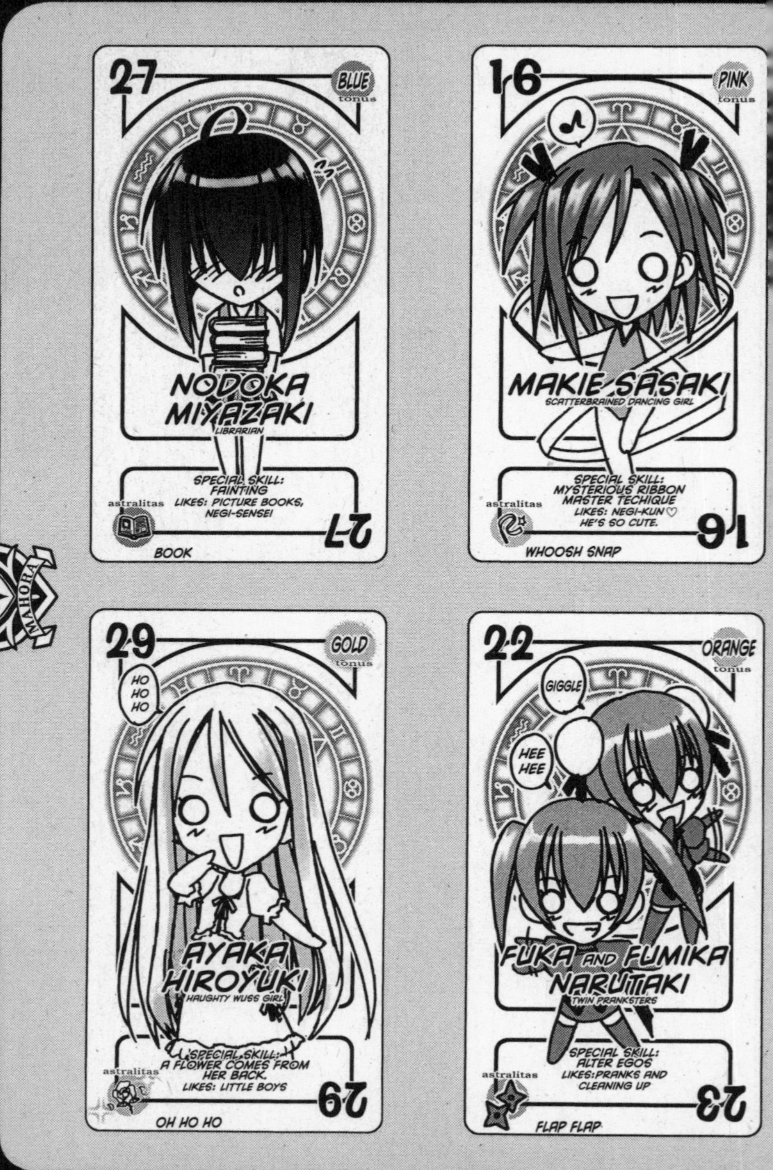
16
PINK
tonus
MAKIE SASAKI
SCATTERBRAINED DANCING GIRL
SPECIAL SKILL: MYSTERIOUS RIBBON MASTER TECHIQUE
LIKES: NEGI-KUN♡ HE'S SO CUTE.
astralitas
16
WHOOSH SNAP
27
BLUE
tonus
NODOKA MIYAZAKI
LIBRARIAN
SPECIAL SKILL: FAINTING
LIKES: PICTURE BOOKS, NEGI-SENSEI
astralitas
27
BOOK
22
ORANGE
tonus
GIGGLE
HEE HEE
FUKA AND FUMIKA NARUTAKI
TWIN PRANKSTERS
SPECIAL SKILL: ALTER EGOS
LIKES: PRANKS AND CLEANING UP
astralitas
23
FLAP FLAP
29
GOLD
tonus
HO HO HO
AYAKA HIROYUKI
HAUGHTY WUSS GIRL
SPECIAL SKILL: A FLOWER COMES FROM HER BACK.
LIKES: LITTLE BOYS
astralitas
29
OH HO HO

COMPILATION OF CLOTHING SKETCHES. SCHOOL FIELD TRIP EDITION.

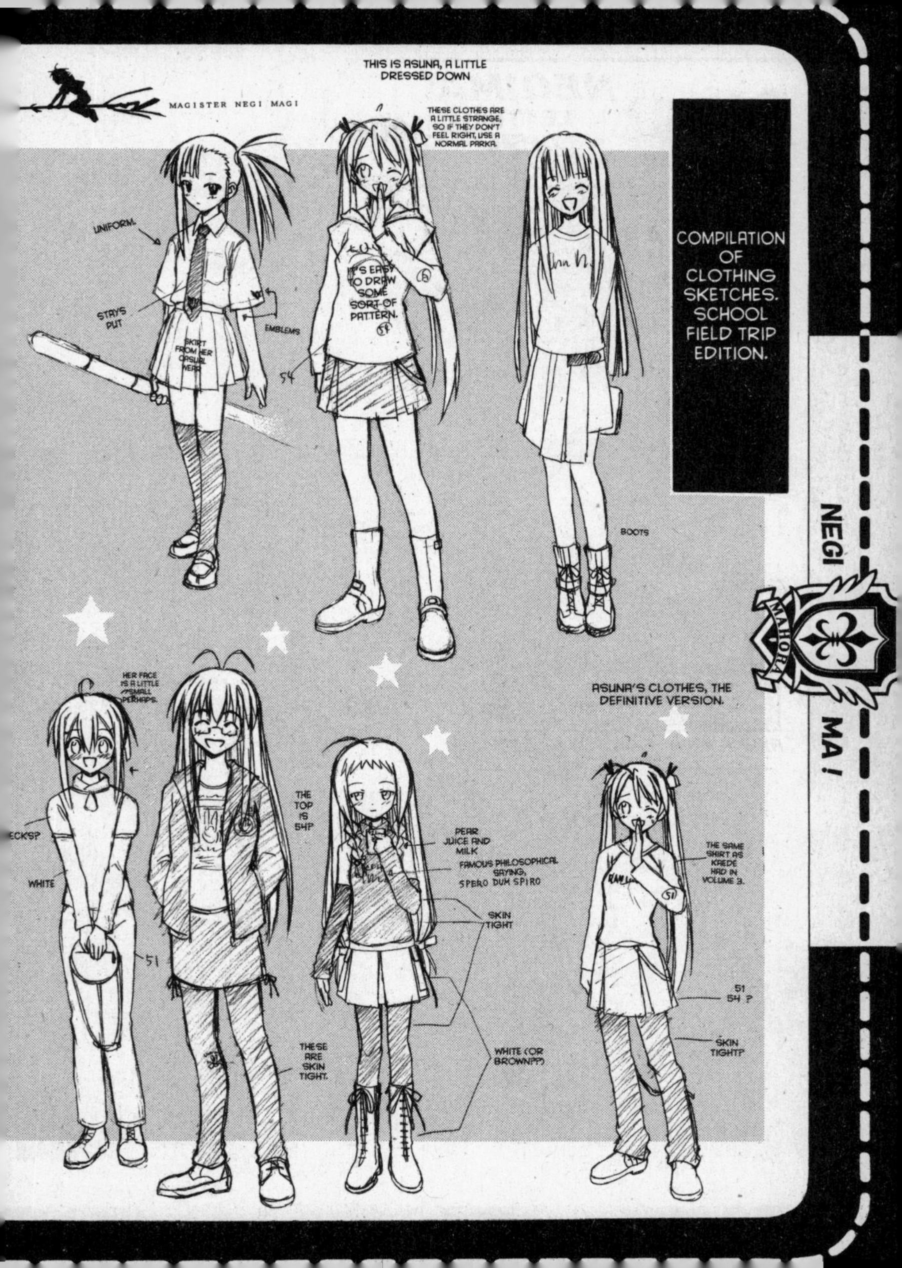
THIS IS ASUNA, A LITTLE DRESSED DOWN
THESE CLOTHES ARE A LITTLE STRANGE, SO IF THEY DON'T FEEL RIGHT, USE A NORMAL PARKA.
IT'S EASY TO DRAW SOME SORT OF PATTERN.
54
BOOTS
UNIFORM.
STAYS PUT
SKIRT FROM HER CASUAL WEAR
EMBLEMS
ASUNA'S CLOTHES, THE DEFINITIVE VERSION.
THE SAME SHIRT AS KAEDE HAD IN VOLUME 3.
51
51
54 ?
SKIN TIGHT?
PEAR JUICE AND MILK
FAMOUS PHILOSOPHICAL SAYING, SPERO DUM SPIRO
SKIN TIGHT
WHITE (OR BROWN??)
THE TOP IS 54?
THESE ARE SKIN TIGHT.
HER FACE IS A LITTLE SMALL PERHAPS.
ECKS?
WHITE
51

NEGIMA! LETTER CORNER ☆

THESE ARE SOME RECENT LETTERS. WE FOCUSED OUR ATTENTION ON THE PORTRAIT ILLUSTRATIONS AND COMPILED THEM FOR YOU! —MAX ASHI.

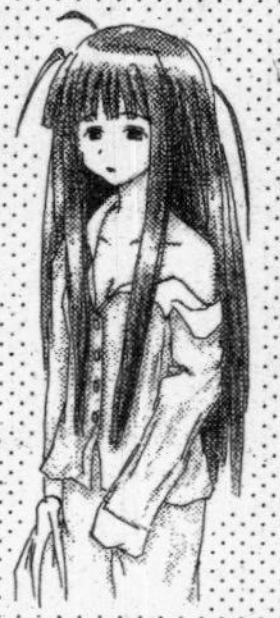

JUST WOKE UP?

G-SUN-SAN, TOKYO CITY.

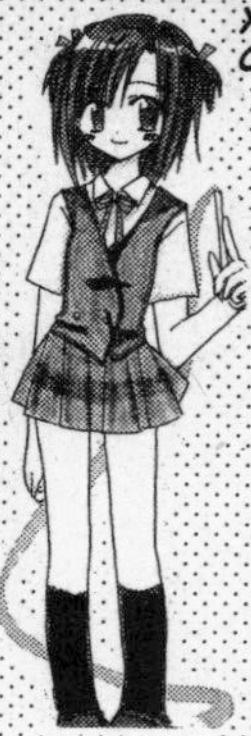

A SUPER-CUTE MAKIE.

YURIKA SHIBA-SAN, CHIBA PREFECTURE.

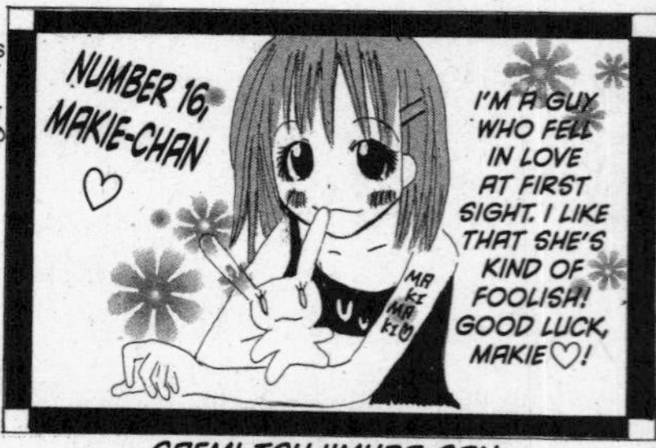
NUMBER 16, MAKIE-CHAN ♡
I'M A GUY WHO FELL IN LOVE AT FIRST SIGHT. I LIKE THAT SHE'S KIND OF FOOLISH! GOOD LUCK, MAKIE♡!
MA KI MA KI

A MAKIE WHO'S EYELASHES ARE SPOT ON (DIFFICULT TO DRAW?)

SAEMI TSUJIMURA-SAN, KANAGAWA PREFECTURE.

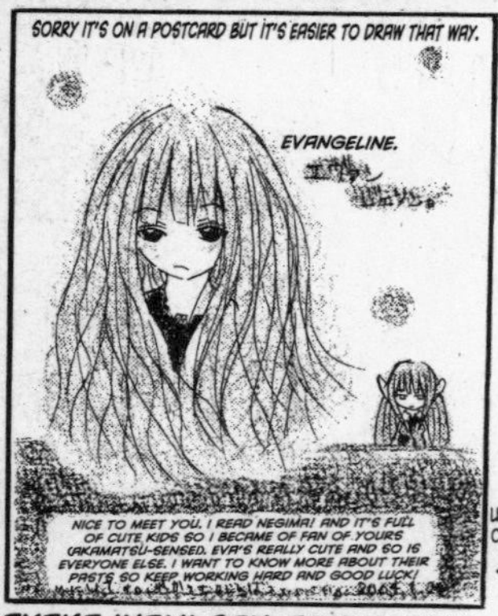
SORRY IT'S ON A POSTCARD BUT IT'S EASIER TO DRAW THAT WAY.
EVANGELINE.
NICE TO MEET YOU. I READ NEGIMA! AND IT'S FULL OF CUTE KIDS SO I BECAME OF FAN OF YOURS (AKAMATSU-SENSEI). EVA'S REALLY CUTE AND SO IS EVERYONE ELSE. I WANT TO KNOW MORE ABOUT THEIR PASTS SO KEEP WORKING HARD AND GOOD LUCK!

AN UNOBTRUSIVE CHACHAMARU.

AYAKA INAMI-SAN, TOKYO CITY.

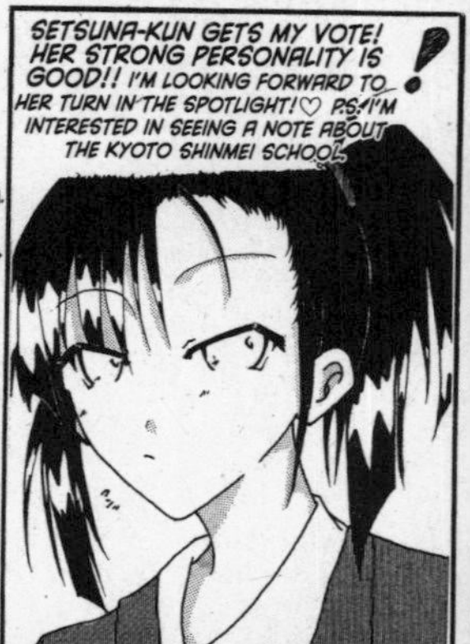
SETSUNA-KUN GETS MY VOTE! HER STRONG PERSONALITY IS GOOD!! I'M LOOKING FORWARD TO HER TURN IN THE SPOTLIGHT!♡ P.S. I'M INTERESTED IN SEEING A NOTE ABOUT THE KYOTO SHINMEI SCHOOL.

KAORI NAKAMOTO-SAN, WAKAYAMA PREFECTURE.

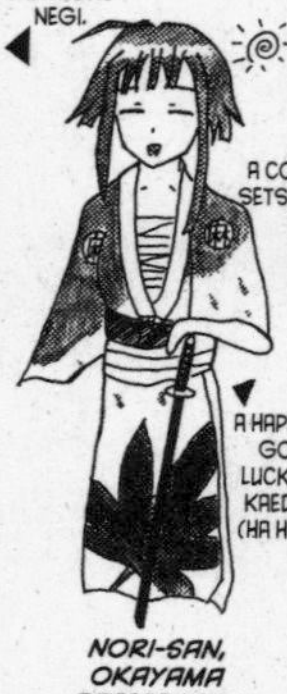

A COOL SETSUNA. ☆

A HAPPY-GO LUCKY-KAEDE (HA HA).

NORI-SAN, OKAYAMA PREFECTURE.

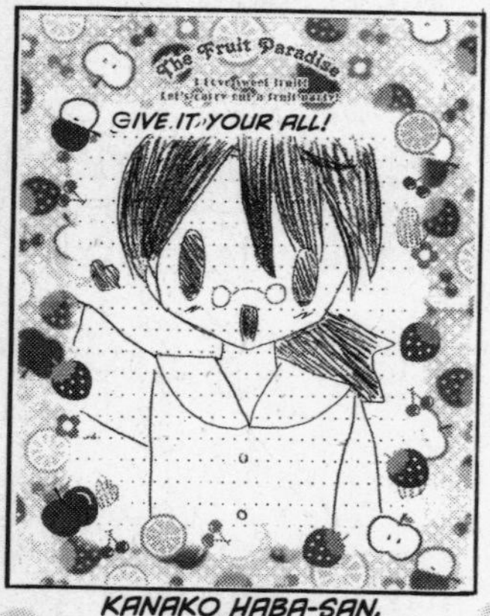
The Fruit Paradise
GIVE IT YOUR ALL!

AN ENERGETIC NEGI.

KANAKO HABA-SAN, SAITAMA PREFECTURE.

Translation Notes

Japanese is a tricky language for most westerners, and translation is often more art than science. For your edification and reading pleasure, here are notes on some of the places where we could have gone in a different direction in our translation of the work, or where a Japanese cultural reference is used.

Seiza, page 10

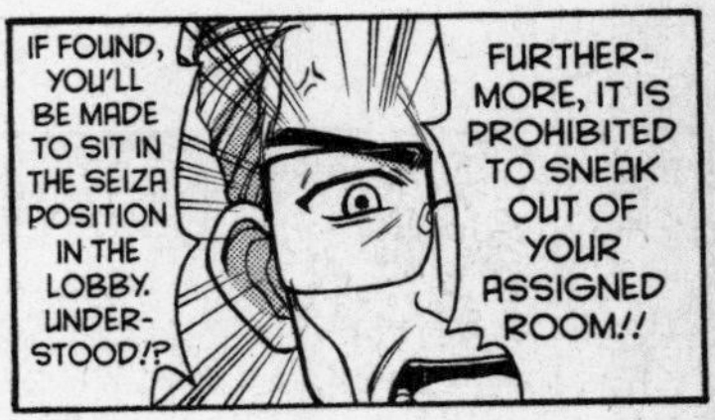
FURTHER-MORE, IT IS PROHIBITED TO SNEAK OUT OF YOUR ASSIGNED ROOM!!
IF FOUND, YOU'LL BE MADE TO SIT IN THE SEIZA POSITION IN THE LOBBY. UNDER-STOOD!?

In Japanese, the word *seiza* is made up of the characters for *correct* and *sit* and refers to the position used in the tea ceremony and in Zen meditation. It involves folding the lower legs under your thighs, and if you're not used to it, it can be very uncomfortable if maintained for prolonged periods.

Katakana, page 20

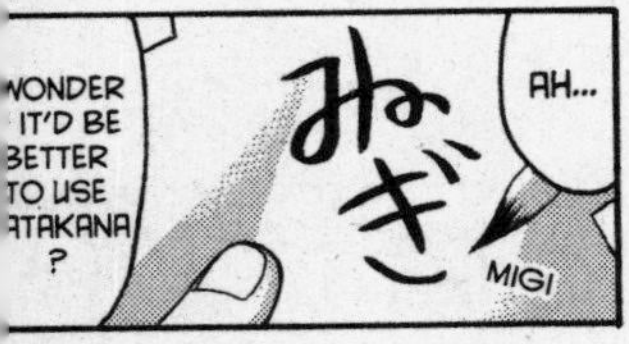
AH...
みぎ
MIGI
WONDER IT'D BE BETTER TO USE ATAKANA ?

Katakana is one of three Japanese systems (alphabets, really) for spelling words (the other two are hiragana and kanji). Katakana is usually used for writing western names or words of non-Japanese origin.

Kouga, page 33

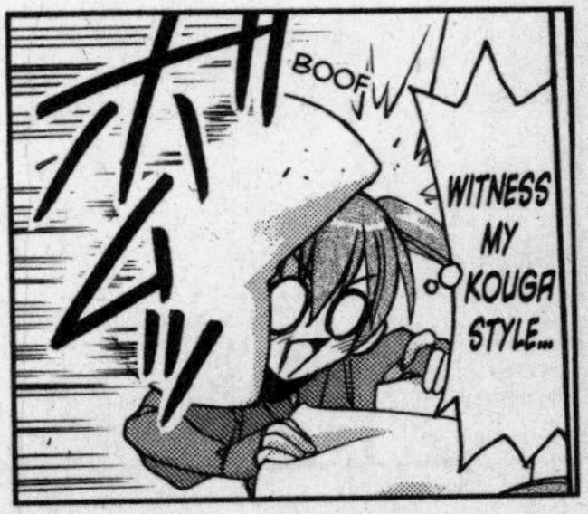
WITNESS MY KOUGA STYLE...
BOOF

Kouga is a county in Shiga Prefecture, and presumably Fuka and Fumika's home.

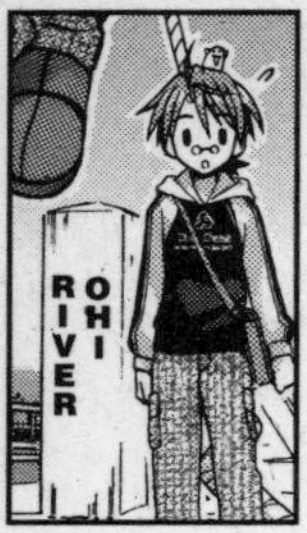
OHI RIVER

Ohi River, page 72

The Ohi River runs through Kyoto. With its source at the southern Japan Alps, it is most famous for the Ohi River Railroad, which used old steam locomotives and is still running today.

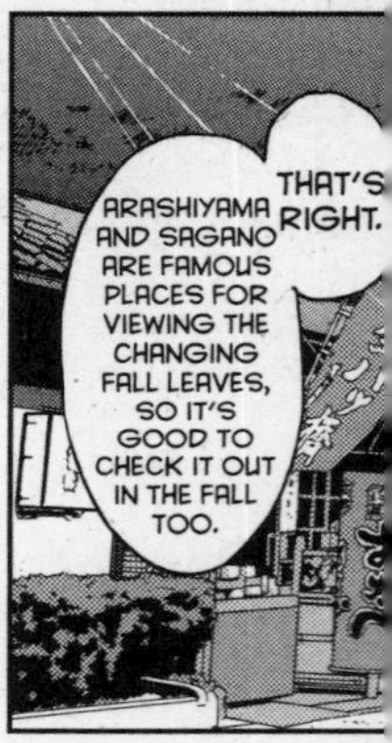
THAT'S RIGHT.
ARASHIYAMA AND SAGANO ARE FAMOUS PLACES FOR VIEWING THE CHANGING FALL LEAVES, SO IT'S GOOD TO CHECK IT OUT IN THE FALL TOO.

Arashiyama and Sagano, page 74

This is the area in the vicinity of Saga in Ukyo Ward in Kyoto.

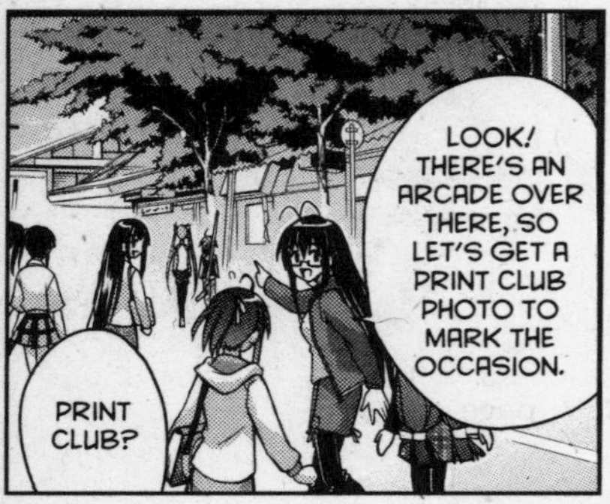
LOOK! THERE'S AN ARCADE OVER THERE, SO LET'S GET A PRINT CLUB PHOTO TO MARK THE OCCASION.
PRINT CLUB?

Print Club, page 75

Print Club (or *purikurabu*) refers to machines in arcades that take your picture and turn them into little stickers that you can customize. They are very popular in Japan.

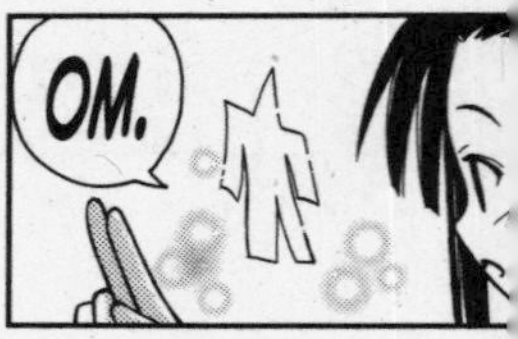
OM.

Om, page 83

The sound used by followers of Buddhism in certain types of meditation.

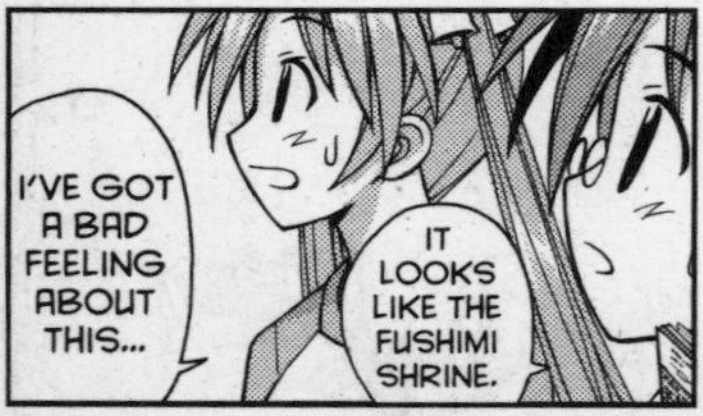
IT LOOKS LIKE THE FUSHIMI SHRINE.
I'VE GOT A BAD FEELING ABOUT THIS...

Fushimi, page 86

Fushimi is a ward in southern Kyoto known for its pure water and, by extension, its delicious sake. Several famous breweries large and small are located here, including Gekkeikan.

O-Shiruko, page 94

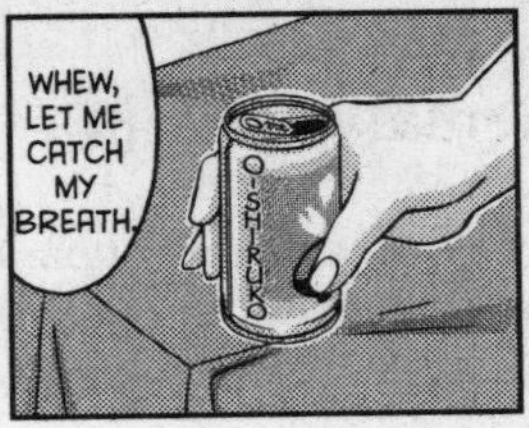
WHEW, LET ME CATCH MY BREATH.
O-SHIRUKO

A beverage made from sweet azuki beans (also called *anko*), water, and sugar.

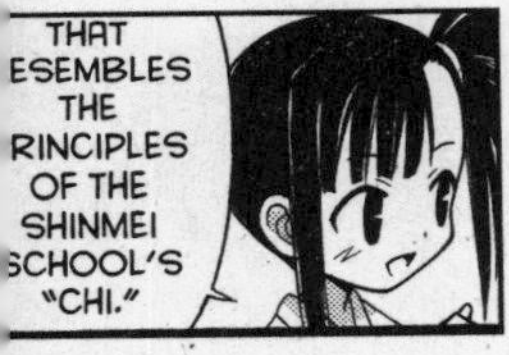
THAT ESEMBLES THE RINCIPLES OF THE SHINMEI SCHOOL'S "CHI."

Chi, page 96

Chi is the power that martial artists and others believe you can harness from inside yourself through training and meditation.

Inugami, page 121

The name *Inugami* is written in Japanese using the characters for "dog" and "upper" or "above."

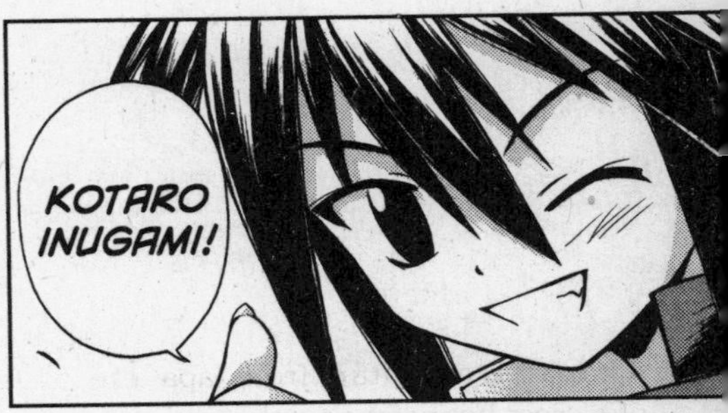
KOTARO INUGAMI!

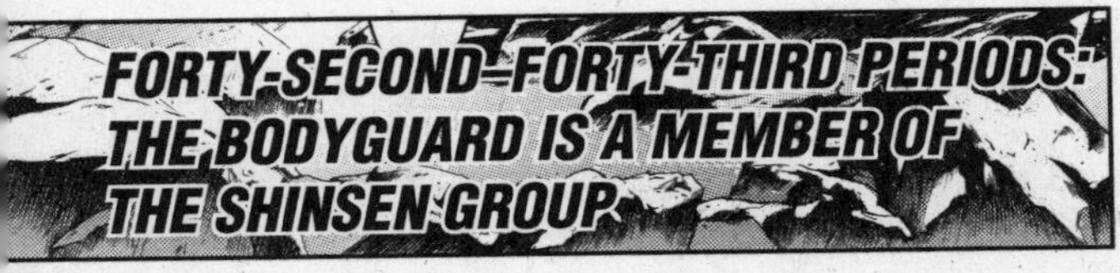
FORTY-SECOND–FORTY-THIRD PERIODS: THE BODYGUARD IS A MEMBER OF THE SHINSEN GROUP

Shinsen, page 145

The Shinsen Group (*Shinsengumi*) was a group of twenty to fifty ronin (masterless samurai) formed at the end of the Edo Era to protect and control Kyoto. They revered the Emperor and sought the overthrow of the Shogunate.

Cinema Village, page 149

There is an amusement park in Kyoto called Eiga Mura (literally, Movie Village), which is a reproduction of Edo-era Japan, featuring reproductions of samurai movie sets, and also actors who recreate the era for tourists.

WHAT!? THIS IS CINEMA VILLAGE.

WATCH OUT, CLASS REP! A HUGE KAPPA IS AFTER YOU!

TROMP TROMP.

KA-PA

GLEAM

Kappa, page 166

A *kappa* is a creature from Japanese mythology. It is an amphibian, sort of a cross between a turtle and a human, that drags people under water and sucks their blood.

AYAKA HIROYUKI STYLE, AIKIJUJITSU! "WINTER FLOWER!"

AikiJujitsu, page 166

AikiJujitsu is a traditional Japanese martial art. Modern martial arts such as aikido, judo and hapkido can trace their roots to *Aikijujitsu*.

Here is a preview of *Negima!* Volume 6.
Available in bookstores now.

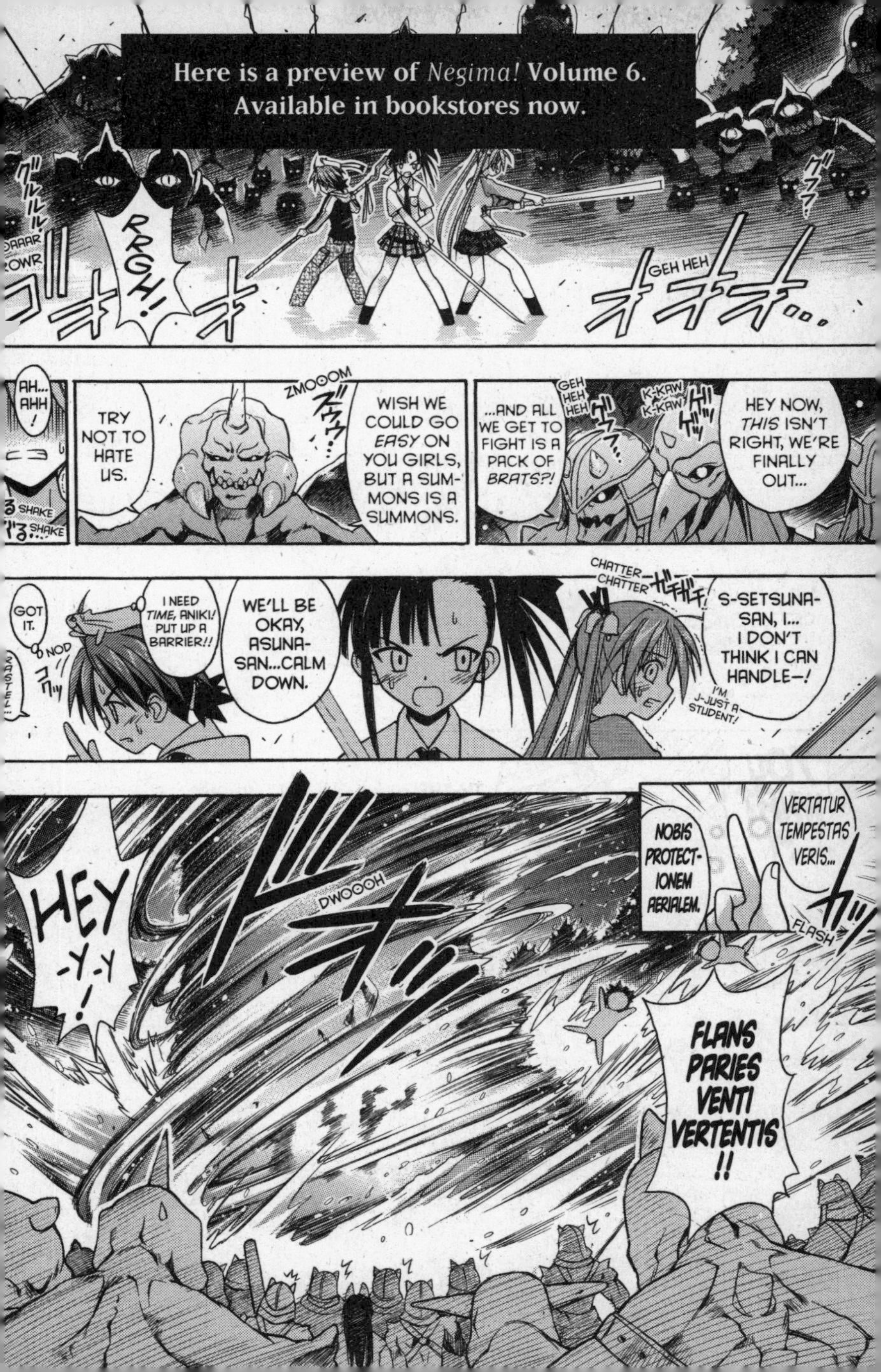
GEH HEH
RRGH!!
ROWR
HEY NOW, *THIS* ISN'T RIGHT, WE'RE FINALLY OUT...
K-KAW K-KAW
GEH HEH HEH
...AND ALL WE GET TO FIGHT IS A PACK OF *BRATS?!*
WISH WE COULD GO *EASY* ON YOU GIRLS, BUT A SUMMONS IS A SUMMONS.
ZMOOOM
TRY NOT TO HATE US.
AH... AHH!
SHAKE
SHAKE
CHATTER CHATTER
S-SETSUNA-SAN, I... I DON'T THINK I CAN HANDLE—!
I'M J-JUST A STUDENT!
WE'LL BE OKAY, ASUNA-SAN...CALM DOWN.
I NEED *TIME*, ANIKI! PUT UP A BARRIER!!
GOT IT.
NOD
VERTATUR TEMPESTAS VERIS...
NOBIS PROTECTIONEM AERIALEM.
FLASH
FLANS PARIES VENTI VERTENTIS!!
DWOOOH
HEY-Y-Y!

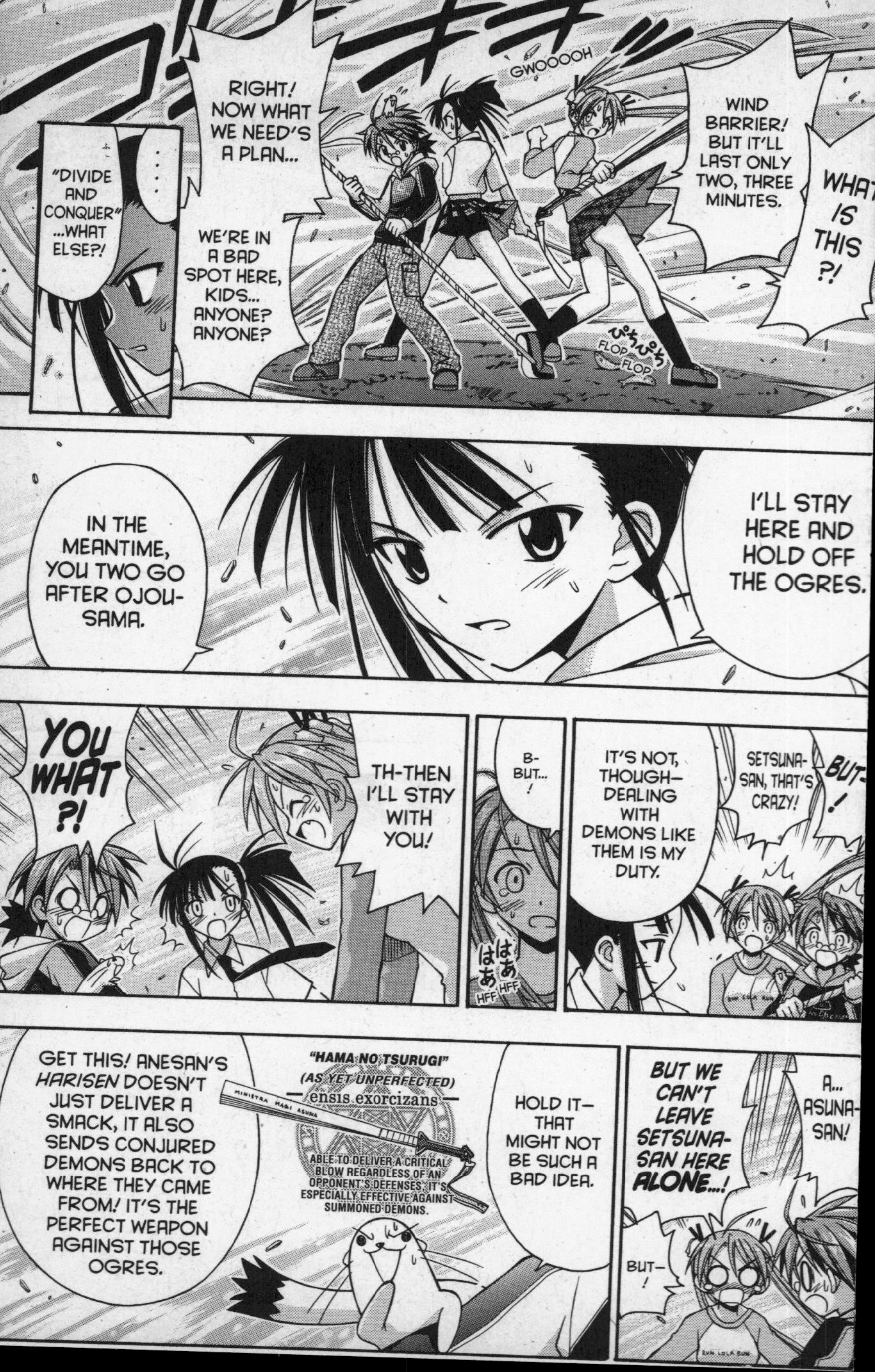
WHAT IS THIS ?!
WIND BARRIER! BUT IT'LL LAST ONLY TWO, THREE MINUTES.
GWOOOOH
RIGHT! NOW WHAT WE NEED'S A PLAN...
WE'RE IN A BAD SPOT HERE, KIDS... ANYONE? ANYONE?
FLOP FLOP
...
"DIVIDE AND CONQUER" ...WHAT ELSE?!
I'LL STAY HERE AND HOLD OFF THE OGRES.
IN THE MEANTIME, YOU TWO GO AFTER OJOU-SAMA.
BUT-!
SETSUNA-SAN, THAT'S CRAZY!
IT'S NOT, THOUGH— DEALING WITH DEMONS LIKE THEM IS MY DUTY.
B-BUT...!
はあ はあ HFF HFF
TH-THEN I'LL STAY WITH YOU!
YOU WHAT ?!
A... ASUNA-SAN!
BUT WE CAN'T LEAVE SETSUNA-SAN HERE ALONE...!
BUT—!
HOLD IT— THAT MIGHT NOT BE SUCH A BAD IDEA.
"HAMA NO TSURUGI" (AS YET UNPERFECTED) —ensis exorcizans—
ABLE TO DELIVER A CRITICAL BLOW REGARDLESS OF AN OPPONENT'S DEFENSES. IT'S ESPECIALLY EFFECTIVE AGAINST SUMMONED DEMONS.
GET THIS! ANESAN'S HARISEN DOESN'T JUST DELIVER A SMACK, IT ALSO SENDS CONJURED DEMONS BACK TO WHERE THEY CAME FROM! IT'S THE PERFECT WEAPON AGAINST THOSE OGRES.

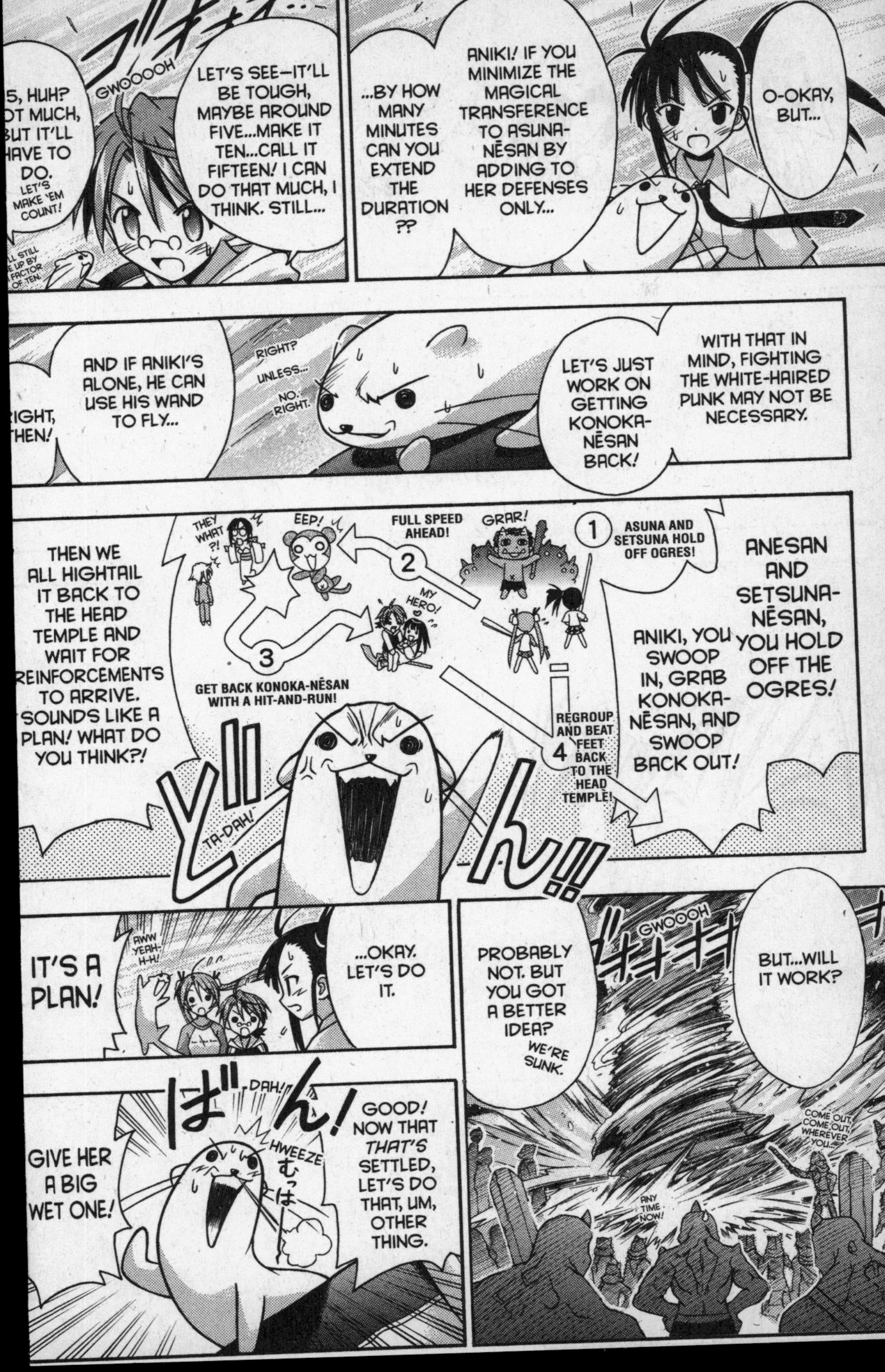
O-OKAY, BUT...
ANIKI! IF YOU MINIMIZE THE MAGICAL TRANSFERENCE TO ASUNA-NĒSAN BY ADDING TO HER DEFENSES ONLY...
...BY HOW MANY MINUTES CAN YOU EXTEND THE DURATION??
GWOOOOH
LET'S SEE—IT'LL BE TOUGH, MAYBE AROUND FIVE...MAKE IT TEN...CALL IT FIFTEEN! I CAN DO THAT MUCH, I THINK. STILL...
5, HUH? OT MUCH, BUT IT'LL HAVE TO DO.
LET'S MAKE 'EM COUNT!
UP BY FACTOR OF TEN.
WITH THAT IN MIND, FIGHTING THE WHITE-HAIRED PUNK MAY NOT BE NECESSARY.
LET'S JUST WORK ON GETTING KONOKA-NĒSAN BACK!
RIGHT?
UNLESS...
NO. RIGHT.
AND IF ANIKI'S ALONE, HE CAN USE HIS WAND TO FLY...
RIGHT, THEN!
ANESAN AND SETSUNA-NĒSAN, YOU HOLD OFF THE OGRES!
ANIKI, YOU SWOOP IN, GRAB KONOKA-NĒSAN, AND SWOOP BACK OUT!
1 ASUNA AND SETSUNA HOLD OFF OGRES!
GRAR!
FULL SPEED AHEAD!
2
EEP!
THEY WHAT?!
MY HERO!
3
GET BACK KONOKA-NĒSAN WITH A HIT-AND-RUN!
4 REGROUP AND BEAT FEET BACK TO THE HEAD TEMPLE!
THEN WE ALL HIGHTAIL IT BACK TO THE HEAD TEMPLE AND WAIT FOR REINFORCEMENTS TO ARRIVE. SOUNDS LIKE A PLAN! WHAT DO YOU THINK?!
TA-DAH!
どん!!
GWOOOH
BUT...WILL IT WORK?
PROBABLY NOT. BUT YOU GOT A BETTER IDEA?
WE'RE SUNK.
...OKAY. LET'S DO IT.
AWW YEAH-H-H!
IT'S A PLAN!
COME OUT, COME OUT, WHEREVER YOU...
ANY TIME NOW!
GOOD! NOW THAT THAT'S SETTLED, LET'S DO THAT, UM, OTHER THING.
ばん!
DAH!
HWEEZE
むっは
GIVE HER A BIG WET ONE!

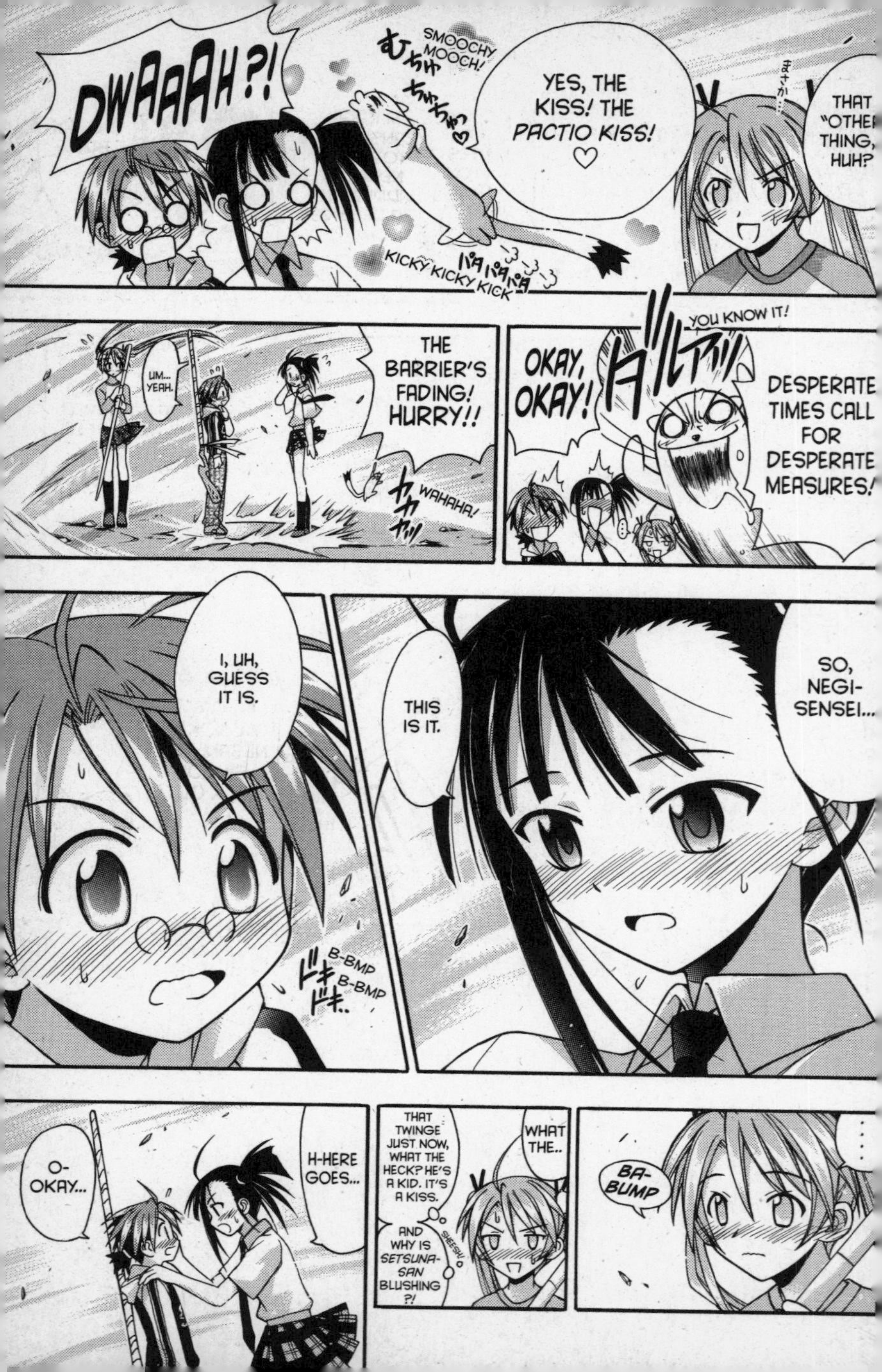
THAT "OTHER THING," HUH?
YES, THE KISS! THE PACTIO KISS! ♡
SMOOCHY MOOCH!
KICKY KICKY KICK
DWAAAH?!
DESPERATE TIMES CALL FOR DESPERATE MEASURES!
YOU KNOW IT!
OKAY, OKAY!
THE BARRIER'S FADING! HURRY!!
UM... YEAH.
WAHAHA!
SO, NEGI-SENSEI...
THIS IS IT.
I, UH, GUESS IT IS.
B-BMP B-BMP
...
BA-BUMP
WHAT THE..
THAT TWINGE JUST NOW, WHAT THE HECK? HE'S A KID. IT'S A KISS.
AND WHY IS SETSUNA-SAN BLUSHING?!
SHEESH!
H-HERE GOES...
O-OKAY...

About the Creator

Negima! is only Ken Akamatsu's third manga, although he started working in the field in 1994 with *AI Ga Tomaranai*. Like all of Akamatsu's work to date, it was published in Kodansha's *Shonen Magazine*. *AI Ga Tomaranai* ran for five years before concluding in 1999. In 1998, however, Akamatsu began the work that would make him one of the most popular manga artists in Japan: *Love Hina*. *Love Hina* ran for four years, and before its conclusion in 2002, it would cause Akamatsu to be granted the prestigious Manga of the Year award from Kodansha, as well as going on to become one of the bestselling manga in the United States.

TOMARE!

[STOP!]

You're going the wrong way!

Manga is a completely different type of reading experience.

To start at the *beginning*, go to the *end*!

That's right! Authentic manga is read the traditional Japanese way—from right to left. Exactly the *opposite* of how American books are read. It's easy to follow: Just go to the other end of the book, and read each page—and each panel—from right side to left side, starting at the top right. Now you're experiencing manga as it was meant to be.